Change

CHANGE

What Really *Leads to Lasting Personal Transformation*

Jeffrey A. Kottler

OXFORD
UNIVERSITY PRESS

OXFORD

UNIVERSITY PRESS

Oxford University Press is a department of the University of Oxford.
It furthers the University's objective of excellence in research, scholarship,
and education by publishing worldwide.

Oxford   New York
Auckland   Cape Town   Dar es Salaam   Hong Kong   Karachi
Kuala Lumpur   Madrid   Melbourne   Mexico City   Nairobi
New Delhi   Shanghai   Taipei   Toronto

With offices in
Argentina   Austria   Brazil   Chile   Czech Republic   France   Greece
Guatemala   Hungary   Italy   Japan   Poland   Portugal   Singapore
South Korea   Switzerland   Thailand   Turkey   Ukraine   Vietnam

Oxford is a registered trademark of Oxford University Press
in the UK and certain other countries.

Published in the United States of America by
Oxford University Press
198 Madison Avenue, New York, NY 10016

© Oxford University Press 2014

Library of Congress Cataloging-in-Publication Data
Kottler, Jeffrey A.
Change : what really leads to lasting personal transformation / Jeffrey Kottler.
    pages cm
Includes bibliographical references.
ISBN 978–0–19–998138–0 (hardcover : alk. paper)   1. Change (Psychology)   I. Title.
BF637.C4K677 2013
155.2'5—dc23   2013016480

9 8 7 6 5 4 3 2 1
Printed in the United States of America
on acid-free paper

CONTENTS

ACKNOWLEDGMENTS

As with most writing projects, this one represents a collaboration with a number of contributors, as well as a remarkable editor with whom I have worked for a long time. I wish to thank Dana Bliss, Senior Editor at Oxford, for his consistent support and critical input for this project, and so many others during the past few years. I'm also grateful for the assistance of Oxford production staff, including Emily Perry and Benjamin Suazo.

There were a number of scholars and researchers who generously agreed to act as reviewers for this book, providing valuable feedback and critical suggestions, at times challenging me to look more closely at issues and alter my thinking. I'm especially indebted to Geoffrey Greif and Meg Selig, who offered a number of suggestions for digging deeper into the subject.

There were hundreds of individuals who shared their stories of transformation with me, only a small fraction of whom are explicitly acknowledged: Katie Robertson, Jamie Littleton, Sarah Childers, Rodney Anderson, Angelica Vasquez, Spencer MacDonald, Sherrill Wiseman, Matt Englar-Carlson, Erica Law, Jamie Alger, Spencer MacDonald, Emily Liwanag, Cynthia Marcolina, Yasamin Amaya, Lori Thomas, Cary Kottler, Lori Drozd, Nadia Muhaidly, Sheila McCabe, Joanna Fick, Meghan Quinn, Christina Spinella, Dawn Hoekman, Jacalyn Schoen, Brian Pfeffer, Katie McAuliffe, Jay Christian, and Briana Hammonds.

PREFACE

Think of a time in which you overcame a significant, chronic, intractable problem that challenged you for years. This was a pattern of self-defeating behavior that plagued and sabotaged you in all kinds of ways. Then, somehow, you managed to completely turn things around in such a way that the changes persist to this day. What is your best understanding of how this happened and what made the greatest difference?

It is entirely possible that your explanation, based on an imperfect and reconstructed memory, might very well correspond with the recollections of a therapist, supervisor, teacher, parent, coach, or mentor who played an instrumental role. It is far more likely, however, that your reasoning might touch on other factors and influences that were never overtly recognized and honored. Perhaps it wasn't what was actually said or done by someone who assisted you that was most impactful, but rather, a cascade of other events that occurred indirectly or tangentially from that experience. If you conduct your own self-study, you will likely identify many of the same factors that will be covered in the pages that follow.

As we begin this journey together, it's important that we are realistic and honest with one another: What are the chances this book will change you? Or more significantly, what's the likelihood that something you might learn within these pages will stick with you long enough to help promote some meaningful improvement in your life satisfaction, happiness, or quality of life? Based on prior experiences, you'd have to admit that the prognosis is guarded, especially if you don't initiate constructive action. To bolster this point, just consider how many books or self-help programs you've consulted in your life that promise some kind of deliverance but leave you less than satisfied. On the other hand, sometimes we seamlessly integrate whatever we learn without an explicit awareness of what happened and why. That's one of the interesting and intriguing things about exploring change processes: even after centuries of systematic study, we still don't really know what's going on.

You'd think after all these years of dedicated research, study, investigation, and clinical practice we would have a pretty good idea about what most consistently and effectively leads to change in people's lives. Philosophers, writers, educators, psychologists, neurobiologists, and other scientists have spent the past few centuries exploring the factors that produce significant transformations in people's lives whether they take place in the context of recovery from trauma or crisis, solitary reflection, collaborative relationships, travel experiences, reading or listening to stories, classrooms, psychotherapy, religious conversions, or serendipitous events. There is certainly no shortage of theories (hundreds) and books (thousands) on the subject, each proposing its own singular answers that run the gambit from finding meaning or initiating lifestyle changes to divine intervention.

I have been researching and writing about change for 35 years, adding dozens of tomes to the stack, each intended to guide change agents such as teachers, counselors, psychotherapists, and organizational leaders in their efforts to more effectively help others. Yet with all this devotion and commitment to understanding why and how people change, I am still often puzzled by what appears to be most helpful. For instance, a client I had been seeing in therapy just left my office and I have no idea what, if anything we said or did during the previous hour, had any lasting impact. He *seemed* to understand what we were doing, that nothing much would change in his life until he stopped dwelling on his situation and instead began reaching out to others, but who knows whether he would actually follow through on his intentions? Did he really provide an accurate report? And if so, could we ever determine what had the most influence?

The truth of the matter is that I often feel confused and frustrated about the impact of my work, whether as a psychologist, professor, writer, or director of a charity, that anything I'm doing is having much of an impact. In spite of all the self-improvement books published each year, it's more than a little ironic that there is an increasing demand for them precisely *because* the lessons learned don't last very long. That's not to say that books such as this one are not useful because there's a lot of evidence indicating that they can be remarkably efficient, cost-effective, and powerful instruments for transforming lives.[1] Similarly, consulting a therapist for problems provides some benefit most of the time (estimated between 75% and 90%).[2] But the really interesting part is that although we *know* that certain actions and resources tend to produce favorable results, we still aren't clear about the underlying mechanisms that initiate and maintain these outcomes.

Making changes is actually the easy part. Relatively speaking, it isn't that difficult to stop smoking, lose weight, end a relationship, stop a bad habit, learn a new behavior, or gain some new insight or awareness; the really difficult challenge is to maintain the momentum over time.[3] And the prognosis for maintaining changes is pretty dismal with the vast majority of programs failing within a few days or weeks. The truth is that as much as we might think we understand about what helps people to improve their lives, we have barely scratched the surface.

This book seeks to bring together much of what is known about change processes, from a variety of sources, studies, disciplines, and approaches, and integrates this knowledge into the most important principles that have proven most effective over time. It represents a lifetime of data gathering, story collection, research, and reflection, on what seems to make the greatest difference in people's lives across a broad spectrum of situations, individual differences, and cultural contexts. It is a compilation of everything that I've learned, plus a whole lot more that fell into place during the past few years talking to people about what not only transformed them, but just as significantly, how and why the changes stick with them over time.

There are several questions that beg for more definitive answers, many of which will be addressed in the pages that follow:

1. Why do people avoid and resist changes that they know are absolutely necessary for their well-being?
2. How is it that people "decide" to change?
3. Why is it that changes can be both gradual and incremental, or sudden and dramatic shifts?

4. When exposed to trauma or disasters, why do some people become incapacitated and dysfunctional while others grow significantly as a result of the adversity?
5. What are the tipping points that spark a cascade of incremental changes?
6. Why don't most changes seem to stick, even when they obviously provide satisfying outcomes?
7. What can be done to prevent relapses?
8. If there are universal features of most successful efforts, how can they be structured in such a way to promote lasting changes?

Although we will be exploring these and other questions, this is not a book that synthesizes *all* the research in the field, nor does it aim to present some kind of unified conceptual framework that explains how change works. The phenomena are far too complex and multilayered to present some simplistic explanation, or a single set of variables. The experts in the field are, themselves, passionately committed to particular models that often contradict one another or present diametrically opposite explanations. There is compelling evidence, for instance, to support the idea that in order to make constructive and enduring changes in present behavior, you first have to come to terms with influences from the past. As persuasive as this argument is, there are equally convincing studies that demonstrate that for some situations and problems it is far better to ignore what already happened and instead concentrate only on what is happening (and possible) in the present moment. Then there is still a third set of advocates who insist that we forget the past and present altogether and instead focus on planning for the future. This leads to a rather obvious conclusion that changes occur for all kinds of reasons, depending on the individual, context, problem, goals, and situation.

To make matters even more challenging, people don't usually know why and how they changed. Of course, they have their own explanations and reasons, but that doesn't mean these self-reports are necessarily accurate and comprehensive. One of the most intriguing results from interviewing patients who visited their physicians or psychotherapists is that frequently what they say was most helpful to them isn't necessarily related to what the doctors believed made the most difference. Whereas helping professionals understandably point to their interventions as being critical, their patients often talk far more about how important it was to be heard and understood. That's why if we ever hope to unravel the mystery of change, we have to listen to the input not only from researchers, clinicians, and theoreticians, but also from the "pilgrims" who have launched quests of self-discovery.

I've long been fascinated by people's stories of how they managed to change long-standing, entrenched patterns that had previously seemed impervious to any intervention. More often than not, such anecdotes didn't include breakthroughs during therapy sessions or some well-meaning family member offering advice, but rather, they appeared to result from life challenges that required developing new resources and increased resilience. You might consider asking yourself the same question that I have posed to so many others. In fact, it is the single most interesting question that I can think of to ask anyone: *Tell me about a time in your life that you initiated a significant change that continues to this day.*

As you find yourself reviewing such seminal experiences in your life, you can't help but consider the variables and influences that played the most significant role. Although the book is divided into discrete chapters, each exploring a major theme that was significantly influential in producing dramatic change, they hardly operate in isolation. So many of the variables work in concert, woven into the threads of each story of change. And this book is, more than anything else, a collection of inspirational stories about growth, recovery, and resilience. You will find within them the essential ingredients, as well as subtle nuances, that help explain one of the most interesting and important aspects of human behavior and how it evolves over time.

After exploring some of the mysteries related to personal changes (Chapter 1), the next few chapters (2–4) review what is essentially known and understood about enduring transformations in people's lives. We will look at examples from addiction (Chapter 5), trauma (Chapter 6), psychotherapy (Chapter 7), and travel (Chapter 8) to highlight the common factors and principles before covering territory that reveals some of the most interesting facets of our subject. Thus, Chapter 9 examines the power of insight to break through these impasses. Whereas a number of stressors and fears (Chapter 10) may compromise efforts to initiate and sustain constructive action, it is through finding deeper meaning (Chapter 11), serving others (Chapter 12), and resolving relationship conflicts (Chapter 13) that personal changes are often stabilized. The book concludes (Chapter 14) with a discussion of how and why most changes don't last very long and what can be done to counteract such inertia.

There is probably no subject more interesting and useful than to study the process of change, whether it takes place within a culture, organization, group, family, or individual life. And there is no undertaking more critical than understanding what *really* makes the most difference to sustain changes over time.

Change

CHAPTER 1

The Mystery of Change

There are all kinds of mysteries related to human functioning. Evolutionary biologists, for example, have a very well-developed theory to explain behavior as it originated in the ancestral environment of the African savannah. This was a time when we lived in small groups of several dozen members, hunting and gathering along a migratory pattern to obtain food sources. Survival was based on the ability to accurately assess and escape from potential danger, and the main goal of life was to ensure that one's offspring flourished.

In spite of the mountain of research that has been completed to explain human behavior in evolutionary terms, scientists continue to be perplexed by exceptions to the rule of survival adaptability—that all behavior persists because it increases the likelihood of perpetuating an individual's gene pool. How, then, do they explain childless couples, altruism, male breasts, homosexuality, female orgasms, suicide, and other such phenomena that don't immediately appear procreativity useful? How do they account for the universality of religious practices when they appear to be counterproductive to survival in difficult environments—limiting food choices, sacrificing valuable resources, provoking intergroup conflict, and devoting energy to worship instead of food collection? Even more perplexing of all is the phenomenon of altruism in which people put their own lives at risk to help perfect strangers with whom they have no kin connection.[1]

Behavior that, at first, does appear to be counterproductive, if not a waste of time, may indeed have functional components, but one must look deeply to discover such utility. Kissing, laughter, superstitions, picking your nose, crying, are just a few illustrations. Weeping, for example, may seem like it is totally useless, leaking water out of your eyes when you feel sad or joyful, but it actually provides all kinds of advantages—communicating in an authentic language, a literal and compelling cry for help, signaling surrender, manipulating others, even leeching excess hormones during emotional arousal.[2]

Among all aspects of human experiences, one that has been most often researched and discussed is the phenomenon related to learning and change processes. There are thousands of studies and books published each year attempting to explain the intricacies and nuances of how we develop, grow, and change. Yet most of these books, papers, and even reference volumes in the field don't even bother to provide a definition of change, either because it is so nebulous, or it is assumed that everyone already knows what it means.[3] In addition, change doesn't necessarily mean that a "cure" has taken place,[4] nor does it actually replace bad habits; rather, it overlays new patterns over the older ones.[5]

When attempts have been made to provide a definition of this mysterious and complex phenomenon, its components are variously described as a process of letting go, an internal negotiation, an unfolding process of learning, a cognitive reorientation, increased self-awareness, a shift in perspective, a progressive series of realizations that lead to action, a redefinition of core identity, and so on. Each of these really describes a particular goal of change rather than a useful description of what actually happens.

This leads to the most basic question of all: What qualifies as change in the first place? Is it a temporary reduction of symptoms? A self-report of satisfaction with the result? A significant improvement from previous baseline performance? A statistical significance of effect size? Does it represent "recovery," "cure," or "maintenance of gains?" How long does change have to last to count as a successful effort?

Even after several centuries of dedicated work on the part of philosophers, biologists, social scientists, and writers, we have barely scratched the surface of this complex and multifaceted process. We have developed all kinds of systems and models for facilitating change in people without really understanding how it occurs.[6] That's not to say there's any shortage of theories available to account for the phenomenon, but the problem is that, at least historically, there has been so little consensus. That, too, is changing.

EVEN EXPERTS ARE CONFUSED

Although people make changes in their lives all the time, they rarely reflect on how exactly they occurred, nor do they offer many coherent ideas about what happened and why.[7] It would seem that such an enterprise would be among the most important tasks for anyone who is interested in being more successful in his or her growth and development.

Psychotherapists are in the business of facilitating change. They are approached by people who are in the throes of misery or dissatisfaction, feeling desperate for some relief. Sure enough, the treatment works most of the time and constructive changes are initiated. Yet ask a dozen therapists what they do that best promotes changes in their clients and you'll hear just as many answers:

- "It's really about coming to terms with unresolved issues of the past, especially related to parental attachment."
- "It's all about perceptions and interpretations of experience and reframing those that are more solidly based in reality."
- "Without formulating realistic, practical, and attainable goals, it's difficult for people to reach their most cherished desires."
- "Forget the past, forget the future; the action takes place in the present moment when people are more fully engaged with their authentic feelings."
- "People are suffering because of a lack of meaning in their lives. We explore underlying issues related to basic values, intimacy and isolation, authenticity, and personal responsibility for their choices."
- "Rather than look at what's wrong with people's lives, I try to balance this by focusing on what is going right, accessing their strengths and resources."
- "Insight is all very fine but often useless; it's all about making incremental, progressive changes in observable, measureable behavior."
- "Self-identity is the core of how we respond to others, and to the challenges we face. My goal is to help people discover and create a new identity that is more in line with their ideal beliefs."

- "I help people to restory their lives, constructing new narratives that are more empowering."
- "Relationships are *everything* in our lives. Without intimacy and close connections, our lives are empty. I try and help people to feel more connected to others through the alliance that we cocreate together."
- "We address some very basic questions, asking what people want most in their lives, what they are doing (or not doing) to attain these goals, and what new choices they could make to get what they say they really want."
- "It's all about the ways we talk to ourselves, substituting more constructive ways of thinking about the events in our lives and how we choose to react to them."
- "I solve problems. First, I get people to stop doing the things that aren't working, then to experiment with alternatives, often the exact opposite of what they're already doing."
- "Most of the people I see have been colonized into accepting roles of oppression by those who dominate power. My job is to collaborate with them to challenge these assumptions."
- "Basically most emotional problems are neurologically based and require some chemical intervention."
- "I work with people in groups because we are all social beings who hunger for stronger tribal affiliations and intimacy."
- "All personal issues take place within a given culture and family, each of which must be thoroughly explored; changes must be made within the context of these systems."
- "Most of the people I help look to a Higher Power for guidance and inspiration. My role is as a companion on this spiritual journey in search of recovery and renewal."

Remember, this is merely a *sample* of the options you would encounter, representing some of the most prominent prevailing theories with familiar names such as psychoanalytic, cognitive-behavioral, existential, reality, person-centered, feminist, constructivist, narrative, strategic, and systemic, among others. The really interesting thing is that they are almost all legitimate paths—and most of them are reasonably effective, at least for some people some of the time. The key question that you must be asking yourself (just as I have for the past three decades) is: *What the heck is going on?*[8] How is it possible that approaches that appear to be so different can produce roughly comparable results?

The answer, which forms the basis for this book, is that almost all effective strategies for producing change are actually relying on similar ingredients even though they might have different names.[9] Based on your own study examining changes you've made in your life, you would likely identify many of the same features that will be presented. Naturally it wasn't just one thing, nor did the change occur in isolation. The nature of change is so complex that there are a host of factors that most likely worked in unison even though we might tend to oversimplify and point to just a few critical incidents. Nevertheless, whether you are looking for change in your life, or take on the responsibility of being a change agent for others (therapist, teacher, coach, parent, supervisor, leader, health professional), you probably have some notion of what best contributes to making the greatest difference.

Given the diversity of opinions available, and the incredible variety of changes that are made in all kinds of situations and contexts, perhaps the simplest and most descriptive definition is that it involves making something different, either by stopping something you're already doing that isn't working, or doing something new that is more constructive and effective. *In all its permutations, change leads to a relatively permanent reduction in distress and/or an enhancement of daily functioning.*

Some Interesting Questions to Further Bolster the Mystery

With that rather simple description, it must also be said that there is hardly universal agreement about what constitutes change, even among experts on the subject. The mystery prompts some interesting questions: When does an alteration in attitudes, beliefs, behavior, thinking, or feeling "count" as change, and how long does it have to last in order to qualify? What if there are reported changes in a person's thinking or attitudes but no observable shift in behavior? How big does a change have to be in order to be included in our discussion? What if it is so small that it's barely noticeable or that the changes aren't really all that meaningful? What if there is considerable disagreement among parties involved in the change in which some people report a big difference but others deny any effect? What do we do with those kinds of changes that appear beyond clear measurement, such as feelings of well-being or spiritual renewal? How do we account for the reality that people often don't report honestly and accurately their experiences? Sometimes they outright lie or distort what happened. The same can be said for observations of change that may not be valid or reliable. Speaking of measurement issues, what about cases of delayed reactions in which the noticeable effects don't really show up for months or even years later? And what do we do with the changes that occur in the "wrong" direction, meaning that the person has deteriorated or regressed significantly?

Some of these points raised add to the mystery and complexity of what happens during psychological transformations, making it even more challenging to study. That is one reason why there has been so much criticism of the methodologies used to study the change processes, arguing that we have failed to fully understand people's inner experiences, looking only at their observable behavior.[10] If we look at feelings as just one example, it's generally agreed that being able to recognize and regulate emotions is one key to producing constructive and stable changes even though these internal states can't be easily defined, much less described.[11] Nevertheless, it is precisely the arousal of feelings that helps us to cement memories and provoke action to reduce those that are uncomfortable or disturbing. And further contributing to the complexity, whereas change usually refers to behavior, feelings, or attitudes, often the first level of modification (especially related to mental or behavior disorders) occurs in the brain long before there is observable evidence in the outside world.[12] With an estimated one billion neurons and one trillion synapses in the cerebral cortex alone, how can we possibly understand all the dynamics of what might be going on, even with advances in imaging technology?

Adding to the mysteries circulating around psychological change is the reality that people are generally pretty unaware of their own behavior and especially the reasons why they do the things they do. Ask someone, anyone, why he or she continues to engage in actions that appear to be so spectacularly self-destructive—overeating, drinking to oblivion, smoking, gambling—and they will likely shrug, or just offer a feeble, "I don't know. Because it feels good." When people are stuck in dead-end jobs, relationships, or predicaments, and asked why they don't try something else, again you'll likely hear a fairly noncommittal response.

Part of the reluctance that most people have to making changes in their lives is related to their misguided belief that they are already fully formed and impervious to most future changes. Called the "end-of-history illusion," investigators found that no matter how old people are they tend to acknowledge and honor the major changes they've made in the past but believe that not much more will happen in the future.[13] Whether speaking about their musical tastes, friendships, hobbies, or interests, most people erroneously think that their preferences will remain stable throughout their lives in spite of fairly compelling evidence to the contrary. Naturally, if you can't or don't imagine that future changes are likely, much less possible, the probability that they will occur is significantly reduced.

In spite of the ambivalence and relative cluelessness that most people feel about initiating many changes in their lives, they may have no compunction whatsoever about fully embracing other kinds of major adjustments. Consumers will stand in line for days to become among the first early adopters of new technology, even though that means learning a whole encyclopedia of new skills and updates to become reasonably adept with the devices. Likewise, they will spend large sums of money to change their wardrobes to the latest fashions or adopt the latest trends in social behavior. In each of these cases, they willingly embrace changes while they stubbornly might resist them in other contexts that are far more meaningful and significant. There is thus tremendous uncertainty, confusion, and vacillation related to change, often a battle between reason ("I really should do this") and emotion ("But I really don't feel like it") that has been likened to trying to steer an elephant that has a mind of its own.[14] Unless there is congruence and collaboration between the rider (the rational mind and long-term gains) and the elephant (emotional responses and instant gratification), you'll not get very far—at least in your preferred direction.[15]

Let's put those questions aside for now, or at least keep them in mind with a degree of humility and skepticism, given that what we are investigating is indeed about as complex and mysterious as anything can be.

A Review of Basic Factors

Let's examine a case from my own life in the distant past as an example and then identity some of the variables that seem to have been most influential, many of which you will recognize in your own experience.

It is my first week attending university [novel environment]. *I'm lost, lonely, and frightened* [high emotional arousal, vulnerability]. *I barely talked my way into this place with an academic record that could best be described as mediocre. They admitted me on probation, and I already realize it was a terrible mistake* [counterproductive self-talk]. *I'm absolutely overwhelmed and need to bail out. I just don't belong here* [feeling lost].

I've been told my whole life that I'm barely average, not particularly bright, and destined for less than greatness [internalized script]. *I accept that this is the case* [negative self-identity]. *Who am I to argue with an undistinguished record? I was tracked into woodworking and home economics classes in high school instead of a college prep curriculum* [haunted by past]. *My test scores were abysmal, confirming my stupidity. I was stuck in right field when I was allowed to play baseball at all. I wasn't popular, attractive, an athlete, or a scholar. Yet with all these crushing defeats, I desperately wanted a girlfriend and some sense of accomplishment* [vision for future].

That's why I'm parked on the steps outside the library, an excellent vantage point to scout prospective candidates for a girlfriend even if I'll never have the courage to approach anyone. When I was in my early teen years, I spent 50 consecutive Saturdays going to the mall ostensibly to meet girls. During that year, not once, not a single time, did I ever even approach a girl much less talk to anyone. I knew I was hopeless and desperate [hitting bottom].

I want so badly to be different but I don't know how [high motivation]. *Glasses helped* [medical adjustment]. *I couldn't see during most of my childhood—fly balls in the outfield, math problems, and grammar constructions on the board (to this day I can't identify the parts of a sentence, nor do I have a clue about how to solve algebraic equations). The world was blurry, and I just thought it was like that for everyone* [self-deception]. *It wasn't until it was way too late that my vision was corrected. Don't ask why it took my parents so long to notice that I used to sit two feet from the television screen* [dysfunctional family system]. *They used to say, "Don't sit so close or you'll ruin your eyes." They didn't seem to recognize that my eyes were already ruined.*

Poor vision might have been one reason I was "stupid," but mostly it had to do with the way I viewed myself [negative self-identity]. *As I sat on the library steps that day, my thoughts turned to the sorry state of my life* [acknowledgment of problem]. *Above all else I wished I could be smart. I wished there was a genie in the vicinity who could grant my fondest desire, but all I was left with was a very interesting question: How can we tell who is smart and who is not?* [constructive goal setting].

I watched other students walk by and tried to identity which ones were bright and which ones were not. I accumulated my data and decided that smart people had two main characteristics: first, they carried around books, and secondly, they knew stuff. That struck me as simple enough [major insight]. *So I decided in that single moment that I would be smart* [an epiphany]. *I would begin by going into the library and checking out some books* [action plan]. *Eventually, since I was lugging them around with me, I decided that I might as well start reading them. Pretty soon, other people started treating me like I was smart since I was always surrounded by books. Eventually I started to believe it myself* [altered self-identity].

Embedded in this brief narrative are several of the most important factors we will be exploring in this book. Change usually begins with someone feeling a level of desperation that leads him or her to take constructive risks and experiment with alternative ways of being that previously felt inaccessible. Motivation and drive are intensified by fear, and often we learn and grow as much from disappointments and failures as we ever do from successes and achievements. It is during conditions of vulnerability and feeling lost that our self-deceptions are confronted and new insights are generated. We try new things because we are now certain that what we've already been doing won't ever work.

A Cascade of Changes

Of course, it takes a lot more than simply *deciding* to be different. If that were the case, someone could simply *choose* to lose weight, stop drinking, or be smart. My own transformation might have been launched on the steps of the library, but there were a whole lot of other things that happened subsequently to reinforce and support those changes. I not only transformed who I was on the inside but also initiated a series of other changes to keep the momentum going, those that involved revisions of my lifestyle, my social network, and especially the meaning I created from this experience.

One of the most interesting mysteries related to change efforts is how small steps often lead to huge gains. If you attempt to trace the trajectory of how and why you ended up at a particular stage or situation in your life, there is rarely a single action or incident that made this happen, in spite of the simple story you might tell yourself and others. Far more commonly, there is a series of events, often initially unrelated, that feed on one another and eventually multiply and pool their influences to lead you in a given direction. These processes can be organized in several broad categories.[16] They basically lend support to the rather obvious idea—so often ignored by researchers—that change can occur on a number of levels (see Table 1.1), leading to significant alterations in the ways that people think, feel, *or* behave (although ideally all three domains would be saturated).

In all their many forms and manifestations, basically what it comes down to is that people finally—and reluctantly—surrender strategies that are clearly not working for them and try something new and different. It is one of the mysteries of human behavior that people will continue to engage in actions that are spectacularly counterproductive and self-destructive and yet not give them up in the face of overwhelming evidence. Someone will attempt to solve a problem, using an approach that has been tried a dozen times previously without success, and yet persist in this strategy even though the outcome is virtually certain to fail.

A parent with an explosive temper is upset because her teenage daughter is obstinate, defiant, and rebellious. "Damn it," she screams in exasperation to her daughter, "I *told* you to go to your room until you can do what I tell you!"

"Screw you," the girl screams back and runs into her room, slamming the door.

The mother runs after the girl and yells at her through the door, "How *dare* you speak to me that way. Young lady, you're grounded!"

Table 1.1. LEVELS OF CHANGE

Change process	Examples
Attitude shift	Self-acceptance, acceptance of events, reduced blame of self or others, patience
Experimentation with alternatives	Shift in attention, letting go, searching for other options, trying new behaviors, doing something different, reinventing oneself
Skill development	Tolerance of ambiguity and uncertainty, resilience, evaluating goals and outcomes systematically, building deficits
Support	Expressing feelings, reaching out to others, expanding social world, resolving conflicts
Cognitive restructuring	Shift in perspective, reframing problems more constructively, confronting self-deception, challenging negative beliefs, looking at big picture
Meaning making	Exploring new ways of understanding life and situation, finding higher purpose, making connections

The girl climbs out through the window and stays out all night, returning early in the morning to face her mother standing at the door in a rage.

It is pretty evident that yelling at her daughter is not only ineffective in stopping the exact behavior the mother wishes to address, but it is actually making things much worse. Yet the mother feels powerless to change what she's doing. Until such time that she recognizes and accepts that what she's already doing is not ever going to work, she doesn't have the slightest chance to try something else. There is no guarantee, of course, that reasoning with her daughter, asking someone else to help, backing off, or any other strategy would work any better—but such experimentation is a necessity in order to discover an approach that might work.

This little scenario captures the essence of how and why it's so challenging to introduce change into existing patterns. Until such time that you are willing and able to stop doing what you're already doing, even though it is familiar and comfortable, there isn't much chance that things are going to be much different.

WHAT WE DON'T UNDERSTAND

It is difficult to determine how much of my story described earlier actually happened the way I reported it. There could have been a whole lot of other factors that exerted influence, things that prepared me for that moment. I could have misremembered the events and distorted their significance. I may have minimized other elements that I neglected or ignored. There could have been accumulative influences that built over time, contributions from all kinds of sources, or delayed effects from prior learning. I don't honestly know what turned my life around during that critical stage in my development, but my best guess is that were more than dozen (or maybe a hundred) influences that all coalesced when I was most ready to pay attention.

This begs the question as to whether people can really know what it was that changed them. When Mira became pregnant, it was an absolute shock considering she was on the Pill and the chances were one in a thousand. After adjusting to the inevitable, she next learned that the baby was terminal and would die soon after leaving the womb. She tried everything to put her life back to some semblance of order—assigning blame, isolating herself to heal, and eventually consulting a therapist who diagnosed her with posttraumatic stress. She had a name for her experience, a condition called *depression*, and that provided some small measure of comfort if not relief. But here's the interesting part of Mira's story: she attributes her eventual recovery not to the therapy, but to a single offhand comment by a friend who suggested she forget medication and therapy and instead just go for a jog. "And in that instant," she reports, "everything changed."[17]

At first she could barely run more than a few blocks, but eventually she built up to completing a marathon. Her husband, who shared her grief, joined her in this enterprise. It was something they trained for together, and it was the one step at a time that she attributes to bringing her back from the brink of despair and grief. Whereas Mira believes in her heart that it was the suggestion of her friend to run that changed her, how can she really know that one isolated element made all the difference? Could the therapy have set the stage for her readiness to hear her friend and follow through with his suggestion? Could the isolation she had condemned herself to have provided the reflective and healing time to clear her mind and heart sufficiently that she was willing to seek out help in the first place? Maybe it wasn't so much the exercise itself that was stabilizing as the vehicle it provided to reconnect with her husband in a common goal? I mention these possibilities because it is so difficult to unravel the mystery of what really makes the ultimate difference.

There have been incredible advances in our knowledge about change during the past 150 years. It wasn't long ago that experts subscribed to theories of animal magnetism, divine intervention, and witchcraft to explain human transformations. It has only been in the last few decades that competing theories have put aside their differences emphasizing early experiences versus present moments, genetics versus environmental factors, cognitive processes versus emotional expression, insight versus action, sudden versus gradual progress, individual versus cultural influences, and relationship factors versus goal attainment. We now know and understand that growth and learning are contextual, depending on the person, the issues, and the situation.

There are now several prominent models to explain the kind of change Mira described with all kinds of impressive names like the "inherent self-healing tendency model," "perceptual control theory," and my personal favorite name: "dynamic systems theory to non-linear and discontinuous patterns of change."[18] What these and other theories attempt to do is describe general patterns and stages that basically follow a sequence in which

1. there is an expressed desire for change that is triggered by a crisis, trauma, or developmental transition;
2. a threshold of pain and discomfort is exceeded that can't any longer be ignored or denied;
3. there is a sudden awareness or insight that something different must be done;
4. there is a gradual process of applying what was realized or learned into constructive action; and
5. there is recovery from inevitable relapses.

Variations of these stage models will be described in subsequent chapters, but they each describe the process as if it proceeds in a somewhat orderly and sequential fashion.[19] I would suggest that things are far more chaotic and serendipitous then that, and are made far more difficult because most people who can definitely attest to the fact that they are irrevocably different still can't supply a definition for what constitutes change.[20]

BASIC INGREDIENTS

With a truce declared, theorists and researchers are looking for "common factors" that are somewhat universal across individuals, cultures, and problem areas.[21] Treatments and interventions employed to facilitate changes are thus customized and specialized, depending on what is presented. Yet even with significant improvements in the quality and efficiency of strategies for initiating change, we can't say, with any authority, exactly what is going on. It is not unlike the phenomenon of climate change: we *know* it is taking place; we *think* it is caused by greenhouse gases; but we don't know for sure where and how it will affect different regions, how serious a threat it is to the planet, or if and when the tipping points will arise.

That is why it is so important to try to reconcile diverse perspectives and discover their common elements. If it is true, as seems to be the case, that so many different approaches to change result in similar results, a useful enterprise is to identify, describe, and flesh out these ingredients. If you were asked, for example, what various fast foods have in common—tacos, hamburgers, fried chicken, salads, French fries (Big Macs alone have 70 ingredients)—you could examine the list and find several universal substances like xanthum gum (stabilizer), soybean oil, salt, and corn syrup. Likewise, if you were asked to remember all the important changes you've made in your life, and then make a comprehensive list of all those ingredients that you believe were operative, you'd have quite an inventory of items. But then if you reduced that list to its common factors, you might end up with a half-dozen of those that seem to capture the essence of many others. That is exactly what we will be doing together in the pages that follow.

Throughout this book I will be speaking authoritatively about what really makes a difference. I will support these statements with compelling examples, research studies, and logical ideas. I also fully acknowledge that change is indeed a mystery, but one that we can sort out if we look carefully at those features that are most powerfully and frequently associated with the significant changes that people initiate in their lives.

Here's the good news: although it is both interesting and useful to understand the underlying mechanisms of how change occurs so you can become more systematic and purposeful in the ways that you undertake such efforts, it isn't necessarily *required* in order to do so. You don't have to even identify the causes of a problem, much less understand them, in order to improve or fix things. There are even some prominent theorists who have argued that such a quest for insight is not only counterproductive and a waste of time but also potentially dangerous.[22] In addition, there are a number of successful treatment programs for problems like autism in which we really don't understand what causes them.[23]

Most of the changes that people make take place at levels that are beyond their understanding, or even awareness. Yet those transformations that really stick, that continue to blossom over time, are those that become an integrated part of who you are. Once you become more educated about your own processes and patterns, you can significantly enhance the magnitude, power, and pace of the changes you'd like to make.

CHAPTER 2

Obstacles and Challenges That Compromise Efforts to Change

Stefan is sick of himself. He's disgusted with the state of his life. He hates his job. He can't stand his living situation. He feels stuck in a dead-end relationship with his girlfriend that only makes him feel trapped: "She has no freaking clue what I'm about or what I want." He feels alone and without hope.

Stefan tried to talk to his girlfriend but he reports that she doesn't listen. After a pause he admits that maybe he just doesn't know how to reach her. They tried counseling for a few sessions, but he found the experience awkward and demeaning. After a series of disappointments at work, he'd also given up looking for other options.

Most recently, he found that smoking pot would at least quiet his overactive mind and help him sleep, but even that was losing its effectiveness. He had also started drinking, but that was making him feel more depressed. "Let's face it: I'm a loser."

Stefan had tried so many other things to get his life back under control, each of them failing miserably. He tried hanging out with a few friends, but that only accelerated his drinking since they'd usually go to bars. He'd read somewhere that exercise often helped, but he couldn't seem to find the energy or initiative to make himself follow through on a regular basis. More and more often, he was thinking about just ending things: "Hey, what do I have to lose? My life is already a complete waste. Maybe I should just finish the job."

Stefan wasn't completely serious about his intention, but it gave him some semblance of peace to know that at least there was one thing he could do on his own terms, even if it was to take his own life. This theme of losing control was actually what was bothering him more than anything else. He could handle his jerk of a boss and the tedious assignments on his schedule. He could probably convince himself to finally end the relationship with his girlfriend and find another place to live. He might even be able to reduce his dependence on alcohol and marijuana. But that still wouldn't fundamentally change how empty and meaningless his life felt, and how little he felt in charge of where things were going.

Stefan felt stuck largely because he was doing the same things over and over again even though they clearly weren't working. He shook his head as he recounted that he and his girlfriend kept repeating the same argument almost every night. He felt completely frustrated because every time he approached his supervisor at work for a change in responsibilities, he'd get the same discouraging answer. But rather than change tactics, he'd keep repeating the same mistakes.

Of course, we have no idea what might help Stefan pull himself out of his misery. There is hardly enough information to form a reasonable hypothesis of what might really be going on with him and how his problems fit within the history and patterns of his life. Nevertheless, he's given us a pretty clear idea of what *won't* work—because he's already tried that action innumerable times with the same disappointing result.

Stefan says he *wants* to change, but his actions say something else altogether. It would seem, on some level, that no matter how miserable and desperate he might feel, there is a part of him that is terrified of the unknown.

WHY PEOPLE CHANGE

On the one hand, change is the most natural, effortless thing in the world. Absolutely nothing ever remains the same. Even mountains are eroding and growing, although the pace is literally glacial and beyond our visible recognition. Everything about you is changing as well, whether you like it or not. Your hair and nails are growing a few millimeters each day, all without any effort or conscious thought. It is when it comes time to choose and act on a needed change that we often get cold feet, stall as long as possible, postpone action, make excuses, and try our best to preserve the status quo.

Anyone who yearns for something different in life eventually initiates changes for a number of reasons. Stefan's expressed desire is hardly enough, perhaps because of the ambivalence he may feel leaving his relationship and job behind. Changing anything is usually hard work, requiring all kinds of new accommodations, learning new behaviors, dealing with different and challenging situations, and letting go of what is familiar in lieu of situations that will feel uncomfortable, if not threatening. As much as Stefan likes the *idea* of having a new job or a new partner, he is actually quite terrified by what that might involve.

In spite of what people say, change is often frightening and disorienting. Russian novelist, Fyodor Dostoyevsky, remarked that taking any new step, even uttering a new word, is what people fear the most.[1] By definition *change* means something completely different from what is known or expected. That's why, ordinarily, people don't make changes in their lives unless one of five conditions is met[2].

1. *Life transitions.* There are natural, developmental processes that force us to make necessary adjustments to changing circumstances, abilities, bodily changes, or environmental factors. Leaving home, marriage, pregnancy, turning 40, menopause, retirement, and similar life events necessarily require changes to adapt to new roles and responsibilities. Whereas such transitions can be extremely interesting and stimulating, they also require a lot of work to handle smoothly; even so, there are likely a lot of uncomfortable and challenging moments.

2. *Boredom.* Restlessness, inertia, and sameness can be as trying for some people as too much stimulation. We all seek a balance between excitement versus boredom; providing sufficient challenges and new experiences enables us to remain fully engaged in our lives. If the stimulation becomes more than we can handle, anxiety kicks in; if too little, then we disengage.[3] Some people make changes for the pure exhilaration of the ride, even though such actions can sometimes backfire or have negative side effects.

3. *Something needs fixing.* It is often a last resort to consider taking action because of the perceived risks involved. People will remain in the most unsatisfying, even abusive, relationships because they are reluctant to deal with the consequences of doing something new, with all the accompanying hard work and adjustments. It is only when people acknowledge that some aspect of their life is irreparably damaged that they will do what is absolutely necessary to move forward.

4. *Rewards.* Given the extra work involved in adjusting usual habits and patterns, there must be some incentive that makes it worth the effort. If the potential rewards for changing existing behavior seem worthwhile, then logically it makes sense that motivation would increase. You might consider altering your commute to work, and learning a new route that forces you to abandon the familiar, comfortable pattern, but only if it saves you significant time and convenience. Otherwise you are subjecting yourself to increased stress and effort without the corresponding profit from the investment. Of course, one possible ancillary benefit might be the stimulation of a novel experience.

5. *Crisis.* Some catastrophic event—a flood, fire, assault, lost job, divorce, death in the family, severe illness, or other such trauma—requires people to deal with a situation they would never have chosen. As we'll see, almost half the time such adversity can often lead to tremendous growth rather than debilitating, lingering problems. As with each of these other conditions, whether voluntary or circumstantial, there are opportunities to experience significant benefits if managed in a particular way.[4]

The "if" is a huge qualifier since, as previously mentioned, the idea of change is often a lot more attractive than the realities of what is involved. This is particularly the case when people realize how much they tend to exaggerate what the changes will actually mean in their lives, rarely leading to the imagined perfect fantasy of happiness that they envisioned.[5]

THE BENEFITS OF AVOIDING CHANGE

There are all kinds of very good reasons to avoid change, not the least of which is that it requires a significant investment of time, energy, and commitment. That's one reason why most people are actually quite ambivalent about change, in spite of stated desires to the contrary. We are often totally oblivious about some of the underlying causes of our discomfort or annoying symptoms, sparking resistance that is both unintended and unconscious.[6] This paradox of wanting to change, but not wanting to abandon the familiar, is at the heart unsuccessful efforts. In other words, "we may be anxious, but not anxious to change."[7]

All kinds of defense mechanisms kick in to help us avoid issues we'd rather not face. If by ignoring the problem we can successfully pretend it doesn't exist, and get away with it for a period of time, then such a strategy works pretty well, at least to buy some time until readiness levels improve. In some ways, it is advantageous to remain blissfully ignorant in that it saves a lot of work. Every change that is made not only involves learning something new, but also usually surrendering something else that is familiar and comfortable. Let's say you take a lesson to improve your golf or tennis swing, which has been somewhat erratic. Adjusting your hand position is likely to feel awkward and take many hours of practice before the change becomes useful. The ball previously may not have been traveling very straight or far, but at least your swing felt comfortable. Now you have to concentrate more, remind yourself to follow new procedures for the grip, and live with a transition that doesn't seem "natural."

Several models have been introduced that chart the stages that people often navigate through during their journeys to initiate relatively permanent changes in a habit or behavior.[8] Reflected in these sequential steps are the ambivalence, confusion, uncertainty, and reluctance that are often felt during this process that progresses along the way. It is during the initial period of reflection (Stages 1 through 3 in Table 2.1)

Table 2.1. STAGES OF CHANGE

Precontemplation: "I don't really want to change."

Contemplation: "Okay, I kind of want to change but I don't know how."

Preparation: "I think I would like to change but it's too much work."

Action: "This feels good to do things differently and see clear results."

Backsliding: "Oops, I thought I was finally free. What happened?"

Maintenance: "This is starting to feel natural."

Termination: "I'm really confident I have this finally under control."

---

that all kinds of reasons and excuses are generated for postponing or avoiding change altogether: "I don't have time," "It's too much trouble," "I'm too overwhelmed right now," "It probably wouldn't work anyway," or "I forgot."

Whereas this stage model plots the usual trajectory of what happens internally as people come to terms with the challenges they face trying to alter a long-standing pattern or habit, it is somewhat rare that progression follows such an orderly and smooth process. In the vast majority of instances, estimated to be as much as 95% of the time, initial efforts fail in spite of the best intentions. This is especially the case with entrenched habits and addictions related to weight loss, gambling, smoking, drugs, and alcohol but also applies to most other behavior in which neural pathways have been grooved in the brain that never really become extinguished.[9]

Although a stage theory, with neat, elegant names for each step in the process, provides an illusion of predictability about people's change experiences, things are usually far more complex than that. In one study of more than two dozen individuals who experienced significant changes in their lives, the participants reported that rather than follow any kind of logical, sequential series of steps, they felt a kind of sudden reorganization as a result of a breakthrough that may have occurred after some gradual progress.[10] It would seem, then, that many existing models aren't necessarily consistent with what people say happens for them during the process.

Hidden Gains

Whereas change is postponed because it involves new adjustments and hard work, the present conditions are also strongly reinforced to remain the same. You do the same things over and over not because they are so effective but because they are both familiar and provide some benefits, even if they might at first appear to be terribly annoying.

Luellen consistently gets herself into trouble when she attempts to speak up in meetings. Her voice tone is strident, her manner adversarial and aggressive. Once she gets going, she comes across as highly inappropriate, and others react by either challenging her or shutting down. She has lost all credibility in her workplace and managed to alienate most of those on her team. Both her supervisor and her coworkers have repeatedly told her to change her style, which they find off-putting and counterproductive, not to mention offensive. Luellen agrees that this would be desirable, but every attempt to change her ways has failed.

It's almost always interesting, if not useful, to ask why someone would continue to engage in behavior that is patently self-defeating. Why would Luellen, or anyone else for that matter, persist in doing things that appear to be getting in their way? Why would you knowingly repeat a pattern that clearly doesn't work?

The answer to these questions is that people "enjoy" certain hidden benefits as a result of even the most self-sabotaging behavior. These are called "secondary gains," which continue to reinforce actions and provide advantages even if they don't immediately seem apparent. In other words, all behavior persists because it is doing something that is useful for the person, even though it might have a lot of negative side effects (like annoying others). This phenomenon was originally observed by Sigmund Freud while working with hysterical patients who seemed to be "clinging to their disease" rather than showing much inclination to change.[11] This idea was later applied to make sense of malingering hospital patients who should otherwise have improved from procedures but only languished without significant recovery. It was observed that they seemed to be enjoying the attention, the escape from work and responsibilities, the excuses they had for being ornery: "Hey, I can't help it. Can't you see I'm sick?" As long as they received such benefits, there wasn't much incentive for them to get better.

Just to clarify, this is not a conscious form of obstruction or resistance, nor does it suggest that people are deliberately being manipulative or controlling, but rather, they are unaware of their ambivalence about what it would mean to launch themselves in a new, unfamiliar direction.

In Luellen's case, it is, indeed, instructive to ask what payoffs she might be accruing as a result of her interpersonal style. For one, she feels powerful and in control. She might be irritating her colleagues and compromising her effectiveness, but she also inspires fear. Coworkers are reluctant to challenge her and choose to back down rather than engage her in battle. She often gets her way simply because others don't want to deal with the aggravation.

Second, Luellen gets to feel like a victim. "Can you believe those assholes at work? They don't even give me a chance. As soon as I speak my mind—and you'd better believe if I don't say something, nobody else will—they cower like a bunch of babies. They're always complaining and whining about this crap about civility. What the hell does that mean, anyway?" She may not have many friends, or enjoy much support, but she can blame others for her problems. It's not her fault but, rather, she's simply misunderstood.

On some level, Luellen well understands that her abrasive manner pushes others away. Not surprisingly, whatever difficulties she's having at work also play out in her other relationships with family and friends. The third benefit of her dysfunctional behavior is that she protects herself by launching first-strike attacks that keep others on the defensive. Although she comes across as fierce and blustery, Luellen is actually quite vulnerable; she is terrified of being hurt and so lashes out at others to keep them off balance.

Finally, her behavior allows her to react and respond to people impulsively and without feeling responsibility. "Hey, I can't help it. I've always been this way. When I was a kid, even my parents would stay out of my way when I was in one of those moods." As long as she believes that her interpersonal behavior is immutable and impervious to change, she can continue that pattern without feeling like it is in any way her fault.

With all these benefits, it makes perfect sense that Luellen would have trouble making adjustments to a style that is already, in some ways, working well for her. It is only when those secondary gains become less attractive (usually through increased self-awareness), or when the consequences of her behavior can no longer be ignored, that she would feel sufficient motivation to take constructive steps in another direction. In Luellen's case, there could be several catalysts to get her attention: (1) her mother stops taking her calls because she is so annoyed by the conflicts that keep arising, (2) her supervisor gives her a poor evaluation with feedback that unless she changes her ways she will lose her job, (3) a guy she likes tells her that she scares the crap out of him. Each of these incidents would bring to her attention to the reality that what's she's doing is definitely not in her own best interest. If such a realization passes a threshold such that pain she is experiencing becomes intolerable, then she may finally feel sufficient motivation to challenge and change a long-standing pattern that has served her well.

Just imagine all the work Luellen would have to do if she gave up her aggressive behavior. She would have to learn other ways of getting her needs met, other means by which to persuade people to do her biding. She would have to surrender all the other benefits she enjoyed as well— especially her most prized strategy of getting others to back down by going "nuclear." It is no wonder, then, that any of us would feel some reluctance to make changes when the payoffs for remaining the same appear so compelling.

Identifying Secondary Gains

This is a concept that is often forgotten, or at least neglected, by those professionals whose job it is to promote change (doctors, psychotherapists, teachers, coaches, managers, leaders, parents). They fail to recognize that until such time that people are willing to acknowledge and "own" the payoffs they receive from keeping things very much the way they are, there isn't much incentive to make needed changes. You can push and push and push someone to do things that you *know* are good for them—and they may even admit that to themselves—but they aren't likely to do much about it until such time when what they are already doing isn't working. For Luellen, and any of the rest of us, that often takes place after our motivation becomes more explicitly evident: It's difficult to keep getting away with something once you are fully aware of what's really going on.

A favorite means by which to promote this insight is to ask yourself (or someone else): *If it is true that even self-destructive behavior persists because it is somehow rewarding, then what benefits are being enjoyed by continuing this pattern, even with all the negative consequences?*

To summarize, most people are just doing the best they can to manage their lives and keep things reasonably under control. They have evolved patterns of behavior that have previously served some useful function, even with the collateral damage. Moreover, they will find it difficult to initiate changes in these patterns until they have addressed some of the needs that are currently being met.

I worked with a man in therapy who was referred by the court because of issues related to anger management, more specifically, road rage. He had been inadvertently cut off on the freeway and went ballistic, chasing down the offender and trying to run him off the road. This was part of an ongoing pattern that resulted in bar fights, screaming matches, and repeated conflicts with almost everyone in his life.

"Hey," the man apologized sheepishly, "I just can't help it. I have a bad temper."

It didn't take long in our conversation for him to admit that he really didn't much like the way he kept losing control. Not only would it eventually land him in jail, but it was also ruining all his relationships. People tiptoed around him to the point that he had few friends; even his family avoided him when possible because of his volatile, unpredictable rage.

It would have been easy to diagnose him with an "explosive personality disorder," a condition that exhibits symptoms of impulsive aggression, but instead I operated from the assumption that this behavior was potentially within his control if he no were longer "rewarded" for it.

"What the hell do you mean by that?" he challenged me. I could see the little vein in his forehead start to pulse, a clear warning signal that I had just triggered his anger. Rather than back down, and give in to the same recursive cycle that was an integral part of his problem, I pressed him further, explaining the idea that even though he said he wanted to rid himself of his uncontrollable rage, I didn't think he could do so until he looked at what it was doing for him.

The man took a deep breath to compose himself and then shrugged. It really is a difficult question for anyone to answer. As long as we are oblivious to what we're doing, we don't have to change.

In this case, there was a whole long list of secondary gains that were operating in his behavior. I might ask you to consider what some of them might be before you continue reading. What strikes you as advantageous about displaying uncontrolled rage that repeatedly lands someone in trouble and undermines any chance for a healthy relationship with family, friends, coworkers—and fellow drivers on the road?

Here are some possibilities that might have already occurred to you:

- By telling himself he has a bad temper, something that is part of his personality, he doesn't have to try to change it.
- He gets to abuse others and it's not his fault: "Hey, I can't help it. You know I have a bad temper."

- He intimidates people and often gets what he wants because others are afraid to challenge him, the consequences of which are that he might go off into a fit of rage.
- He gets to feel like a victim most of the time—misunderstood and unappreciated. The only reason he gets angry is because others deserve his wrath for their stupidity or wrongdoing.
- He loves the drama that accompanies his outbursts. It makes life exciting.
- Ironically, the loss of composure provides an illusion of control—that he engages the world on his own terms without restraint or rules that apply to others.

You can readily see that this guy would have his work cut out for him to alter this pattern unless he is prepared to find other ways to deal with some of the underlying issues of insecurity, impulse control, and a sense of injustice. In this example, he is frightened and threatened by intimacy. He has felt that life has given him a raw deal and owes him something for past disappointments and failures. And within his family, anger was the only thing that ever seemed to get him any attention.

Within such a stable system that perpetuates the same self-defeating behavior, one strategy designed to circumvent resistance simply and subtly involves creating a balance sheet listing the costs and benefits as a result of the current state of affairs.[12] Sure, the man with the explosive anger enjoys tremendous power and control as a result of his behavior, but he also pays a dear price for this pattern. When invited to explore these side effects, he found that time and again he was preventing any kind of sustained intimacy in his life because others were so afraid of upsetting him. Yes, he got what he wanted a lot of the time but at the cost of alienating most of those around him.

OBSTACLES TO CHANGE

Before we review some of the influences that do work consistently well to promote and maintain changes, it's important to recognize the factors that block these intentions. It is often a lack of awareness and self-knowledge, as well as a degree of self-deception, that allows people to continue along a destructive path without apparent concern for the ongoing consequences.

Widening the scope of this phenomenon, geographer Jared Diamond explored the reasons why certain cultures like the Anasazi, Inca, Mayan, Easter Island, and Norse Greenland collapsed in a relatively short period of time.[13] Many of these critical errors apply equally well to an individual's problems that persist and seem intractable. The first lapse in judgment was a failure to anticipate or predict a problem, being caught totally unprepared for some natural or human-induced disaster. This was followed with the even more indefensible excuse that once the problem or crisis did appear, people refused to recognize and acknowledge it. Third, even when the problem was identified, people procrastinated and refused to deal with it, crossing their fingers and hoping it would go away. If that didn't work, then they'd rationalize that the problem was just part of the natural course of events or part of some divine plan. If this sounds more than a little familiar to our present predicament related to global warming, that's because the circumstances are virtually identical to what happened throughout history when inhabitants refused to become responsible custodians of their environment. The final fatal error, once the severity of the problem was recognized (soil erosion, extinction of species, depletion of resources, overpopulation, conflict with others), was that only feeble, tentative solutions were undertaken. By then, it was too late.

When we apply this same analysis to the obstacles that block personal changes, we can readily see some parallels—although it's almost never too late to make needed adjustments and changes even if the situation is no longer optimal or ideal.

It's About Attitude

As much as psychotherapists would like to believe that it is their brilliant strategies that are the most potent factors in producing excellent results and accomplished goals, the best predictor of a successful outcome is actually more often related to the client's own characteristics, especially those that relate to an absence of severe psychopathology, high motivation, lack of impulsivity, absence of substance abuse, and realistic expectations for the treatment.[14]

When people do find themselves stymied, frustrated, and discouraged after repeated efforts to initiate changes, it is most often the result of their own unrealistic or counterproductive attitudes that are getting in the way. Usually these take the form of the following themes:[15]

1. "Maybe change isn't really necessary." As long as you feel ambivalent or uncertain about whether it is critical that you actually have to do something differently, it is far more comfortable, or at least familiar, to maintain the status quo.
2. "This really isn't my idea in the first place." Good point. It is often the case that pressure to change comes from external sources or other people, rather than from some internally based desire. Until you "own" the problem and acknowledge intense interest in doing something about it, efforts are usually futile.
3. "I'm overthinking this." Some of the most effective defense mechanisms for avoiding or sabotaging change are those that involve intellectualizing, analyzing, and ruminating about options and possible outcomes. Change is really about action rather than reflection.
4. "What's the point anyway?" Futility and hopelessness arise from a sense of powerlessness, that whatever changes you make won't fundamentally improve the quality of your life. Needless to say, this belief would discourage any persistent effort.
5. "I'll do it later." We tend to procrastinate and put off those things for which we don't feel a personal investment. You seem to find time to do the things that matter the most to you (and are the most fun); if you find yourself avoiding action, it's often because you don't see a clear connection between its completion and the investment of time and effort involved.
6. "I know what I have to do; I just can't seem to stick with it." Knowing what is good for you is one thing, but acting on that understanding is quite another. There are all kinds of evidence supporting the idea that insights, self-awareness, and self-knowledge may be interesting but they don't necessarily lead to constructive action—and in some cases can doom you to inertia.
7. "I just lost interest." As we will discuss repeatedly, initiating changes is the easy part—the real challenge is to sustain the momentum, especially when there are setbacks and disappointments.
8. "It's too much work." This is clearly the case: it *does* take tremendous effort, energy, resources, sacrifices, risks, and consistent

self-monitoring in order to get serious about change, at least the kind that feels grandiose and potentially life altering. Sometimes it doesn't feel like it's really worth it. And that's why taking things in small, realistic, achievable steps can often counteract most of these internal obstacles.

Another important lesson is that change is not seen as a trial, a job, an annoyance, or a task to be completed if it's perceived and experienced as enjoyable and satisfying. When a visitor to a game park remarked to the ranger that he was pretty lucky to see a lion that was perched on top of a rock and wondered how they managed to train the lion to sit there so patiently, the ranger just laughed. It turns out they didn't have to train or make the lion do anything because the rock was temperature controlled, providing a warm spot in the winter and a cool spot in the heat: "No need to train the lion or tie him to the rock or hope he likes the view. Just make the rock a place he *wants* to sit."[16] Each of us has to find a place, a *different* place, where we actually like to sit.

In other words, the ability and willingness to change is certainly sabotaged or empowered by your own personal qualities, interpretations, choices, attitudes, and beliefs. Although these are supposed to be rather stable characteristics, once you are intimately familiar with your own strengths and resources, as well as limitations, you can take definitive steps to customize plans in your own best interests.

Personality Traits

Those who have a more optimistic and upbeat disposition are naturally going to have an easier time taking action than those who always imagine the worst. Those who routinely attribute their circumstances to luck, fate, poor genes, negligent parenting, bad weather, the economy, God's will, or other circumstances outside of their control won't do nearly as well as those who demonstrate a "hardy personality," meaning that they are generally optimistic, rise to challenges, and feel some degree of control over their choices.[17] Likewise, those with a diagnosable personality disorder (a severe self-sabotaging characteristic style), or who are typically impulsive, indecisive, and lack the ability to be self-reflective, are also going to encounter greater difficulty changing themselves.[18]

I presume it makes sense that certain people have an easier time making new adjustments because they are more open to such changes in the first place.

Another important dimension is related to recent research that indicates that some people's brains are wired differently than others, making them far more susceptible to habit formation and addictions (Figure 2.1). You can shake your head all you want at the apparent craziness of compulsive gamblers, wondering why they are so stupid to think they can actually beat the casinos, but it may actually be true that at least some of them really can't control their behavior.[19] Some studies have indicated that pathological gamblers' neurological systems are far more responsive to the temptations of gaming, distorting beliefs that they can actually win. They just flat out get more aroused and excited by even the *prospect* of hitting the jackpot.[20] Near misses count as wins in their minds, which is why casinos, poker machine manufacturers, and lotteries design their programs so it appears if the players almost win, even when they lose.

Even with the biologically programmed challenges that are embedded in personality traits considered relatively stable, there are still

Figure 2.1: Developmental plasticity refers to someone's inborn ability (neural connections) to adapt to changing circumstances, contexts, and environments. It is one of several personal characteristics that often determine—and sometimes limit—the potential for initiating and maintaining behavioral, attitudinal, and habitual alterations. Evolution has favored those organisms that are most adaptable to the ever-changing nature of context and environment. (Photo courtesy of Shutterstock © Gornjak)

innumerable ways that people have learned to cope with their limitations and disabilities. There have been legions of historical figures who struggled with debilitating depression, including Georgia O'Keeffe, Virginia Woolf, Vaslav Nijinsky, Ludwig Beethoven, Sylvia Plath, Ernest Hemingway, John Adams, Isaac Newton, Meriwether Lewis, Winston Churchill, and Abraham Lincoln, to mention a few. Each of them found ways to circumvent their struggles and use the suffering to further their creative or productive goals.[21] They taught themselves to adapt to the challenges they faced, as well as to accept those variables that were truly outside their control (such as biologically based severe depression).

There are vast differences in a person's ability to change, depending on a host of different factors, including such things as your characteristic cognitive style, tolerance for discomfort, access to social support, and coping skills.[22] Each of us manifests different levels of patience, frustration tolerance, resilience, and adaptability, which, while possibly inherited and physiologically programmed, can also be significantly improved with enough diligence and commitment (see Table 2.2). But first comes the honest acceptance of what you can and can't do realistically.

Negative Moods

Those who cope with lifelong depression, anxiety, or other physiologically based mood disorders (as opposed to those that are situational

Table 2.2. PERSONAL FACTORS THAT AFFECT THE CAPACITY FOR CHANGE

Past experiences	Previous trauma
Perceptual sensitivity	Cultural background
Cognitive deficits	Cognitive rigidity
Self-discipline	Emotional regulation
Tolerance for ambiguity	Willingness to explore unknown
Willingness to take risks	Interpersonal skills
Social support or isolation	Peer pressure and family dynamics
Impulsivity	Tendency to externalize blame
Openness to feedback	Resilience
Hardiness	Optimism versus pessimism
Debilitating emotional problems	Emotional volatility
Stress inoculation	Tolerance for pain and discomfort
Self-reflection	Capacity for insight

and reactive to events) have got their hands full just trying to keep their heads above water, much less trying to stay afloat. On a different scale, chronic stress impairs your ability to think clearly, control mood swings, make sound decisions, and follow through on intended goals.[23] In all of these cases, your attitudes and responses to life challenges are largely determined by your attitudes and the ways you metabolize experiences.

When Charlene was first told that her husband wanted a separation, she was understandably devastated. The announcement came as a complete surprise even though their level of intimacy had been waning over several years and their companionship had become habitual rather than mutually satisfying.

Charlene went into a complete tailspin. She found it difficult to get out of bed, much less show up for work. She stopped exercising because she just didn't have the energy: "Besides, what's the point? I'll never recover from something like this and I'll probably never find anyone else."

What began as legitimate and normal reaction to a fairly upsetting life situation descended into profound depression. Charlene stopped taking care of herself altogether. She gained weight and fed herself on junk food to "medicate" her pain. That and a few glasses of wine each night were about the only things that seemed to provide an hour or two of relief. She stopped taking calls from friends and isolated herself. Under such circumstances it is perfectly understandable why it would be so difficult for Charlene to implement any constructive changes to get herself back on track. Every time she tried to follow through on some commitment ("Tomorrow I'll go for a walk just to stretch my legs"), she found she just didn't have the strength or wherewithal to leave the house. Each time she vowed to go to the fitness club or join her friends for a meal, she offered excuses for why it just wasn't convenient. But the reality is that she felt so down and listless that she couldn't mobilize the energy to do much of anything except feel sorry for herself.

On a less severe scale, there are plenty of other emotional states that will likely interfere with attempts to change. These might run the gambit from having a very low tolerance for frustration, hypervigilance (extreme self-monitoring), volatile mood swings, obsessive ruminations, and emotional overreactions to situations that feel like they are outside of one's control. In addition to the more severe mood and personality disorders mentioned previously, there are also chronic "low-grade" versions that predispose certain people to dysthymia (mild but functional chronic depression), stress, and other excessively strong responses.

It should be mentioned also that expressive and passionate emotional reactions to situations have also been labeled as pathological and problematic largely because the authors of diagnostic systems and manuals have been men in positions of power and influence who favor logic and rationality as preferred values over expression of feelings. This has changed in recent years with the increasing influence of feminist approaches to mental health that advocates greater balance between traditional male and female processing resources.[24]

That's not to say that in cases like Charlene's that her emotional responses aren't hindering her (because they are) but, rather, that for most of us it is perfectly normal and natural to feel all kinds of negative emotions when we face disappointments or difficult situations. In many cases, acknowledging, expressing, and working through these feelings are a critical part of the healing process, especially if they are handled constructively.

Coping Skills

In addition to inheriting certain personality characteristics, each of us also learned and developed a number of abilities and skills that we employ to function in the world. Even as children, the earliest signs of optimism, curiosity, perseverance, and determination predict success in later life.[25] What we are able to do in life depends, to some extent, on the repertoire of options at our disposal. Here is a sample of some skills that might be useful to those who are planning to make significant changes in their lives, whether this involves breaking a habit, stopping an addiction, ending or beginning a relationship, losing weight, beginning an exercise program, changing a job or living arrangement, altering a lifestyle, or implementing any other desired life-enhancing goal. While reviewing the list, you might take inventory of your own level of ability in each of these areas.

- Feeling clear about what is most important in terms of core values and life goals
- Being honest with yourself about strengths and weaknesses, as well as resources that are available

- Taking care of unfinished business that might intrude, interrupt, or sabotage intended progress
- Collecting maximum data and information that will be useful when implementing a change effort
- Making decisions that are well founded in the data gathered
- Reflecting honestly and meaningfully about most cherished values, priorities, and goals
- Setting goals that are specific, incremental, and realistically attainable
- Making public commitments about your intentions so you are held accountable for your plans
- Postponing immediate gratification and impulsivity
- Patiently waiting until the optimal time for taking action
- Practicing and rehearsing anticipated and planned actions prior to implementing them
- Taking constructive risks and experimenting with new behaviors
- Evaluating systematically the relative impact of an action and making needed adjustments
- Talking to yourself in constructive, helpful ways during times when you feel discouraged
- Soliciting feedback, input, and suggestions for those in a position to be most helpful
- Avoiding high-risk situations that invite unnecessary temptations
- Monitoring carefully internal conditions that increase risks (hunger, fatigue, stress, sadness, anger, loneliness, frustration)
- Managing stress *before* it becomes excessive
- Asking for help when the need arises
- Reaching out to sources of social support
- Recognizing triggers that increase the risk of relapses
- Bouncing back from inevitable setbacks and disappointments
- Forgiving yourself for mistakes and failures and learning from these experiences
- Taking proactive steps to make sure that the changes stick as long as you want
- Applying what was learned to other aspects of your life also in need of upgrading or improvement

Even if you were able to master all of these skills, there are still restrictions on what is possible, given the practical limits of free will. We might prefer the myths that "anything is possible" or that we live in a "land of opportunity," but there also restrictions placed on our capacity for change. There is a self-regulating system in each of us, integrated into our biological systems to maintain homeostasis at a cellular level. Any slight change in temperature, pressure, or volume, any introduction of a "foreign" body, any departure from usual routines, kicks into gear all sorts of immune and regulatory responses to return the organism to its previous settings. Raise your body temperature a few degrees through exercise, and sweat glands will immediately activate to return things back to "normal." We may perceive that we have control over other aspects of our life, but similar operating systems make it challenging to alter existing habits and routines. Just as the autonomic nervous system controls the respiratory, circulatory, and other body functions, so, too, are we predisposed to create and maintain habitual behavior systems to save time and energy.

At the most basic level, the "fight-or-flight" response is one example in which we are programmed, without conscious thought, to respond instantaneously to a perceived threat. The cerebral cortex is bypassed altogether (too slow!), instead launching a barrage of endocrine functions to activate systems that will be useful if you have to do battle or flee. Eyes are dilated to better perceive danger. Hunger and excretory systems are shut down as they aren't needed, instead redirecting nourishment (oxygen) and support to increase heart rate and breathing. All of this occurs without your permission, or even awareness, because your survival depends on an immediate response to perceived danger.

Much of your behavior is similarly regulated through habitual responses, "mental butlers" that take care of things for you.[26] This definitely makes our daily lives easier as we automatically take care of chores, brush teeth, get dressed, commute to work, and groom ourselves, following habitual patterns that have become long-established routines.

Here's the problem: What if you want to change, alter, or revise one of these "mental butlers," much less an important part of yourself? Once neurological pathways have been grooved into our system, it takes a *lot* of effort to reroute them, much less set up a roadblock or carve a new, more efficient highway. No wonder it's so challenging to reprogram our mental butlers and why relapsing is the norm rather than the exception.

False Hopes and Resolutions That Fail

As we shall see, maintaining progress is far more difficult than making the initial changes in the first place. People make all kinds of promises to themselves and others that they are unable or unwilling to deliver. Take New Year's resolutions as just one example, a practice followed by the vast majority of Americans even though most of these commitments are never achieved.[27] Most people resolve to do the same things each and every year—stop smoking, lose weight, exercise, call home, get out of debt, spend more time with family, give up drinking, get a better job— and yet they rarely, if ever, meet those expectations or change the goal in light of previous failures. The average person tries at least 10 times before successfully (and often temporarily) following through on such commitments.[28]

Researchers investigating this phenomenon wonder why people even bother to keep trying to change with so many repeated disappointments.[29] They cite absolutely dismal prognoses for losing weight, stopping smoking or gambling, and other negative habits as well over 90% failure and provide a number of reasons for the poor outcomes. It's not so much that people are interested in avoiding change as they are just extremely delusional about their abilities and unrealistic goals. Then they make things far worse by persuading themselves that the reasons for the failure are one or more of the following:

1. I didn't try hard enough.
2. I wasn't motivated enough.
3. I ran out of time or energy.
4. I used the wrong approach.
5. It was just bad luck.
6. I'll do better next time.

Interestingly, what most people don't realize is that maybe their initial goals weren't realistic in the first place. As a result they conclude that it was some inadequacy or shortcoming in themselves that sabotaged the effort but they'll produce a different outcome next time. It's certainly reasonable to question whether you tried hard enough or used the right approach, but gee, after a half dozen times you'd think it's time to do a thorough reassessment.

Sure, they might be benefiting from secondary gains, but just as likely, they hold unattainable expectations for what's reasonable. People tend to overestimate their abilities and underestimate the amount of time and energy it takes to complete a task, especially one that is complex, intractable, and long-standing. Taking weight loss as one example, dieters believe that once they slim down *everything* in their lives will change for the better and they'll live happily ever after. When that doesn't quite work out as expected, discouragement leads to a faltering spirit.

The more often that someone fails at a task, the more likely that confidence and self-esteem will be compromised, reducing the likelihood that future efforts will be successful. It's as if there is a limited reservoir of willpower that is systematically depleted after each failed attempt. Imagine trying eight different times to tell your boss you don't appreciate the way he treats you and runs the department, and each time you are met with scorn and further abuse. Now you're ready to try once again but with appreciably less optimism that the attempt will be successful.

It turns out that a number of myths are perpetuated by the self-help industry, that all it takes to change your life is good intentions, positive thinking, self-affirmations, grandiose expectations, and force of will (Figure 2.2). But as it turns out, it is precisely these illusions and myths that lead people to overestimate what is realistic and possible, dooming them to disappointment and discouragement.[30]

The solution, of course, is to be as realistic as possible, assessing what is likely contributing to the failures, no matter how close to the target the effort might seem. Is the disappointing result really a function of insufficient commitment or motivation? Would a different approach to the problem be indicated? Or, does the goal need adjusting to something else within reach? It turns out that that aiming for small, incremental goals that are more easily within reach produces far more successful outcomes than going after more ambitious achievements all at once.[31]

WHAT WE PROBABLY KNOW AND UNDERSTAND ABOUT WHAT LEADS TO CHANGE

Okay, enough of the bad news, or at least the obstacles faced when making changes. And enough of the mystery surrounding such efforts.

Figure 2.2: Most people have a genuine interest and commitment to change some aspect of themselves that is getting in the way or is less than desirable—they just want the process to be effortless, simple, and painless. That is one of the appeals of the billion dollar self-help industry in that it promises easy quick fixes to whatever plagues you, whether it is losing weight, stopping addictions, or extricating yourself from a lousy job or relationship.

What is it that we *do* know and understand about how change occurs?[32] Although this will form the basis for the rest of the book, here is a list of some of the most important operative factors we will be discussing:

- Dissatisfaction with life (depression, anxiety, stress, unhappiness)
- External events (economy, war, natural disaster)
- New insight ("I'm smart," "I don't have to like it," "It's finally over")
- Hitting bottom (loss of everything, desperation, nothing to lose)
- Trauma (abuse, assault, neglect, death of loved one, illness)
- Life transition (developmental stage, age-related crisis)
- Keystone behaviors (little changes can lead to big things)
- Travel (adventure, novel environment, new resources)
- Counseling (psychotherapy, coaching, consultation, instruction)

- Spiritual transformation (relationship with God, scriptures, transcendence)
- Validation (affirmation, support, feeling understood)
- Narratives (stories, books, resources that made a difference)
- Mortality (close brush with death or confrontation with limited time)
- Self-deception (confronting a truth or lie, coming to terms with self)
- Risk (experiment, facing fears, trying new behavior)
- Lifestyle (exercise, health, consumerism, interests)
- Support (groups, friendship, family, social engagement)
- Solitude (reflection, contemplation, meditation, centering)
- Meaning making (value clarification, making connections, life's purpose)
- Altruism (serving others, involvement in a cause, making a difference)

Reviewing this list of factors most often associated with personal transformations, one obvious conclusion is that there are, indeed, many variables at work. People have been changed by things small and large, from reading a book, watching a film, having an intense conversation, becoming lost, attending a group, seeking therapy, going on an adventure, recovering from illness, facing death, listening to a call-in radio show, being touched by God, receiving support from family, losing or finding a job, creating meaningful work—the list is potentially endless.

If we delve more deeply into the research on happiness, well-being, and life satisfaction, rather than only look at problem resolution, the conclusions we can draw are somewhat clearer and more focused (see Chapter 11). The studies are unequivocal, consistent, and overwhelming—and you can pretty much guess what they discovered in answer to the question: What most often leads to people's happiness and greater well-being (see Table 2.3)?[33]

What's intriguing about these results is that everyone already knows most of this but rarely acts on the findings (although it may be surprising to see what research indicates *isn't* important, like health and education). So much of our lives center around attaining status, material wealth, accumulating possessions, pursuing measureable goals, and yearning for a bigger home, more luxurious car, and more attractive climate. Yet what research tells us is that none of this matters much in terms of life satisfaction: Given all other things equal, people living in

Table 2.3. WHAT MOST OFTEN LEADS TO HAPPINESS

What matters most	What doesn't matter
Hopeful optimistic disposition	Health
Resilience and adaptability	Income beyond a "moderate" level
Solid friendships and social support	Material possessions
Involvement in a romantic relationship	Education
Faith/spiritual beliefs	Race
Meaningful work	Gender
Wisdom and experience	Geographical climate

South Dakota, Nebraska, or Mississippi are just as happy as those living in sun-drenched California or Florida. Once you have enough to live on comfortably, having more things or making more money does not significantly improve anything—except the levels of stress associated with holding onto what you've amassed.

Questions related to these "big" issues of what gives life meaning are at the heart of our exploration. There is no sense going after goals or making changes if, once you reach them, they don't make much of a difference in the way you feel about yourself, your life, and where you are headed. That's one of the reasons why people become discouraged after they discover that all the hard work they invested didn't pay off with the miraculous benefits they had anticipated. And that's also why it's so important to have realistic goals regarding what is ultimately within your grasp.

CHAPTER 3

When Lives Are Transformed

*C*hange is such a simple little word to describe making something different. Yet there are so many different kinds of change, even when only applied to human behavioral alterations. There are little changes and big ones. Change can be fast and furious, sudden shifts without warning. Change can occur gradually at a pace that is so barely noticeable that you don't even realize it happened. It can take place on the surface or at a deeper, "second-order," structural level. It can vary in its magnitude, rate, level, consistency, and significance. It can be vivid and intense or muted and subtle. It can spark constructive actions or lead to a downward spiral. It can be temporary or stable, planned or serendipitous.

We have lots of names to describe the kind of change that results in dramatic, life-altering transformations, the sort that forever impacts who you are and how you walk through the world. That, after all, is what interests us, rather than relatively minor adjustments that often take place beyond awareness. There is an assortment of different terms used to describe such "quantum" or "transcendental" shifts that lead to radical changes in self-identity or worldview.[1] These can involve, for example, deep shifts in feelings with corresponding insight (corrective emotional experience), a spiritual awakening or religious conversion, or a dramatic reconceptualization of one's place in the world. What they all have in common is an emphasis on relatively significant and permanent modifications that have been internalized, resulting not only in altered beliefs and priorities, but also in new, more effective behavior, as well as continued growth that may even take place at a cellular level in the brain.

When related to recovering from addictions, personal transformations have been described as a form of death and rebirth, in that "a new person within a body once occupied by another" takes over.[2] These are the kinds of events first described by Abraham Maslow as peak experiences, transcendent moments that shape the directions of a person's life.[3] Although Maslow originally attributed these transcendent shifts to highly functional, self-actualized individuals, those who are most psychologically healthy, it turns out that roughly half of Americans report such an experience during their lifetime.[4] Most often, you don't go looking for this life-altering event; it arrives when you least expect it—busy fighting a battle, facing a challenge, recovering from a setback or tragedy. At least half the time, epiphanies occur at the absolute low point of people's lives, when they are desperate and feeling hopeless.[5] But the other half of the time we make conscious choices to improve the quality of our lives. We pull the plug on something that clearly isn't working, institute a major turn in the direction we were heading, follow some dream, quit a job, begin a new stage of life, or otherwise reinvent ourselves.

TRANSFORMATIONAL CHANGE

When I was in my early twenties, my mother was dying of cancer and had only a few days left to live. I made a nonstop, 12-hour drive home in the middle of the night to visit her on her deathbed. I spent most of that long drive crying and grieving, utterly exhausted and vulnerable. I rushed into the hospital and sat in the waiting room until my mother's physician could speak to me.

"Son," he said to me, with almost no preamble, "your mother passed away a few hours ago."

Tears started pouring down my face. I was too late to say goodbye and offer her any comfort. I was not only flooded with grief, but also regret for not having been a better son. Because of the sleep deprivation and internal distractions, I hadn't realized that the doctor was still speaking to me.

"So," he said in a voice that sounded almost bored, "there was really nothing we could do. The cancer had metastasized..."

I could barely concentrate on what he was saying, so I interrupted to ask him to repeat what he'd said.

"Look," he said, now visibly impatient. He actually looked over his shoulder at the door to make a quick escape. "With your genes, kid, you don't have much of a future—unless you take care of yourself."

The doctor was referring to the fact that while my mother, still in her forties, had died of cancer, at the same time my father was in another hospital going through quadruple bypass surgery; he would have a stroke a few years later that would leave him paralyzed and brain damaged.

"What are you saying?" I pressed the doctor. I didn't understand what he was telling me. I thought he was talking about my mother dying but now he was saying something to me—and I didn't even know the guy very well.

The doctor just shook his head and started to head back through the door. But he turned to look at me and leaned closer. "I'm saying that you don't have the greatest longevity in your future. You'll be lucky to live to be 40." Then he walked through the swinging door.

I was so furious at this jerk who had the interpersonal skills of a gerbil. How dare he frighten me like that, especially when I was so overwrought and vulnerable! Who the hell did he think he was, pronouncing a death sentence on me? He knew nothing about me or about my own medical history.

I walked out of the hospital in a daze, not only because I was about to become an orphan (I didn't know if my father would survive his surgery), but also because I had just been told that my life was extremely time limited.

It probably wouldn't surprise you to learn that this five-minute conversation changed my life, although there are many such seminal events that occur but merely dissipate over time. In this case, I was so overwhelmed with feelings, so disoriented and lost, so frightened, that it never felt like I had a choice to do anything other than make some significant changes in my lifestyle. It was the very next morning that I made a commitment to completely change almost everything about my life. If my time were, indeed, so limited and I only had a few years left, then I wanted to make the most of it. Furthermore, I would do whatever was in my power to extend my life: I started running the next morning, barely finishing a few hundred yards before I ran out of breath.

Eventually I worked up to running 10K races, then marathons, never missing a single day of exercise for 15 consecutive years! This means I ran through blizzards, below-zero temperatures, sickness and fevers, sprained ankles, never giving in to an excuse. I convinced myself that if my few years left on earth were, indeed, so precious, I would make the most of the time. I made a commitment, one that I have followed ever since, to live every day as if it were my last. That choice has guided so many decisions of my life, to avoid postponing anything that seems important, to assertively go after what I want, to go to sleep each night reasonably content that I have made the most of whatever time I have left.

Remarkably, this life-changing transformation took place as a result of a brief conversation with someone I didn't know very well and would never see again. Granted, it occurred under circumstances that were highly emotional and under conditions in which I was both vulnerable and impressionable. Nevertheless, it illustrates the way certain kinds of quantum changes can be ignited without warning or even voluntary choice. Such events, whether they are spiritual awakenings, recovery from addiction, transcendent awareness, new insights, or spectacular growth, have certain qualities. Many of them have been catalogued as a result of studying life-transforming experiences of individuals that led to historical movements.[6]

Think of major religious figures who launched a revolution or new movement, and you will often find within their background a seminal transformative event that set them on their spiritual path: Mohammed, Jesus, Moses, Buddha, St. Augustine, Martin Luther. Consider, as well, more contemporary figures such as Malcolm X, the Dalai Lama, or Bill Wilson, the founder of Alcoholics Anonymous, and again their commitment to enlightenment began with a singular event that transformed them. Whether occurring in a religious context, or one related to personal growth, such experiences are often characterized by certain features: They were unplanned, sudden, brief, vivid and intense, positive, and long lasting. They occurred during a time of personal crisis. They involved a requisite amount of solitude that permitted reflective contemplation and opportunities to make sense of the experience and put the new insights into constructive action. Such experiences didn't so much change behavior as launch a rebirth.

One of the most prevalent themes evident in transformative change is that it most often occurs during period of crisis, transition, difficulty, and trauma. It is during such events that people remain open to experiences that they might otherwise seek to avoid. When you are desperate and helpless, you will grasp at options that you would never have considered previously. You are willing to do whatever it takes to find your way, especially when you've lost almost everything that's dear to you.

THE GIFTS OF CRISIS

It's the bottom of the sixth inning. The Pittsburg Pirates are up, one to nothing, on a solo home run by Willie Stargell in the second inning. Dock Ellis, the mercurial starting pitcher, is struggling on the mound in more ways than one. Not only has he lost his pitching control, but he also seemed to be having trouble picking up the ball sitting on the mound. Ellis looked up, momentarily startled, as if he couldn't remember where he was and how he got there.

Ellis visibly shook his head, took a deep breath, then another. It didn't seem to help. The ball now firmly trapped in his glove, he looked at the catcher for the sign, but that seemed hopeless. In truth he couldn't even *see* the catcher, much less the batter or umpire. He just felt, no *sensed*, that the batter must be standing there waiting for the pitch, although at this point he couldn't even tell if the hitter was batting right- or left-handed. He wondered if maybe it was better to kind of aim down the middle and hope for the best.

In spite of his resolve, the pitches were sinking into the dirt, or flying high, out of control; sometimes he couldn't even tell where the throws were going. He could hear people yelling, all excited about something, but couldn't quite figure out what was so damned important that it was worth screaming about.

Damn, he must have walked the first batter because now he could see him on first base, although he couldn't remember how he got there. "Gotta concentrate. Gotta *focus*." But it was so damned hard when the ball kept changing size and shape. Sometimes it was so big he could barely lift his arm, or even hold it in his oversized hand; then, suddenly, it was reduced to the size of a grape so he could barely see the damned thing, much less grab it with two delicate fingers.

What was he thinking? Oh yeah, new batter. Time to start over.

Ellis looked over his shoulder and noticed that Nate Colbert, the guy who had been on first, wasn't there anymore! He looked around, confused, and saw the smug son of a bitch standing on second. Shit, the guy stole the base when he wasn't looking!

Ellis regained his composure, at least enough to have a vague recollection of what's going on. He was "high as a Georgia pine," as he would later describe his internal state after ingesting LSD hours before the game and then a handful of amphetamines to help him function well enough to walk out to the mound.[7] He looked up at the scoreboard and noticed that not much had changed in the seconds (minutes? hours?) since he had been standing there. Then he turned and saw Jimi Hendrix standing at the plate, ready to take a swing with his Stratocaster guitar. Ellis just started to giggle into his glove, pretty sure this part wasn't real. A few innings earlier, he thought he'd seen Richard Nixon behind the plate calling balls and strikes. He shook his head, closed his eyes for a moment, and tried to keep his focus. It was hard, so hard, because he couldn't keep track of the count, much less the score. "I'm throwing a crazy game," he recalled afterward. "I'm hitting people, walking people, throwing balls in the dirt, they're going everywhere."[8] Yet in a very strange way, Ellis found it easier to pitch when he was high. Or at least he'd gotten so used to it that it had become normal for him.

Miraculously, the next two batters flied out, and the sparse crowd of less than 10,000 people in the stands seemed to get all excited about something again. They were making noise but it seemed very far away. *Everything* seemed very far away—especially home plate.

Rather than feel better as things progressed, Ellis felt himself drifting away, and losing his focus again. It was like there was a war going on inside his head, a battle between the hallucinogenic drug that should be wearing off soon, and the speed that was now kicking in with it's full power. If he could just get out of this inning, he was sure he could get back into a groove.

Somehow—and even Ellis doesn't remember much about how exactly—he completed the "perfect" game, a no-hitter, even though he had ended up walking eight batters, throwing pitches in the dirt, high, low, even though he had trouble even catching the ball when it was lobbed back to the mound. Eventually, the catcher, Jerry May, had to put white tape on his fingers because Dock claimed he couldn't see the signals. The catcher wasn't sure that helped much.

Ellis had made history as the first person to pitch a no-hitter, maybe the first athlete ever to reach the pinnacle of his sport, while hallucinating on LSD. It is from such stuff that legends are made. But it is also from such myths that a person's struggles and suffering are overlooked because it all makes for such an amazing story, one that has found itself translated into songs, films, poems, and even comedy routines that celebrate the improbability of the whole crazy episode.[9] But that one afternoon in Dock Ellis' life, and even the 12 years he spent in the major leagues as an eventual Hall of Fame player, were only a small part of his life and his legacy.

Living in a Haze

Ellis had arrived in San Diego a few days earlier than his scheduled game so he could hang out with his childhood friend, Rambo, and Rambo's girlfriend, Mitzi, in Los Angeles. This was a frequent refuge for him, a place he felt safe, where nobody could bother him. He had grown up in this part of the city, and it was still the only place he felt he could truly be himself.

As was their custom, the three of them went on a 24-hour, drug-fueled binge, smoking marijuana, drinking vodka, snorting lines of cocaine, and popping amphetamines or whatever substances they could lay their hands on. Ellis just liked to tune out all the pressures of the world, all the stress of being a starting pitcher in the Major Leagues, especially an "uppity" black player with an attitude that often offended the owners (see Figure 3.1). It was just unbelievable what everyone expected from him, what everyone wanted from him. Every few days he'd have to put his whole job on the line. Teammates were depending on him. The manager was always on his ass. The racist media was driving him crazy with their critical comments about his rather eccentric outspoken style. His damned arm hurt all the time, but he couldn't say anything; just suck it up and get ready for the next start. Fans were always pestering

Figure 3.1: Dock Ellis wearing one of his signature hairstyles that infuriated his team's owner, as well as the powers of major league baseball. Their punitive actions only inspired him to tweak management whenever he got the chance. This made him both a hero to many, and reviled by others. (Photo courtesy of Associated Press.)

him for autographs and pushing him to say something funny or memorable. He could hardly trust anyone—except those in the 'hood, and even they were sometimes suspect. When he was home, when he was high, nobody could get to him. He'd listen to Jimi Hendrix sing "Purple Haze," which had become his anthem. He *lived* in a haze.

Dock Ellis became famous not just for his extraordinary athletic prowess, but also for his eccentricities and erratic behavior. For anyone who knows his story, it is hard to say his name without giggling. Indeed, throughout his lifetime, Ellis loved to kid with people, repeat the legend of his LSD trip on the mound, and talk about his drug-crazed adventures.

Underneath all the comic antics was a deeply wounded man who did the best he could to hold his life together under the harsh glare of public scrutiny. He was perceived as a big, angry black man who didn't give a shit about anything. Like many addicts, the drugs he relied on were as much to help him get through the day as they were to have fun. He *needed* the drugs to function in his job, as well as to deal with the pressures of daily life. It wasn't just his insanely difficult job as a starting pitcher that got to him—it was dealing with money, health, relationships, and ghosts from his past.

Ellis has been repeatedly, annoyingly interviewed about the fateful day. When one reporter remarked to him that it must have been the scariest experience of his life, trying to keep himself together and perform at the highest level when he could barely keep himself literally grounded, Dock just laughed.

"That's not true," he said. "The scariest time was in 1973, when I tried to pitch completely sober. We were in San Francisco, and when I went to the bullpen to warm up I couldn't even figure out how to wind up."

When the catcher, Manny Sanguillen, asked him what the hell was wrong because he looked so out of sorts, Ellis just shrugged. "I don't have my shit."

"Well, you better go get it then."

Ellis nodded. He went back into the clubhouse, located some amphetamines, downed them with strong coffee, and then started to feel normal again.

Thinking back on that day in the spring of 1972, Ellis could only shake his head in wonder.

"It was [actually] *easier* to pitch with the LSD because I was so used to medicating myself," Ellis recalled. "That's the way I was dealing with the fear of failure. The fear of losing. The fear of winning. It's part of the game, you know. You get to the Major League and you think, "I got to stay here. What do I need to do?" I was functioning as a baseball player but I was addicted to drugs and alcohol."

Sure, Ellis was wounded, haunted, and at times spectacularly self-destructive, but he was drowning and had to no idea where and how to get help. Any effort he made to change the pattern of his behavior lasted only as long as the next temptation. It was only the Benzedrine, marijuana, LSD, booze, and cocaine that seemed to bring relief.

For Ellis, drugs and alcohol weren't just a means by which to deal with the unrelenting stress but also a way to stave off his fear of failure.[10] Yet far more than that, he also struggled with what it meant for him to truly excel: "I was frightened to death of succeeding, and subconsciously, I did a lot of things to tear that down." Indeed, Ellis' career was filled with volatile ups and downs that reflected his own ambivalence about what he'd accomplished—and what he really could have done if he'd set his mind and will to it. Although Ellis earned a spot in the Hall of Fame, he never managed to maintain enough consistency to win 20 games in a season. Ellis believed he could have reached that milestone "if I'd had a chance to consult someone who was an authority on stress management. I felt my drug problem would have been arrested."

Feeling Completely Lost

After his retirement from baseball, Ellis was forced to face the emptiness and chaos of his life. He couldn't even remember the last time he hadn't gotten high at some point during the day. His first few marriages had already failed. He had a young son whom he barely knew, limited financial stability, few employment prospects, and no clear future. He knew that somehow he had to get clean; he had to turn his life around, but he had no idea what to do. He had dabbled with half-hearted attempts previously but with little success. It was going to take something radical to get his attention. Every previous attempt to get himself clean ended in utter defeat. He had moved from a contemplation stage in the process of change to a heightened state of readiness in which he was prepared to take constructive action.[11] As a last-ditch effort, he decided to enter a treatment program one more time, perhaps his last chance before he continued the trajectory of a slow death.

The prognosis for a chronic drug addict entering a 30-day treatment center is guarded at best. Relapses are so common that aftercare programs teach patients to *expect* to fail as part of their ultimate recovery. Yet we know well that it is the person's initial motivation, drive, and commitment that best predict positive outcomes. So it was with Dock Ellis; he was absolutely determined that this was going to be the absolute end of his self-destructive behavior. He'd had enough of the craziness. He'd lost almost everything that was important to him—his wives, his family and friends, whatever money he'd managed to squirrel away; even his reputation was trashed.

What was the source of Ellis's resolve to change a lifetime of destructive behavior virtually overnight? Certainly the structure of the program must have had something to do with it, as well as the accompanying support: "There was a big old redheaded dude in my face every day and he had a lot experience with what I was going through." Ellis paused for a moment, remembering that his mentor had killed himself: "Some of us live. Some of us don't make it."

Ellis had never considered himself worth saving. But once his son was born, that changed everything. It was no longer about ruining his own life but also the life of this helpless child: "I was wearing a lot of jewelry at the time," Ellis remembered, "and when I'd hold him, I'd grab his arms and whatnot. Then I read these stories about parents who shake their kids and kill them. I asked myself, I wonder how hard I'm grabbing him. Then I realized the truly fucked-up thing: that I had to ask myself at all. That's when I knew, something's wrong with me. I went to treatment the next day."

It's not like things were easy for Ellis in his recovery. He struggled and fought with the staff just as he had opposed anyone else in his life who had tried to control him. He actually tried sniffing ping-pong balls to try and get high. When one of the psychiatrists interviewed him during the intake and asked him to list all the drugs he'd taken in his life, the doctor concluded that Ellis had to be suicidal since anyone ingesting that many substances *had* to be trying to kill himself.

Ellis thought long and hard about that. It pissed him off that people, especially these professionals, thought he was a hopeless cause. Shit, he'd been behind in the count, bases loaded, plenty of times, and somehow managed to finesse himself out of an inning. This wasn't going to be any different except that he wasn't just trying to complete a game but save his life, and that of his child.

Ellis decided, then and there, with that psychiatrist giving him the pitiful look, that this was it: "I told him nobody will ever have to worry about me getting high ever again." The incredible part of the story is that he was true to his word and never touched another drug or drop of alcohol for the rest of his life!

In this powerful example of transformative or quantum change, Ellis's story supports the compelling evidence that such a process is not necessarily incremental and gradual but can occur as a sudden, dramatic, irrevocable shift that is maintained over time. In one study that contacted participants 10 years after their initial interviews in which they related major life changes that had taken place, remarkably none of those in the original sample lost what they had found or returned to their previous state. One participant in the study described her epiphany that occurred during a meditation class when the instructor reminded her that she wasn't becoming a different person but, rather, becoming the person she was always meant to be:"Right there, at that moment was when I began the serious thought, 'I'm ready to accept that person—warts and all.' A door opened and I walked through it and the door behind me closed and I never worried about opening that door again. It was just a total opening of myself."[12]

Although certainly an inspiring declaration, one supported by evidence in this case, I'd take issue with the part about never having to worry about that door opening again. For most people, especially those recovering from addictions and habitual patterns, a crucial part of preventing a relapse is to remain *extremely* concerned about falling back into old patterns.[13] In the case of Dock Ellis and other recovering addicts, he quite literally had to "live one day at a time" in the parlance of 12-step programs.

Maintaining Momentum

In order for behavioral changes to be sustained, especially health-related issues such as weight loss, smoking, and addictions, there are several conditions that must be met:[14]

1. The benefits and functions of the behavior have been disrupted and no longer provide satisfaction without fairly awful side effects (estrangement from family, loss of income, increased suffering, health risks).
2. Choices have been reduced or eliminated. It is no longer an option (or feels that way) to engage in prior behavior because of the likely consequences.

3. The underlying causes for the behavior (loneliness, stress, boredom, fear) have been addressed through other means.
4. There was some meaning attached to the changes that permitted the person to find some greater purpose to his or her life.

Dock Ellis became so determined to remain clean and sober that he decided he'd found his own greater purpose in life. He wanted to do something to redeem himself, maybe even to help others who were like him. Ellis went back to school and trained to be a drug counselor, eventually specializing in working with inmates within the California Department of Corrections.

In an interview shortly before his death, Ellis remained unapologetic about his past even though he had rehabilitated himself for the previous 20 years. It was precisely the experience with his dark side that made him so effective as a counselor for other addicts and incarcerated inmates. He had found a way to use the mistakes and calamities of his life for the benefit of others, thereby providing even greater incentive to remain on his chosen path. One of his previous clients, Dwayne Ballard, observed that it was precisely Dock's own checkered past that gave him credibility with the "losers" who had been abandoned by everyone else.

During one of his last public statements, before he succumbed to liver failure, he summarized the most important accomplishment of his life—which wasn't pitching a no-hitter, winning the World Series, or being elected to the Hall of Fame. "I try to help people," he said simply, with a shrug, "but I can't save them—they have to do that themselves."

MAKING SENSE OF CHANGE PROCESSES

What is it that really made the difference to Dock Ellis, allowing him to alter a lifetime history of self-abuse and neglect? His counselors would propose one theory, that it was their structure and therapeutic community that allowed Ellis to turn himself around. Ellis himself reported that it was absolutely hitting bottom, sinking so far out of control he had nowhere else to go but recovery. Perhaps another part of the equation involved him finding a greater purpose, a way to use his own painful experiences to be of help to others.

We can readily see in this story that there are so many different factors at work that it's hard to sort out which one(s) made the most difference. Dock Ellis, himself, settled on his responsibility as a parent, which got his attention in a way that nothing else had previously. His friends noted that, as a public figure, he had no choice but to get his act together with the sports world scrutinizing him so carefully. His own clients believed that *they* were the inspiration for Dock to remain clean and sober.

Cases such as this, and others presented in this book, provide glimpses of the forces at work that coalesce together to inspire actions that would have seemed inconceivable previously. If Dock Ellis had been asked earlier in his life if he could have imagined that there would ever be a time when he would be able to function without chemical assistance, he would have laughed hysterically: drugs were the fuel that kept him going.

So, what are we to make of this mysterious process of change? We are flooded with information, bombarded with research, overwhelmed with explanations, and left spouting some simplistic approximation of truth that we barely understand, much less explain in terms that really make sense. Dock Ellis had some understanding of what helped him most, but it didn't exactly jibe with what experts had told him.

When examining transformative changes as they occur among individuals who are experiencing severe distress, there are several predictable stages along the journey, including variables that correspond to the chapter titles in the rest of the book. Drilling down to the essence of this process, we find a couple of signature features that are worth highlighting.[15]

Passing a Threshold

Most of the reputable stage theories of change include some component that describes a point after which continuing along the same path is absolutely intolerable.[16] This is a critical moment when you can't stand living with yourself any longer. Although under such conditions you can hardly be as rational and logical as you'd prefer, if you did a simple spread sheet tallying up the relative costs versus gains of your current way of being, there would be overwhelming evidence that things are not sustainable. It is as if you no longer have a choice since it feels like your very existence depends on making some kind of adjustment.

Of course, everyone has a different pain threshold that not only applies to bodily reactions but also psychological suffering. There is, first of all, a congenital sensitivity to pain that varies according to one's physiological makeup. Yet the experience of pain is also a learned response based on how you have taught yourself (or been conditioned by others or events) to interpret and respond to such sensations. One of the attributes that distinguishes world class athletes is that they have trained themselves to interpret pain differently than amateurs, reframing it merely as useful feedback rather than pure misery.[17]

"You can always go harder," confesses pro cyclist Craig Lewis. He should know. He was riding in one of the premier international races, the Giro d'Italia, when he crashed spectacularly into a road sign, breaking the femur in his leg in half, fracturing four ribs, and injuring a nerve in his arm. Although still in excruciating pain after multiple surgeries, he was back racing on his bike in just a few months, his leg still broken. "Suffering is the coin of the realm in cycling," observed commentator Bob Roll.[18] Indeed, this is the case with pro racers like Lewis who spend up to six hours each day with their physiological systems maxed out to the point they burn over 9,000 calories and can barely walk when they fall off the bike at the finish line.

The function of pain is essentially to get your attention so you stop doing whatever is creating the problem. It is a messenger that becomes more and more strident and persistent if you ignore the first signals. Some people learn to "enjoy" the sensation, or at least associate it with something productive. That is one explanation for the deliberate self-harm that is common to those who continue engaging in behaviors that are clearly not in their best interests—addictions, cutting, and other self-destructive habits.

The first step in any successful change effort involves acknowledging that there is a problem in need of resolution. This may seem rather obvious, but is a lot more complex than we might imagine. Fred, an extremely depressed and lonely man, was described by coworkers and his few friends and family as being extraordinarily rigid. Everything had to be done his way, on his terms, and to *his* exacting standards. One day he and his wife decided to go for a walk, but it had to be along his determined route, at his pace, and to his preferred destination. His wife tried her best to negotiate a compromise: "Hey, couldn't we go a different way this time? I want to check out the neighborhood."

"That's fine," Fred answered curtly. "If you want to go that way, I'll just head the other way." He then started off on his own, leaving his wife standing there in exasperation. Would it be any surprise to learn that she soon after filed for a divorce?

Fred had no clue what the problem was, nor would he accept any responsibility for their difficulties. He didn't understand why his friendships were so fractured and why he had a reputation at work for being difficult. As far as he was concerned, he didn't have a problem in the world—except that others were so frustrating for him to deal with. And in one sense he was perfectly correct: he didn't have a problem in that he almost always got his way. Until he was willing to acknowledge and own his rigidity and stubbornness, there would be little incentive or motivation for him to change (see Figure 3.2 for another example of resistance to change).

A Push Past the Threshold—With a Little Help From Some Friends

Pain, suffering, and discomfort act as negative reinforcers to increase the likelihood that people will cease doing things harmful or unproductive and substitute other strategies that may be more beneficial. In that sense, they operate as powerful motivators. But the desire for change can arise just as strongly from positive visions of what might be possible.

"I had just filed for bankruptcy and I was flat broke," relates one man who refashioned his life. "I owed everyone money, and even though the slate would be wiped clean and my debts canceled, I still felt awful that I couldn't keep my commitments. I lost my home after 15 years of making payments. My kids would soon be going to college, and I had no idea how the hell I could finance it. On top of it all, we had to move into a small apartment which none of us was crazy about."

Figure 3.2: Changes are often involuntary and made without one's consent. There is natural resistance to such alterations in what is most familiar which is why people (and animals) desperately hold on to what they know, regardless of how limiting such options might be. Willie B. spent most of his life in a small cage at Zoo Atlanta. Because of protests at this inhumane treatment, they built him a brand new, state of the art facility, complete with mock jungle to roam around. Yet the gorilla was so used to his prison that he absolutely freaked out at being forced to leave his familiar surroundings and had a panic attack after a raindrop fell. He fled back inside his cage. (Photo courtesy of Shutterstock © Jerry Sharp)

There is the pain and suffering part of the man's story: he was definitely in trouble and he knew it. He had been holding onto a job in an industry that would soon be obsolete. He was earning less and less yet working harder and harder without much to show for it. Yet he was still reluctant to make the changes he needed. "I kept convincing myself things would improve even though I knew it was never going to happen." Whereas the pain and discomfort got his attention, it still wasn't enough to push him past the threshold.

"My whole professional life I had always worked as an individual contractor," he explained, "so I never really had a boss or had to work within much of a structure. But at this stage of my life, for the first time, it sounded pretty good to me to have a stable salary and regular benefits. I yearned for the structure that I had avoided previously. I was tired of working on my own and thought it might be fun to actually have colleagues and a regular office and all."

So it wasn't just what he was escaping that acted as a catalyst for him to make a change in his lifestyle but also a new, exciting dream for the future, one that would be even better than before. It is this intense desire for something different that is driven as much by future rewards as it is by avoiding further punishment.

It is also through connections to others that people find the support they need to do that which is most difficult and walk through a portal into an unknown world. Without Dock Ellis's friends, and without the incentive to take care of his family, he never could have altered the course of his self-destructive life. Without the help of his counselors, he never would have had a model of who he could have become. Without the close connections he felt with his own clients, he would have found it difficult to stay his course.

In another example, someone else with a long-standing addiction found inspiration from the need to get outside himself to help others: "The changing point for me was my brother had suffered for a very long time with depression...I had to be strong for him and for my family."[19] It would be virtually impossible to underestimate the power of such loving connections to others as the main incentive to take charge of one's life. Above all else, human beings are tribal beings, programmed at every level of our existence to work on behalf of the community, as well as our own survival. That is one reason that living creatures will deliberately put themselves in harm's way for the benefit of others: It is one of the best explanations why individuals sacrifice themselves for the group. And it also provides one of the most powerful and compelling reasons for people to transform their lives, if not for their own sake, then for others.

New Insights, Modest and Profound

As mentioned previously and as will be discussed further throughout the book, change can be a gradual process of small, incremental steps, or one gargantuan, earth-shattering moment of clarity. Jack Kerouac, famous for his travel memoir, *On the Road*, awoke one morning in a strange motel room (granted, he probably had a hangover) to find that he wasn't sure who he was. "I wasn't scared," he insisted, "I was just somebody else, some stranger, and my whole life was a haunted life, the life of a ghost."[20]

Although awareness or insight alone may not make much of a difference, it sure helps get the ball rolling. There have been people attending therapy or self-help groups, reading self-improvement books, or participating in growth seminars, for *years* without any visible improvement in their day-to-day functioning. They may be able to trace the origins of their core issues, have perfect understanding of their difficulties, demonstrate interconnections between the past and present, and talk authoritatively about the underlying metaphors, thought patterns, unresolved issues, yet still be unable to translate any of this into constructive action.

Comedian and filmmaker Woody Allen spent most of his life in therapy focused on understanding his past and yet without much apparent change in his behavior. "On balance, I would say it has been helpful," he disclosed in an interview, "but not as helpful as I had hoped and helpful in a way they didn't intend."[21] What he meant by that is that the sessions had become a habit and a crutch. "There were no dramatic moments, there were no special insights, there were no tears, there was, you know, nothing special."

The interviewer, herself a psychoanalyst, pressed him further, incredulous that after several decades he couldn't point to any significant changes that he'd made.

Woody nodded, keeping a straight face. "I lay on the couch. I did what I was told. But after eight years, I got up one day and offered my analyst a draw. We shook hands."

Then he started all over again with a new therapist and a similar result. He concluded the interview with an awareness that does seem pretty insightful: "The only thing standing between me and greatness is me."

It would seem as if Woody had learned a thing or two that was helpful to him. But the kind of insight we are interested in is more often classified as an epiphany, a transcendent moment of awareness when everything seems to come together, and the course of action you must take is crystal clear. This clarity is so overwhelming that there is no choice but to act on what is now understood.

REDEFINING YOURSELF

It is one thing to change behavior, or some aspect of daily functioning, but the process of change becomes infectious, sometimes to the point that it leads to a whole new way of defining oneself. We are often filled with "I'm's," self-descriptors that purport to describe who we are: "I'm a loser," "I'm not good at math," "I'm not assertive," "I'm a smoker," "I'm overweight," "I'm an addict," and so on. In so many cases, our identities are compressed into a single label, one that is often not exactly self-enhancing. We think of ourselves as fitting neatly into boxes that supposedly capture and define our essential nature, but most of the time these labels are self-limiting and highly inaccurate: nobody is shy, awkward, depressed, anxious, or insecure *all* the time but, rather, only in certain situations and contexts. It is the exceptions that define us as much as the convenience of simple labels.

In the previous chapters, we covered different types of change that occur on different levels. There are the "little" adaptations that refer to surface alterations of behavior, and then there are those quantum changes that take place on a deeper level. This is sometimes referred to as structural or "second-order" change because it represents a change in the underlying system or core of a person's being.[22]

In one study of people who successfully stopped smoking, lost weight, or made other significant health changes, the investigators found that the initial impetus for permanently altering this behavior arose from some life crisis, such as the case of Dock Ellis.[23] This was followed by the other factors mentioned in the chapter—fewer opportunities to engage in the behavior, reduced enjoyment or benefits from continuing the actions, and a clear understanding of the consequences of that dysfunctional behavior. Most crucially, these significant lifestyle changes led to a new identity for those who managed to maintain the progress over time. They redefined themselves in such a radically different way that some ended up moving from a position of "sloth" to running marathons or becoming fitness trainers or nutritionists. Whereas the stories told about these cases might make them appear as if they were the result of sudden inspiration and decisive action, it is far more common that the changes took place over much longer periods of time and with small, incremental adjustments.

It is truly quite an amazing, mystical phenomenon when people manage to completely transform who they are. Intention and motivation certainly play an important role, often empowered by crisis or intense dissatisfaction with the present state of affairs. Dock Ellis altered his self-image from "drug addict" and "baseball star" to drug counselor and advocate for the oppressed.

It is just incredible to think about what *could* be possible. There is a wide assortment of limits placed on what we are permitted to do in our lives, restrictions placed by laws, moral codes, cultural traditions, family history and expectations, geographical location, economic realities, genetic determinants, physiological capacities, and racial and gender attributes, but mostly by our own self-definitions. We limit ourselves based on what we believe is possible, or within our grasp.

Second-order, quantum, or "major" changes might not begin with the decision to be different, but somewhere along the line the opportunity to make such a choice will follow the first small steps in that direction. It is, indeed, a cruel myth to spout platitudes such as "you can be anything you want to be." That is clearly not the case since there are realities based on your ability and resources. No matter how much you dream about being a quarterback in the Super Bowl, winning the lottery, or winning an Academy Award, that probably isn't going to happen for more than one in ten million. That's not to say that we should give up our dreams but, rather, that there is a compromise we make between what we really, really want, what is possible, and what we are willing to do to reach that goal. There are certain fantasies that are probably beyond reach, but there are so many others that can be achieved with sufficient drive and determination—plus luck, support, preparation, and practice.

CHAPTER 4

Life-Changing Stories

You are holding in your hands a book that purports to offer something instructive and useful about understanding change processes. Whether you continue reading depends on whether you believe it is a worthwhile investment of your time. If you review what has seemed most memorable to you, it is likely related to one of the stories that have been told. A lot of the concepts may have seemed interesting, but if they weren't embedded in a story, you may have been unable to hold onto them.

Stories are the DNA of memory. Our brains are biologically programmed to organize and store information as narratives, a process that happens automatically during dreams and waking life. In some ways, the brain treats fictional scenarios as if they are real, firing neurons in much the same way as if you were immersed in active experience. Regardless if you are watching a film, reading a book, or involved directly in a situation, you quite literally feel the similar emotional responses.[1]

Stories are embedded in almost every aspect of life, from reading or watching films for pleasure, to sharing myths and legends, engaging in gossip, and telling tales of murder, sex, war, conspiracy. Stories shape our attitudes and values, teach morality, instruct us on life lessons, and allow us to live a thousand other lives through the characters we follow. It is the power of stories that makes us uniquely human and, in some cases, shapes our whole identity (Figure 4.1).[2] In one sense who we are is defined by our own constructed story.[3]

Figure 4.1: A storyteller among the people of Southern Africa. Their oral traditions have been passed on for tens of thousands of years, telling stories of their ancestors, the origins of their land, and the spiritual forces that guide their lives. Along with music and dance, stories are the primary means of instruction and healing. (Photo courtesy of istockphoto © Davor Lovincic)

STORIES AS REHEARSAL FOR LIFE'S CHALLENGES

Think of a book or film or television show or story that changed your life. What immediately comes to mind?

Actor Michael Caine vividly remembers a half-century ago when he found his calling in life: "I was taken to the Tripoli pictures when I was a little kid by some bigger boys, and the curtain went up, and *The Lone Ranger* came on, and I knew what I wanted to be. Not a cowboy— I wanted to be an actor. I didn't even like horses."[4]

Back to my question: Consider a particularly influential or impactful book you read, as a child or an adult, and how it continues to exert its powerful effects. Or think about a movie or show that knocked you out, that haunts you to this day and, in its own way, played a crucial role in some choices you made or patterned your life. I had such an experience that literally saved my life.

I was backpacking in New Zealand, taking a break from teaching responsibilities at a university there. With a brief time available, I set off on my own on the Abel Tasman Coastal Trail after checking with a ranger about the route and conditions. I was advised that the best place to spend the first night was across an inlet where a hut was situated. As it was growing dark and cold, I stripped off my clothes, restrapped on my backpack, and started across the wide estuary.

With each step I took, the water rose higher and higher, past my knees, thighs, then up to my waist. I hoisted my pack onto my head to keep it dry. This was really strange because the ranger had specifically told me it would be low tide and the water would only be knee deep at most. I shrugged and continued onward, starting to shiver with cold and apprehension. The water continued rising, now up to my chest, and I wasn't yet even halfway across the body of water. I thought about turning back but the prospect of sleeping in the forest gave me the creeps. So I soldiered on.

About the time I got to the midpoint, the water was touching my chin, the pack precariously balanced on my head. I was standing on my tiptoes, frozen in fear, undecided what to do. I noticed the shivering had stopped and that was a very bad sign, indicating the early stages of hypothermia. My mind felt like mush, and I had trouble organizing a thought, much less making a decision about what to do next. For some reason, all I could think of was how embarrassing it would be if someone found my body, naked and exposed.

I don't remember a lot that happened after this point. For some reason John Wayne came to mind, and I pictured what he would do in such a life-threatening predicament. As a kid I had seen every movie he'd ever made; he was the model of composure and courage under fire. I thought to myself that he wouldn't be standing out here frozen in panic; he'd *do* something heroic. So I forced myself to continue tiptoeing forward, finally noticing that the water level seemed to be dropping as I approached shore.

I'm pretty sure I was hallucinating at this point, completely losing control of my mind and body. My last conscious thought before I fell unconscious was to remember Jack London's story, "To Build a Fire." For some reason I recalled that the protagonist, himself on the verge of death from the cold, started running to increase his body temperature and prevent freezing to death. Ultimately it didn't work out for the fellow, but it was the only thing that came to mind under these dire circumstances.

I started running, buck naked and covered in icy water, toward a light. That's all I remember before I passed out.

It turned out that I had apparently been making some noises as I had been running through the forest. The light I had seen was actually the hut where there happened to be a guy who had been stationed in Antarctica and was an expert on hypothermia: he knew just what to do to bring me back to life. I don't know if John Wayne's film character or Jack London's story truly saved my life, but they provided a last thread of hope that kept me going a few more steps.

That's the thing about stories: they provide life lessons and instruction for solving problems we might encounter in the future (Figure 4.2). Whether awake or dreaming, most stories present challenging or life-threatening conflicts that are resolved, providing windows of illumination about what might be faced in the future. The content of dreams, for example, are so often menacing that it has been estimated that three quarters of them involve some physical or social threat, rehearsing a fight or flight response.[5] Human brains have thus evolved over time to become exquisite instruments designed to acquire, code, and retrieve

Figure 4.2: Stories contain within them the moral lessons of a culture, designed to provide guidance for appropriate behavior, and often, strategies for survival during periods of adversity. Although structured to provide entertainment and a sense of drama, they hide within them symbolic, mythological, and metaphorical features that operate on multiple levels within humans' storied brains. Photo courtesy of istockphoto © Christopher Futcher

memories as storied sequences. Those ancestors who were most accomplished at receiving, recalling, and telling stories about hunts, battles, food gathering, conflicts, mistrustful or lazy members of the community, dangers and obstacles in the environment or among neighboring tribes would be most likely to survive and produce offspring who would be similarly enhanced in these dimensions.[6]

Stories often provide alternative experiences, a different kind of "reality," that supplies us with moments of support and validation. They can show what *might* be possible if you let go of limiting visions. Melanie, for instance, had always wanted to be a writer as long as she could remember. This was especially surprising because she had been a late reader and struggled with dyslexia.

So she put aside her dream, worked hard to compensate for her disability, and earned a distinguished academic record in college and law school, eventually working as a prosecutor for the district attorney of a large city. "I became a prosecutor for moral reasons," Melanie explained. "I was raised by a Dominican sister and Franciscan friar. I'd had *way* too many early experiences with violence and injustice. And then, of course, there were my own feelings of having been mistreated because of my reading problem. I watched how those of us who had learning disabilities were called lazy, careless, dumb, or unmotivated."

In the DA's office, Melanie devoted herself to launching new task forces to deal with the sexual exploitation of girls, to reform prison reentry programs, and to educating teachers about gangs, keeping her dream alive to fight on behalf of important social issues. And late into the night she continued to write—mostly for pleasure— because she knew she was "damaged" and limited because of her disability. Whoever heard of a professional writer who has trouble decoding words?

And then there was a life-altering experience, at least partially initiated by a story she read: "My college roommate sent me a novel, *Let the Great World Spin*, that changed everything! This novel helped me to realize that it wasn't the dyslexia that had always stopped me from becoming a writer but my own guilt for not doing something more worthwhile with my life." The book thus provided Melanie a model for how a writer can be "an instrument of justice, shining light on things that people would prefer to hide.

Soon after reading this story, Melanie quit her job and started graduate school in fine arts in another country where she could begin her life again. Can we say, with any authority, that it was truly this one book that made all the difference? More likely this was a culminating event that followed a series of other cumulative insights and experiences, each of which contributed some small influence to the decision. But it was still the story she read that put her over the top.

There is sometimes an incredible realism and authenticity to a story, one so well crafted that we are quite literally transported to another world, one where we have the kinds of relationships or opportunities that seem to escape us in life. Writing about the impact of the television show, *Friday Night Lights*, had on him, one man was moved to tears after every single episode. And this was a guy who hadn't cried since he fell off his bike when he was six and had been told by his mother that crying wasn't manly. How interesting that we sometimes won't allow ourselves to feel and express strong emotion for events in our own lives, but we are perfectly willing to do so for characters who don't really exist, except in our imagination. But it's also interesting the *power* these fictional people hold over us. In this particular case, as a recently married man, the author "studiously watched Eric and Tami and used them as a model for my upcoming years of marriage." They were, in his own words, "a platonic ideal of what human beings can be like."[7] Actually, the *best* in what we might become.

Universal Themes

There are universal myths, as well, that transcend any individual culture and have been around since ancient times. This folklore contains common threads, whether told by a schoolteacher, witchdoctor, psychotherapist, healer, mystic, lama, or performer.[8] They are constructed not only as a form of art or entertainment but also to describe a rite of passage leading to resolution of life's riddles. Whether the protagonist is Zeus, Oedipus, Dorothy, Nemo, or the Lion King, the hero must confront great obstacles in order to resolve life's riddles, proceeding through a series of stages: (1) "call to adventure" in which the hero is invited or coerced into beginning a quest; (2) "refusal of the call," showing reluctance, as well as expressing fear and apprehension;

(3) "supportive aid" often appears in supernatural form (godmother, Merlin, angel, the Good Witch) to provide protection or advice; (4) "crossing a threshold" into the unknown, a world filled with mysteries and danger; (5) "facing trials" that will test the resilience and courage of the hero, but resulting in greater wisdom as well as the spoils of victory (Holy Grail, crown, hand in marriage); (6) "return to world" in which the hero must reenter his or her previous life while retaining new skills and knowledge.

It doesn't take much of a stretch to recognize that this classic story is largely a metaphor for change and the challenges that must be faced during such a journey. By the time we reach adolescence, we have been thoroughly indoctrinated into what to expect when confronted with adversity—it is going to be a grueling test of determination and courage, but one that can be passed if we are well prepared. A child glued to the computer screen killing zombies, or watching the same animated feature a dozen or more times, is actually in training for future imagined challenges. Stories thus act as simulations for real life, as much as historical artifacts. They shape who and what we become.

In a catalog of the most influential people who never lived, the authors list over a hundred memorable fictional characters who not only have changed people's lives but also helped shape the world we live in.[9] I am talking about the likes of mythological figures (Pandora, Prometheus, Icarus), folktales (Santa Claus, Pied Piper, Cinderella), legends (King Arthur, Don Juan), monsters (Jekyll and Hyde, Frankenstein, Dracula), fictional characters (Gatsby, Captain Ahab, Don Quixote), children's books (Hansel and Gretel, Peter Pan, Wizard of Oz, Ugly Duckling), figures from films (Captain Kirk, Buffy the Vampire Slayer, Harry Potter), and also a collection of characters from advertising (Smokey the Bear, the Marlboro Man, Joe Camel). Even with the diversity of contexts and media represented, there are still some universal themes that make these fictional characters memorable: they faced challenges that were overcome by following a moral compass. They were sympathetic individuals, often with handicaps or tragic flaws, who triumphed over adversity through force of will, resilience, and passionate commitment to a goal or cause. Such stories raise our own spirits by instilling hope that if we, too, lead a good life, we will be rewarded here or in the afterlife.

Stories Leave Big Impressions

"Some see the world with fresh eyes through wild adventures. For me, the revelations always come via books." So writes journalist Marie Arana, whose life can be measured by the stories that changed her.[10] Memoirs, in particular, have been particularly influential: "I've seen people I might have been. Or people I might become."

As an immigrant and bicultural child, Arana struggled with her place in the world. It was during her most impressionable age of early adolescence that she read Vladimir Nabokov's memoir, written in English even though he was Russian. It absolutely astounded her that someone could master a second language and command it so poetically, giving her hope she might do the same. Other books by authors of color similarly inspired her in such a way that she eventually found her own voice. It was these authors, as much as any other mentors in her life, who spoke to her.

Childhood and early adolescence might, indeed, by the most impressionable ages to be profoundly impacted by stories. It is a time when we have love affairs with books, passionately and uncritically.[11] The books and stories are about courage, loyalty, friendship, acceptance, and identity, exactly the struggles that are most present in our lives. Rattle off a list of popular titles, and they bring tears to your eyes in remembrance: *The Velveteen Rabbit, The Little Prince, Chronicles of Narnia, The Diary of Anne Frank, Twilight, Harry Potter, The Hunger Games.*

During childhood, when we are most impressionable, is a time to be introduced to some of the important moral lessons of a culture. The most famous fairy tales of Aesop, Hans Christian Andersen, or the Grimm Brothers were as much designed to teach lessons as they were to beguile the intended audience of small listeners/readers. Some of the most well-known and beloved stories focus on a theme of empowerment for children when they feel so insignificant and powerless. Children so fluently navigate between the worlds of fantasy and reality that they have little trouble imbibing the implicit messages.[12] For creatures who feel small and insignificant, there is nothing more empowering than hearing a story like *The Little Engine That Could* about how being big and strong doesn't necessarily lead to doing great things. The Little Engine relies on determination and belief in herself to compensate for a small stature.

Continuing with the theme of children's empowerment, two of the most beloved stories ever, *Peter Pan* and *The Wizard of Oz*, pursue a theme of children's capacity to make a difference in a world populated by Captain Hooks and Wicked Witches. The worlds of Neverland and Oz are *still* among the most popular fantasy locales for children's imagination after a century of productions on stage, film, and books. This tradition has continued more recently with *The Hunger Games* and *Harry Potter* series in which children fight forces of evil by relying on their own resources and the loyalty of their friends.

Erica was having a really difficult time in her life. She had just turned 21 and was grieving the death of her father as well as the end of a three-year romantic relationship. A friend recommended reading the Harry Potter series as a way to distract herself: "I read the first book in high school but lost interest early on because it seemed to be for kids and I didn't want to waste my time. I thought I should be reading the classics because that's what adults expected of me."

When Erica says that she didn't want to disappoint "adults," she was really thinking about her boyfriend who had ridiculed her childish interests: "I had spent most of our relationship always doing what he liked and I wanted to totally disconnect from his influence to find out what I really enjoyed. I kind of liked the idea that he'd hate that I was reading a children's book so I picked it up."

Initially, this act of rebellion and assertion of independence was an important part of how changes were in store for Erica. The book gave her permission to be childish and less inhibited: "I completely lost myself in Harry's journey and spent the whole summer reading the books and watching the movies. In some ways it was like my job that summer; it's what I did—living in Harry's world."

Given that Erica's father had recently died, she took comfort in the idea that Harry's parents still lived within him. "My father was a patient and kind man and I'd like to think that others can see those qualities in me." Although the books helped her resolve her grief and move forward, Erica also found she could also identify strongly with Hermione because of her dogged determination to stand up for what she believed in. This inspired her to be more assertive in her own life.

It may seem improbable that reading children's books can help someone recover from a tragic loss, or become more assertive, but Erica credits Potter and his friends for helping her find her way during a time when she felt completely lost. "I have two Harry Potter tattoos," Erica said with a laugh, "and I certainly get teased by friends about my excessive enthusiasm for the series." She recently came across a quote by C.S. Lewis that captured what the books did for her: "When I became a man, I put away childish things, including the fear of childishness and the desire to be very grown up." Erica paused for a moment in reflection, and then smiled: "Harry Potter is a reminder for me, even now, to not take myself too seriously and to embrace the part of me that is silly, irreverent, and spontaneous."

That's the thing about good fiction: it allows us to enter another world in order to imagine other possibilities, other ways of thinking about ourselves. The power of these stories sneaks up on us in such a way that we sometimes unconsciously consume certain messages that we later internalize and make part of ourselves.

One of the purposes of children's literature is as much to teach as entertain. And it isn't just books that have exerted this kind of life-changing influence in children's lives. Comic books, as well, have been extremely influential, spawning characters like Batman, Wonder Woman, Superman, and Spiderman, all of whom enjoy secret powers that are used to right wrongs and fight crimes to aid helpless victims. These stories with social justice themes follow templates from the past, such as *The Adventures of Robin Hood*, in which a hero or heroine fights on behalf of those who have been marginalized or oppressed. This is part of our cultural indoctrination in which we train our young citizens to show empathy and compassion for others within the community who are less fortunate. Without such instruction, it would be every one of us only looking out for our own best interests to the detriment of collaborative goals.

STORIES HAVE A PURPOSE

One original function of language during preliterate times was to tell stories that passed along important traditions, history, and rituals, as well as crucial knowledge related to births, deaths, dangers, battles, hunting, and food gathering. Stories served other functions as a display of skill or creativity, a way to demonstrate superior intellect or verbal skills to achieve status, or as simply a form of play.[13] They have been described as the "social glue" that holds a group together through a shared experience.[14]

Even after printing was invented several hundred years ago, we still use conversations primarily to tell stories about ourselves and others. Stories are also an integral part of religious congregations, along with their sacred texts that are used to define the group, regulate ethical behavior within the community, and provide incentives for cooperation and selflessness (heaven) or punishment (hell). Stories of the past have led to world domination in the sense that Zeus and the Trojan War inspired Alexander the Great's conquests, which, in turn, influenced Napoleon's invasions, followed by Adolph Hitler, who took his turn trying to conquer the world.

Studying stories of history can assist in avoiding mistakes of the past, but it seems that fiction can often be a more powerful and effective influencer than nonfiction in terms of changing beliefs.[15] Don Quixote, Frankenstein, Sherlock Holmes, Romeo and Juliet, King Arthur, Captain Kirk, Dorothy, and Scrooge are almost as alive as anyone else you know intimately.[16] In fiction you surrender control and critical thinking, allowing yourself to enter the fantasy world. During sleep your unconscious mind makes up its own stories, weaving together threads of images, fragments, and neuronal firing into a bizarre storyline that contains encrypted messages or perhaps works through conflicts that you may someday face. As mentioned earlier, most dreams are about peril and danger and may provide practice scenarios that could be faced in waking life.

People are especially fascinated, even obsessed, with stories that enact violence. Some of the most popular shows, films, games, and books are about true crime or feature zombies, vampires, serial killers, and psychotic criminals. There is an attraction we feel to flawed, morally suspect antiheroes who are killers. They face many of the same problems that we do—financial instability, children who are acting out, midlife crises, fractured relationships—but they resolve these difficulties by employing methods that are beyond our own moral code.[17] They engage in behavior that may be reprehensible, but it feeds our own fantasies of living outside the normal bounds of what's acceptable.

There are many possible reasons for the attraction to violent stories in terms of what it might teach us to prepare for possible life-threatening scenarios (What would you do to protect your family or save your life?). In addition, in many cases they appear to serve a cathartic function of leeching aggressive energy. They allow us to vicariously experience things that we might never otherwise consider—even survival of death.[18] Stories like this provide alternative experiences of travel, adventure, stimulation, and relaxation, all without leaving the comfort of your seat. They serve a fundamental purpose that far exceeds their value as a form of diversion or entertainment.

STORIES TO PROMOTE CHANGE

Any self-respecting teacher, coach, therapist, trainer, or leader has developed and collected a series of stories that are designed to inspire and impact others. Some arise from personal experience (self-disclosures) or they are collected from others' lives. These are tales told in such a manner and context that they work at subtle and unconscious levels to motivate constructive action. Through the use of metaphors, they have the advantage of operating indirectly and bypassing resistance; they engage in active imagination and require listeners/viewers/readers to personalize the lessons in a meaningful way.[19] Interestingly, it isn't even necessary that stories make sense since sometimes the more ambiguous the narrative, the more actively people have to create their own personal meaning.

One example of that phenomenon comes from a friend and colleague who devoted his life to the study of transformative metaphors within stories.[20] Noted psychotherapist Steve Lankton had made a pilgrimage, at great expense and inconvenience, to study with one of the master therapists of the era, psychiatrist and wizard Milton Erickson.[21] Erickson was known primarily for his ability to weave incredibly complex stories into life-changing hypnotic inductions that operated on many levels that are yet to be fully understood.[22]

Steve patiently waited his turn in a supervision group with Erickson when the great man abruptly asked him why he was really there. "Why, of course to learn to put people into deeper trances," he answered.

Erickson studied him for a minute, then nodded his head, and ordered Steve to leave immediately, to go out in the desert and not return until he found the fabled Boojum tree. Dejected and shocked by this incomprehensible assignment, Steve slowly walked out of the room, unsure what else to do next. Just as he was about to exit, Erickson called out to him, "One more thing, watch out for the creeping devils. And when you do find the Boojum tree—and you *will* find it, you are going to say to yourself, 'I don't believe it!'"

Steve wracked his brain, trying to recall where he'd ever heard of a Boojum tree before and thought he remembered it from a poem by Lewis Carroll. But that hardly inspired much confidence. Like Moses he wandered the desert in search of his elusive goal when, lo and behold, he stumbled upon a strange looking succulent-like tree that he immediately recognized might be his holy grail. Just at that moment, he stumbled upon a vine that tripped him (which he later learned was called a Creeping Devil), mumbling to himself, "I can't believe it. I can't believe it."

Now here's the *really* interesting part of this story: Steve has spent the past 40 years trying to make sense of what this whole episode was about. Why had Erickson sent him out to look for this tree? What did he think was going to happen on this quest? And how the hell was it related to what Steve was in the group to learn, or what brought him to Erickson in the first place?

When asked to explain what happened, Steve just grins. At first he thought it was a ploy to get him outside of his intellect. Then he decided it was designed to encourage him to take risks, to launch a quest for important answers that had eluded him. This is consistent with the healing trials of most indigenous healers who eschew any kind of talking or insight cure in favor of tasks that must be completed, often those that have no apparent connection to the presenting problem.[23] Or perhaps it was to help him confront his self-doubts in many areas of his life? Maybe it was all a practical joke Erickson had been playing on him? Eventually Steve concluded that Erickson probably only had the vaguest idea of what this assignment might elicit—the goal was quite simply to create a powerful experience and then allow *him* to create story to make sense of it.

This formula, one that creates stories that are rich in complexity and metaphoric opportunities, has become the hallmark of Steve Lankton's clinical style when assigning therapeutic homework to his clients: "I try to think of something that's *not* relevant to a client's problem and tell him or her to go do that; and, when the person comes back, the outcome is often far more profound than I ever imagined."[24]

Stories As a Collaboration Between Author and Consumer

The most potent action from stories takes place at a level in which the viewer/reader/listener does a lot of the work. Editors and writing teachers advise any budding novelist not to *tell* readers what is happening but to *show* them through dialogue so that the implied action can be surmised or interpreted. The more actively involved the consumers of a story are, making their own interpretations, filling in gaps, visualizing the details, the more easily the narrative feels real. A good story is actually a *collaboration* between its author and reader or viewer, and sometimes leads to outcomes that could never been anticipated.

Margie thinks back to her adolescence, that impressionable age when books exert such powerful influence, and remembers reading Somerset Maugham's *Of Human Bondage*, the story of a boy with a clubfoot: "That book surfaces in my mind every year, at some point, for one reason or another. It created an unrealistic idea of what was possible in unconditional romantic love. What I thought at 13 led me to an unhealthy obsession that could never be met in any relationship."

In another more recent example of the power of a story, Margie read a novel, *The Final Diagnosis*, about a woman who was told she had cancer. "I read the book so fast," Margie said with a laugh, "that I missed the point that the shadow on her bone found by the radiologist might have been a bruise caused by diving into a swimming pool." Margie mistakenly interpreted this to mean that the woman had given herself cancer by getting banged up in the pool. "For the next few years I lived in terror that every time I might have bruised myself that I was giving myself cancer. I spent a lot of time in a terrorized cold sweat, lying on my bed, picturing myself with one leg because I'd need an amputation. The fear only went away after I reread the book and realized my mistake."

Obviously we make our own interpretations of stories, sometimes distorting what was intended, other times simply creating our own meaning from what was offered. Stories are not static objects but, rather, open sources of narrative that can be reshaped in a variety of ways. Symbols and metaphors speak to people in different voices. Characters resonate and touch people according to their own needs and desires. Even within the realm of music, the lyrics of songs may speak in a way that provides a breakthrough.

Callie had been in a marriage of 14 years, and she had known for some time that the relationship was in trouble. She had married young, *way* too young, and the couple had grown in very different directions. They had consulted a therapist for their problems, which provided interesting insights but didn't lead to any noticeable changes except the increased awareness that they wanted different things from life: "I was struggling with the whole idea of being divorced and worried about how a split might affect our two-year-old daughter. I just couldn't make a decision: should I stick things out for the sake of my baby or get a divorce?"

The pressure was taking a toll on Callie's health and well-being in so many ways. It was tough enough to endure the pain and annoyance of feeling trapped in a marriage that was so conflicted, but things were even worse because she was beating herself up over being unable to make a decision about what to do. And then—in almost an instant—everything changed. "I was driving home from work one day," Callie recalled. "I was listening to the radio, when Kenny Rogers' song, "The Gambler," came on, telling the story about the player who can read people's faces and sees that this guy sitting across from him on a train is "out of aces" and in great misery. As soon as he sings the chorus, "You got to know when to hold 'em, know when to fold 'em,'" it just hit me that it was time to walk away and start over."

Callie recognizes that she was most likely already heading in that direction even if she failed to recognize it, but hearing those words "made it clear to me what I needed to do. It changed everything for me. It was the words in this simple country song that made me realize that it was time fold 'em and walk away. Sure, I've had some regrets but, overall, I know I did the right thing."

This example is particularly interesting considering that we listen to an average of three to five hours of music per day (if you count commercials, background "elevator" music, sound tracks, etc.), and yet sometimes the words from a particular song can seep into our consciousness in such a way that a lever switches in our brain.[25] We read something into the story that resonates with our own experience, that reveals a part of our own life that feels important. The fact that it occurs in the context of music, with all the accompanying sensory stimulation and arousal, potentially makes the impact that much more powerful.

It's also intriguing how song lyrics from a particular era reflect the dominant stories of that time. Comparing the stories told 25 years ago to those of today, the lyrics of popular music today reflect a far more narcissistic and self-oriented flavor. They tend to use more first-person singular pronouns ("I" versus "we"), fewer references to social interactions with others, more focus on loneliness and isolation, and more frequent expressions of anger and antisocial behavior. These songs appear to reflect the resonance that listeners feel with many of these issues, struggling more than ever before with feelings of alienation and disconnection with others.[26]

Professional Storytellers Who Teach and Heal

Teachers, psychotherapists, health experts, and professionals in positions of leadership often use stories to instruct or heal, to inspire and motivate their clients, employees, students, or patients. Some helping professionals even view their main role is as a master of narrative whose primary strategy involves telling stories that lead to change.[27] There is considerable research support for the ways that stories impact people's behavior and promote changes in their lives.[28] All such professionals have a catalog of narrative tools at their disposal, each of which may be geared to produce a particular outcome including such tasks as providing new insights and ideas, stimulating imagination and creative options, planting hope, inspiring action, demonstrating resilience and recovery, revealing solutions to problems, teaching skills, clarifying values, and resolving conflicts, among others.

The whole idea is to promote change through subtle and indirect means, capitalizing on unconscious and intuitive processes, bypassing defenses and resistance, and evoking strong emotional reactions that correspond to activated resources and greater self-awareness. Tyra, for example, is adamant that she doesn't really need to lose weight. Sure, she carries an extra hundred pounds, resulting in a host of health problems including high blood pressure, borderline diabetes, and osteoarthritis, but she insists that people in her family have always been a bit "full figured." And that is really the way she sees the problem.

Her physician had tried everything in her power to help Tyra at least make an effort to improve her health condition but nothing seemed to work. Diets and referral to a nutritionist didn't make a dent in her status. The only options that Tyra would seriously consider were those that would not require her direct involvement in sustained self-control—surgery to install a lap band or gastric bypass and medications. The doctor realized that the prognosis for such procedures would be less than ideal given Tyra's limited motivation and self-control.

"I had a patient once," the doctor shared with Tyra, "who had a similar condition. She didn't do well on diets. She was a poor risk for surgery. Just like you she had a history of obesity in her family. She had all but given up because nothing seemed to work for her."

"And you're telling me this story because...?" Tyra interrupted. "Because she followed your wise advice and lived happily ever after?"

The doctor paused for a moment. "No, actually she died of a heart attack while bending over to lift bags of groceries out of the trunk of her car."

There was another long silence, after which Tyra took an exasperated breath. There was something about that particular story that bothered her, then later *infected* her: She couldn't get the image out of her head, especially later in the week when she went shopping and thought about retrieving the bags from the back seat. Somehow she had steadfastly refused to put them in the trunk even though she didn't realize she was trying to ward off the prospect of her own impending death.

Psychotherapists have long recognized the power of stories to reveal deep psychological insights. Sigmund Freud was a huge fan of novelists like Dostoyevsky who presented him with the earliest recognition of unconscious motives. Contemporary therapists often make frequent use of recommending particular books or films to their clients, even basing their treatments on what has been called *bibliotherapy* or *cinematherapy*. One practitioner has compiled a collection of movies that inspire people to overcome their problems, organizing them according to the issues they highlight such as abandonment, abuse, addiction, codependency, family conflict, mental illness, and physical disability, and prescribing them as needed just as a physician might do so with medications.[29]

Regardless of the particular form, whether films, songs, poems, novels, short stories, biographies, television shows, plays, operas, puppet shows, ballets, blogs, social media, nonfiction, or videos, stories provide us with alternative realities that we would (or never could) pursue ourselves. They teach us important lessons that we internalize. They populate our world with living beings who inspire, frustrate, sadden, and touch us. We feel their pain and share their joys. And if we're very, very fortunate, they transport us to another dimension where we transform ourselves into someone we've always wanted to be—and then return from the journey with the lessons learned fully intact.

CHAPTER 5
The Benefits of Hitting Bottom

"It's no big deal, really." He shrugged and then looked at his watch. I couldn't help but notice it was a gold Rolex.

I just looked at him and waited. I still wasn't sure what he wanted or why he had chosen to schedule an appointment for this "little problem that was no big deal."

"I don't know how much detail you want, but sometimes I just need a little pick-me-up. I'm under incredible pressure, so a guy's gotta do what he's gotta do, know what I mean?"

"Not exactly, no," I said, already not liking this guy very much. He was obviously wealthy, certainly successful, if I could judge by his appearance. Beyond the expensive watch, he was wearing a custom suit, silk tie, and monogrammed shirt. His nails gleamed from a recent manicure.

"Well," he began, settling into the couch with resignation, "it's like this. I've got a little problem—I'm not sure it's a problem exactly—but my wife thought it would be a good idea to talk to you. At least one time anyway."

"Okay, then, what's the problem?" This guy was definitely getting on my nerves and I was impatient. I had already formed a first impression that he didn't seem all that serious about therapy but was only showing up just so he could tell his wife he'd been a good boy. I was also aware that my negative reaction to this man was triggered by something he touched in me—envy? Resentment? Threat? I took a breath and tried to access greater neutrality, if not compassion.

"My wife thinks that I do a little bit too much cocaine." He said this simply and matter-of-factly, then smiled and crossed his arms. It was as if he dared me to judge him.

I thought about saying that *any* amount of cocaine was too much, but instead I just nodded, gesturing that he should continue.

"It's just that sometimes the pressure just gets to me. I have all these deals going, and it's like 20 hours a day of one thing after another. I don't sleep all that well, and a lot of the people I talk to are in different time zones so I have to be alert, you know."

"So, the coke helps you concentrate."

"Exactly!" He said it like he had finally gotten through to me. "But to be perfectly honest, I also kind of do a few lines for fun, you know what I mean?" He actually winked at me.

"So," I clarified, "you also use the drug for recreational purposes, as well as to boost your productivity." Excellent summary, I thought—neutral, clear, concise.

"Yeah," he agreed, "that's about it."

"Okay, then," I pressed him, almost rubbing my hands together because I knew where this was going, "what's the problem?"

"Well as I said, my wife thinks I might be doing a little too much and it's a problem."

"What do *you* think?" This was it: the moment of truth. We had only known each for a few minutes and I was asking him to admit to a serious drug problem.

He shrugged. "It's possible I guess."

"May I ask you a few more questions?" I wanted his explicit permission before I started to push him—and I knew this was going to get pretty uncomfortable fast.

He held his hands out, palms up, as if his life was an open book. We'd see about that.

"Exactly how much cocaine do you consume?"

"What do you mean?" he answered, knowing exactly what I meant but stalling while he decided just how honest he was going to be.

It turned out that he was going through a few grams a day, maybe more considering the likelihood he was minimizing the problem. I did the quick mental calculations and figured he was spending more on his habit than most people earn.

"Look," I said, far more abruptly than I intended, "I just don't think I can help you."

He looked at me like I was deranged. "What do you mean?"

"Just what I said. I don't think I can help you."

"But aren't you a therapist? Isn't this what you do? I mean, don't you help people like me?"

"Well, you're right that I help people. It's just that I don't think I can help *you*."

"What are you saying?" He wasn't used to being told no, and I'm ashamed to admit how much I was enjoying this. I was certainly aware that my choice to confront him so quickly was premature, if not misguided, but I really was feeling hopeless about his prognosis.

"I don't know how to be any more clear about this so I'll try one more time." Now I had his complete attention, and I decided this was going to be a huge dose of reality for him. "People with your sort of, ah, problem, don't do well in therapy—not just with me, but with *anyone*."

"So I'm a hopeless case? I told you it was really no big…"

"I heard you," I interrupted, but I was frustrated. This was a time when cocaine was the rage among the privileged, a sign of status. I had already seen more than my share of users and had almost no success working with them, other than to persuade them to get into a Narcotics Anonymous or similar program. At the time there were very few inpatient programs available to deal with the drug; even so, it was nearly impossible to get anyone to enter such a facility unless they were absolutely desperate. And it was clear that this guy wasn't even at a point that he admitted he had a problem.

"Here's what's going to happen next," I said, before he could go into defensive mode. "No matter how much money you have, you're going to lose it all. Your wife is going to divorce you. You'll lose custody of your children. Your business is going to go down the tubes. You'll try and borrow money from all your friends to support your habit, but eventually they'll write you off as well. You'll lose your house, your fancy car, even that gold watch."

Okay, maybe I was being more than a little harsh with him. But he seemed to take each of the predictions in stride, at least until I mentioned his watch. He grabbed it with his right hand and held it tightly as if I was threatening to take away his soul.

"Wait, there's more," I said, while I had him reeling. "You'll likely reach a point where you can't beg, borrow, or steal the coke any more, so you'll try to find other ways to deal with your little problem—and let me tell you, it isn't the cocaine, but it's all the things in your life that you're hiding from."

I knew I was pushing him too hard, too fast, but it was as if all my helplessness with clients just like him had reached a point of complete exasperation. I felt just as helpless as he did.

"So, that's it?" he said, still so shocked he wasn't sure how to respond to me. This was going so much differently than he expected.

"Yup," I agreed. "That's it. There's just not much I can do for you at this point."

"At this point?" He was grasping at whatever he could get. His composure was gone. His posture was slumped. His perfectly pressed cashmere slacks were now wrinkled where he'd been gripping the fabric as a lifeline. I could see sweat forming at his brow.

"That's right. For now, there's not much I can do for you. But after you lose everything, after everyone has abandoned you, after you've hit bottom so far into the depths of despair that you see no hope whatsoever, after you have completely run out of choices or options, after your 'little problem' is acknowledged as one that has completely taken over your life, then—*maybe*—I can help you."

I'm not saying this was good therapy, or that I was behaving in the most compassionate, responsive clinical mode; as I said, this guy just pushed my button, and I became—how should I best say this?—overly dramatic in my attempt to apply some tough-love leverage.

"Are we done here?" he mumbled, looking down. He was deflated. He was resigned. One thing was clear in that he seemed to have heard me. But I just knew the impact would last only as long as he got home, or to the glove compartment in his car, and he snorted a line of coke. I wasn't proud of my behavior; in fact, I was ashamed.

The guy left, and that was that. I never heard from him again, nor did I expect to. I thought about calling him to apologize, but I honestly didn't think that would help with damage control.

Years went by, at least 10 or 12 as best I can figure. I thought of him occasionally, as much in regret at my own behavior as I did out of concern for whatever happened to him.

My brother called me one day and said he'd run into a guy who once knew me when I lived in Michigan.

"Oh yeah? Who's that?"

"He said he was once one of your clients."

I didn't say anything in this kind of awkward moment when I couldn't acknowledge a past connection to a client.

My brother laughed because he knew I wouldn't say anything. "Sounds like it was a pretty interesting case. He told me the whole story."

"Really?" I answered, now curious about who this was and whether I'd remember her or him after so many years.

My brother then went on to describe that first session with the cocaine addict, in far more detail than I could have imagined. "Man," he said, laughing, "you were a sonofabitch, weren't you?"

I just waited.

"Well," be continued, "it seems your approach worked pretty well for him."

"Oh yeah?" I tried to sound casual but I was holding my breath.

I then heard the saga of what happened after the client left my office. Apparently, the guy just stopped cold turkey. I scared the living crap out of him. He was shaking when he walked out my door, furious at me, but just as terrified of himself. It turned out he *did* have a vial of cocaine in his car and, before he could even think about it, tossed it in the trash wondering if some lucky guy would find it. He stopped using that day and, at least up to a dozen years later, had never used again. According to my brother, who has been active in 12-step groups his whole life, the man never went to Narcotics Anonymous or any other support group, and never went back to therapy; that brief 20-minute conversation was enough to get his attention in a way that nothing else had before.

Now, I would like to take full credit for this client's recovery, or at least believe his version of events that it was our conversation that made all the difference and saved him. Heck, I don't know—maybe it did. But I'm awfully skeptical of those kinds of so-called instant cures, especially when they appear to be the result of some epiphany that occurred in a therapy session. Furthermore, premature confrontations of this type more often backfire and alienate or harm the person than do much good.[1] The best sorts of confrontations are not those *between* people but, rather, when someone comes face-to-face with him or herself in such a way that there is reasonable safety and support.[2] Obviously, these features were missing in the example above, so I'm certainly not presenting the case as an object lesson for good therapy.

As we've already covered, I think there's an awful lot more complexity and variables at work, most of which we will likely never identify, much less understand. Here's the thing: in spite of all our research and theoretical advancements, outcome measures, client self-reports, therapist perceptions, and clinical trials, at best we only have the barest inkling of what most contributes to people changing their lives, whether freeing themselves of an addiction or a debilitating relational or emotional problem. This leads to the central question of this book: What is it that really made a difference to this man who so abruptly and successfully changed his life in a matter of 20 minutes?

WHEN THERE'S NOTHING ELSE TO LOSE—OR TO GAIN

Whether discussing a case like the one just described, or the one about the baseball player, Dock Ellis, addiction specialists have a name for the level of desperation it takes to overcome resistance—hitting rock bottom. In the parlance of researchers on change, it is also referred to as someone's relative degree of "functional impairment," their level of pain and desperation that leads to acknowledgment of a problem. Of course, "the thing about hitting bottom is that, in the middle of it, sometimes you don't know if you're really hitting bottom or just bouncing off ledges on your way further down."[3] Indeed, it is often a slow, progressive deterioration that has been described with alcoholics, beginning with initial relief of stress or pain from occasional drinking.[4] This is followed by increasing dependence on alcohol to manage daily life, leading to repeated promises and resolutions to stop that inevitable fall. Physical deterioration follows with corresponding, vague spiritual desires for deliverance. Finally, complete surrender and defeat are admitted, intermittently exchanged for continued drinking. It is at this point, with nothing left to lose, that there begins an opportunity for recovery.

It is when it feels like you have nothing left to lose that you are open to trying things that previously had seemed like too much bother or work. On the other hand, those who are most severely impaired are those less likely to benefit from therapeutic treatments.[5] There is, thus,

Table 5.1. BALANCE SHEET OF BENEFITS VERSUS COSTS

Remaining in my job		Changing my job	
Benefits	Costs	Benefits	Costs
Easy and predictable	Stress from workload	New challenges	Risk it won't work out
Safe and predictable	No variety of tasks and little learning	Better salary	Starting over with retirement plan
Position of seniority	Too much isolation	Opportunity for advancement	There will be a learning curve
Finally know what's going on	Leaving unfinished business behind	Can redefine myself in new ways	Difficult to make new friends

a "decisional balance" that takes place in which ambivalence toward change is resolved by weighing the costs of remaining the same versus the benefits of doing something different. It sounds like this is a rational, logical process in which a psychological "spreadsheet" is plotted similar to the one in Table 5.1.[6]

Whereas it might, indeed, be possible to consult a list of costs and benefits when considering actions like a job or relationship change, there is often far more emotion and intuition involved that goes something like this: "I can't frigging *live* like this anymore! Can't sleep. Can't get out of bed. Can't think straight. Can't do anything except think about how wasted my life has become. I've got to *do* something!"

Becoming Worse to Get Better

It is one of the realities of change that it is rarely sought after or embraced until such time that it seems there is no other alternative. Resistance comes in many different forms—avoidance, denial, distraction, distortion—and its particular manifestation depends on the underlying motive. Of course, people tend to resist those things that don't make sense to them or don't seem clearly connected to a desired result that seems worth the investment. When the outcome is uncertain or ambiguous, it actually makes sense to drag your feet.

Most often people tend to show reluctance when things appear potentially threatening, especially when it seems there is a lot to lose. You might not be all that happy in a relationship, job, living situation, or lifestyle, but at least you've learned to live with the annoyances, even with their side effects. But the alternatives could be far worse.

Nobody walks out on a relationship that is just okay; it's got to be pretty awful to make such a change. Rarely do people quit a job that is only acceptable or move to another region just because they are only moderately content with the status quo. Likewise, people don't quit drinking, drugging, or acting out until such time that the consequences for continuing become absolutely untenable. We are talking about a level of desperation when it feels like there really isn't any longer much of a choice.

Hitting bottom has long been considered a prerequisite for recovery among addicts and alcoholics. "It is the essence of getting hold of AA," Bill Wilson, the founder of Alcoholics Anonymous, once observed.[7] That is why 12-step programs like AA, Narcotics Anonymous, Overeaters Anonymous, and others so strongly urge their members to acknowledge they are powerless and helpless. It is believed that recovery can't truly begin until such time that the addict is willing to accept there is nowhere else to go except sobriety. "The first step is not resurrection," reports one of the earliest AA advocates, "it is crucifixion. It is the crucifixion of pride, narrowness, stupidity, ignorant prejudice, and intolerance."[8] Perhaps not surprisingly, this was from a minister who believed that without surrendering to God's will recovery would be far more difficult.

In a study of what led to an increase in readiness for alcoholics to finally give up drinking, it was found that "hitting rock bottom" was a significant factor.[9] It isn't as if it is only an all-or-nothing condition of absolute despair but one that can even be classified as "high bottom" and "low bottom"; the first one is likely to lead to self-referral for help whereas the second one is usually referred by the court.[10] In either case, there was some culminating experience, voluntary or involuntary, that led to recovery.

It seems important, therefore, to increase the awareness and intensity of *negative* feelings about the current state of affairs, to feel worse in order to feel better. Reaching the end of the line, by definition, means that it is an unsustainable position that is impossible to maintain indefinitely. Eventually you simply run out of options and have to do *something* to adapt to an unstable situation. This leads to one of two possible outcomes: either people fall so deeply into a hole that they can never climb out, ending up homeless, in prison, or dead, or they try some things that they've long been avoiding.

Interpersonal Support—And Sabotage

Most people who are hovering back and forth between change and inertia are likely being enabled by others in their world. It just isn't possible to get away with consistently dysfunctional behavior without some level of collusion on the part of others. Cassandra has tried for years to lose weight, experimenting with each new fad diet on the bestseller lists. They all worked—for a little while anyway.

Then inevitably Cassandra would gain the weight back. She felt awful about herself and was terrified that her obesity would end her marriage before it would eventually kill her. This was not an unreasonable fear given that Cassandra's husband frequently threatened that he'd leave because she was so fat and unattractive.

Desperate and more motivated than she'd ever felt, Cassandra became determined that she'd hit bottom and could drop no further. She was depressed and despondent. She couldn't stand to look at herself anymore and so avoided mirrors altogether. One sleepless night she announced to her husband that she'd had enough and that things were going to change. She went shopping the next day and brought into the home only those foods that would help her resist the impulsive snacking that was her downfall.

Given her new public commitment to change, and her husband's expressed desire that she lose weight, it was all the more surprising when she returned home from work to find open packages of junk food sitting on the counter. These were temptations that her husband knew she couldn't resist, which is why she vowed she'd never have them in the house again.

"Honey," she asked her husband, "what are these things doing here? I thought we agreed that I was serious this time about losing weight?"

"What?" he answered. "So because you've got a fat ass, I should deprive myself of the stuff that I like? Hey, it's *your* problem, not mine."

So here we have a case in which Cassandra's husband is deliberately sabotaging her effort to change even though he says this is what he really wanted. In reality, the man was highly threatened by the idea his wife would become more attractive to others because of his insane jealousy. He actually preferred his wife to be the way she was because it gave him the power to continually control her and use threats to leave her as leverage. Throughout the pattern of their relationship, he was pushing her in one direction while pulling in the other. It's no wonder she had been so unsuccessful.

RECOVERING FROM A CHRONIC PROBLEM—WITH A *LOT* OF HELP FROM FRIENDS AND FAMILY[11]

Hitting bottom only becomes a fulcrum for change when it actually leads to constructive action—and that can't easily happen on your own: it takes a "village," a community, a group in your corner, to provide needed support. Without the caring and concern of people you trust, it's hard enough to initiate changes but virtually impossible to maintain them. As is evident from the previous case example with Cassandra, in spite of what most people say they are often threatened by changes you aspire to make. Once someone changes it often makes others feel uncomfortable with their own laziness and mediocrity. They will either have to make adjustments to their behavior, which is hard work, or alternatively, somehow persuade or sabotage the person to backslide. I know that sounds rather pitiful, especially because we're talking about friends, family, and loved ones, but that is the nature of stable systems—they're very difficult to change. And that's also why most of the stories that clients bring to therapy (85%) are about family members who are disappointing, frustrating, disapproving, or annoying to them.[12]

The single best predictor of a successful change effort is the degree of support you receive from others. This is even more critical with the kinds of stubborn problems like addictions, entrenched habits, and impulse disorders that have such a poor prognosis in the first place and are so affected by social influences.

Birth of a Coping Strategy

Sarah wakes up in the morning to start her first day of college. She is incredibly anxious and excited about the first day of school and her new life. She has so many hopes and dreams about what she'd like to do to escape the drudgery and challenges of her life. This is a new beginning, an opportunity to reinvent herself in this new environment.

She sits down for breakfast, consisting of a single orange, while she studies the map of her campus for the third time that morning; she feels overwhelmed by the prospect of navigating through the maze of her new school. Part of this orange is all that she will allow herself since she is trying to lose weight.

While she tries to concentrate on the map, carefully separating the orange segments into those that meet her approval, she hears her parents fighting in the background. Like most of these daily arguments, this one began as a simple discussion over something stupid and meaningless. Her family has a troubled past, so it doesn't take much for almost any conversation to escalate into a major crisis. Painful memories are usually stirred up, enough so that her parents do their best to inflict serious injury on one another, seeing revenge and retribution for imagined slights. It is a serious game they play with the goal to produce serious injury; there is no concern for collateral damage to the noncombatants in the war zone.

Sarah just shakes her head in disgust at her crazy parents. Don't they have any idea how important this day is to her? Why do they have to get into this crap now, when it's so important for her to keep calm with everything she must face? Can't they at least keep their voices down?

Not going to happen. If anything, she can anticipate that this fight is going to be a sustained campaign—and a bloody one. She blocks her ears as best she can, glances at the clock, and wonders if she can make a quick escape. Now that she hears her older sister entering the fray, she realizes it won't be long before she is dragged in as well, expected to take sides. She pushes the half-eaten orange away.

Just One More Bite

Sarah arrives at her new campus and is stunned by how big it seems, so much more intimidating than it looked on the map. There are thousands of students rushing around with purpose while she stands frozen, staring at her map, wondering if she made a huge mistake trying to take on this added pressure with everything she has to deal with at home. She can't remember a time when she's ever felt this anxious—and that says a lot considering the usual levels of stress that she has carried most of her life. New situations and challenges like this make things even worse.

Much to her relief, Sarah managed to survive the first day of college without major trauma or visible scars. But that didn't appease the anxious voice inside her head. As she drove home from school that first day, she could feel a panic attack starting to build up momentum, so she calmed herself as best she could. It was in moments like these that all she could think of was food—potato chips, French fries, cinnamon rolls, chocolate doughnuts, chocolate milkshakes, chocolate cake, chocolate *anything*. Even though she'd only had a half of an orange that morning, she wasn't actually hungry—but she craved food like a drug, like the only thing that would save her. There was comfort in food. There was relief from her anxiety. All her stress and pain and sadness seemed to vanish, at least for a little while.

Sarah felt a rush of excitement, almost an erotic charge, as she entered the drive-through line of her favorite fast-food place. She ordered a family meal that was supposed to feed four. "I hope your family enjoys dinner," the guy in the drive-through window said with a smile.

As soon as she arrived home, Sarah quietly sneaked into her room and laid out her feast: two cheeseburgers, a 10-piece chicken meal (with ketchup, barbecue sauce, and ranch dressing for dipping), a breakfast sandwich, large order of fries (more ketchup and ranch dressing), large chocolate shake, plus a Coke. She meticulously arranged each of the items in a circular pattern on the floor, satisfied that everything was in its assigned place, and then began working her way around the circle, beginning with the burgers and breakfast sandwich (red meat always goes first). After arranging the various condiments in their proper location, she then proceeded to dip the chicken pieces in the ranch dressing, barbecue sauce, and then ketchup. This process was proceeding in a blur, both hands working, her eyes anticipating and planning the next steps. All of a sudden, in midswallow, she realized with horror that she had just dipped the chicken in the ketchup *before* the barbecue sauce! Before she could rectify her error, she could hear footsteps in the hallway. Of course! This was the punishment for her terrible mistake: she gets busted and then disowned. She should have known better that any departure from the ritual could have serious consequences.

Fortunately, whoever was walking by continued on their way, so she was safe, at least temporarily. Sarah threw away the "ruined" piece of chicken and started to concentrate once again on the task at hand. She wanted so badly to stop. She felt sick and nauseous. But she realized she had to force herself to keep going so there wouldn't be any evidence. She noticed that she *was* feeling calmer and more in control. Besides, the best part was yet to come: the French fries and milkshake.

After cleaning up all the wrappers, putting everything back in their bags, Sarah tiptoed outside to dump everything in the garbage and then cover the bags. This was her secret, and it was the only thing she could do that seemed to work consistently. And work it did! Although her belly was bulging, it was clear that she was less anxious and almost optimistic about the future. This satisfaction lasted the better part of an hour before the guilt set in. She couldn't stop thinking about the thousands of calories she consumed, all of it the most unhealthy food choices she could imagine. She felt like a glutton, as if she might explode. She promised herself that this was the last time. But whom was she kidding? This happens almost every night.

I Ran Out of Space

Sarah first began binge eating soon after she had stopped cutting and mutilating herself. It felt like progress in a way that she substituted one form of self-harm for another, one that seemed an improvement at the time. "I first began cutting the inside of my arms when I was 14 years old," Sarah recalled. "I had just entered high school, and during this period I was very obsessed with death. I read every single book on it at my local library and planned on going to mortuary school after I graduated. I stared wearing dark clothing and along with this image came a new set of 'Goth' friends who shared similar interests. For the first time in my life, I felt accepted by my peers, however weird we might have seemed to others. This drove my parents crazy, which is probably one reason why I so enjoyed my new life."

Sarah became a scapegoat in her home, the main source of arguments among her parents. "They were always yelling at me," she explained. It was during one of these screaming matches that she dug her fingernails into her arm, surprised by the pain: "I was actually not trying to hurt myself, but when I looked down at my arm and saw the blood trickling down to the floor I was mesmerized. I stared at my arm and saw the three puncture wounds from my nails, each welling up with blood that I thought was so beautiful. It was strange, but for the rest of that night I didn't even notice my parents fighting. It was almost as if the cuts gave me an invisible shield to protect me against them, against the sadness and anger I felt."

The next morning, Sarah remembered to wear a long-sleeve shirt even though it was 85 degrees outside: "I figured that as long as nobody else saw the wounds, then my pain wasn't real. I could live in this imaginary world where everything was fine. Cutting would keep me safe and insulated."

Yet when she returned from school that day, the fights began anew: "It was clear that I was such a disappointment to my mother in every way, the worst daughter imaginable. Since there didn't seem to be anything I could ever do to please her, I would punish myself with a razor. This had the added benefit of temporarily freeing me from my anxiety and depression. The only problem is that I ran out of space to cut on my arms so I began making incisions on my thighs."

Discovering a Substitute

Sarah was able to keep the cutting a secret from her family for almost a year. It was during one particularly difficult night that Sarah's sister joined the fray attacking her. "My sister was upset because I was ruining her high school experience. After all, who wants to be related to the high school crazy girl who's obsessed with mortuary science?" As the argument and yelling escalated, Sarah realized she couldn't take it anymore. She had reached rock bottom with such brutality that she couldn't live for one more minute inside her shredded skin.

Sarah took her father aside, the one person to whom she felt she could confess what was going on: "Daddy, I'm just not right. There's something seriously wrong with me and I don't know what to do. I think I need help."

Sarah could see the confusion on his face when she rolled up the sleeves and showed the mutilated arms. But for the first time, her parents started to take her problems seriously and insisted she join a therapy group for self-injurious teens. She looks back in retrospect and laughs at the idea that the therapist and group members would like to take credit for her recovery although she strongly believes her "cure" came from a very different source, one that was very much against the rules: "I started dating one of the guys in the group. Even though we were both damaged goods, we sought comfort in one another. All the things we couldn't say in the therapy group itself we told one another in private. Each of us felt so relieved that we could relate to one another, that we weren't alone. It felt amazing to be loved for who I am rather than having to hide my arms and legs and feelings. Each of us felt understood for the very first time."

Sarah laughed again as she told this part of her story as all this was supposed to take place *in* the therapy, not outside of it: "It's ironic that the only thing the therapy did for me was to introduce me to my boyfriend, but I'm sure if you asked the therapist, he'd say that I'm just in denial and minimizing the actual effects of the treatment."

Sarah and her boyfriend both stopped cutting themselves soon after they began dating. They became one another's support system in a way that group never could because it didn't feel safe: "The truth is that I stopped cutting because I cared so much for my boyfriend I wanted *him* to stop. If I continued to cut, then that would have made me a hypocrite, and I'm sure he felt the same way about me."

Sarah doesn't want to give the impression that her boyfriend was the sole reason for her recovery because in so many other ways it was a very unhealthy relationship. That's one reason, of course, why they have rules about not dating someone else in the group. The fact is that she did learn a few things in the group that taught her to be more aware of what triggers her to cut and how to control those urges. That may have helped her to stop this self-destructive behavior, but it never really got to the heart of the matter, which is why she just ended up substituting one method of self-harm for another. With a little improvement and reduction of her pain, she was no longer at the intolerable depths of despair that came with hitting bottom.

Healing Herself

Sarah did the best she could to manage a life that felt totally out of control. Her eating disorder and self-mutilation were actually adaptive coping strategies that worked for her—until they didn't any longer. It wasn't until she reached a point of complete and total despair, with no other options, that she finally, and reluctantly, confessed her problems: "I've always been inclined to deny my feelings, much less ever express them directly. I became more aware that my tendency to overeat occurs during those times when I feel depressed or anxious, or stuff my feelings. I so fear rejection and critical judgment from others that I haven't been willing to talk about what I really think and feel, much less ever talk about my problems." Sarah admitted that is the reason she is telling her story here, even though it is so difficult for her to be honest: "After all, I'm talking about the worst parts of myself in the most public setting imaginable."

Sarah tried a number of other ways to stabilize herself. She tried Overeaters Anonymous groups, but the religious preaching didn't work for her. She had already had a negative experience from her previous therapy group, so she was resistant to going that route again. It wasn't that she was turned off by therapy altogether, just *bad* therapy led by incompetent professionals. Interestingly, that is what inspired her to become a therapist herself!

"It was while learning to be a therapist that I finally had a breakthrough," Sarah recalled. "I was talking about my most honest feelings to people who could hear me without judgment. In my early classes, I was required to talk about my issues in practice interviews with peers. Although some of my classmates chose to disguise certain things, or talk about safe subjects, I jumped in with both feet. In some ways I felt like I had nothing left to lose."

Ah, the benefits of hitting bottom.

As much as Sarah anticipated scorn and ostracism from her parents, they actually showed tremendous support and love. They acknowledged their own shortcomings and invited her to be even more open about her feelings, especially those that have led to her self-destructive behaviors. Of course, this was far easier said than done: "I've been an expert at hiding my feelings all my life, so it is a constant struggle to push myself to avoid reverting back to old habits. It helps to remind myself that this is *exactly* what my own clients need to do."

Perhaps in a movie or fictional story, Sarah would have lived happily ever after once she acknowledged her problem and reached out to her family. She would ride off into the sunset, Super-Healer, righting wrongs and saving others with her afflictions. But often self-healing is not quite enough, so she recruited the help of a professional to cement the "cure."

"It felt wonderful to confide my secrets, to talk about my problems without feeling judged. It also reminded me of the sheer power of telling one's story and making sense of that life experience in the context of presenting problems," Sarah explained. She feels fortunate that her therapist was both smart and very skilled, able to penetrate her usual disguises and games: "But I honestly don't think that any of her techniques and interventions were all that important in the grand scheme of things. It just helped that she was fully present with me, that I could depend on her."

Sarah realizes all too well that her recovery and healing hardly took place in a single transformative moment but, rather, result from an accumulation of events that occurred both within therapy and in her life. She also knows she will likely struggle with some of her core issues for the rest of her life: "But I've found a kind peace with my past. I have also learned to embrace my differentness; I think being 'normal' is overrated. I know that my passion to help others comes, in part, from what I have suffered. I have so much compassion and empathy for people who are struggling with eating disorders or overeating, as well as other forms of self-harm."

So, What Made the Biggest Difference?

As I've mentioned repeatedly, it is next to impossible to isolate any single experience that truly "made the difference" in anyone's life because so many factors are involved. Certainly being in group therapy early in Sarah's life, even though she didn't seem to get much out of it (except meeting her boyfriend), and attending individual therapy for a few months were part of the recovery. So was her own self-study and research. And then there are so many other influences and incidents that led to such excruciating self-loathing that she felt she had no choice but to change.

When Sarah was asked what she believed helped her the most, she minimized the usefulness of therapy (even though it led her into the same career) in lieu of some disturbing life events: "It certainly got my attention when I lost a friend to suicide, just as it did having my parents' support. Both of these factors are consistent with a lot of what I now know and understand about how and why change takes place—so much is connected to relationships."

Sarah was impressed with her last therapist, who she found to be both highly intelligent and skilled, but she was not much influenced by their sessions: "She knew a lot about eating disorders and all but it never felt like we connected. She may have thought she understood me but I never felt understood by her."

This last statement is profound in that it highlights the essence of what makes a difference in therapy, or any other helping relationship, at least as reported by clients. It may be that professionals are in love with techniques and interventions, but the people they see, especially those who are already stuck in the muck of a deep hole, want desperately to feel like someone truly understands them. "I didn't feel safe, so I just shut down," Sarah remembers. "I hid what I was really thinking and feeling because I didn't think she could hear me." Fortunately, however, for the first time she felt unconditional support, compassion, and love from her friends and family. It also helped tremendously that she is able to use the experiences of her own pain to help others. We will be revisiting that theme in a later chapter when we discuss the value of service to create meaning.

Sarah experienced the best and worst of what it means to reach out to others for help. These models provided her with a clearer vision of what she wants to do for others to make a difference: "I have had a very strong support system for about a year now, and my life has significantly improved as a result. Sometimes that's all someone needs. At least that was the case for me."

Of course, if all it took to help people was love and caring for them, then we wouldn't need doctors, therapists, health professionals, teachers, and clergy. Compassion and understanding may indeed be critical pieces of the puzzle, but, as we've seen, there are many others needed to complete the picture.

In the next chapter, we examine a more specific kind of hitting bottom that results from trauma or some catastrophic event. As you'll see, more often than not, such difficult life challenges can result in tremendous growth—depending on how they are handled.

CHAPTER 6
Growth Through Trauma

SCENE I

The first thing Rodney was aware of after regaining consciousness was the annoying sound of some kind of Darth Vader–like machine. It was breathing in and out in a monotonous whisper, its pace regulated by a higher pitched sound.

Beep.... Beep.... Beep.... Beep....

When he lifted his head with some difficulty, he saw that there was some kind of life support system by his bed, attached to him with multiple cords. On some level he realized he was in a hospital, but he couldn't figure out exactly how he got there or why. He concentrated really hard trying to remember, but the last thing he could recall was leaving the house for some reason that now escaped him. It was then that he looked up and saw a nurse in the room puttering around the machine. She was smiling at him.

"Wannalee," Rodney said to the nurse with considerable effort. It was hard to talk, especially over the sounds of the machines next to him. Beep.... Beep.... Beep.

The nurse just stared at him and smiled. She continued adjusting the machine but otherwise ignored him.

"Iwanalee," he said again, mumbling louder.

Rodney was trying to tell the nurse that he wanted to leave this place, to take him home. Now he remembered that he had to get ready for the last basketball game of the season against New Mexico State. Coach said he'd get some playing time even though he was a freshman, just a few months out of high school.

The nurse acted as if Rodney were invisible, as if she couldn't hear him. He was speaking as clearly and distinctly as possible, but she still wouldn't listen to him or respond in any way other than to keep smiling. He started to call out to her again when he realized there was some kind of tube in his mouth. He could feel himself start to gag as he realized there were tubes running down his throat. No wonder the nurse couldn't hear him: He wasn't making any sounds except those inside his own head.

Rodney looked around the room, at least the part of it that he could see lying flat on his back. There were more tubes connecting him to the machine, at least one connected to his chest, another to his arm, and something snaking along his neck. He could see a bag of blood on a stand next to the bed, plus another one containing some kind of fluid— all of it was connected by the damned tubes.

Rodney tried to concentrate once again, but the pain was absolutely unlike anything he could ever imagine. As an athlete Rodney knew pain. He had suffered through drills on the court that would surely destroy a lesser man. He had played hurt. His coaches had taught him that pain was nothing. He had learned to ignore pain, to play through it. Pain was nothing.

Whatever was going on in Rodney's body felt like something beyond pain. It was as if he were lying on a bed of needles with the point of each sharp tip sticking into him, penetrating the skin to the core. He could feel hundreds, thousands, of sharp points sticking him, hurting him everywhere. His neck. His back. His legs. His arms. Even the inside of him hurt so much he couldn't stand it.

Rodney tried to move, to get away from the needles, but they had him tied down to the bed for some reason. He tried to move his arms, but they were apparently strapped to the bed. His legs felt even more immobilized. He struggled again to get up, to get away, to escape the pain, but he couldn't move anything except his head. When he looked up, he saw the nurse still smiling at him and fooling with the damn machine.

"Help me," he cried out in a gurgle. "I want to go home. I'm tired of this," but he realized that the sounds coming out of his mouth were not intelligible because the nurse kept ignoring him. Why wasn't she listening? Why wouldn't she help? Why couldn't she turn off the machine so he could concentrate? With each sound he could feel the needles digging deeper.

The most likely scenario—the *only* possible explanation that occurred to Rodney in his fogged state, was that he was part of some kind of experiment at the university. Maybe this wasn't a hospital after all. He must be in the health clinic on campus, and they're doing some kind of study on him. They've tied him down to the bed, and they're hurting him to see how much he can take. He'd been trying to tell them that he can't take any more, he'd had enough, but they weren't listening. If only the nurse would quit smiling.[1]

THE GIFTS OF TRAUMA

The trauma from a gunshot wound, debilitating disease, catastrophic event, natural disaster, death of a loved one, or any other form of abuse or neglect, is often a life-altering experience. It was always assumed that such a traumatic event would necessarily lead to all kinds of future problems and misery—there's no doubt that there are extra burdens to bare and healing to take place. But imagine the surprise when it was discovered that in at least half the cases of trauma that the supposed "victim" (*survivor* is usually the preferred term) actually experienced significant growth and positive transformations as a result of the events.[2]

In a classic example, one of the worst maritime disasters in history, the sudden sinking of a cruise ship in the English Channel in 1987, resulted in the death of nearly 200 passengers, leaving the survivors to literally swim for their lives in the freezing water (Figure 6.1). Psychologists were called to the scene afterward to assess the damage and provide whatever support might be useful, leading to systematic studies of the effects on the passengers over the next several years.[3] It was, indeed, the case that many of the survivors resorted to alcohol and drugs as a means of coping with the trauma and others experienced severe depression and anxiety, as might be expected. But what was most surprising is that 43% of the survivors interviewed some months after the incident reported that their outlook on life had *improved for the better*! They were more appreciative of the relationships in their lives. They found themselves more willing to be expressive with others. Their

Figure 6.1: Herald of Free Enterprise cruise ship, which sunk in a matter of minutes en route to Belgium from England, leaving hundreds of survivors to scramble for their lives and live with the consequences of the tragedy for the rest of their lives. Incredibly, as many people who reported significant trauma also said they experienced positive transformations, appreciating their lives and loved ones more thereafter. (Photo courtesy of Associated Press.)

life goals crystalized. And a whopping 90% said that they no longer take things for granted, inspiring them to engage more fully in their daily activities.

Far from unusual, it turns out that posttraumatic stress is *not* the universal consequence of tragedy or unfortunate events. Sure, there is initial misery, and considerable adaptation required, but many people find a way to move beyond their previous level of functioning and actually make significant gains beyond what they imagined possible. There have been a host of benefits documented, many of which could not have been gained any other way except by facing difficult challenges and overcoming them (see Table 6.1).

Table 6.1. POTENTIAL BENEFITS OF POSTTRAUMATIC GROWTH

Engagement in the moment	Greater appreciation for relationships
Hardiness and toughness	Tolerance for ambiguity and uncertainty
Psychological mindedness	Ability to deal with stress
Resilience and self-reliance	Renewed passion for life
Emotional expressiveness	Greater compassion for others
Altered priorities and values	Spiritual renewal
Deeper insight into the meaning of life	New interests
Increased tolerance for pain and frustration	Higher self-esteem

This is a fairly important finding considering that 80% of people will experience significant trauma in their lifetime from a variety of circumstances, whether diagnosed with an illness, losing a loved one, being the victim of a crime, or the survivor of a tragedy.[4] Most of these events occur without warning and could strike anyone at any time. But the reassuring news during major life changes is that it is precisely the high level of emotional arousal (fear, confusion, frustration, anxiety) that creates opportunities for significant change.[5] It seems that those episodes of our lives that we experience as most trying and difficult are exactly the ones that propel us to new levels of enlightenment and growth. It is also the case that people who have lived through significant and multiple forms of adversity in their lives often end up far happier and less impaired than those who have avoided such encounters.[6]

SCENE II

Right after Rodney was gunned down on the street, they took him to the nearest hospital, which happened to be the Martin Luther King Jr. / Drew Medical Center in Los Angeles. It has since become famous as one of the most poorly run facilities in the country, eventually losing its national accreditation because of persistent health and safety violations. Fortunately, because of its prime location near one of the most gang-invested territories in the country, there is no better place to be treated for a gunshot wound. Doctors in the critical care unit often function like combat surgeons after a major firefight. By the time Rodney had been brought in, with three bullets still embedded in his body, it was business as usual—just another gang shooting.

Incredibly, Rodney had remained completely aware after he had fallen on the sidewalk. He faded in and out of consciousness during the ambulance ride, awaking to the feel of something shaking him.

"Can you hear me? Are you awake?" a doctor asked, standing over him with the rest of the trauma team.

Rodney opened his eyes and tried to focus.

"We have to do emergency surgery and we have to do it quickly. Do you want to be awake or asleep?"

Rodney smiled. He thought this was very funny that they were giving him a choice. "Sleep," he said, "please sleep."

There was a .38 bullet lodged in Rodney's neck from the first shot that had come in through his back. There was another bullet that had gone in lower, through his kidney and spleen. A third shot hit his arm and shattered his elbow. The fourth went straight in his back and out through the side, puncturing a lung along the way. The doctors knew that their patient was most likely a lost cause, but King/Drew is a teaching hospital for the University of Southern California Medical School, so maybe the residents figured he'd be good practice. Later, after they had removed Rodney's kidney and spleen, repaired his lung, reset the bone in his arm, assessed the damage to his spinal cord, and repaired the holes in his body, the doctors told his mother that he would never make it through the night. It was best to make peace with that and say her good-byes. Besides, even if there were a miracle and Rodney somehow survived the next 24 hours, there was little chance he could survive much longer than that. The trauma to his body had been catastrophic.

NO REGRETS

Wounds suffered from combat, shootings, or other violence forever change someone in ways that would be difficult for anyone else to understand. There are often physical disabilities and limitations that will follow—spinal cord injury, lost limbs, neurological damage, reduced functioning of motion—but also severe psychological trauma. It has always been assumed that recovery would be limited and the deeper emotional wounds would last a lifetime, resulting in nightmares, chronic stress, and psychological impairment. Although it is certainly true that posttraumatic stress symptoms are one logical consequence of extreme tragedy, they are not the *inevitable* result. Richard Tedeschi and Lawrence Calhoun were among the first researchers to ask how it might be possible for survivors of trauma to go beyond returning to their previous "baseline" functioning and actually experience significant growth as a result of the events.[7]

Suffering and adversity have long been viewed by some philosophers and religious figures as "good for the soul," to teach humility, tolerance, and greater appreciation for life's offerings. Many of the existential philosophers talked about suffering as part of the human condition, depending on the meaning created. Soren Kierkegaard, Friedrich Nietzsche, and Paul Tillich described how suffering can become an excellent teacher, one that instructs about courage and resilience, as well as motivates action. It also helps people to take greater responsibility for their lives and how they choose to respond to things. Psychiatrist and concentration camp survivor Victor Frankl famously created a whole system of helping based on what he learned from what he experienced and witnessed.[8]

According to the Buddhists, suffering is simply a judgment about experience that is neither good nor bad. It is up to each of us to determine how we will respond to *any* situation we might face, much of it guided by the choices of interpretation we make.

Pointing to his leg constructed of plastic and steel, one Iraq war veteran said, "This right here is a minor setback."

When he was asked whether he would do it all again if he could, that is, if he could change anything, the ex-soldier vigorously shook his head. "The guys I served with were awesome guys... Yes. Absolutely. I wouldn't change it for the world."[9]

That might be difficult for many of us to understand, how someone who lost a limb, or is paralyzed, or who contracts a terrible disease, refuses to regret what happened. But that is the essence of a healthy coping strategy (or denial) in circumstances when choices might be limited.

So the interesting question is: what determines how someone responds to crisis or trauma? Why do some people fall apart while others rise to the occasion and view the events as a seminal growth experience that changes them for the better?

It turns out that posttraumatic stress and posttraumatic growth aren't exactly opposite responses. Based on studies of prisoners of war who lived under very adverse conditions, it was the feeling of being out of control and powerless that most contributed to poor adjustment and recovery.[10] Yet many prisoners found positive benefits from their experience. In fact, a whopping 61% of POWs from the Vietnam War who had been tortured, isolated, starved, and abused said years later that they benefited significantly from the experience.[11]

There are several factors that have been discovered that best predict whether trauma will lead to positive gains:[12]

Severity and kind of event. There are many different kinds of trauma—floods, earthquakes, fires, tsunamis, tornadoes, bombings, plane or car crashes, heart attacks, cancer, shootings, battlefield injuries or deaths, bereavement, sexual assaults—each of which presents its own unique challenges.

Personality traits. There are certain kinds of personality traits that better prepare someone to deal with adversity. Those who are generally optimistic, are confident, and exhibit "hardiness" and resilience are more likely to have the best prognosis.

Prior experiences with adversity. Those who have led a relatively sheltered, privileged life may have more difficulty dealing with challenges than veterans of prior difficulties who have already developed coping strategies and know what to expect.

Preexisting conditions. What was going on in the person's life before the trauma occurred? If the person were already under stress, unhappy, or dealing with multiple challenges, then it would be far more difficult to recover successfully from a catastrophic event.

Absence of blame and shame. Given that helplessness and lack of control usually accompany trauma, it doesn't help much to wallow in guilt, self-blame, and ruminations about fault finding. Rather than dwell on who is to blame and what could have been done differently, it seems far more productive to move forward.

Drugs and alcohol. Those who rely on prescriptive medications, illicit drugs, or alcohol to self-medicate do far worse than those who manage without these chemical crutches.

Personal resources. It's obvious that those who have financial resources, access to quality care, a good job with benefits, and a functional family have distinct advantages over those without such assets.

Support system. As we've discussed earlier, relationships are key. Those who can rely on others for love, caring, and guidance are more likely to make the best of things.

Spiritual beliefs. People who have strong religious or spiritual beliefs often cope better and have an easier time accepting "God's will." A less religious form of this might involve comparing someone who says, "Why does this always happen to *me*?" versus a shrug and "Oh well. Shit happens."

Meaning making. Ultimately, it all comes down to what sense you make of the experience and how it is framed in the context of your life.

It is precisely the crisis and disequilibrium that makes big changes possible. Take away what is familiar and safe and put in its place a life-threatening or extremely stressful situation, and there is going to be a lot of internal action taking place, for better or worse. It is during such times that you question everything, that you're open to new alternatives. It is when your world collapses that there is an opportunity to rebuild a new, even better structure.

SCENE III

Rodney awoke again...minutes?...hours?...days?...later. He was still in the same place, still part of some kind of experiment. They were obviously holding him prisoner. They were keeping him in this place to test him. The machine was still going, breathing over and over in its raspy breath, interspaced with the annoying beeps.

The pain was worse than ever. The needles were deeper. They were pushing them into him harder and harder. "I want to go home," he kept saying to himself over and over. That's all he could think about.

Rodney glanced around the room and the nurse was gone. She had been standing to his left next to the machine. He turned his head—it was the only thing they hadn't strapped down—and saw Monique, his girlfriend, sitting in a chair on the right. She had a book on her lap and she was smiling at him, just like the nurse.

"Monique! Girl! Listen to me. Get me outta here. Take me home. I want to be with my mom. Find my mom. Tell her I'm here. She'll take care of this. Stop smiling, will you? Help me. Why won't you help me?"

Monique kept reading her book, glancing at him every once in awhile, but most of the time just ignoring him. She was part of the experiment, too. Either that, or she couldn't hear him. He kept trying to talk, but with the tube down his throat and the drugs in his system, the voice remained in his head. Rodney could talk all he wanted, but he was the only one who could hear the cries for help. If only his mother could hear him, she'd take him away from here. She wouldn't just smile at him; she'd do something. She'd get rid of these tubes and the needles and the machine. She'd make it all better.

Rodney lifted up his head. Monique turned a page and looked up, smiling, which infuriated him. Why couldn't she see what these people were doing to him? Why wouldn't she listen to him and go get his mother? She was the only one who could save him now.

There were tears flowing down Rodney's face and he couldn't even wipe them away. His arms wouldn't move, and the pain from the needles was too bad. Monique continued to smile, thinking that her fiancé was crying tears of joy because he was so happy to be alive, so pleased to have the love of his life sitting by his bedside.

Rodney was now completely terrified, crying because he was confused and frustrated and because he didn't know what else to do. He cried until he passed out from the pain.

HELPLESSNESS AND POWERLESSNESS

The title of Stephen Joseph's book, *What Doesn't Kill Us*, says it all. One of the foremost researchers on posttraumatic growth has found that trauma and crisis can present each of us with a critical turning point in our lives, which can either beat us down and destroy us, or make us so much stronger. I suppose a third option is that it would have negligible effects, which might also be common.

When Melanie was in college, she had been kidnapped at knifepoint, held captive for 48 hours, and repeatedly raped until she was released. I had the chance to speak to her about the incident while her family sat in stunned grief in another room. Melanie seemed cheerful and relaxed, which was my first surprise. The second was the casual way she told the story of what happened. Sure, it was frightening and disgusting. She did the best she could to talk the guy into releasing her (which worked!). Now her biggest problem was that her family in the other room, and all the media covering the story, expected her to be a basket case. But all she now felt was relief that it was over and anxious to get back to school.

Now, one might easily conclude (as I did) that Melanie was in strong denial, that her defenses were kicking in and surely she would be due for a crash after such a horrific, life-threatening assault. But I checked in with her several times over the years, including last year (which was 40 years after the incident occurred!), and she still insisted that she had never experienced ill effects from the episode. It was just a difficult thing that happened to her that was over and it was time to move forward.

I would suppose that if you can manage to stay in denial until you die, then you win—it was an excellent coping strategy after all. But I remain convinced that Melanie was neither in denial, nor minimizing the consequences of her rape and assault. She just seemed to have the resilience and attitude to put the trauma behind her. And I say "seemed to" because there is also some evidence that we can't always trust self-reports by survivors as accurate.[13] It's not that people exactly lie to themselves and others but that they create a story of change after the event that may not match actual, observable changes in their lives. And often those memories of what really occurred are fractured, fragmented, and distorted since survivors have a distinct problem recalling an accurate and coherent picture of the events.

In almost all circumstances, Melanie's case notwithstanding, trauma either kills a part of you or makes you stronger. It creates a state of acute instability and vulnerability. It shatters your most cherished beliefs that you are safe and the world is essentially benevolent. It contradicts your assumption that you are in control of your life. You realize, in one swift moment, that you are, indeed, frail, mortal, and helpless in the face of events way outside of your power to control.

SCENE IV

Rodney drifted in and out of consciousness throughout the week. Each time he'd awake, there would be someone else in the room. Sometimes it would be Monique. Another time it was some of the guys from his basketball team or his neighborhood, or several of his sisters. And there were always nurses and doctors.

One day Rodney awoke to the sensation of his bed moving. At first, he was afraid to open his eyes, fearful as to what torture they could possibly devise next. He couldn't imagine anything worse than the needles and being strapped to the bed, but who knows what they might have in store for him next—maybe turning up the volume on that beeping machine. He drifted in and out of consciousness, each time awaking to the feeling that he was going somewhere. He was trying to work out how the bed could possibly be moving when he decided to risk a look, confirming his worse fears: the bed *was* moving. There were two men, attendants of some sort, who were pushing his bed into the hall. For the first time in as long as he could remember, the sound of that machine was gone.

Rodney had no idea what had been going on outside his insular world, but he came to learn that hundreds of people had visited him every day. The waiting room was a mob scene with newspaper reporters, TV people, magazine writers, friends, family, well-wishers, and strangers who wanted to get a glimpse of the mortally wounded celebrity. It had become a very big deal in the media that a neighborhood boy who had gotten out of the ghetto was supposedly murdered by the gangs he had managed to avoid. There was a death watch going on with people waiting to write his obituary. The hospital couldn't control the access, not to mention their fears that maybe some gang members would come by and finish the job.

The doctors thought it would be better for Rodney's safety if he were moved to another facility that could provide care after they had stabilized him. Nobody explained any of this to him. In fact, nobody even talked to him directly. They just smiled and wheeled him out of there to Somewhere Else.

He awoke to the sound of a doctor's voice. "I'm sorry," he was saying in a grave voice. He was a neurosurgeon, and he looked uncomfortable giving bad news, so he made everyone else feel that way, too. "I've reviewed your son's scans, and it is clear that one of the bullets permanently damaged his spine."

Rodney could still see his mother's back but not her face. She was looking down at the floor but not saying a word. That's when his sister,

Theresa, jumped in: "So what are you saying? What does that mean?" She sounded angry and Rodney liked that. He had been feeling so helpless all week. Finally someone was talking for him.

The doctor was either used to irate families or completely oblivious to the emotional nuances. He remained perfectly calm, as if he were giving a weather report. "I'm afraid the prognosis is rather poor. He's lucky to even be alive."

"So what are you saying?" Theresa interrupted him. Her voice was shrill, and now Rodney could see that his mother was crying. Rodney felt like he had already died, that he was totally invisible, with his body inhabiting the bed but his mind and spirit hovering somewhere overhead, watching this surreal conversation as if they were talking about somebody else.

The doctor looked at his watch, then fiddled with the stethoscope surrounding his neck. "I'm saying that your son—I mean, your brother," he said, correcting himself, realizing that now he was talking to the patient's sister rather than his mother, "is completely paralyzed from the neck down. He will never walk again. He may regain some use of the lower extremities of his hands, but that's about it. He'll be in a wheelchair that can be operated with a few of his fingers. You'd be amazed at the technology these days." The doctor paused, then added: "Of course, he can still lead a relatively normal life."

Rodney was trying to digest what the doctor was saying. He wasn't supposed to be listening to this conversation. For the longest time, he thought they were talking about someone else, perhaps another patient in the room. Then, all at once, he realized they were talking about *him*. He remembered what had happened on the sidewalk outside of his house. He had been shot—four times. He would never forget the sounds of the gunfire.

In the fog, drifting in and out of consciousnesses during the preceding week, Rodney had thought he was part of an experiment but that wasn't it at all. They were saying he was paralyzed—that's why he couldn't move. There were no straps. No needles. Rodney lifted up his head and saw there was nothing attached to his arms and legs. They were perfectly still, covered by a sheet. He willed his legs to move, but it felt like he really was tied down.

Rodney heard his sisters and mother whispering and arguing about something. There were some harsh words for the doctor, but at this point Rodney started to lose focus. It was like he left them in the room still talking about this guy who looked like him lying in the bed. But he was now gone.

Rodney kept thinking what he was going to do with his life. They were saying his legs were gone. His legs had been his life. His legs were *everything*. This was the end for him. They're saying he's going to be in a wheelchair for the rest of his life.

"Why didn't I just die?" Rodney wondered. "Why am I still here? I can't live like this. I can't. I can't. I can't."

To this day Rodney has never told anyone that he overheard this conversation, that he knew the truth almost from the beginning. His family tried to protect him. They told Rodney that he was going to be okay, that he'd be up and walking again, maybe even playing ball again. They kept smiling at him.

Just a few weeks earlier, Rodney had been having a conversation with a friend. They were just fooling around and talking about the worst thing that could possibly happen to you. She was saying that it was being blind—that she couldn't stand the idea of not being able to see. She'd rather die than lose her sight. Rodney told her that the worst thing that could ever happen to him would be to lose his legs. Without his legs, he'd have nothing. He'd be nothing. He'd depended on his legs for so long. They carried him out of the neighborhood. They got him into college. They brought him fame and respect. It was like he had lost his soul.

Rodney tried to lift up his head again, to look around the room one last time to see if this had all been a dream. He was wishing that he was back in the experiment. But he could still hear the voices talking. He couldn't hear what they were saying, but he heard his mama, say, "Oh God, Oh God, my baby, no." She was saying it over and over. Then he was asleep.

STRATEGIES FOR COPING AND GROWTH

"Coping" is actually a fairly benign word that refers to simply managing a situation, dealing with it in such a way that you can continue on the present course. But we have been talking about the ways that crisis events spawn incredible, positive transformations that go way beyond mere recovery.

We are looking at the ways that people flourish after difficult challenges. This state is characterized by several features: (1) positive feelings about the experience, (2) increased engagement in life, (3) improved confidence and self-esteem, (4) sense of optimism and hope about the future, (5) improved relationships and deeper intimacy, and (6) resilience to face future problems with greater ability and adaptability.[14]

It is more than a little interesting that this last factor, resilience, may actually *prevent* those who are high in this dimension from enjoying the benefits attained through growth.[15] Because such individuals already have solid skills to manage and bounce back from adversity, they often take such challenges in stride, returning to their previous level of functioning but not necessarily spring-boarding to higher levels. That means that there is actually a learning effect from novel stimuli in which the first time or two that you face difficulties you are presented with maximum opportunities for quantum change.

Ideally, it is the goal of any strategy to deal with trauma not only to reduce suffering and return the person to "normal" functioning but also reach further for potential growth and learning. This is actually the goal of the "positive psychology" movement, which has become increasingly popular as the means to help people not just to address dysfunctions and disorders but also to promote quantum changes in well-being and happiness.[16]

What's Going Right Instead of Wrong?

As you are probably well aware, most mental health professionals operate from a position of figuring out what is *wrong* with people and then trying to fix it. They employ diagnostic models of psycho*pathology* that identify debilitating symptoms, self-destructive behaviors, chronic conditions, mental illnesses, and incapacitating disorders. Initial diagnostic interviews usually begin by asking someone, "So, what's your problem? What's wrong with you that you sought my help?"

Moving beyond mere recovery or fixing problems, however, the ultimate goal is to actually learn something meaningful from the experience in such a way that enhances the quality of life and provides you with resources that you can rely on in the future.

Clinicians now routinely ask their clients not only to talk about their problems, but also to elaborate on exceptions in which they managed to handle things reasonably well. I recall working with one woman who was experiencing all kinds of unpredictable symptoms as a result of advanced-stage multiple sclerosis. Each week she would report some new disturbing set of physical problems—loss of balance, numbness in her face, dizziness, confusion, and bladder dysfunction, each of them completely unpredictable in its sudden appearance. She felt understandably helpless. It also made sense that she wanted to talk a lot about the latest problems she was facing, but by allowing her to do so it only seemed that she became more depressed and discouraged. Eventually, we made a rule together that she was more than welcome to talk about her problems, but only after she first spent 10 minutes of the session speaking *only* about things that were going well in her life. This was really, really hard for her to do, but eventually she would come in prepared to balance the complaints with things about which she felt grateful.

It is so often useful for any of us to focus on what's going well in our lives instead of harping on the disappointments, frustrations, and problems. Even when struggling with difficulties that feel overwhelming and all encompassing, it is almost always useful to look for exceptions when you have managed temporarily to demonstrate a degree of control, if not mastery.

Avoidance Versus Action

Strategies for recovery and coping are usually divided into two groups, those that are avoidance oriented and those that are approach oriented. Avoidance methods can be appropriate at times, providing opportunities for reflection, recovery, adaptation, and proceeding at more comfortable pace. This gives you the chance to gather your energy, make sense of what happened, and plan what you want to do next. It isn't so much stalling as buying some time until readiness is at a more optimal level.

Avoidance can also be counterproductive when it kicks in defenses that lead to denial or extreme procrastination. You stall and stall, put off action at all costs, wallow in suffering, and feel incapacitated to move into any kind of action. Under such conditions, guilt, rumination, and blame are common.[17]

On the other hand, it has been assumed for many years that encouraging people to talk about their trauma and relive the experience was the best way to work through unresolved issues. Firefighters, police officers, soldiers, and emergency personnel who had been exposed to disturbing effects of violence or death were virtually required to participate in critical incident stress debriefing programs. The focus of these programs was well intended, encouraging supposedly traumatized professionals to talk about the awful things they witnessed.[18] But it turns out that there was little evidence to support many of the assumptions of the treatment, especially considering that only about 5% of workers actually suffered any symptoms. In many cases, forcing workers to talk about incidents only made things worse.[19]

Of course, there are those who benefit from having opportunities to talk about what is bothering them, but only at a pace and in a context that works for them rather than one imposed by some outside authority. People often shut down when pushed to do something for which they don't feel ready or don't yet see a value. More recent research indicates that it might not be necessary at all to relive disturbing incidents in order to work through them.[20]

Approach options involve doing something constructive. They can involve specific tasks such as learning new skills, increasing flexibility, reaching out to others, and repairing damage. They can also focus on expressing and working through feelings related to the events that occurred, making sense of the experience. Such an active strategy might involve renewing interest in religious or spiritual traditions, consulting with a therapist, joining a support group, talking to friends and family, and also talking to oneself more constructively. Which of these options are chosen depends a lot on how you view the situation, whether you genuinely believe things will improve with time, or whether you think you must do something to make things better.

Regardless of the situation, there are some guidelines that have been developed as a consensus from current research.[21]

1. *Responses to crisis are often guided by how you conceptualize them.* If you think of yourself as a victim and view the situation as a terrible crisis

from which you will never recover, then that is how it will remain framed. If, on the other hand, you interpret the situation as a difficult challenge that can be overcome with time, patience, and effort, then you significantly increase the probability of achieving that outcome.

2. *Accept that transitions, crises, problems, and even tragedies are a part of life.* You have not been singled out for special treatment (even if it might sometimes feel that way). Everything is in a constant state of motion, flux, and change; that is true of relationships, careers, family situations, and especially anything related to Nature, health, the economy, government, and culture.

3. *Clarify what it is you really want.* Goals have to be realistic and attainable, but also those that take you further than you've gone before (the difference between coping and flourishing). Make sure the goals are incremental so you can make small steps in the desired direction every day.

4. *Make commitments and then take action.* The goals set in the previous step are worthless unless they lead to actual movement.

5. *Reflect rather than ruminate about the situation.* It does little good to obsess about what might have been, what you could have done, or what you wish you could do. It is far more useful to search for meaning in the struggle and discover new parts of yourself about which you were unaware. Also, work to keep things in perspective by looking at the big picture. Sure, you'd never deliberately choose suffering, but now that you find yourself in this situation, remind yourself of your blessings.

6. *Maintain hope and optimism.* Your attitude is everything. Inevitably there will be setbacks, even times of despair and incredible frustration, but things *will* get better if you will it so.

7. *Reach out to others.* Those who have reported the biggest gains after trauma are often those who have recommitted themselves to loved ones through greater intimacy and sharing. If your life isn't already populated with a solid support system, then now is the time to create or expand one.

8. *Take care of yourself.* During difficult times, it is even more important to do the things that soothe and relax you. Meditation, prayer, exercise, social support, and recreational activities should become a priority.

To this list I'd add one more item: Redefine who you are. All transitions and crises provide opportunities to be more like you've always wanted to be. Once you are confronted with the reality of disappointments, failures, tragedies, and even death, you can't help but ask yourself what is most important for you to do—and be—with the limited time you have left.

SCENE V

Fast forward a year. Rodney has been released from physical therapy and instructed that it was time for him to begin his life again. The problem is that all Rodney had ever been prepared to do was play basketball. He had been raised in South Central Los Angeles in a gang-infested area; the only way out of there was shooting hoops, and he was among the best high school players in the state, having led his team to several championships. He had been offered a full ride out of the ghetto with prospects of a pro career in the NBA. Basketball had been his life. It was what made him a celebrity both on campus and in his old neighborhood, which was steeped in poverty and ruled by vicious, violent street gangs. It was a miracle, and a great source of pride to his family, that Rodney managed to stay out of the clutches of criminal elements. He would become a professional athlete—and a college graduate—the second in his family.

Rodney may have survived the shooting, but he was now paralyzed, a quadriplegic confined to a wheelchair with only limited movement in his wrists. His basketball career was over; in fact, he would never run, jump, walk, or even be able to move most of his body again. A guy who used to have a 38-inch vertical leap would never again leave the confines of his wheelchair. Someone who defined his life through the sport of basketball could never again hold a ball.

It is certainly understandable that Rodney lapsed into depression and despair, crying himself to sleep. School was over since the only reason he was there in the first place was to play ball. He had no academic preparation or success in that area. His relationship with his girlfriend would soon be over as well—Monique would not want to stay with a broken man who had no future, who no longer had any dreams.

To make matters even worse, Rodney was now confined to his family home as a virtual prisoner, unable to navigate himself into the kitchen or the house's only bathroom. A contractor who had been hired by the state to refurbish the dilapidated dwelling had knocked down a few walls, punched some holes through the floors and roof, and then took the money and run. The house would soon be condemned even though Rodney's sister and her family had moved in to help take care of him. The children were sleeping on the floor. The rooms had no doors. The only heat source was from the gas stove. The only bathroom had no sink. When Rodney's mother had to quit her job to help take care of her son, and when his father was involved in a car accident that limited his ability to work, their already desperate situation became hopeless. The only bright spot was that for reasons he couldn't fathom, Monique, his girlfriend, was determined to stick by his side.

LEARNING THROUGH THE PAIN OF OTHERS

Studies of posttraumatic growth after life-threatening illnesses have consistently found results that parallel those who recover from terrorism, bereavement, and catastrophic events.[22] Recovering patients from cancer, spinal cord injuries, HIV, and other illnesses expressed surprise and delight at how their family members, friends, and even perfect strangers came to their aid during this time of crisis. This often led to a complete reappraisal of the importance of relationships in their lives, coupled with a similar reassessment of all life priorities. They became less concerned with their physical appearance and yet more concerned with taking care of their bodies. They felt less need to be in control and found it easier to go with the flow. Even with their new physical limitations, they began to think of each day as a "gift" to be treasured and no longer taken for granted. They lived more in the present and expressed greater appreciation for simple things. They reported feeling less fear of death. They felt more prepared to take risks with future career options; in many cases, they went back to school or learned new skills for other jobs. They often described the physical illness as a catalyst for change, one that launched them in directions they never imagined but that, in many ways, was far better than what they were doing previously.

It's unfortunate that it takes a catastrophe or trauma to get our attention in this way. In these studies, people had to lose a part of their body functioning in order to take greater responsibility for their own health and well-being. There are obvious lessons here for all of us.

There is a phenomenon known as "secondary trauma" or "vicarious trauma" in which people experience acute stress as a result of observing others' suffering close at hand. If you've ever had a loved one or friend who has died, committed suicide, or been grievously injured or ill, then you know exactly what I mean: You are haunted as a result of standing by helplessly as someone close to you struggled.

We can learn a lot by observing the ways that people handle their life challenges. We can feel inspired by their courage and determination, even under incredibly difficult circumstances. And as we've seen in a previous chapter, this can easily happen through the stories told by others, whether fictitious or real. If you've ever read a book (or seen the movie) like *Johnny Got His Gun*, *The Color Purple*, *We Need to Talk About Kevin*, *The Lovely Bones*, or *Diary of a Young Girl*, you would never be the same afterward. Their stories will penetrate you as if you were *there*, as if you stood by helplessly and watched the tragedies unfold.

SCENE VI

One day, Rodney and his family heard a knock on their door. It was ABC Television's *Extreme Makeover* crew. They had selected Rodney for a major life transformation. The television staff completely tore down his home and rebuilt another one, two of them actually—one for his parents and a specially designed, technologically advanced dwelling that had every appliance and aid imaginable for someone so severely disabled. The episode, presented as a special two-hour show, was among the most popular, memorable, and acclaimed in the history of the series.

This break was just the spark that Rodney needed to redefine his life. He could no longer be an athlete, so it was now time to become a scholar. This was all the more audacious considering that he had so little preparation for this role—he had always been scheduled to take "jock" classes to make more room for basketball practice.

Through hard work, pure stubbornness, and plain desperation, Rodney became an honors student at the university with a major in human services. He took the energy he used to pour into his game on the court and transferred it to the classroom. He was determined to work with at-risk youth in the inner city, helping the same gang members who had shot him. He received support and encouragement from all over the country. People sent him money. The university retired his basketball jersey. A crowd of thousands turned out in a rally for him. The president of the university adopted him as a surrogate son, offered him a scholarship to complete his graduate education in counseling, which he managed to do through a sheer act of will.

With the media attention over, Rodney was still left to continue to pick up the pieces of his life. It was assumed by the millions of viewers, as well as by the thousands of people who offered emotional or financial support, that their hero lived happily ever after in his spectacular new home. Yet with the improvements to the property, the taxes assessed were now 10 times higher than before. Rodney felt the burden to help his family keep their newfound prize. He wondered how he could do that when each day it was a struggle just to get through the day, keep up with his studies, and make a new life with Monique, who was now his wife.

ADVICE FROM EXPERTS

How do survivors best recover, if not thrive, after trauma? What have we learned from stories of success, as well as systematic research, that would be most instructive to the rest of us who are also doing our level best to make the most of our lives?

As with any other significant disruption of life or severe problem, it takes a combination of strategies that address issues that occur at the biological, interpersonal, emotional, and cognitive level. Every system has been profoundly affected by the trauma. There are likely physical injuries with accompanying pain and adjustment. Depression, anxiety, anger, guilt, shame, frustration, and feelings of helplessness are not uncommon. There is plenty of counterproductive thinking going on, including recriminations, self-blame, rumination, and other negative thoughts. And, of course, all primary relationships will have been affected, exacerbating conflicts and presenting difficult areas for negotiation. The survivor really isn't the same person anymore and may never return in the same form.

Here are several key messages from experts in this area that work together to help the person to heal and grow:[23]

Normalize the Experience

The only thing worse than losing what you believe are the most precious things you have—your stability and health—is thinking that there's something wrong with you because of your reactions. It is perfectly normal, appropriate, and reasonable to fall apart when faced with catastrophic events—at least as an initial response. This does not reflect poorly on someone's character but, rather, simply indicates the severity of the event. It really helps to realize that healing and recovering from any trauma takes time and patience. But it's also important, as mentioned earlier, to hold on to optimism and hope.

Control the Debilitating Emotions

As long as stress, anger, depression, and self-pity continue to take over, it's nearly impossible to regain normal functioning, much less grow from the experience. Survivors must be taught how to talk to themselves differently about what happened and what this means in their lives. It isn't possible to change what already happened, but there's so much that can be done to alter one's perceptions of the past and the future. Until such time that negative feelings are reduced to manageable levels, it's not likely that much other progress is going to be made.

Take Care of Yourself

When you are wounded, it is crucial to prevent "infection," keep yourself comfortable, and allow yourself time to heal. There is never a better time to make sure you get proper medical and psychological care, maintain good sleeping and eating habits, and get exercise to keep your system running optimally. There are a host of anxiety reduction and relaxation strategies that have proven helpful for most people, especially during times of crisis when your system is flooded with excess stress hormones.[24]

Talk to People

Whether survivors reach out to friends, family, clergy, doctors, or a psychotherapist, it is absolutely imperative that they have an opportunity to tell the story of what happened and what that means to them. But as mentioned earlier, although it is useful to extend an invitation to talk about the experience, individuals should not be *forced* to do so. Whereas talking about the experience is important, it is just as critical that they feel heard and understood. They don't want to be told platitudes like, "Get over it," or "It's all in the past now," which only confirm their worst fears that the listener really *doesn't* understand. One of the reasons that Holocaust survivors have done so poorly in therapy is because their therapists, with their eternally optimistic, hopeful attitudes, refuse to accept that there are certain things that happen to people that are so horrific that it really *isn't* possible to fully recover.[25]

Discover Meaning

This can occur through renewed religious or spiritual pursuits, or by exploring existential issues that examine personal responsibility, isolation, death, service, and especially how what happened creates new opportunities for life goals and priorities. This is where survivors reconstruct a different, more robust narrative in which they begin to see things in terms of strengths instead of weaknesses, growth instead of damage, and new options instead of limitations.

Do Something . . .

. . . useful and constructive. It's important to do way more than just think about issues and wrestle with their meaning, or talk about them to others. Transformation may occur purely from new insights but, more often than not, it stems from action. This means trying new things, experimenting with behaviors and options that never occurred to you before. And just a reminder: You don't have to wait for a trauma or crisis to get your attention that your life is passing you by and you don't have nearly as much time as you think to do the things that are most important.

Transform Personal Identity

In Rodney's story, which has formed the foundation of this chapter, he was able—with more than a little help from family and friends—to completely change the way he sees himself as a person. His whole life he had defined his worth and value in terms of the number of assists, rebounds, and points scored during a game. He was an athlete, a basketball player, a refugee from South Central L.A. In the aftermath of his tragic shooting, Rodney lost almost everything that he thought was most important, yet he rededicated himself to those he loved most and made a choice to become someone completely different. It's ironic that without the trauma he suffered, realistically he may have completed a few years of college while playing basketball but may not have committed himself to complete his studies and begin a distinguished career.

SCENE VII

I first met Rodney when he applied to our graduate counseling program with the ambitious plan to work with gang members or athletes who were unprepared to succeed in a career outside their "hobbies." Although I was certainly impressed with his life story, and the obstacles he had overcome, I was skeptical that he could make it in such a rigorous academic program. To add to the challenges he faced, being confined to a motorized wheelchair with limited use of his hands, Rodney was also painfully shy. My first reaction was that we'd give him an opportunity to succeed, but I didn't think the odds were in his favor.

During the next decade, I became one of Rodney's mentors and confidantes. I couldn't believe the things that man had to face on a daily basis. I learned, for example, that he couldn't yet drive a specially equipped vehicle, so his mother drove him from the inner city to our campus an hour each way and then waited in the parking lot all day for him to finish his classes.

I once asked him how he managed to take notes in class, or from his textbooks, given that he couldn't type or write. Again, there were classmates and friends who came to his aid. His family was so incredibly proud that he would be the first in his family to obtain a graduate degree.

I also noticed that Rodney was becoming more confident and articulate in his verbal speech, more and more willing to speak in class about his experiences and express his opinions, which were often very different from other students who came from very different backgrounds. He started talking about dreams he had, perhaps to work in a university like ours and help mentor students from disadvantaged backgrounds.

I am still amazed at what Rodney has managed to accomplish in his life. He now works as a counselor at our university where he does exactly what he hoped to do—provide support for minority students (Figure 6.2). He is completing his hours to become licensed as a marriage and family therapist. And just to show that there's no limit to what

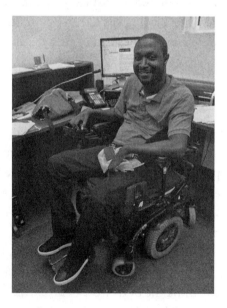

Figure 6.2: Rodney Anderson working in his office where he serves as a counselor to minority students at the university. (Photo courtesy of author.)

he can do, Rodney is attending a doctoral program to conduct his own research and eventually teach.

Looking back on his journey, I asked Rodney the central question of this book: what exactly made the most difference to him in all these incredible transformations he has undergone?

He thought for a minute, the question catching him off guard. There were so *many* sources of help, how could he pick just one? There was this eight-year-old kid who kept writing him letters during his convalescence and that meant a lot. There were the rallies held on campus to raise money for his medical bills and honor his courage. Then there was his family and all that they'd done to keep his spirits up. He thought for sure his girlfriend, Monique, would end up abandoning a cripple like him, but she became his biggest cheerleader (and his wife).

"My strength comes from God, for sure," Rodney said. "But my driving force has been not to let others down."

"That's a lot of pressure," I commented.

"I didn't want to be another statistic. From where I came from, none of us were expected to do much. I wanted to be the exception that others in my neighborhood could look up to and say to themselves, 'Why couldn't I do that, too?'"

Rodney just shook his head in amazement at how his family came together to support him. His four sisters, brother, and parents made so many sacrifices on his behalf, just as so many others did in the community. And he just had to show them that their investment would pay off.

Rodney remembers that if there was one thing that motivated him more than anything else it was this doctor who told him that he wouldn't be able to do much after his recovery. It made him furious! "I didn't want to become the story of the guy who used to play basketball and then got himself shot and now he sits in a chair at his parents' house. I just refused to accept that."

Rodney thinks of his father and the difficult life he had raising five children while working in a steel mill and then painting lines on the highway. "Now he calls me professor," Rodney says with a smile. "He's so proud of me. I always wanted to be someone my parents would admire after everything they did for me."

Rodney thinks it's a load of crap when people say they wouldn't change anything, that they accept what happened to them: "I'd always take back what happened if I could. Who would ever *choose* to be in a wheelchair?"

Yet he is also very clear about how different his life would have been if he had never been shot. He wonders if he would have ever graduated college. Would he be working some 9–5 job in a factory or a mall? Would he have gotten sucked into his neighborhood gangs? It's doubtful, but he's damn sure he never would have found his current resolve and mission in life.

"The thing about basketball is that it's instant gratification. You shoot. The ball goes through the hoop. Or not. That was my life." Rodney shakes his head, still in awe how different his life has become. "But now I have to get up every morning and start each day with a long list of things I have to do just to get out of bed, get dressed, drive to work, all these things I used to take for granted. It taught me patience and to think long-term."

With all that Rodney has accomplished, all those he has inspired and helped, he feels like he's just getting started. "With everything that I've done, I'm not close to where I want to be."

SUDDENLY EVERYTHING CAN CHANGE

Rodney's story, however dramatic, is hardly unique. There are so many instances of people who have found courage and achieved their greatest triumphs after recovering from catastrophic events. Katie is one such individual whose life took an unexpected turn as a result of circumstances completely out of her control. Like Rodney, she uncovered aspects of herself that could only be discovered through adversity.

Katie was looking forward to her last semester of college. She was an excellent student, taking a full academic load, while also working full-time for a law firm. She had an ideal job as marketing coordinator waiting for her upon graduation. She was also planning her wedding. "I was so ready to enjoy the fruits of my hard labor," she remembers, "everything I had earned."

"Oh how things can change so quickly," Katie says with a laugh. It was a beautiful summer afternoon, and Katie was planning dinner with her fiancé. She was looking forward to a romantic evening, saving time for her usual study ritual afterward. This would be her last memory for a long time.

Katie met her fiancé at the grocery store to pick up a few things for their dinner. All of a sudden, she remarked out loud that she didn't feel well and then collapsed on the floor, cracking her skull. She was rushed to the hospital, where they performed emergency surgery to remove a portion of her skull to reduce the pressure and to try and stop the internal bleeding. She was then connected to a ventilator while the doctors and her family waited to see if she would survive, and if so, the extent of her brain damage.

By the time Katie woke from her coma, she had lost most of her voluntary functions. She couldn't talk, walk, or eat on her own, much less move most of her body. "But I never gave up," she says. "I was determined to regain my life."

Determined, indeed. Just as Rodney found support among his family and friends, so did Katie rely on others to help her recover. She spent months in physical therapy, speech therapy, and occupational therapy. She had to wear a helmet to protect her fragile skull: "There were so many things I had to learn all over again. I was reminded of the things that were truly important to me. And not a single moment went by that I ever thought about giving up."

Fast forward several months later, and Katie was reenrolled in 18 credits in school. The only concession she made to her condition was to postpone working full-time while completing her studies. She remembers sitting in class the first day back when she noticed her hands shaking uncontrollably. "That's when I realized how terrified I was of not ever being able to function at the same level as I had been before. Each day, each exam I faced, I had to make the conscious choice to overcome my fear."

Katie graduated with straight A's and never felt more proud of anything she has (yet) accomplished in her life. As she walked across the stage at graduation to receive her diploma, her family was there, as well as her neurosurgeon.

"I would never have guessed that my life could change so quickly, so dramatically, and so completely," Katie admitted. "I have gone from near death to accomplishing the greatest achievements of my life, so the daily struggles I used to stress over no longer seem insurmountable and oftentimes seem insignificant. Each new day and each breath I take has become a cause for giving thanks, and I will never again take for granted the ability to care for myself."

Katie looks back at what she has done with awe, now left to wonder about what happened and why. She believes she was saved for a reason, but now she is left to figure out what that might be.

Katie and Rodney's stories highlight how, with support and perseverance, even the most tragic of events can lead to extraordinary growth that couldn't have happened any other way. But such significant changes often take place incrementally, and often under the guidance and care of a helping professional. Such changes that occur in the context of psychotherapy will be described in the next chapter.

CHAPTER 7
Changing in Psychotherapy

Let's face it: Psychotherapy is usually a last resort after all other options have been tried and failed. It is time consuming, expensive, inconvenient, and often painful and intrusive. As we've already seen, most changes that people make in their lives take place in the outside world, as a result of circumstances, challenges, adventures, disappointments, conflicts, transitions, traumas, opportunities, and other critical incidents. It is only when people have exhausted their current resources that they seek professional help—or are pressured to do so by others.

The arenas of psychotherapy and counseling are places that have been specifically designed to promote change. Almost every aspect of the experience is thoughtfully arranged in such a way to make it possible for pilgrims who journey there to find the answers for which they are searching. People who are unhappy, unsatisfied, troubled, anxious, depressed, frustrated, or lonely, or who just want someone with whom to discuss plans and ideas, can find something of benefit. Perhaps those with addictions or chronic personality disorders might not have the best prognosis, but otherwise, somewhere between 80% and 90% of clients report positive outcomes from their treatments,[1] although about 5% become worse.[2] There is even some evidence that more than one quarter of clients get what they want and improve after a single session![3] Of course, the particular results depend on a lot of different factors—the severity and chronicity of the presenting problems, the client's motivation, characteristics, and external support, the approach employed and kind of treatment, and the ability and experience of the clinician, to mention a few.

There have been thousands of volumes and 10 times as many studies completed to investigate and describe the inner workings of therapy and how it leads to change. Some of these works have been instrumental in highlighting the common features of almost all therapeutic approaches, continuing a long line of distinguished works beginning almost a hundred years ago.[4] I've written dozens of these books myself, each of them intended to explore a particular aspect of the therapy experience from the perspective of the client, the therapist, and their relationship.[5] You'd think with a lifetime of experience and so many volumes under my belt, I'd have a pretty good idea of what is really going on. But one of the main reasons I began this project was to pull together what is known (or *assumed* to be known)—not just from the reports and studies of professionals but especially from the consumers of these services, who often present a very different picture from what clinicians and most researchers claim is going on for them.

Here's the bottom line, to cut through all the smoke and mirrors: Therapists are absolutely in love with their theories and techniques. We tend to worship at the altars of our false idols. We treat the sanctioned and approved volumes representative of our favored approach as sacred texts, handed down by divine intervention. At our conferences, major leaders in the field are treated like rock stars, literally thousands of their disciples (most of whom have medical or doctoral degrees themselves) stand in line for autographs. At workshops and conference presentations, participants are hungry, even desperate, for handouts that describe some new, innovative technique that is promised to revolutionize the field. Every few years another fad comes along—waving your hands in front of clients' eyes to cure their trauma, watching the direction of their eye movements in order to match some linguistic metaphor, rechannel their energy fields, or put them in meditative trances; the list goes on and on.

Now that I have thoroughly offended and annoyed most of the therapists who are (or were) reading this book, let me confess that I'm as hungry as anyone else for any possible clue, intervention, or magical cure that will allow me to help people more effectively. During the past 40 years, I've been a huge fan of at least a half-dozen major approaches and I loved them all! I've long been amused when I've read reviews of my books and I'm described as a leading existentialist, or psychodynamic, or cognitive-behavioral, or integrative, or social justice therapist. One reason for this is that I believe fairly strongly that the particular approach we take should depend on the client, his or her particular needs at any given moment in time, and even our own unique preferences, mood, and skills.

When researchers attempt to unravel what it is that they do that appears to be most helpful to their clients, they seek to compare treatment methods or particular variables associated with certain approaches. Matters are complicated by the fact that therapists have different goals in mind, as well as define their successes and failures in very different terms.[6] Consistently (and incredibly) more recent studies have found that the therapist's techniques account for only about 15% of a client's improvement compared with triple that figure (45%) for so-called "common factors" that are evident in almost all approaches.[7] This includes things like the quality of the relationship, client expectations and characteristics, the opportunity to talk openly about their concerns, feeling supported, taking constructive risks, and developing new understanding of themselves and the source of their difficulties.[8]

Most therapists know this. The strongest movements in the field during the past decades have been to transform clinical practice into an empirically validated and evidence-based treatment. Task forces have been recruited, trained, and launched into the battlefields to sort out what's really going in during sessions by isolating and measuring variables and conducting "meta-analyses" that look at research results across hundreds of studies.[9] Yet even with the flood of compelling results that demonstrate that it often doesn't matter so much which techniques therapists use, we are still obsessed with finding the latest, best method that will provide that elusive Holy Grail.

ASKING CLIENTS WHAT'S REALLY GOING ON

Therapists continue to believe that it is primarily our insightful minds and brilliant interventions that make the most difference, and I suppose this is true among surgeons and plumbers. But then things start to get confusing when patients who consult their physicians report much higher satisfaction with treatment when they feel heard and understood by their doctors. Likewise, our patients in therapy often report all kinds of things we did that we hardly remember, yet glossing over those interventions about which we felt the most pride. It is hardly a surprise anymore when we discover that those sessions that seemed like the biggest waste of time were reported as those that were most memorable; likewise, sessions that seemed to produce breakthroughs at the time are often not even mentioned by clients as significant weeks later. The ugly truth is that a lot of the time we don't have a clear idea what matters most, nor can we reliably predict what it is that we do that has the most positive influence.

I was consoling a young woman who had recently had a catastrophic brain injury. She experienced chronic feelings of dizziness and disorientation that were literally driving her crazy. She couldn't concentrate, focus, or think coherently. She was both depressed and highly anxious. She couldn't sleep or even rest without feeling like she was losing control. Suicide was a real option that she was considering.

I spent several hours with her that first session, and I must admit, rather modestly, that I was absolutely brilliant. I reassured her that what she was going through was perfectly normal. I convinced her that the symptoms would eventually abate but she would have to be patient with herself. I listened to her fears and provided a safe place for her to talk about how terrified she felt. I could see almost instant relief, and by the time that session ended she seemed both calm and much more grounded. I have never felt more potent in my therapeutic skills.

Here's the problem: I never saw the woman again—and this wasn't because she was cured. I heard through a third party that she had been terribly annoyed by my manner and felt angry with me after the session ended. She felt like I didn't really understand what she was going through, that I was impatient and frustrated with her because she wasn't buying what I was selling to her. The most confusing part of this whole report is that I had no clue how little connection I had made with her. This is pretty consistent with some studies that report how we dramatically exaggerate our own effectiveness in sessions while drastically overestimating the dropout and failure rates of our colleagues: We are all exceptional practitioners while our peers are merely average.[10] The fact that 90% of therapists describe themselves as more competent than their peers is consistent with other self-deceptions by professors, college students, graduate business students, and drivers who also describe themselves as far better than average in their skills.[11] This would be almost comical if it didn't lead to so much self-delusion.

If you're wondering why I didn't ask my client at the end of the session how the experience had been for her, soliciting feedback to make needed adjustments, the reality is that I *did* ask her—but she lied. Apparently she hadn't felt safe enough to tell me how she'd really been feeling. I suspect that this is often the norm if you consider how often we tell other service professionals that we are satisfied because it is just too much trouble to complain.

In one of the defining moments of my practice as a therapist, I was saying good-bye to a client who had made spectacular progress in sessions when I remembered that it would probably be a good idea to do an assessment of the outcome—what happened and why. This was a time when I was a workshop junkie. Not only had I attended a program in which the speaker had virtually shamed us to do systematic outcome studies of our own clinical work, but I had also been studying a lot about all kinds of new innovations that had then emerged. I was particularly entranced with some training I had done in therapeutic metaphors, so I was really excited to hear about its effects on my client's significant improvement. But, of course, the changes could have occurred as a result of any number of other brilliant maneuvers I had introduced with her—vigorous confrontations, hypnotic inductions, psychodramatic enactments, all kinds of things too numerous to mention.

Needless to say, pressing this client to tell me what helped her most was not as helpful (or at least as affirming) as I had hoped. She simply pointed to a hole in my shoe, claiming that she would stare at it session after session since I would sit with my legs crossed. These were my favorite shoes, so I did wear them frequently (but had no idea the sole was damaged). Anyway, to make an uncomfortable story as a brief as possible, she disclosed that she found me to be an arrogant know-it-all and yet took comfort from the fact that I wasn't nearly as well put together as I imagined. "Somehow," she said, "it made my problems not seem like such a big deal to know that you also have problems that you don't even know about."

Well, surely that wasn't the real catalyst for her remarkable progress, was it? I tell this story a lot, and every time colleagues reassure me once again that she was just in denial, or unwilling to credit my excellent work, or dealing with some unresolved resentment toward authority figures, or... You get the idea. But the reality is that most of the time we really don't have a clear idea what happened with our clients and why. We have our assumptions, and theories, and our hypotheses, but they are just possibilities that are difficult to validate and confirm.

A number of researchers such as Hans Strupp, Michael Lambert, Bruce Wampold, Scott Miller, Barry Duncan, John Norcross, Timothy Carey, and David Burns, to mention a few, have been urging us for decades to become more systematic and intentional in soliciting client feedback. Clients are not only the customers we serve, but the experts on their own experience. Contained within their stories is an extensive history of what has worked for them in the past, not to mention clues to what they need most.

So, the central question of this book, as well as the profession at large is: What leads people to change self-destructive behavior? Psychotherapy is often a significant part of that process, but one that represents only one piece of the puzzle. There are all kinds of other forces and extraneous events (improved economy, family support, new opportunities, spontaneous remission of symptoms, self-initiated actions, impulsive gestures, random conversations, films, and books) operating outside of sessions, and within the client, most of which we will never identify, much less understand. We attempt to deal with the uncertainty, complexity, and ambiguity by honing in on specific, measurable outcomes or by looking at discrete, isolated variables. Sometimes we go way beyond self-reports by the participants in the process and instead attempt to carefully assess reduction of symptoms or increases in target behavior. That may assuage our own need for scientific precision but often doesn't actually capture the essence of what really happened.

SAYING GOOD-BYE TO AN OLD FRIEND

Jacqui has struggled with bulimia since she was a teenager, but it really took hold of her life for most of her twenties. She is now pixie-cute, a dedicated exerciser, and in remarkable shape, so you'd never guess she ever had such a problem.

"It was a lot more than just being obsessed with my weight," she explained. "It was a way to control my life when things seemed so chaotic. After I graduated college, I married a professional athlete and entered a world where I was constantly judged based on my looks, my weight, the car I drove, how I dressed, the size of my diamond, and the purse I carried. My job was being an 'athlete wife,' and that seemed mostly to present a particular image of affluence and a sparkling trophy."

Jacqui confided her eating disorder to another woman while they were watching their husbands play one day. The woman jumped all over Jacqui, confronting her vigorously about what a dangerous line she was walking, how she was risking her health and her life. The woman urged her to get some help and kept pressing until Jacqui agreed to see a therapist during the off-season.

Catalyst for Change

One of the things that therapists don't often recognize and appreciate is how the change process for clients doesn't begin with the first session but *way* before that when the decision is first made to seek help. During all those months when Jacqui anticipated calling for an appointment, she began a dialogue with the future therapist in her head, planning what she might say, imagining what the experience might be like, and talking to herself and this professional she hadn't yet met about her life and her problems. Like many other clients report, this already made her feel better.

Fortunately, Jacqui didn't stop with just the *intention* to seek help; she eventually called for an appointment. Like many chronic conditions, especially addictions, impulse disorders, and eating disorders, the prognosis isn't nearly as good as it might be for other kinds of problems like adjustment disorders in which people are upset because of some even that occurred in their lives.

"Once I began treatment," Jacqui explained, "I would say the biggest factor that helped me to change was the idea of having children, although the conversations were interesting and provided some relief. My husband and I were desperately trying to have a baby, and I knew I had to stop what I was doing because I would have a baby to care for.

At the time, that was enough for me to stop binging. I wanted to be a mom, and I realized my unborn baby was the reason I wanted to live more healthfully. Learning to be responsible for another life took the selfish focus off of me."

Jacqui is referring to "extraneous" and "participant" factors that occurred outside of her sessions and that seemed to make the most difference in getting her attention. This is consistent with a lot of the research that I mentioned earlier that it is often not only the therapist's actions and techniques that matter as it is also the relationship connections that are made with others, as well as serendipitous events that occur in the person's life.[12]

While the realization that she was going to become a mother, and the initial confrontation by a friend, got her started on recovery, it still wasn't nearly enough to maintain the changes. As we'll examine in the last chapter of the book, launching changes in your life is relatively easy compared with maintaining them over the long haul.

The Power of Hope

Although Jacqui managed to stop binging during her pregnancy, she relapsed several times thereafter: "I found myself resorting back to my bulimia as a means to control my life that was still fluctuating wildly. I went back to see my therapist, who had warned me that it would take some time and would be a constant battle. He told me it takes the average person at least seven years to fully recover."

I find this part of Jacqui's story interesting because people will often conform to expectations that are set by people in authority. It was once assumed that therapy would necessarily take many years of treatment, with sessions scheduled several times per week, in order to be helpful. There are still practitioners who hold this belief and insist that real, deep changes are not possible without intensive, long-term treatment that gets at underlying issues that are hidden or masked. Although I also think this might be useful for a small percentage of individuals who have the time, resources, commitment, and appropriate presenting issues for this type of treatment, the vast majority of people require some kind of relief in a few months if not weeks. Fortunately, in the last decade there arose many well-researched and tested therapies for eating disorders, and most other complaints, that can be successfully implemented in a *much* shorter period of time.

If someone is told it will take a long time to recover from a problem or illness, then probably that expectation will be fulfilled. On the other hand, in most brief therapies, clients are often presented with realistic but hopeful expectations that they will begin to notice significant improvements almost immediately. After all, it is hope and the "placebo effect" that also have a big impact on the eventual result.[13] If you go into therapy, a class, workshop, adventure, or book, with the initial belief that it is going to transform your life, and do so almost right away, you're far more likely to achieve that goal than if you are skeptical, are resistant, or believe that it isn't going to help much.

Imagine that you come in for a first session, and I tell you, "Look, I don't know whether this is going to work or not. You've got some *big* problems and the prospects don't look promising, but what the heck, let's give it a try and see if it works. If there is going to be some favorable result, trust me when I tell you it's going to take awhile." This might be a good strategy if I want to lower your expectations and keep you coming back for a long time, but it won't maximize the potential of hope.

The Power of Listening

Jaqui's symptoms returned most recently during a time of increased stress when she returned to graduate school to study to become a therapist, inspired by her previous experiences as a client, as well as her wanting a deeper understanding of her own experiences (this is a very common motive): "I was constantly fighting the urge to resort to my old friend, bulimia. Again I didn't feel in control of my life, and ole bulimia seemed to do the job in the past, even with the side effects. I just didn't know what else to do. I was killing myself to get good grades and be "good enough" in the eyes of my fellow students and professors and for myself. I wanted to fit in and feel as smart as my classmates. I wanted them to like me."

Jacqui began pushing her husband away, but this only incited him to cling tighter, which in turn, led her to push back more vigorously. This is the kind of "circular causality" that forms the basis for much of what we understand about family systems in which the behavior of one person becomes both the cause and effect of a vicious, recursive cycle: "I wanted to be left alone to sort through some complicated thoughts and feelings, and I wanted to binge and purge to feel better. But it wasn't working."

One of the lovely benefits of therapy is that it "ruins" you in the sense that it brings to light motives, desires, intentions, and patterns that can only be continued when you remain oblivious. That is the optimal beauty of insight when it forces you to face what you're doing without turning a blind eye. In Jacqui's case, she refused to go down the same road again with everything she'd done to recover.

One of the most interesting research findings is that beginners can be trained in basic helping skills in a matter of a few weeks or months and often do solid work in paraprofessional or crisis intervention roles, often comparable to professionals with advanced degrees. About 80% of what most experienced therapists do anyway is apply the most basic listening and responding skills that beginners learn their first semester. Of course, it's that additional 20% that makes a clinician truly exceptional.[14]

Jacqui was required to participate in mock counseling sessions with a classmate to practice basic "active listening" skills. "Although this was supposed to be role plays, I was a mess. I was ready to tell my husband I wanted to separate because I no longer knew what I wanted out of my marriage. And then, hearing myself talk about this to my peer counselor, it just hit me all at once: it wasn't my husband. It wasn't the new stress of grad school. It was *me*! My counselor helped me realize that simply by reflecting back what I was saying, but helping me go deeper. It's interesting that I felt safer with her than I did with my previous therapist. I knew we had limited time together, only a half-dozen sessions or so (not seven years!), so I didn't waste time."

Jaqui's therapy didn't only take place in her practice sessions for one class but also in joining a supportive community of peers where she felt such caring and respect, without being judged: "There were these amazing new people in my life who accepted me for who I am, not for who I had to pretended to be. For the first time, I felt permission to slow down and focus on what was really important. There is this incredible feeling of empowerment once you figure out what the inner conflict is all about. It's given me such internal peace and a sense that I can accomplish anything. I feel like we've finally parted ways, and I no longer need my old friend, bulimia. Therapy gave me a gift that I couldn't get anywhere else, and that's the gift of truly finding myself."

WHAT CLIENTS REPORT MATTERS MOST

Jacqui is describing one of the key facets that therapy, or a therapeutic community, can provide: supportive, caring, respectful, and accepting relationships that give permission to explore areas that previously had been ignored or inaccessible. There is less fear of being judged, and then shunned for taking the risk of saying and doing things that are outside the "normal" domain of what is expected. This is one of the key features that Carl Rogers and others described decades ago as the most important part the process: the primacy of the relationship. For many years, this went out of fashion as therapists fell in love with the illusion of technique and theoretical allegiance. Time and time again, when clients are asked what was most important to them in their therapy, what was most instrumental to the changes they made, they point to things that their therapists often forget to mention. The following feedback was collected from a dozen research studies that investigated clients' perceptions of what was most helpful to them.[15]

Hope

We already covered this, but it's worth mentioning once again. Hope is at the core of all change efforts, regardless of the situation or context. There is a clear connection that the more hope that people have to improve, the better the likely outcome, whether related to psychological issues or health problems.[16] What is it that people actually hope for? Well, for one thing hope, simply stated, is the belief that goals are possible. Without that faith, effort is often doomed.

Nietzsche claimed that hope was the "worst of all evils because it prolongs the torments of man." It's quite true that false or delusional hope is, indeed, a setup for crushing disappointment, especially if it isn't realistic. But we are talking about the ways in which hope is instrumental to therapy in that it is the bridge that builds meaningful goals, followed by behavior that is directed toward achieving those objectives.[17] Almost without exception clients mention increased hope and optimism as one of the main benefits they received from therapy during a time when they were most filled with despair.

Relationship Connections

In one study clients participated in a highly structured from of cognitive behavioral therapy for depression, with treatment consisting of procedures for identifying, evaluating, and changing dysfunctional beliefs. Perhaps not surprisingly, the therapists valued most of their own interventions and interpretations, believing they were the most potent force in the sessions—and perhaps they were. However, when the clients were asked what made the most difference to them, they said it was being safe in the relationship and feeling understood. They repeatedly mentioned the human, personal aspects of the encounter. One client, referring to the therapist, said, "She laughed, which helped so much. When you can't cope with something, you make a joke."[18]

The clients were also grateful for new insights they gained: for example, the connection between their underlying thoughts and subsequent feelings. Although this was, in fact, part of the program, they also attributed positive outcomes to simply feeling more comfortable with themselves. "I don't feel as if I've been real to myself for a long time," one client mentioned, "and this brought me back to reality."[19]

Researchers are often most interested in validating their own favored theories even if they are mandated to remain as objective as possible to avoid polluting their results. Their biases, assumptions, worldviews, and agendas may predispose them to "discover" what they think they already know, even with supposed safeguards in place as part of the experimental method. It has been somewhat rare to ask clients to share their own assessment of what was most influential to them, perhaps believing that their opinions are less valid than other measures. In almost all the studies that have been conducted, time and time again, clients talk about so-called nonspecific factors like the therapeutic relationship that helped them feel a greater sense of self-control, self-acceptance, and safety to explore new aspects of themselves.[20] In addition, clients are sometimes found to be very intelligent, discerning, skilled, and critical observers of their own experience, providing clear, cogent, and seemingly accurate descriptions of what worked for them and what didn't work very well, providing persuasive reasons and rationale for their opinions.[21]

There are, of course, many different kinds of therapy, each of which has different emphases on the kind of relationship that is created with clients. Some therapists see their role primarily as an instructor, others as a parental figure, coach, confidante, collaborator, or provocateur. Each would lead to a different relationship configuration that optimizes those facets that are deemed most therapeutic. Regardless of its form, clients appear to be extremely forgiving of their therapists' lapses, mistakes, and imperfections, as long as they perceive that the relationship between them is solid and generally supportive.[22] More than any other single factor, clients reported that feeling trust and caring in the relationship empowered everything else that occurred.[23]

Talking Things Out

Therapists might be in love with their techniques, strategies, and interventions, but their clients consistently report that they most appreciate the opportunity to talk about things that are disturbing to them.[24] This hardly has to happen in therapy since people find similar relief talking to all kinds of trusted confidantes in their lives, whether clergy, coaches, teachers, hair stylists, bartenders, friends, or family.

Some approaches to therapy make the "talking cure" (as Freud originally described it) the main focus of treatment, encouraging clients to use the time primarily to share their life stories, dreams, fantasies, thoughts, and feelings. Yet even so-called brief and problem-solving therapies that emphasize specific, behavioral actions still provide opportunities to share what is most bothersome so that clients feel heard and understood during these disclosures.

"We can tell what our therapists like the most," one ex-client said with a laugh. "Ha! They think we aren't watching, but we can tell a lot about that kind of stuff. My therapist just loved to tell me stories—and most of the time they were pretty good ones—although sometimes she'd repeat them. Inside my head I'd be rolling my eyes but I'd pretend to listen. Hey, I liked her a lot! Anyway, what I appreciated the most is that I could talk about anything—*anything*—and never feel judged. Whatever else we did in those sessions, I just really enjoyed being able to talk things through with her, even though most of the time we didn't actually resolve things in any session. But it just felt so good to have that time."

This example highlights what every good therapist knows and understands—that whatever else we do, whatever favored approaches we take or brilliant interventions we introduce—they *must* be accompanied by opportunities for deep talk about important, upsetting, or exciting issues.

Learning New Stuff

This is one of the aspects of therapy on which both clients and therapists seem to agree: Clinicians like to teach things and their clients appreciate learning them—*if* the lessons are relevant, applicable, practical, and useful. Too often therapists teach what they feel like rather than what a client actually needs during a particular moment.

"I liked therapy—mostly," one person shared. "But it bugged the shit out of me that my therapist would launch into these long-winded stories about... You know, I don't know what the hell they were about because I never really understood them. But it seemed so important to the guy that I never had the heart to tell him."

Clients often mention that one of the things they liked most about their therapy experiences was gaining new knowledge about themselves. They liked being able to talk things over and sort them out, especially when confused or frustrated. Sometimes they even mentioned appreciating specific techniques to reduce stress, deal with conflict, or process negative feelings. But all of this was predicated on an experience in which the therapist appeared caring, compassionate, empathic, open-minded, attentive, and understanding.[25]

Fred can't figure out even where to begin to talk about what he learned in therapy, but it all starts for him with a simple statement: "It took my internal dialogue and made it public." He means by this that it helped to talk about things out loud, and in doing so, it led to powerful realizations: "I think I lacked the skills to understand myself, maybe because I'm a guy and not used to talking about stuff. It's just so hard to pull apart the muck that engulfed me and see what was right in front of me. My therapist taught me things about how to think and interpret data in a way that I had not previously considered."

Fred appreciated the times when his therapist would probe and push and ask tough questions for him to consider. He feels like he probably would have learned many of the things on his own—eventually—but therapy made the changes much quicker. It even helped how often he was teased and ridiculed by family and friends for being in therapy in the first place. He felt like he was pursuing a noble cause, even with the criticism. "My first significant moment in therapy came when I was trying to decipher why two good friends of mine made me feel abandoned and deeply wounded emotionally," he recalled. "We had spent three months in Australia, surfing and living out of our vans, and for much of the trip I felt like I lacked any connection with them. Subtle things in the way we communicated with each other eventually created a huge riff between us."

Fred explored with his therapist aspects of his personality and interpersonal style that were somewhat unique and at odds with this two friends: "My therapist wanted me to look at the way the others were relating with me and see it not as a flaw, but as simply different. It wasn't right or wrong, it just was, or is. He was so calm and matter of fact about the whole thing that I think I started to take on his calm demeanor and acceptance into myself."

Most importantly, Fred was able to generalize what he learned in that situation to many other aspects of his life. It is the ultimate gift of therapy when someone is able to take the lessons learned and apply them to other situations and contexts.

WHAT THERAPISTS BELIEVE

Here is where it gets tricky. Therapists are a very opinionated group of professionals. We have some rather strong espoused beliefs about what we do that matters the most. And it's all very confusing because many of those passionate statements, all supported with research and clinical experience, sometimes contradict one another. Some therapists believe strongly that the best work has to do with resolving issues in the past while others think that is a stupendous waste of time and we should instead be focused on the present—or the future. Some therapists believe that the action takes place at a cognitive level, but then they can't agree whether this occurs in the form of narratives, beliefs, or neurological processes. Then there are whole schools of thought that say it is far more important to work through unresolved emotions, or to conduct reenactments of negative feelings, or create corrective experiences. Other therapists advocate working only at a behavioral level, targeting specific goals for intervention. I could list a dozen or more other approaches, but you can easily see the point that there appears to be a lot of disagreement about what matters most.

This Gets Personal

One of the earliest books I wrote about what leads to change in therapy explored the complex mysteries of how it's possible that therapists can appear to do such different things in their work and yet still get similar results.[26] The initial spark for the project arose not only because of my ongoing professional frustration with heated debates in the field about who had found the true path to enlightenment, but also from a very personal search for some resolution to my own personal struggles.

This was a time when I felt totally burned out in my work. I felt restless, bored, trapped, uncertain about what to do next. Okay, I was depressed and highly anxious. During the preceding six months, I had gotten in two very serious car accidents and barely escaped with my life.

Once I acknowledged that I was in trouble, I tried everything I could think of to address my problems, failing miserably, sinking into deeper despair. It was fairly obvious to anyone that I needed help, but I knew enough about myself, and past experiences, that I'm a terrible client in therapy. I play games. I intellectualize. I hide. I second-guess every intervention. I appear compliant and cooperative and then present excellent excuses for why I didn't follow through. I set expectations that are impossible to meet, either for myself or my therapist. I'm not saying I can't be helped; it's just that I'm a handful.

In searching for someone who might best help me, there was no way I was going to trust just one therapist who could meet my standards. I scheduled initial appointments with *three* professionals in the same week, figuring I could interview them individually and then decide who might be the best match.

My first awareness, after taking this initial step, was that I already felt much better. As mentioned earlier, clients have reported this relief frequently, how during their process of rehearsing what they want to say, they already begin a dialogue with the therapist they haven't yet met. I began to have second thoughts about whether I really needed to see someone after all; surely I could figure this out myself.

I had another close call in traffic and now began to wonder if I was only distracted or negligent, or perhaps suicidal? What could it hurt to keep my appointments? At the very least, I'd gather some useful experiences I could use in my own work.

Dr. Genghis

I was not a very happy kid growing up. It wasn't just the vicious divorce between my parents, but that I was left to take care of my depressed mother and younger brothers after my father moved out. I could often hear my mother crying behind closed doors, and to this day, when I think of her the memory is associated with the smell of Scotch on her breath.

There were times when I became so frightened that my mother would hurt herself that I would call her psychiatrist to ask what to do. From about age 14, I consulted with the doctor about my mother's condition and treatment. Years later, when I hoped to avoid the draft during the Vietnam War, I met the psychiatrist in person for the first time, and he agreed to write me a letter stating that I was too emotionally unstable to be subjected to people trying to kill me.

It seemed logical that this doctor would be the first person I would consult for my deteriorating condition. After all, he knew my family history, had treated my mother for so many years, and was somewhat of a mystical figure who had been hovering on the periphery of my life all these years.

Dr. Genghis (as I call him for reasons that will soon become clear) had an office appointed just like a Hollywood set for the classic psychoanalyst. As soon as I entered his office, he came from around his cavernous desk to greet me formally. I looked around to get my bearings and noticed a swoon couch in the corner, leather-bound collected works of Freud on the shelves, and also separate entrance and exit doors so that his patients would never see one another.

I settled myself in the leather chair opposite his desk, took a deep breath, and waited for him to begin: He pounced on me like a predator. If I thought this was going to be an analytic session in which I would do all the talking and he would listen, I was definitely misguided. Dr. Genghis fired question after question at me: What was I doing here? Why had I come to see him? How was my mother? (She had died years earlier.)

I explained that I had been practicing therapy for a number of years but was no longer satisfied with the work. All my clients sounded the same. I didn't really think I was making much difference. Or more to the point, I felt like I wasn't doing anything meaningful anymore. I wanted to stretch myself or do something else, or at least work in less isolation.

Dr. Genghis steepled his fingers under his chin thoughtfully, then jotted a note on a pad sitting on his desk.

Rather than follow up on my presenting problem, he directed a question at me that I thought was pretty interesting: "What is your earliest memory?" It felt like I was a prisoner during interrogation and he was using misdirection to keep me off balance.

I stammered a bit, stalling until I could figure out what he was looking for—I so wanted to please him and sensed I was failing miserably. One of my fantasies was that I thought he'd be so proud that I had become a therapist, too.

"I think it was my brother," I answered finally.

He just lifted his chin as a gesture to continue. I noticed he was writing notes on a pad but couldn't imagine what he could possibly have concluded so far after five minutes of contact.

"Well, I remember my brother right after he was born. We were at the hospital and I was..."

"How old were you?" he interrupted. Next I thought he'd be asking for my serial number and rank.

"I guess I was about three."

The chin lift again, the signal to go on.

"I remember we were leaving the hospital. My parents must have brought me with them to pick up my brother after he was born. And I remember I was sitting in the back seat and they were in the front. And they put my brother in my lap to hold him for the trip home."

"Uh huh," he said with a smug look on his face, "and how did you *feel* in that moment?"

"Feel?" I answered without hesitation. "I was terrified."

Genghis cocked his head, inviting me to elaborate.

"It's just that I was only three years old and my parents were putting this little infant just a few days old in my lap. I didn't know what to do with him. He was crying and I was scared."

The doctor made another note on his pad and then drilled me with a look. "See," he said, "that's your problem."

"Excuse me?" At this point I was more than confused by our inter-action. I could feel sweat dripping down my back. This guy really frightened me, not only by his abrupt manner but his unpredictability. Maybe that was part of his method.

"It's simple," he said to me, like I was a child, "You don't want to grow up."

"I don't? Well, I suppose that could be..."

"See, even now you intellectualize. You talk around things. You don't say what you mean."

"Well, I was just saying..."

"You are afraid of responsibility," he interrupted again. "*That* is your problem." He leaned back in his chair and crossed his arms, smiling.

"I'm sorry but I don't know what you mean."

"I think you do," he answered.

I was so dumbfounded by this whole conversation that I didn't know what to say or do next. I'm all for confrontation, but I had no idea where this was going.

"Look," he explained. "Your earliest memory is of being afraid— terrified you said—with the responsibility of taking care of your brother."

I nodded, agreeing, but not at all sure where this was going.

"It's the same thing now. You are trying to run away from your fears."

"I am?" Now I was starting to get riled up, angry at the way I was being treated. I was already feeling so vulnerable, and this was making me feel more unbalanced.

"Come on, grow up! Doing therapy is hard work. You've been doing this for, what, 10 years?"

"Longer," I whispered, my arms now wrapped around my chest.

"Whatever," he shrugged. "The point is that from your earliest memory until now you have consistently run away from responsibility, especially when things get tough."

Well, he wasn't exactly off base. I did have a pretty low tolerance for frustration, boredom, patience, all kinds of things. He sort of had me pegged. I could see where he was going with this now. If I stayed with him in treatment, he'd help me to become more like him. I'd be more responsible and stick with my obligations instead of dreaming about something else.

I stumbled out of his office in a fog. I felt so drained I could barely walk. By the time I got into my car, I sat still for a few minutes before tears started flowing. Then I started to sob and scream.

Now I wondered whether I should I go back to this guy? A part of me was intrigued by his bluntness and assault on what I thought was my reality; another part of me was convinced he was a lunatic, a self-important bully like Genghis Khan. He was everything I never wanted to be as a therapist. He was neither warm nor accepting, but critical and judgmental. He was one of the meanest bastards I had ever met. But maybe that's what I needed?

Once I recovered I realized that Dr. Genghis did actually help me. It was interesting because I felt neither heard, nor understood by him; if anything, I felt attacked and shamed. I didn't even agree with much of what he had to say, but he shook me to my core. He pushed me, prodded me. Against my will, I admitted that I really appreciated his brutal honesty and directness. The force of his personality was so powerful that I got a kick out of his eccentric style (at least after the experience was over).

I knew that if I could muster the courage to return to Dr. Genghis, I would definitely get my money's worth. He would challenge me in ways such that I could not hide or play games. He did get me to think about things in a distinctly different way, not as he expected me to conform to his vision of responsibility but, rather, quite the opposite: In that single encounter, I felt a bit clearer about what I *didn't* want to do anymore. He would never have any idea that the primary impact he had on me was to push me more vigorously in a direction that I had been considering for some time but was feeling too terrified to pursue because of the risks involved. I knew that I wanted to change my life in some dramatic and significant ways, perhaps relocate with my family to another region, abandon full-time practice, and completely redefine my life. But I also felt myself wavering, reluctant to give up all that I had worked for to begin again.

I kept hearing Genghis's admonishments over and over—that I was irresponsible, that I wanted to escape commitments and avoid the really hard work of sticking with my profession. And yet I felt furious that he would be so casually judgmental of me, especially when I sought him out in the first place for validation and support. It has been more than 20 years since this encounter, and I *still* talk to the guy in my head—defending myself, justifying my choices, proving to him that I was right and he was wrong by pursuing my own dreams.

What is interesting to me now, a revelation that just hit me as I'm reliving the experience, is that Genghis unknowingly and unintentionally reactivated a familiar pattern in which someone in authority told me I couldn't do something because of my limitations. My parents used to tease me that I would never get into college because of my laziness and marginal intelligence. My school counselor tracked me into a career preparation curriculum because she didn't believe I was college prep material. My whole life I've been rebelling against people in power who hold my fate in their hands. If I had been teetering on the edge of reluctance to follow a difficult, challenging path, then this arrogant jerk pushed me over the cliff.

Dr. Glinda

I was now having second thoughts about whether looking for a compatible therapist was actually a very good idea. Maybe I'd be better off trying to work things out on my own? Maybe I could be my own therapist? After all, I didn't really have the time for this sort of thing—and

I was reluctant to spend the money. Besides, I figured I was too old to change my ways.

As much as I longed to accept my excuses, I knew I was being a complete hypocrite. These were the same sorts of things my clients tell me all the time: Why waste money paying someone to listen to problems when you can just do it yourself?

I finally justified my continuing quest under the guise of an academic study; after all, I was doing this as much to broaden my understanding of therapeutic work as I was to help myself personally. Yeah, I know: what a load of crap!

If there could be a therapist more unlike Dr. Genghis, it would have to be Dr. Glinda, who reminded me of the "good witch" from Wizard of Oz. Whereas Genghis was combative, critical, confrontive, and even a bit scary, Glinda was the embodiment of nurturance and kindness.

The first thing I noticed about Glinda was her incredible smile that was at once warm and inviting yet completely genuine: She actually seemed happy to see me, which immediately led me to put my guard up. What's this lady up to, I wondered, still more than a little reluctant after my last experience with Genghis.

Glinda had that look, you know, the one we therapists display that implies we know some deep, dark secrets about people before they even open their mouths. She sat patiently, just smiling, waiting for me to begin in my own way, at my own pace.

I began by telling her that I was recovering from the trauma of my previous session with another therapist, who basically told me I was irresponsible and a coward. I almost dared her to do the same.

As I retold my story, focusing on my dissatisfaction and frustration with my work, feeling trapped in my life, Glinda just nodded, encouraging me to continue without interruption. Even though she wasn't saying much, I had absolutely no doubt she was following me closely.

"So," she offered after my first pause about 20 minutes into the session, "it really sounds like you do know what you want to do and where you want to go, but you don't feel the support to follow your heart."

I opened my mouth to respond, then shut it abruptly and just nodded, tears flowing down my cheeks. YES! I wanted to say but couldn't quite get the word out. I just lowered my head and felt total relief that someone heard me.

Glinda reached across and touched my arm, which only invited me to feel more understood. It felt so good to get this out, to tell someone what I was feeling, and to not feel judged or criticized.

During the next half-hour, I poured my heart out, and Glinda responded just as I would have done (or would have liked to have done) with a new client like me. She listened carefully, so, so carefully. She reflected my feelings. She supported and validated me. She genuinely seemed to care about me, that I wasn't "just" a client but, rather, someone she respected and valued as a person. She made it clear that she would go at my pace, honoring where I was at, holding me until I was ready to go further—and deeper.

It came as somewhat as a surprise that as good as it felt to be with Glinda, to feel heard and understood by her, I didn't think she would help me much. I got the sense that she would be reluctant to confront me, to push me, to challenge me. I didn't just want someone to listen to me but, rather, to call me on my stuff—but to do it in such a way that I wouldn't feel attacked and humiliated.

Although I'm treating each of these episodes as discrete events, I suspect the impact was accumulative. Genghis set me up to feel extremely raw and vulnerable, playing the "bad cop" to Glinda's "good cop." If they had been working in concert, they could not have been a better team to set me up for what followed.

Dr. Wright

To this day I feel a little guilty that I never called Glinda back to reschedule, much less thank her for being so kind and compassionate. Maybe I'll track her down now and tell her. But I felt clearer that I needed someone who would be both direct and honest with me, but also do so in a way that was sensitive and respectful.

Dr. Wright was a psychiatrist, which put me off immediately. I didn't need medication, I did not present any organic difficulties, and more than anything, I wanted someone who would not play shrink games. My prior experiences consulting with medical colleagues were that there were precious few of them I'd ever met who really loved to do therapy. Nevertheless, this guy came highly recommended from a colleague who knew me pretty well and thought we'd be a good match.

It took exactly five minutes before I decided this was *just* what I needed most. Maybe I was prepared to like him, no matter what, after the two previous visits that felt unsatisfactory. In some ways it did feel like a last chance, that if this one didn't work out I was going to abandon ship altogether and just resign myself to my fate. Yet Wright did feel just right: He was direct and honest with me, yet soft-spoken and kind. He was masterful at listening carefully to me, yet going way beyond mere reflections or surface interpretations to describe things in ways that really made sense. He was calm, reassuring, and authoritative. He asked me questions I couldn't answer and probed in areas I hadn't considered. He called me on my reticence and avoidant behavior. Most importantly, he gave me permission to go where I needed to go.

After the sessions, and even now when I look back, I could never put my finger on what it was about his style or approach that helped me the most. I suppose now, over so many years later, this is partially what led me to write this book, to answer the questions that have been plaguing me all these years: What really does make the most difference?

The best I could answer then—and now—is that it really wasn't about what he *did* but, rather, who he *was*. It was his essential kindness and accessibility, his authentic, easy-going manner, his directness and no-nonsense approach, his flexibility and willingness to really *see* me, that gave me the support and courage to consider the major life changes I wanted to make.

Most of the time I walked out of his office confused. I didn't understand a lot of the time where he was going with me. And I liked that. I liked not knowing and understanding and still feeling okay with that. I don't think that was part of his agenda. I don't even imagine that he realized exactly what I was taking from our sessions and that still resonates with me. It's a reality that a lot of the time we don't really know what it is we are doing that is most helpful because we don't take the time to find out.[27] But what it came down to is this: I felt reassured that no matter what I decided to do, or however things fell in place, I'd still be alright anyway. I had been terrified of making a wrong decision, one that would have devastating consequences for my family. When our sessions were completed, I still didn't feel any clearer about what I was going to do. For all I know, he may have counted our work as a failure— I never asked him about that.

What Are We to Make of This?

We had a glimpse into the workings of three different therapists, each of them with a sterling reputation, but with radically different styles. If I had stuck with *any* of them, I would have been helped, even with my protestations to the contrary.

If you were to have difficulty with your car, say the vehicle was overheating, and you took it to a half-dozen different reputable, honest, and competent mechanics, presumably you'd get basically the same diagnosis of the problem with roughly the same recommended solution—it's a faulty thermostat or maybe a nonfunctioning cooling fan that needs to be replaced. But imagine consulting with just as many therapists, and you'd likely get as many different answers.

To complicate matters further, although clients in therapy provide their own explanations as to what happened, the responses are often ambiguous and unsatisfactory. When one client reminisced about her experience, she was asked how it was most helpful to her. At first, she paused, then shared: "One night he walked me to my car because it was late and the parking lot light wasn't on. I remember he said something incredible. At the time it changed my life."[28]

Wow! That's pretty significant, don't you think? But when she was asked what extraordinary life-changing thing the therapist revealed to her during that magic moment, she hesitated.

"Oh, gee, I don't remember."

When the therapist was asked about the incident, he couldn't recall either, leading him to conclude that it's impossible to know what makes a difference and what most influences people. It may be difficult and challenging, but hardly impossible. And since we are having this conversation together (and it *is* very much a dialogue between us as any active reading experience should be), our main priority is to cut through all the fog and make clearer what really makes a difference. In spite of therapists' insistence that it is the unique features of their particular approaches that are most important, there is a lot more evidence to indicate that it is really what they all have in common that matters most. If we sort through all the major theoretical models, each of which emphasizes particular dimensions, and pay closer attention to what *clients* report helped them the most, we can summarize an interesting list (see Table 7.1).

Table 7.1. WHAT MAKES A DIFFERENCE IN PROMOTING CHANGE IN THERAPY?

Positive expectations and hope	Relationship factors (trust, caring)
Disclosure and processing of content	Permission to explore new areas
Telling a personal story	Feeling understood and heard
Emotional arousal	Emotional regulation
Facing fears	Constructive risk taking
Reduction of stress	Honesty and directness
Rehearsal of new skills	Task facilitation
New insights and understandings	Sensitive confrontation
Challenge of dysfunctional beliefs	Suggestions for resolving problems
Focus on present, past, and future	Modeling of new behaviors
Modeling new behavior	Creation of meaning
Public commitment of intentions	Social support
Reframed narrative	New options and alternatives
Secondary gains eliminated	Responsibility for consequences
New resources accessed	New solutions generated
Understanding past behavior	Planning for future
Interpretations of behavior	Tolerance for ambiguity/complexity
Inviting and responding to feedback	Flexible adjustments over time
Integrity and mutual respect	Follow-up and accountability

A Counterpoint to Shake Things Up

There actually is somewhat of a consensus among most theorists and clinicians about a few key ingredients that are considered important in any therapeutic approach. These are the "common factors" mentioned previously that include the relationship, the power of hope, and helping people to restory their lives through interpretation, explanation, and challenging beliefs.

There is a radical counterpoint to the passion that most of us feel toward the value of constructive narratives and alternative life stories in therapy. Bradford Keeney, one of the innovators of experiential therapy, believes we should move way beyond any "talking cure" to one that is best conceived as a "performance" in which all the participants share roles as actors, directors, and audience in the unfolding drama. According to Keeney, "Change, by its very definition, requires something new."[29]

It is novelty that makes a difference in grabbing attention and having the greatest impact. This is true with therapy, travel (see

Chapter 8), or any other setting or context that leads to transformation. Yet think about how therapy is usually constructed in such a way to emphasize a stable, predictable "holding environment." Sessions begin the same way ("So, what would you like to talk about today?") and end exactly the same ("Same time next week?"). Participants sit in the same place, claiming the same chairs and postures. The procedures have been "manualized" and standardized as much as possible, bowing to the demands of managed care providers and "empirically supported treatments."

If you ask clients, they will say they prefer this kind of arrangement, which they can count on. In lives filled with chaos and uncertainty, a marked lack of stability and predictability, therapy is often designed to provide an experience that follows a particular template. In fact, clients become visibly disturbed if something in the office is out of place or if things depart from the usual plan.

But here's the interesting question: If the object of therapy is truly to promote maximum, positive change in the most efficient period of time, why are we doing what is precisely designed to keep everything the same?

I usually see clients in my home office. We were having some remodeling done that would make such an arrangement unfeasible, so I cancelled some appointments. There was one client (another therapist) who I contacted to see how she'd feel about scheduling our session in another locale—there was a private room in a local coffee shop a few blocks away. I felt uncomfortable proposing this option, but I convinced myself that it would be an interesting experiment. Indeed, it was.

When the client showed up, we walked down the street, talking along the way, and settled ourselves in oversize chairs with cappuccinos in hand. I found it really interesting that we broke new ground and got into new areas that we never had previously. It was a breakthrough session of sorts.

The next week, I decided it probably wasn't a good idea for us to meet in a public setting, so I suggested we sit at my breakfast room table and share a cup of tea. Again, we got into new areas we hadn't discussed before.

The following week I suggested we meet on the back patio and again there was another breakthrough. But even more intriguing is that in the months that followed we each had perfect recall of those three sessions while the others seemed blurred together. The experiences we shared were far more vivid and intense because they took place in novel environments. Ever since then it's got me thinking about how much more potent therapy could be if we changed the setting, locale, structure, patterns, pace, and procedures in *every* session. Imagine what it would be like if every time a client entered the office, the furniture were arranged in a different configuration—the chairs moved around, different pictures on the wall; maybe even one day there would no furniture at all but just yoga mats, a trampoline, dance floor, or kiddie pool.

Okay, maybe that's a little much, but you get the main idea that change occurs through the acquisition of new behavior that most often occurs in novel situations. When faced with a predicament or environment that you've never encountered before, you are forced to develop new ways of dealing with the situation because what you usually might do won't fit very well.

"It is time to take a prophetic stand," Keeney proposed, "and declare that a retreat into 'safe interpretation' is little more than an act of cowardice and grotesque irresponsibility. There is nothing safe about interpretation—it is often destructive, imposing, and inherently limiting."[30]

Keeney has long adopted the methods of indigenous healers he has spent the last decades studying and imitating.[31] He sees himself as a shaman or "trickster" whose main job is to help guide transformative journeys, most of which have little to do with talk and more to do with healing rituals.[32]

I once joined Keeney on such a journey in the Kalahari, documenting his methods to see what contemporary therapists could learn from the oldest healing tradition on the planet among the Bushmen (Figure 7.1). In one of the most transformative experiences of my professional life, I was interviewing a Bushman shaman about his healing methods when he turned the tables and said that he understood I was a healer among my people.

I told him that was so, after which he asked me about the ways that I work. We had spent the previous night dancing, chanting, and shaking as part of a community healing ritual that is designed to evoke the

Figure 7.1: Indigenous healers around the world, from the Kalahari Desert of Southern Africa, to the jungles of South America or Indonesia, among the Native peoples of North America, or the Aboriginals of Australia, all subscribe to somewhat universal rituals that employ spiritual, physical, and community based strategies that almost always include music, dance, and movement and almost never conversation or talk. In this photo, the author is being inducted as a shaman among the Bushmen with Bradford Keeney supporting him. (Photo courtesy of author.)

spirits as a healing force. I described what we do in our culture, how we sit and have conversations about problems. The shaman found this absolutely hilarious, especially after he discovered that I don't use fire, or dance, prayer, or music when I work with people. He laughed uproariously when he learned that the whole community wasn't present during these healing sessions, even though I tried to explain that my "community" of Southern California has over 20 million people, not the 144 inhabitants of his village located in the most remote part of the world.

Once he caught his breath, the shaman regained his composure and asked me with all seriousness, "Tell me, have you ever helped anyone just talking to them?"

Good question, huh?

Compared with the multifaceted therapeutic strategies of indigenous healers around the world, most of whom utilize a combination of movement, music, dance, chanting, community rituals, plus natural drugs and evoking the spirit of all the ancestors who ever lived in the village, our methods pale in comparison. When you think about how ridiculous it is to expect that major changes are going to occur merely from a weekly conversation of a few minutes, it gets us thinking about other alternatives that reformulate transformation as part of a life journey. And that is where we are traveling in the next chapter.

CHAPTER 8

Transformative Travel and Spiritual Journeys

Tanya was ordinarily very eager to please, an accomplished approval seeker since childhood. If you asked people who know her what she's like, they'd use descriptors like "sweet" and "considerate," mentioned repeatedly. As such, she was very reluctant to assert herself, and she was almost never involved in conflict.

Perhaps that's why her husband, Jake, is so shocked by what he's just witnessed. They had just arrived at the airport of their destination, weary and irritable. After claiming their luggage, they walked outside to find a taxi where an airport guard pointed to a spot they should stand while waiting. As they proceeded to the appointed station, they overheard the guard yelling at them to stand somewhere else; apparently they had at first misunderstood him. Just as they adjusted their position, they heard him yelling at them once again.

Tanya had put up with quite enough. She calmly walked up to the guard, and in a voice that neither she nor her husband had ever heard before, proceeded to unload her frustration: "I don't know who you think you are or what right you think that uniform gives you, but there is no reason you have to be so rude or yell at people. If this is how the people in your city behave to newcomers, then you should be ashamed of yourselves."

The guard looked at her like an insect he debated squashing. "Look, lady, are you deaf or something? Just get out of the way and let me do my job."

"You, sir, are not a nice person—and you certainly are not very help-ful." With that, Tanya turned and strode away with a determination her husband had never seen before.

Whatever made her act that way, so out of character?

Actually several factors were at work. Tanya was tired and vulnerable, her nerves stretched tight. Second, her husband had not been feeling well. Whereas normally he would take care of everything, his relative docility throughout the journey stimulated Tanya to take a more active role in their relationship. When one person in a family alters character-istic behavior, it often leads to changes in others within the system. But most of all, it was being away from her usual environment, the normal cues and obligations, the people and schedules that ruled her life, that permitted her the option and freedom to be someone different.

TRAVEL AS A FORM OF THERAPY

It may occur to you that there are some similarities between what hap-pens in good therapy, or other growth-producing experiences, and what occurs in a particular sort of travel experience that ignites perma-nent transformations. But the big question is whether Tanya will hold on to this new behavioral option of being more assertive when she returns home.

If you came to me and said you wanted to change your life, and you wanted to do it fast, and most importantly, you wanted those changes to really last, I couldn't in good conscience recommend therapy as the first option. Sure, it's reasonably convenient and would only require you to show up once per week in a comfortably appointed office. All you would have to do is talk to someone about your problems, which prob-ably wouldn't hurt *too* much. It might be a little expensive, and it does take a bit of time, but all in all it's a quite civilized arrangement that almost always produces some kind of good outcome.

But remember, you said you want to change your life in a *major* way. You want quick results, and you don't want to have to deal with annoy-ing relapses and have to return for additional tune-ups.

I'm actually a frustrated travel agent. Although I've profited from the times I've consulted therapists in my life during difficult times, and also learned a lot from supervision, workshops, books, and teachers, nothing has come close to rocking my world as particular travel experiences that forever changed the way I think about myself and the world.

I spent a semester teaching and doing research in Iceland, as well as working on a photographic book of spectacular winter scenery. My final shooting location was a remote mountain hut located on a glacier crawling down the side of an active volcano. The plan was to spend two days in this spectacular location, capturing the waterfalls and winter scenes.

The moment after I arrived with two companions, the weather turned treacherous, making visibility impossible. It snowed so much and the wind howled so hard that we had to retreat inside the hut for safety. To stay warm, we marched in circles most of the day and huddled together at night. What little food we had froze solid. Our fuel ran out, so we couldn't any longer boil snow for water. For some reason our radio didn't work, the batteries frozen, so we couldn't call for help. We were running out of time and had all but given up hope.

We were eventually rescued after the fourth day, dehydrated, on the verge of hypothermia, and terrified. We had accepted that death was inevitable when it seemed there was nobody coming to retrieve us. Although we were eventually saved, and it took several days to recover, I wouldn't trade this experience for anything. It would have taken years of therapy to get me to the same point this misguided adventure did. During those four days trapped in the hut, believing our lives were over, we talked about things we'd never discussed, confided secrets of our lives, made amends with the past, and came to a kind of peace with our fate. There was nothing else to be done.

THE IMPORTANCE OF BEING LOST

In Tanya's experience, or my own (and this is only one of a half-dozen such travel transformations I've had), there are several factors that had such a powerful effect and influence on producing quantum changes in our lives. For the past few decades, I have been systematically interviewing people who, like me, have experienced major life changes as a result of a trip. Almost everyone has a story to tell (I'm sure you are thinking about one at this moment). Interestingly, although the trip probably did not confront you with mortal danger, it likely did present its own challenges for you to overcome. In fact, it appears that most constructive life-altering trips were those that involved some sort of uncomfortable or traumatic event that forced the person to develop new resources, increase confidence, and solve problems in new ways.[1]

The stories you hear after a particularly "amazing" adventure sound fun, amusing, and quite enjoyable. But remember, these are just stories that have been crafted after the fact to present memorable details. Quite often the experiences involved being hopelessly lost, miserable, and terrified. "Traveling is a brutality," writes novelist and poet Cesare Pavese. "It forces you to trust strangers and to lose sight of all that familiar comfort of home and friends. You are constantly off balance. Nothing is yours except the essential things—air, sleep, dreams, the sea, the sky— all things tending towards the eternal or what we imagine of it." In other words, there was a high level of emotional arousal that made the person ripe for altered perceptions. You would recognize this as a feature of any of the other kinds of personal change I've described earlier.

The implication of this premise is interesting because it means that the best stuff that happens on trips are those events that were unplanned and unanticipated. As long as people stay on tour buses, reside in comfortable hotels, eat familiar food, stick with guides and planned itineraries, they may have a lovely time, but they will probably not experience major life changes. They may return rested and relaxed but the result will not last long. Yet once people stray from what is predictable, force themselves to take constructive risks, pursue the unknown, embrace unstructured time, wonderful things can happen—if the person is not seriously traumatized and has the opportunity to process the experience in a systematic way.

There is a long and distinguished tradition throughout the centuries of travelers who were searching for far more than adventure, willing to suffer the travails of such a sojourn.[2] Consider Marco Polo's journeys in the Far East, John Wesley Powell's exploration of the Grand Canyon, or Lewis and Clark's expeditions, all filled with grandeur but also terrible physical and emotional challenges.

At the very end of the 19th century, Ewart Grogan became the first person to cross the entire length of Africa, from the tip of Cape Town to Cairo, covering almost 5,000 miles of swamp, jungles, and crocodile-infested rivers. During his epic journey, he encountered cannibals, bandits, angry rhinos, civil wars, clouds of malarial mosquitoes, and all manner of other dangers. Almost every single day of the months he spent climbing over mountains, navigating rivers, and crossing deserts, he faced challenges that left him limping, wounded, and sick. Once he returned home and reflected on what he had done, he remarked simply and modestly, "A few dangers avoided, a few difficulties overcome, many disappointments, many discomforts, and those glorious days of life are already dim in the haze of the past."[3]

It may not appear as if the experiences remained prominent in his memory, but the trip inspired for Grogan a lifelong hunger for new adventures and renewed stimulation throughout his more than 90 years. In fact, there is some compelling evidence that those who live abroad or travel extensively, and are thus exposed to enriched and stimulating environments, tend to be more creative and flexible in their thinking.[4] This can also translate into improved problem solving skills in many other areas of life.

Although they have received relatively little recognition for their accomplishments compared with their male counterparts, several women have undertaken major expeditions to stir their sense of adventure or promote healing. Isabella Lucy Bird, a 19th century writer, suffered from lifelong depression and insomnia, as well as chronic pain from a spinal disorder. She embarked on a world journey spanning decades, climbing mountains, riding horseback, crossing deserts, and searching out the most remote regions of the globe. Freya Stark, a contemporary of Bird, spent most of her 100-year life exploring the Middle East. "To awaken alone in a strange town," wrote Stark, "is one of the most pleasantest sensations in the world. You are surrounded by adventure. You have no idea of what is in store for you, but you will, if you are wise and know the art of travel, let yourself go on the stream of the unknown and accept whatever comes in the spirit in which the gods may offer it."[5]

"Challenges build character like nothing else," writes adventuress Kira Salak. "They teach you about yourself and others; they give you deeper perspective on life."[6] Salak would know: she was the first woman to cross Papua New Guinea on foot. She rode her bike across Alaska, climbed the Himalayas in Bhutan, and kayaked on the Niger

River: "There is something to be said for the challenge of going where most people don't want to travel. I find that such unfamiliar places fuel my imagination."

The "unfamiliar" can also include the most pedestrian of experiences within your own neighborhood. Tony Hiss began his book on what he calls "deep travel" by running out of the house to do a few errands and returning transformed by the most ordinary events along the way. As he walked out the door of his home, he began to notice things around him with an almost mystical appreciation for their beauty. "Each thing I looked at," he marveled, "seemed now to have a story curled inside it."[7]

It is entirely possible to have therapeutic-type travel adventures almost anywhere, as long as you are willing to immerse yourself in the unknown and surround yourself with experiences that you don't really understand. "Even when I'm not speaking pidgin English in Hanoi," writes Pico Iyer, "I'm simplified in a positive way, and concerned not with expressing myself but simply making sense."[8] Travel thus forces us to return to the most basic needs and engage life in its simplest form.

WHAT LEADS TO CHANGES DURING TRAVEL?

Transformative travel refers to the kind of life-altering, permanent changes that result from a disorienting or challenging situation while on a trip. It is precisely this exposure to "difference on every level of human interaction" that makes travel so potentially powerful as a change agent.[9] During the experience, a person develops new resources and problem solving skills, which can become internalized and generalized to other aspects of life. They become classified as peak experiences, so often triggered by travel and interactions with Nature.[10]

Transformative travel can occur in a number of different forms and structures, from an ordinary business trip that presents unusual opportunities or extraordinary departures from the agenda, to an adventure-based exploration to the top of a mountain (see Table 8.1). Regardless of whether you take a trip to a neighboring city, plan an adventure, or travel to an exotic locale, there are some common ingredients that most often lead to transformations that continue long after you return.

Table 8.1. TYPES OF TRANSFORMATIVE TRAVEL

Professional conference in a new city	Business trip that goes astray
Initiation ceremony	Vision quest
Service learning	Volunteer travel
Aboriginal walkabout	Religious pilgrimage
Research in the field	Ritual ceremony
Cultural immersion	Armed service deployment
Adventure-based travel	Meditation/contemplation
Photographic safari	Diverted trip
Study abroad	Wilderness adventure
Travel writing	Immigration to new land
Missionary	Physical conquest
Rite of passage	Tourist trip that goes off the grid
Retreat	Time travel (Just kidding!)

Mindset Ripe for Change

Just as the placebo effect and positive expectations operate so powerfully in psychotherapy, so, too, do optimism and hope program a trip to be a special experience. If you go into it with an open mind, wishing for something magical to occur, you increase the likelihood that it will be the case. It also helps to look for and remain open to opportunities that will present themselves along the journey.

Preparation for a trip not only means carefully packing luggage and reading tour books or consulting travel guides, but also getting into a mind-set in which you fully *expect* to be transformed. Conversations you have with family and friends prior to departure signal your intentions—and warn them you will come back different. Keeping a journal or blog to describe what you hope to gain also keeps you accountable, especially if you continue documenting the experience along the journey.

When Alice's husband had died unexpectedly after routine surgery, she had been understandably devastated. They had been married for 12 years, never had children, and had been devoted to one another. Alice described herself as an "emotional cripple," and even a year later she could barely hold herself together. She was tired of the numbness and her unrelenting grief, frustrated with the lack of progress trying to talk things through, first with friends, and later with a therapist. She decided it was time to put this sad part of her life behind her and try to move forward as best she could. She concocted a plan and decided to put it into motion.

Alice needed some kind of ritual to help her let go of her husband and yet honor his memory in a special way. She spent months trying to figure out what would be suitable, what he would have appreciated as a gesture, and also what would be most meaningful for her. It would have to be something dramatic, if not spectacular.

Alice laid out the plans for a scheme as if her life depended on it (and maybe it did). She researched the logistics, studied the place she would be visiting, and meticulously considered all the little details about how she wanted things to unfold. All of this thinking, in advance of the trip, was part of her self-therapy. All the time she anticipated that her departure was devoted to acceptance that this would mark the end of her formal grieving. She reminded herself repeatedly that once the ritual was completed, she would force herself to move on with her life. She announced this to others so they would know what she planned and hold her accountable.

Alice left for India with an airtight container in her luggage that contained the cremated ashes of her husband. She had arranged for a guide and porter to escort her on a trek in the Himalayas that would eventually end at the sacred Ganges River. It was at the side of the riverbank, in sight of water buffalo drinking their fill, that she ceremoniously spread her husband's ashes while saying a prayer she had rehearsed. Given the amount of time and effort she had devoted to planning the trip, it is no wonder that this action made all the difference to her.

Insulation From Usual Influences

Aside from the ritual Alice planned, one of the healing elements of her transformative travel experience involved finding space between herself and her world back home. She felt so much pressure from family to behave in a particular way—they thought she was weird and a little crazy for mourning her husband's death so long. She felt guilty with her friends because she found it hard not to talk about her lingering grief and she knew they were tired of pretending to listen. Most of all, the memories of her husband were kept so alive because his possessions were all over the house. She had to get away from all these reminders and somehow isolate herself so she could clear her head. That wasn't going to happen unless she could get away—far, far away to a place that held no associations or reminders of their past life.

What's so special about travel to promote change, and why is it necessary to leave home? Well, for one thing, you are isolated from family, friends, and others who may control and influence aspects of your life. Of course, if you keep yourself tethered to them through daily texts, e-mail, social media, and phone calls, it will seem very much like they are with you every step of the way. That companionship and shared experience can be quite satisfying but is not necessarily ideal if, indeed, the goal is to initiate changes.

Time and time again, I have heard people report that the reason they were able to reinvent themselves while on the road is that nobody knew who they were, or who they were supposed to be. They could be anyone they wanted to be, and nobody knew that wasn't the "real" them.

In part, it is the novel environment and all the accompanying stimuli, rituals, and "foreign" culture that make us most ripe for change. We are forced to let go of what is most familiar, whether in the form of support we usually rely upon or our usual behavior. We are freed from all the typical influences that rule our lives.

A foreign exchange student spent a semester in Costa Rica and made the decision to live with a family instead of with other friends. Although a bit frightening and challenging for her, knowing she'd only be able to speak in Spanish and eat local foods, the payoff was huge compared with that of others who made a different choice. "I stepped out of my world," she related, "and I went into a whole entirely different world, and I really got to see how other cultures are living and they are healthy, perfectly happy, and doing just fine."[11] You can know something like this intellectually, but when it is part of your own lived experience, the lessons tend to stick far better and longer.

Problem Solving

Any trip or adventure presents a series of challenges along the way. It begins with what you take with you, not only in terms of luggage but also companions. What you plan for yourself depends very much on what you are looking for and what you wish to accomplish. There are several possible motives for why people plan a trip.[12]

- *Escape from daily pressures.* This is the type of typical holiday that people plan in order to rejuvenate themselves. The goals are selective and modest, focused primarily on entertainment, fun, and relaxation.
- *Pursuit of pleasure.* Related to the previous category, these trips are designed to provide pure stimulation, accompanied by relaxation, drinking, massage, and other forms of recreation.
- *Time out for contemplation.* In order to reflect on your choices and life path, it is often useful to get away from normal routines. Whether in a retreat setting or structured time for solitude, the goal is to sort out future plans and perhaps initiate an action plan.
- *Social interaction.* People often travel to meet other people, or deepen relationships with existing family members and friends. In other scenarios, travelers join tour groups for the companionship as much as the convenience.
- *Adventure.* People pursue all kinds of challenges to test themselves or feel a sense of accomplishment. Options might include river rafting, backpacking, mountain climbing, caving, or all kinds of exploration or discovery.
- *Education and learning.* People choose to travel to see the sights, visit museums, or study art, architecture, culture, or history.
- *Service.* Some people plan trips that involve some type of volunteer work to assist others.

Each of these reasons for travel has its own unique benefits and opportunities, as well as special challenges. Some have a much greater chance of fostering quantum growth, if they present opportunities for participants to solve problems in such a way that they build confidence, strengthen resources, and provide new skills and behavioral options. In many cases, they teach people how to overcome their imagined limitations.

Regardless of the original intention behind a trip, invariably some things won't unfold as expected. There are always situations in which you will have to navigate through unknown territory in which you aren't certain of the terrain, don't really understand what is going on, and don't quite know how you will resolve matters. Sometimes they can involve seemingly insignificant matters that result in huge personal consequences.

One example of this occurred when I was working in South Asia, staying in a hotel for several months. For the life of me, I couldn't figure out how to work the electricity in the room to engage the air conditioning (It was 90 degrees and 90% humidity). In my frustration and impatience, I became rude and overly demanding, insisting that there was something wrong with the system. Eventually I discovered it was my own ignorance about the culture that led me to make inaccurate assumptions. I was completely embarrassed when I learned that I had made a complete fool of myself by refusing to ask the right questions.

This may seem like a simple mistake, one easily forgotten, but it changed my life in so many ways. It was because I was jet-lagged, tired, disoriented, confused, and vulnerable that I overreacted to a relatively simple problem to be solved—all it would have taken was a request for help. But I became stubborn, and progressively more rigid and unreasonable, as the conflict escalated. I have never forgotten that incident that could have only occurred while traveling because it has since reminded me to take a deep breath during times of conflict, especially with apparently irresolvable problems. I learned to ask myself what I'm missing.

That's the thing about travel—it is really about solving a series of little problems in which you can't so easily rely on what you already know or think you understand. Some behaviors don't generalize appropriately to other cultures and contexts. Some actions just plain don't work and might aggravate things more. I'm not just talking about huge cultural differences in foreign countries but also a bunch of little things that differ across the continent. For example, it is ironic that in car-crazy California pedestrians are considered sacrosanct when strolling across streets in crosswalks. I've been almost killed dozens of times forgetting that this isn't the case in the other cities.

When spending time in any new locale, it is virtually certain that you have to invent new ways of dealing with difficulties and figure out how to get your needs met. You are forced out of your comfort zone and required to try alternative means to navigate through puzzling challenges. In the best of circumstances, these critical incidents can train and prod you to be far more flexible when you return home.

Pursuing New Adventures

The best things can often happen when you depart from the planned itinerary, throw away the map, and embrace whatever you encounter along the way. When things go according to the agenda, you probably won't remember what happened for very long afterward. Listen carefully to people's chosen travel stories, and so often there will be themes of facing adversity, challenges, discomfort, and fear.

In a collection of stories by great travel writers, they were asked to share their favorite adventures, those that that were best remembered and whose effects still endure.[13] "Everything good that has ever happened to me or come my way has been unplanned," said novelist Mary Morris. "Everything interesting has been an accident."[14]

That might sound intriguing, but the fact of the matter is that the writers in the volume humorously relate stories of being attacked by army ants, deluged by falling scorpions, freezing to near death at the North Pole, detained in a holding cell, and being lost *way* off course from their intended destinations. Yet it seems to be precisely the drama of the events that cemented their memories and solidified the effects of what they experienced. Again we revisit the theme of Chapter 6 in that what doesn't destroy you can very well make you stronger and more resilient.

There are both legitimate and exaggerated fears that will likely be faced during a transformative trip, especially when fully immersed in the adventure. Naturally, there is always a fear of the unknown and unfamiliar because they will require a high degree of adaptability and employing new skills that will feel awkward. There is also the fear of anything that is different from what you are used to—strange customs, confusing situations, exotic but unfamiliar situations. There are fears of not being understood, especially with language barriers and local norms. Finally, there is a fear of failure that, ultimately, you won't be able to handle what you face along the way.

It isn't only fear or adversity that makes experiences more memorable but almost *any* intense emotion, including joy, passion, and exhilaration. Watching a sunset, standing on top of a mountain, walking along a beach, viewing or experiencing anything that feels transcendent, stays with us long afterward—especially when it is unexpected and takes us by surprise. Changes most often occur when the experience is *way* outside the boundaries of a traveler's expectations, assumptions, and worldview.[15] There is a renewed sense of wonder, observes environmentalist Rachel Carlson, who reflects on what we lose after childhood and wishes she had the power to ask the good fairy to provide each of us with this enduring gift "that it would last throughout life, as an unfailing antidote against the boredom and disenchantments of later years, the sterile preoccupation with things that are artificial, the alienation from the sources of our strength."[16] She goes on to say that it is precisely this interest in the novel and unusual found in travel that inspires greater joy, excitement, and mystery.

Altered States of Consciousness

Transport yourself to a new environment, and you become much more attentive to new stimuli. Smells, sounds, sights, and feelings become intensified because of their novelty. You notice things that you would otherwise ignore back home. You become far more sensitive to your surroundings, and especially to cultural differences. You become open to experiences that you might otherwise not consider. In this heightened state of attunement, you also become far more susceptible to influence because you are in a more vulnerable condition. In a sense, you sometimes enter an almost hypnotic state when traveling, an altered state of consciousness that matches the alternative reality you face, one that features things you've never encountered before.

Although there are times when you are able to enter a trance state back home (television, books, watching a fire, etc.), it's so much easier when you are moving through time, space, and place. There is something about being on the move that makes us open to new experiences that otherwise would be out of reach. That is why all great travel writing is a "reflection of the heightened perception and awareness that travel itself is already set in motion within these writers' minds."[17]

Teachable Moments

There is little that you learn on a trip that you couldn't really learn at home; it's just easier to hold your attention and gain a different perspective when you are in the kind of wide-eyed receptive mood that accompanies travel.

Morgan is ordinarily quite shy. It's not that he is exactly reticent to approach others as much as he simply enjoys spending time alone. This has worked out fine most of his life, especially in his work, which involves creative design, in which he spends a lot of time in front of a computer screen, rarely needing to interact much with others. But lately what once felt like solitude is feeling more and more like isolation and loneliness. There's a part of him that would really like to connect on a deeper level with others, but he just isn't sure how to go about approaching others. He feels awkward and reluctant, fearful of rejection.

Morgan signed up for a service trip to help rebuild a school and tutor local children. As was his usual custom, he immediately headed for a solitary task of painting the trim along the roofline of the building. This allowed him to work alone at his own pace but also isolated him from others in the group of volunteers. This would have been his normal pattern except that during a lunch break he did something he'd rarely, if ever, done before: He approached a circle of follow travelers and sat down to join them for the midday meal. This might not sound like much of a major breakthrough but for Morgan this was unprecedented. He *always* ate his lunch at his desk while at work.

This first attempt to join the group was, indeed, awkward and uncomfortable for him. Throughout most of the lunch break, he sat quietly and just listened to the others bantering with one another. Even though he didn't contribute much, it felt strangely satisfying to him that he was part of the group; they seemed to accept his presence in a casual way. This led him, slowly, to continue throughout the week's expedition to sit with others, even if he didn't contribute much beyond his presence. And it started to feel good!

Morgan's experiment with becoming more social and engaged with others never would have happened back home where he was too entrenched into long-standing patterns of self-protection and isolation. It was because he was in a foreign environment, his usual habits disrupted, that he was open to a "teachable moment" in which he would try something that he desired but that had previously felt inaccessible. A key question is whether Morgan will carry with him what he discovered about himself when he returns home. Will he join other coworkers for lunch back at his office or continue to sit alone at his desk? Will he have had a sufficient taste of intimacy and engagement that he is willing to reach out for more?

One major difference between what you do on home turf versus when on a sojourn is that while traveling you are given the opportunity, if not required, to experiment with new behavior, and new ways of being, as well as to reflect on the results. One object of therapy is to get people to do things that they know are good for them but they don't necessarily want to do. Travel often makes this possible: If you want food, or to get from one place to another, you must figure out a way to do some things that are uncomfortable. The path of the pilgrim is often suffering.

TRIAL BY TRAVEL

Okay. Your turn.

Think of a travel experience that forever changed your life. This could have been a conference you attended or business trip that presented challenges you hadn't anticipated and forced you to define yourself in a new way. You may have chosen some adventure or journey that required physical stamina, emotional resilience, or mind-blowing revelations. It could have been an ordinary vacation that ended up far differently than you imagined was possible. It could have involved activities or circumstances that required you to do things you'd never done before. It could have resulted in new relationships or deepened those that had previously been superficial or limited. Regardless of the context, you returned a different person from the one who left. You might have looked the same to others; you might even have resumed your normal, previous activities, but you felt like a profoundly different person.

I've been taking groups of volunteers with me to Nepal for more than a dozen years as part of a foundation we run to support at-risk, lower caste girls and prevent their induction into domestic or sex slavery. Each year we raise money to support the girls with scholarships to attend school, as well as visit with them, their families, and teachers, to mentor them. In many cases, they are the first girls in their villages to plan realistically for higher education with dreams of becoming engineers, doctors, teachers, and other professionals.[18]

Although the trips sound exotic, interesting, and fun, they are also brutally difficult. I've brought hundreds of volunteers with me over the years, each of them breathlessly excited about the opportunity, and starry-eyed over visions of the spectacular Himalayan scenery and Nepali culture. They are never disappointed by those expectations but almost universally unprepared for the hardships that accompany this kind of mission. Squat toilets, sudden snowstorms, crowded lodges, strikes, long days walking up and down and up the sides of mountains (there is no flat land where we operate), and even threats of violence from ongoing civil unrest challenge the most experienced traveler. And these physical hardships are nothing compared with the emotional strains of working with children who are so desperately poor and neglected. There is *always* someone in our group who is crying (me included) because of physical exhaustion or feeling emotionally flooded (Figure 8.1).

Figure 8.1: This woman is exalting in the joy of overcoming challenging obstacles, both physically and emotionally, as she climbed to the top of a high Himalayan peak. The journey was hardly "enjoyable," at least as I remember the complaints, oxygen-deprived rest stops, and exhaustion. The interesting thing about transformative travel experiences is that they are often terribly uncomfortable and difficult at the time; only afterwards do we create narratives that make the experience seem far more fun and interesting. This offers important insights for understanding the process of change that is often fraught with trails that test our resilience, commitment, and perseverance. (Photo courtesy of author.)

Remember my dream of becoming a travel consultant as change agent? I specifically design these visits to maximize the possibility of change, not only for the hundreds of girls we support, but also for the volunteers. There is mutual and reciprocal influence in these interactions in which the lives of the travelers are transformed almost as much as those of the people we are helping. Yet when we look deeply at what aspects of the trip had the most impact, invariably people mention the trials they faced along the way.

When Zack planned to complete the John Muir Trail along the spine of the California Sierras, he had no idea what he was really getting into. He had minimal wilderness experience and little preparation for this remarkable adventure that takes a month or more to navigate 220 miles walking up and over dozens of mountains, some of which exceed 14,000 feet. The biggest challenge for Zack was not so much the strenuous physical demands as the need to remain mentally strong for days at a time when he felt discouraged and frustrated, and almost lost heart: "My only cure was to take step after endless step. I had to know who I was in order to accept what lay around the next bend or over the next pass."

The changes that Zack experienced, and the essence of his adventure, resulted from the times that his meticulous plans and preparation had failed. He learned to let go of expectations. "When gazing at the stars at night," he recalled wistfully, "if you expect to see a meteor or shooting star, you will be unlikely to appreciate the beauty when one occurs. In preparation for many journeys, as you purchase tickets, make reservations, and buy gear, your heart may become attached to an expectation set rooted in self-imposed pressure to have the ideal experience. What is joy? What is challenge? What will I eat? These questions start to be answered before your journey begins. Under stress, the heart and mind draft a narrow definition of a successful journey."

This was a powerful revelation for Zack after he realized that preparation does indeed reduce future stress but at the cost of remaining basically unchanged. His journey was one of discovering what was unplanned and unanticipated, and that was his ultimate gift he could take back home.

Zack realized that travelers often mistake restoration for transformation. They stay in posh resorts, which may "do wonders to restore us to our normal selves, but rarely can they transform someone who is challenging his physical and mental limits. We don't have to climb a mountain or walk an endless road, but it helps to view our lives as tiny in context to the beauties, vistas, and challenges of our big Earth. For me the transformation didn't occur all at once, but instead with each step I took. Living in the moment, whether traveling, or throughout each day, allows us to realize our constant transformation. Would I have realized this without my trip to the Muir Woods? Perhaps, but it is along the trail where the thought came to mind."

SPIRITUAL JOURNEYS

In one sense, Zack's adventure was as much a spiritual journey as a physical one. As important as it was for him to control as much of the walk as he could, ultimately the weather, terrain, and unexpected encounters taught him to surrender to the experience and let go of control. He was exploring as much of himself as he was the Sierras.

Historically, human travel has occurred for several prominent reasons: (1) exploring and migrating to new territory for occupation, hunting, or food gathering, (2) scouting movements of potential threats and enemies, and (3) spiritual quests to sacred sites. The whole idea of recreational travel is a relatively new phenomenon among our species, given that such journeys were fraught with danger, discomfort, and annoyances. The earliest pilgrimages were thus often communal affairs in which groups of travelers would visit sacred sites to pay homage and demonstrate their religious devotion.[19]

During the 14th century, Ibn Battuta, a devotee of Islam, followed Muhammad's advice to seek knowledge through travel: "Swayed by an overmastering impulse within me, and a long-cherished desire to visit those glorious sanctuaries, I resolved to quit all my friends and tear myself away from my home."[20]

Battuta spent over 30 years on his spiritual journey, visiting more than 40 countries, and keeping meticulous records of his reflections and revelations, as well as observations about the cultures he encountered. Although his contemporary Marco Polo earned greater recognition, it was Battuta who remained focused on learning and growth rather than commerce.

To someone on a spiritual quest, in search of enlightenment or to honor a deity, the discomforts and challenges are considered to be just a part of the noble task. The birth of most world religions began with a spiritual quest in search of greater meaning and purpose. Granted, Moses' exodus across the desert to Mount Sinai was hardly a search for transcendent experiences as much as an escape from his enemies. Buddha chose to pursue enlightenment by roaming the Indian countryside starving himself half to death. Similar journeys of self-restraint, hardship, or service were undertaken by Jesus, Mohammed, Brigham Young, the Dalai Lama, and Mahatma Gandhi.

Among more contemporary religious leaders, many of their spiritual paths were first launched as a means to heal their own suffering or come to terms with personal issues that plagued them.[21] Arun Gandhi learned kindness and forgiveness after encountering his nemesis on the street. Thomas Moore encountered a total stranger who became his mentor during a time of crisis. Dan Millman began a journey of recovery after almost losing his life. Donald Neale Walsch transported himself from homelessness to penning his "conversations with God" after a transcendent journey. Jhampa Shaneman traveled to India to live in a spiritual community. Caroline Myss found her path to "mystical activism" after a small act of kindness she experienced. Each of them, and so many others following a spiritual path, traces his or her "awakening" or enlightenment to a particular journey that presented obstacles to overcome, both in the physical world and within himself/herself. This is but one of several possible precipitating factors that may lead to religious conversion[22] (see Table 8.2).

In a study of religious conversions, including both historical figures (Luther, St. Paul, Buddha) and more contemporary examples, the transformational changes usually included several features.[23] First, there was an initial period of discontent or crisis, followed by forced or voluntary isolation. This time alone seemed to be critical to intensify the struggle and create space and openness for what would follow in the form of a breakthrough experience that often took the form of a mystical or physical journey. "Suddenly the room lit up with a great white light," describes Bill Wilson, the founder of Alcoholics Anonymous, about his religious awakening that led to sobriety. "I was caught up into an ecstasy which there are no words to describe. It seemed to me, in the mind's

Table 8.2. PRECIPITATORS OF RELIGIOUS
OR SPIRITUAL TRANSFORMATION

- Hitting bottom
- Loss of power or control
- Crisis or trauma
- Near-death experience
- Acute stress
- Interpersonal conflict
- Insecure attachment with partner, family, or community
- Shame and unrelenting guilt
- Surrender of false pride
- Acknowledgment of personal inadequacy
- Mystical vision
- Communion with others
- Oneness with Nature
- Fasting/meditation
- Drug- or substance-induced vision
- Coercive peer pressure
- Visit to sacred site
- Pilgrimage
- Intellectual or aesthetic awareness of divine

eye, that I was on a mountain and that a wind not of air but of spirit was blowing. And then it burst upon me that I was a free man."[24]

Whether described as ecstasy, revelation, surrender, awe, forgiveness, or enlightenment, critical review of the experience resulted in some kind of validation, first from within and later by joining a shared community. It would appear that the communal support is a significant factor in solidifying the changes and maintaining the chosen path. Indeed, it is the shared experience of a religious or spiritual community, the mutual commitment to their beliefs and one another, that help to maintain devotion and continued loyalty.

Among all the kinds of transformational change we will discuss in this book, religious/spiritual awakening is potentially among the most sudden in onset and long lasting in duration. This occurs, in part, because of all the structures in place (prayer, meditation, retreat, study groups, religious services, confession, social events, rituals) that are designed to help participants maintain their faith and devotion. Considering that 90% of the world's population actively participates in some form of spiritual or religious tradition, it is also a context for change that is most universal, at least among younger people. By the time you reach later maturity, around age 50, transcendent spiritual experiences are much less frequent and dramatic, prompting adjustments rather than radical shifts.[25] But here's the good news: Older adults, with their life experiences, are far better equipped to deal with challenges and crises they face, recovering relatively quickly from distressing situations.[26] It helps that their spiritual foundation is already well grounded.

Keep in mind that religious beliefs are hardly all the same. Those that emphasize values of love and forgiveness are far more likely to promote constructive changes than those that feature punishment and guilt as major factors. In addition, there are different stages of religious/spiritual development that evolve from extreme rigidity to greater openness and flexibility, critical reflection, and acceptance of alternative points of view.[27]

Religious transformations that are ignited by a solitary revelation or spiritual quest were first described by William James as a way to unify the "divided self" and establish a more solid emotional grounding.[28] There often alternates a cycle between "seeking" and "dwelling," in which the pilgrim begins searching for greater meaning through a relationship with a Higher Power and then continues with a period of contemplation and meaning making or integration into one's life. This leads to further searches and quests for deeper commitment, followed by additional reflection.[29]

SPIRITUAL COMMUNION WITH NATURE

What if there were an extraordinarily effective treatment for reducing a range of physical and psychological complaints, as well as increasing well-being, life satisfaction, and cognitive functioning? It is well supported by research and has been employed for thousands of years with consistently positive outcomes across a wide spectrum of populations, regions, and cultures. It has no known side effects and costs absolutely nothing. Even more remarkable, it is readily available to almost everyone.[30]

For the secular pilgrim, or someone not strongly connected to religion in a traditional sense, Nature or wilderness settings may provide an alternative way to access peak spiritual transcendence. Henry David

Thoreau perhaps embodies this kind of transformation, exemplified by his refuge at Walden Pond. "Nature is full of genius, full of the divinity," he observed. Others such as naturalist John Muir found spiritual solace within the natural world, describing it as God's temple.

When people were interviewed about spiritual transformations that occurred for them while immersed in Nature, they reported themes reminiscent of any other peak experience that has been described.[31] They felt a greater connectedness to the natural world, accompanied by a heightened awareness and deeper appreciation for what it offers. They also found it possible to generalize what they learned in such a way as to initiate other changes in their lives to pursue more meaningful goals and escape from pressures within the human world.

Wilderness or natural environments have the potential to become restorative because of several distinctive features (Figure 8.2).[32] They are free from distractions that occur in daily life—traffic, congestion, technological interruptions, and the squalor and chaos of urban settings. They provide intrinsically alluring landscapes that are perfect for sensory stimulation. They arrest attention in such a way to elicit awe and inspiration. There is also a certain degree of risk that is known to be associated with quantum changes, especially if people don't monitor and honor their own limits and resources.

QUESTIONS TO CONSIDER WHEN PLANNING A TRANSFORMATION

One of the fastest growing segments of the travel industry is "mystic traveling" for those who are seeking enlightenment.[33] Whether visiting sacred sites such as the Vatican, Mecca, Mount Sinai, Notre Dame Cathedral, Meiji Shrine, Luxor Temple, Stonehenge, Machu Picchu, or New Age spiritual centers such as the vortexes of Sedona, the initiate traveler begins a rite of passage that has been followed for millennia. Many of the sojourners are wounded physically, emotionally, or spiritually, while others are searching for deeper wisdom, simplicity, or enlightenment. These sacred sites are believed to hold special spiritual powers that provide a boost to those searching for greater meaning, relief, or enlightenment.

We have talked in Chapter 6 about how one of the correlates of post-traumatic growth was increased interest and commitment to spiritual

Figure 8.2: Nature provides the perfect sanctuary and place of worship for many who search for spiritual enlightenment, restoration, or communion with the world at large. The peak experiences and changes that people undergo during such a quest are often the result of the environment that frees them from normal restraints and focuses their attention on thoughts, feelings, and revelations that are blocked by the "noise" of daily life. (Photo courtesy of author.)

lives. This has been true for traumatized soldiers and prisoners of war, but equally the case with those recovering from addictions.[34]

Based on the interviews I've conducted over the years, and the research I've accumulated, if you wanted to construct a transformative trip, the sort that may very well change your life, here are some questions that may be useful to consider:

- What would you like to achieve or accomplish as a result of a trip?
- What are some specific ways that you would hope to return different from before you left?

- How do you intend to make public commitments of your goals to keep yourself accountable after you return?
- Regardless of the plans you've made, and itinerary you've created, to what extent are you prepared to abandon this structure in order to capitalize on serendipitous opportunities and spontaneous moments?
- What sacrifices, inconveniences, and uncertainties are you prepared to tolerate on the trip?
- What can you do to begin the travel before you leave, setting in motion forces that will maximize the impact of the trip?
- What forms of support will you access when things become really difficult and challenging?
- What will you tell yourself when things don't go as expected and you are forced to change plans or embrace a different perspective?
- What will you do to fully immerse yourself in the new culture instead of seeking the safety and familiarity of what you already know and enjoy?
- How do you plan to meet and engage with new people along the journey, initiating encounters and deepening these relationships?
- How do you intend to insulate yourself from pressures, responsibilities, obligations, and communications from back home so that you are free to fully pursue new possibilities?
- How will you follow through on applying what you learned and generalizing from this experience to other aspects of your life?

Although it may appear from these queries that life-changing trips can be strategically structured and planned, I hope you've heard the message that such experiences are most often discovered when you go with the flow. You are busy and focused on one particular agenda (heading to a museum, about to reboard a tour bus, following the pathways on a map, checking off the next site on your list) when, perhaps impulsively but certainly spontaneously, you shift in a different direction. You meet someone who invites you to his or her home. You wander aimlessly through back streets. You do something wholly uncharacteristic and outside of your usual pattern. You initiate an adventure (for you) but one that is reasonably safe rather than reckless. You search for opportunities to function outside what is familiar to provide you with new, stimulating experiences that widen your world and push you to discover new aspects of yourself.

Among all the questions you might consider, perhaps the most important of all is related to how you are going to take what you learned from the journey and incorporate it into your daily life. This is the meaning you make from the experience and how you choose to process what happened in such a way that the lessons stick with you. A number of studies have consistently documented, with students studying abroad, Peace Corps volunteers working in the field, Outward Bound participants traveling in the wilderness, or pilgrims heading toward sacred sites, that the effects of this experience are far more enduring when people take the time to systematically make sense of the experience through contemplation, reflection, dialogue, journaling, or in therapy.[35]

To summarize, there are three distinct components of a life-altering trip. First is what happens before you leave and how you program the experience. Then there is the actual experience in which critical events occur and memories are created. Finally, last but hardly least, is what happens afterward and how the experience is processed, folded into narratives, communicated to others, and understood by yourself. Trips are soon "forgotten" when you resume previous patterns without taking the time and investing the energy to keep the new insights and behavior going.

TRAVELING AT HOME

It isn't necessary to travel to a foreign country, or even a different city, in order to experience quantum changes from a journey; it's just easier to do so when you are immersed in a novel environment. Taking a trip, even an adventurous or unstructured one, is no guarantee that you will grow significantly as a result. Just getting out of bed in the morning in a particular way, facing the day with a spirit of adventure, encountering people with openness and flexibility, pushing yourself to do things differently, is what sparks personal growth.

While it is often easier to do this during a trip, away from usual influences and restrictions, these changes can take place anywhere you choose to make them happen. In fact, if travel teaches you one important lesson, it is that life is too sweet and short to limit your freedom to mere vacations. Travel is not really an escape from normal life, nor is it an insulated reality; rather, it acts as a reminder of what is possible for you to experience every waking moment of your life.

CHAPTER 9

Moments of Clarity That Change Everything

It was just a few minutes past midnight when the doorbell rang. Meghan was awakened from a deep sleep, having just gone to bed on a school night. She was groggy and disoriented as she heard voices downstairs, then sobbing. She knew instantly that something was terribly wrong.

Meghan leaned over the banister of the stairway, looking down, to see something utterly shocking: her father was crying, trying hard to choke back his tears and clear his throat. "There's been an accident," he said in a hoarse voice, looking up at her. "It's your sister. She didn't make it."

With those words, everything in Meghan's live changed instantly: "I completely lost control of my body. My legs collapsed, and I fell to the ground, unable to move. I heard my younger sister running through the house, screaming, like something you read about in a Greek tragedy. It didn't seem real."

Meghan and her sister were brought downstairs where their minister waited to provide comfort. "I couldn't look at him," Meghan remembers. "I could only stare at his chest. I remember thinking that he had taken the time to dress with his starched collar. But as he was talking to me, I finally looked up into his eyes and realized that he had no answers. I had to find them myself."

Meghan's first thought after the house calmed down and she returned to bed was that now she could have her sister's blue sweater. She felt terribly guilty that this thought went through her head, but it was all so surreal that she wouldn't have been surprised by anything she thought that night. Everything changed literally overnight.

Meghan watched her mother totally fall apart, which was typical because she had never been very stable in the first place. But here's the part of her story that's so interesting: Meghan remembers consciously and deliberately deciding not to be a victim. It was her sister's last gift to her: "I put my feet on a path of wanting to understand life and why things happen a particular way." The first attempt to do so was related to why the blue sweater popped into her head, but it was immediately followed by so many other questions: "For so long I had felt trapped by my parents' idea of who I had to be, and now I chose to be free of all that."

Looking back, Meghan doesn't solely attribute her life-changing moment of clarity to her sister's death. It wasn't that simple: "That part of me had already developed in terms of my values and goals, even if they were buried inside. My sister's death burst the bubble that I was living in. It was the external event that just cracked open the seed in the center of me and allowed everything to just spill out." What poured out of her was the determination to build a different life than the one that had been planned for her.

"I grew up sheltered and privileged," Meghan admitted. "I believed that nothing could touch me. And now, after my sister died, I realized all at once that my life wasn't a game I was living. It was real. And it was time for me to start living on my own terms."

Isn't it interesting that people can react so differently to the same set of circumstances? A tragic death in the family and some members are "ruined" for life while others reach deep within and find the seeds for renewal. Whereas Meghan attributes her newfound independence and freedom to this terrible loss in her life, her sister and parents reacted to the tragedy quite differently. So it is with other things that happen which people interpret and respond according to their belief systems.

A flight is delayed and some travelers go ballistic while others calmly take the annoyance in stride. Of course, the particular interpretation of that adjustment depends on what is waiting at the other end of the trip. If the delay means a missed connection, cancelled meeting, or lengthy postponement, its significance looms far larger than for those who have flexible plans or a fluid agenda. On a far larger scale, consider the different ways that people respond to life's disappointments, catastrophic events, or tragedies. Some become devastated and forever wounded, while others recover within a relatively short period of time, all the better for the experience.

What determines the varied responses? Ultimately, it depends on several factors, including what else is going on in the person's life at the time and the person's characteristic outlook and disposition, as well as cognitive style and contagious influence of peer group.

Almost everyone has had the experience of a startling moment of insight, in which things all at once seem to make sense in a way they never have before. That epiphany forever changes the way you see yourself. And depending on how it is processed and internalized, it can often lead to a torrent of additional changes.[1] One individual described the paradox: "One day I felt really good, but when I thought about it, I had been feeling better before that…it was gradual but the realization was sudden."[2] It would seem, then, that significant changes often involve both a slow, unfolding process, and surprising moments of clarity when things seem to come together.

REALIZATIONS BEYOND DESCRIPTION, EVEN BY THE WORLD'S GREATEST WRITERS

Moments of life-altering clarity can occur either suddenly as epiphanies, or as gradual evolutions in understanding. Whereas the latter are far less dramatic and noticeable, often the effects last longer because of the increased opportunities to reflect on their implications, practice the new behaviors, and generalize the insights to other aspects of functioning. Nevertheless, as we've seen throughout this book, quantum changes and epiphanies may also endure when their intensity is sufficient and the timing is right.

Insights are also not merely experienced and then accepted as truths but, rather, are "imaginatively shaped."[3] This is most visibly recognized in the memoirs of writers who struggled with their demons, those that fueled their creativity but also drove them to the edge of madness. In some cases, it was a single insight that brought them back from the abyss.

In a study of writers' autobiographies, it was observed that the great Russian novelists, Fyodor Dostoyevsky and Leo Tolstoy, suffered terribly as a result of their life circumstances. In Dostoyevsky's case, he found himself standing in front of a firing squad, saved at the last second by the Czar's pardon. Most of his companions became psychotic as a result of their terror while he was sentenced to hard labor in Siberia. It was while working in the gulag, interacting with his fellow convicts, most of whom were murderers, rapists, and anarchists, that he felt himself sinking lower into the depths of despair. He felt nothing but disgust for the other prisoners, that is, until he felt himself changed as a result of putting together several fragments from his early childhood. He felt himself utterly transformed, not only internally, but also in the way he viewed others: "I suddenly felt that I could behold these unfortunate men with a wholly different outlook, and suddenly, by some miracle, all the hatred and anger completely vanished from my heart."[4] What was left for Dostoyevsky, and what remained throughout his life, was compassion and empathy for the downtrodden, a theme that was pervasive throughout his stories.

Tolstoy suffered as well, but from internal misery rather than the kind that had been imposed on him by jailers and oppression. At a time in his life when he enjoyed widespread notoriety and international fame from *War and Peace* and *Anna Karenina*, he was severely depressed and suicidal. Like many other notable writers such as Virginia Woolf, James Joyce, Jack London, Victor Hugo, Emily Dickinson, Walt Whitman, John Keats, Edgar Allen Poe, Ernest Hemingway, and Sylvia Plath, his creativity was sparked by a dose of madness.[5] Yet it was his revelation to reunite with God that turned things around: "And more than ever before, all within me and around me lit up, and the light did not again abandon me."[6]

With both Tolstoy and Dostoyevsky, as well as with other writers who have documented their life-changing insights in their memoirs, the experiences exhibit intensity, vibrancy, and a degree of power that can't be ignored. They "do induce awe and challenge articulation, for their expansive mystery suggests non-cognitive sources of imaginative power."[7] They are beyond description, which is not all that unusual considering that most people can't really describe very well what they are feeling.[8] One reason for this is that emotions can occur at both a primary and secondary level, the first of which involves deeply rooted, evolutionary adaptive responses that help protect us from danger.[9] That is both an important distinction and a potentially critical insight to understand that although the instinctual fear of strangers, spiders, or snakes is hardwired as a protective mechanism, other secondary emotions like feeling angry or depressed are the result of personal judgments that can be altered through other interpretations—much of that misery is self-inflicted.

INSIGHT COMES IN ALL KINDS OF FLAVORS

There are many different kinds of insights, little ones and big ones, gradual moments of realization, and sudden bursts of inspiration. But when people are asked to describe such occurrences in their lives, they might look thoughtful for a moment or two, but then their faces break out into immediate smiles of recognition. They often describe their experiences using a variety of metaphors that all represent a seminal moment (even if it really took place over a much longer period of time): "As if someone has pressed a button," "It suddenly clicked," "It was like a wee volcano," "It was like 'ping' and then it was like I could see things clearly."[10]

Psychotherapists are in the business of promoting insights, or at least traditionally that has been the case. From Sigmund Freud's early observations that that unconscious desires must be uncovered to deal with present problems, or Carl Rogers' contention that it is critical to understand unacknowledged feelings, to cognitive-behavioral formulations by Aaron Beck and Albert Ellis that emotional suffering results from internal interpretations that must be identified and challenged, insight has been the bread and butter of therapeutic sessions (see Table 9.1).

Identifying Causes

Regardless of the therapeutic approach or type of treatment, and apart from whatever behavioral changes were initiated as a result of sessions, most people feel grateful for what they learned about themselves and their characteristic patterns. Although insights generated through conversation and reflections don't necessarily lead to subsequent changes,

Table 9.1. MODELS FOR PROMOTING INSIGHT

Type of insight	Theoretical framework	Skill employed	Example
Awareness of feelings	Person-centered	Reflection of feeling	"You're feeling upset because you don't like giving up control."
Unconscious motives	Psychoanalytic	Interpretation	"The anger you are expressing toward me seems related to feelings you have toward your mother."
Cognitive distortions	Cognitive	Guided discovery	"Even if you don't get what you want, how is that absolutely terrible?"
Inauthenticity	Gestalt	Confrontation	"You say you are really angry about this, but you appear quite calm."
Personal meaning	Existential	Immediacy	"I notice that right now you are withdrawing from our relationship just as you have done with others."
Problem redefinition	Strategic	Reframing	"When you say you have a bad temper, what you really mean is that you are sometimes very passionate."
Family dynamics	Systemic	Restructuring	"I want you to move over there and sit with your wife instead of your children. Talk to one another about what this is like."
Power imbalances	Feminist	Exploring gender roles	"How have you limited yourself by the ways you have defined what it means to be a man?"
Sources of influence	Narrative	Outcome questions	"How did you manage to overcome the anger when it tried to control you?"
Social influences	Constructionist	Restory life circumstances	"Which roles have you adopted that were not of your own choosing?"
Consequences of choices	Reality	Challenge decisions	"Is what you are doing getting you what you want?"
Family constellation	Adlerian	Interpret early recollections	"Which of your parents do you most resemble?"
Contingency contracting	Behavioral	Identify reinforcers for target behaviors	"What is it that sustains this behavior?"

Adapted from: Kottler, J. A., & Shepard, D. (2014). *Introduction to therapeutic counseling: Voices from the field* (7th ed.). Belmont, CA: Wadsworth.

they do offer a foundation upon which to make sense of what is going on and why. Hopefully this also results in a deeper understanding of how to prevent recurrent problems.

If someone is depressed, for, example, it often helps to understand the source and causes of the suffering before an effective strategy can be planned and implemented. Is the depression a logical and reasonable reaction to disappointment? Does the depression reveal an underlying sense of emptiness and meaninglessness in the person's life? Is it the result of a delayed reaction to early trauma or unresolved loss? Might the depression be caused by an inherited genetic condition or a neurological disease, which would imply a very different kind of intervention and lifestyle adjustment? Or perhaps the symptoms aren't even "owned" by the person who presents him or herself in therapy, but rather, this "designated patient" is there on behalf of the dysfunctional family. The point being that understanding the underlying causes of problems can often suggest the best possible way to deal with them.

Jamie had been attending group therapy for a period of several weeks to work on issues related to poor self-esteem and ongoing fears that her eating disorder might return with increased stress in her life. There are some distinct benefits of any group support experience, as she describes: "I could be vulnerable and emotional and talk about taboo issues and then walk out feeling closer than ever with these incredible people. I felt alive and free in the group in a way I never had before, and it got me thinking that this was a new standard for future relationships. I felt accepted as I was, loved for my flaws, and not judged for being imperfect."

Among all the things she learned in the group, Jamie felt most grateful for the realization that she wasn't nearly as messed up as she thought: "There was this one incredible moment when I realized that although I was really screwed up, so was everyone else in the group! There was a point when I was afraid everyone thought I was a bitch and weak, and maybe they did, but that was okay, too. There were times when people pushed my buttons and I was able to safely react. There were times of great intimacy that further deepened our bond as a group. There were times when it felt as though people looked way deep inside of me and saw things that have taken my friends and family years to see, but they recognized it in a matter of weeks. It was intense, and at times, it felt like too much for me to handle, but we all got through it together. There were times when I felt I was going to fall flat on my face, but I had a group of people who held me up, even when the stuff I was learning about myself seemed too painful to bear."

Another insight important for Jamie, and for almost anyone who has experienced a therapeutic group experience, is the "universality" that is considered a major ingredient of the process, apart from any individual goals that are attained: "Sure I felt alone and defeated, unlovable and unworthy, but that was okay because we all felt that way at some point or another. All of these feelings can make me feel so small, but then I realized that these feelings are universal and that is *so* powerful. This has never happened to me before. The feelings that made me feel alone and isolated were the very things that united us all in the group. Sure, my role in group included my normal, motherly, nurturing self, but I got to be so much more than that as well. I will forever be thankful to these people for what they taught me about myself. It was so special, and our time together was invaluable. I do not think they will ever know the extent of my gratitude, but I hope what I took with me that was so life changing was useful to them as well."

Limits of Insight

It's important to acknowledge once again that understanding how and why you have problems doesn't always result in changes that are needed. Some brief therapists consider time devoted to self-understanding to be, at best, a waste of time, and at worst, dangerous because of the excuses provided for avoiding the hard work of initiating action.[11] Some therapists aren't even particularly interested in understanding the underlying mechanisms of their procedures, much less promoting insight in their clients. They follow empirically supported treatment manuals, most of which cover the same basic things.[12] Each of them follows a regimented protocol that provides some instruction (which is a kind of insight after all), normalizes the condition, capitalizes on positive expectations, encourages autonomy, improves communication skills, introduces problem solving, and targets specific goals with specialized procedures. But there may be little effort to intentionally help people understand how they got to their present circumstances, or to make connections between past events and present behavior.

There are people who have devoted years to their therapy, and others who read every book ever published on their problem, or have a collection of self-help books that rival a library, or who have become personal growth workshop groupies, but who never seem to alter the destructive patterns of their behavior. They understand all too well why they are messed up. They have deep understanding of all the probable causes, make connections between the complex dynamics in their early childhood, and recite innumerable reasons why they have difficulty, but they still don't *do* anything differently in their lives. Of course, the job of a good therapist is to accept the initial reluctance, which is both normal and even wise, and patiently wait, probe, and prompt the person until such time that he or she is prepared to do the hard work that lies ahead.

There was one client, Fred, who I saw over a period of years, and I can't say with any confidence that I ever noticed any difference in his observable behavior. He was absolutely committed to his therapy, never missed an appointment, seemed to enjoy the sessions and appeared to make good use of the time we spent together, but nothing ever seemed to change. When I would confront him about this state of affairs, expressing my own frustration and impatience, he would just shrug and look at me like it was *my* problem—which of course it was! Eventually I had to accept (which I did not do very graciously) that he wasn't coming for help to change, but for a weekly spirited conversation about things that interested him. It bothered *me* a lot that he was so isolated and lonely, so stuck in rigid patterns, but he had learned to live with this situation quite contentedly.

So change isn't always on the menu for people who ask for help. Or to state this differently, there are many different kinds of change that can occur, some at a purely intellectual level, some at a deeper emotional level, and some that do, indeed, translate into measurable, observable changes in behavior.

Moment of Clarity After Screaming Your Head Off

So far I've been talking about moments of clarity as they result from therapeutic-type conversations, but it is far more common that they arise from life experiences, especially those that make you feel like you are on a roller coaster. In Bethany's case, that is quite a literal description of what happened.

"I went on an old wooden roller coaster at a park this summer and one I've wanted to visit for years," Bethany says with a laugh. "Play and laughter have always been important to me."

Although she describes herself as fearless when it comes to physical risks, Bethany was terrified of intimacy with people. Somehow she had never been able to apply what she could do jumping off cliffs to the interpersonal arena.

This time, on the roller coaster, there was a very different outcome. "I don't regret going on the thing," she says, "but I ended up with a bruised ankle and sprained neck. I got to scream my head off and my lungs out. I didn't know I could scream like a horror movie actress. I thought I was going to lose my voice by the ride's end. Even the little boy in front of me turned around to look at the crazy lady who was so out of control. I couldn't help it and I didn't care!"

The breakthrough for Bethany was that she was scared out of her mind and wasn't afraid to show it: "I was really letting it rip, letting out a bloodcurdling scream, when this sad thought flashed through my mind and I started to tear up. I decided in that moment that I didn't really need to cry when screaming was just as cathartic."

Going on that roller coaster, Bethany says, "gave me a chance to find out how well I can scream. I hadn't realized, until that moment, how uninhibited I could be instead of holding in all my feelings. I learned from that ride that next time I feel blocked, I'm going to scream my bloody head off!"

This might not seem like much, but it is a good example of how we discover inventive ways of coping with situations, dealing with difficulties, and creatively solving problems through serendipitous events. After all, some of the most useful inventions ever discovered—penicillin, X-rays, the pacemaker, the microwave, Velcro, super glue, Teflon— happened by accident.

It is also the case that most opportunities for learning and growth occur when you are busy doing something else. Most of the time, we don't go looking for change—it comes to find us when we're looking the other way.

TIRED OF WAITING FOR CHANGE TO SHOW UP ON YOUR DOORSTEP

If you're hanging around, waiting for deliverance, you'll be waiting a long time. That's true as much for change as it is for winning the lottery, that ideal job you were hoping for, or the perfect mate. Most of things in life that are worth having are also worth going after. With that said, insights and moments of clarity can't be forced; they take place when the timing is right and you are open to the opportunity. As we've seen, often these realizations occur when you've hit bottom and have no other choice but to confront the issues head on.

Chris begins his story with the observation that with any good redemption story, you have to begin at the bottom. In his case, it meant sinking to the lowest point imaginable, described in what he says is one of the longest and saddest run-on sentences imaginable: "I accepted a basketball scholarship to college, played one great individual yet utterly dismal team season (I think we were 6-22), stopped attending church regularly, started drinking and ditching class on a regular basis, collapsed on top of a pile of beer cans in my dorm room, had heart surgery at the age of 19, was not allowed to play competitive basketball again, spent the next three years pissing away my scholarship by a deadly cocktail of ditching more class, drinking more alcohol, and sleeping with more girls, cheated on a midterm, got caught for cheating, got suspended for cheating, returned to school to become the quintessential hanger-on; i.e., rather than shape up and work hard in school or get a job like an adult, I just hung around my friends when they partied, drank when they went to class/work, and never had my portion of the rent when it was due. Oh, I failed to mention a failed half-ass suicide attempt, but trust me, it was not all that glamorous."

I look at Chris now and the transformation is remarkable. He has since graduated university and law school and now works as a lawyer and advocate. He is a model of a family man and successful beyond his own wildest imagination. Prior to his fall from grace, the only way he could picture his escape from a small town was to play basketball in the NBA.

So, here's the big question that we've been wrestling with: What insight or moment of clarity finally got through to Chris after so many years languishing in mediocrity and a wasted life?

Chris considers the question for a few minutes and first offers a trite response—that he was saved by a new girlfriend. Unfortunately, the recovery didn't last long before he spiraled back into old patterns. He then admits that religion played an important role. It occurred to him, in a rush of revelation, that he had lost his faith. Once he began attending church regularly, he felt grounded in a way that hadn't experienced in a long time.

That may have brought him back to earth, but he attributes his turn-around to the realization that he had been avoiding hard work. Chris acknowledges that he knows he is smart and talented even if he wasted a lot of those abilities until he hit bottom. "For all of my posturing and soul searching I engaged in during my crisis period," Chris says, "the one inescapable truth was I was just a bum—and there is no way around that fact. I did not experience any sustained growth or change until I put my head down and started working."

It was Chris's background as an athlete that he says helped him to renew his dedication to work. He was never the most talented, or smartest, player on the court, but he flat out worked harder than anyone else. And he drew on that experience to get himself back on track. He finally realized that he had extraordinary resources that he could access: "The inner voice that tells you that some days are good and some are awful. But each day you gotta show up, and you gotta run that last sprint and put in the time if you want to reach your goal. Everyone has that inside them, and it's the only thing equal in this world that we all have when we are born, and it is the only thing we can control. In my case, I stopped making excuses for myself and worked. And I have never been happier."

Talking to Yourself

There are certain moments of clarity that you can make happen all on your own. They don't require anyone else's permission or cooperation. They are not subject to the whims of fate, Nature, or happenstance. They aren't limited by circumstances or context, nor are they vulnerable to external intrusions. In fact, all the action takes place inside of you, regardless of what's going on around you—or *to* you.

For those who are already familiar with these concepts, whether as dedicated readers, veterans of therapy as clients, or mental health professionals, cognitive approaches to personal transformation are maximally effective the more often you monitor your internal thought patterns. I have been applying and practicing these ideas most of my adult life, employing them on a daily basis with clients, students, and myself, and yet I still need constant reminders that I am potentially in control of my internal thoughts most of the time. I may not be able to control what happens in the world, what challenges are thrown my way, what obstacles are placed in my path, and how other people choose to act—or react to me—but I surely can make decisions about how I choose to interpret these events and respond, both inside my head and in the external world.

Insight number one: Nobody or nothing can make you feel anything, or cause you to react in a particular way, without your permission and consent. One of the most popular and research-supported therapeutic approaches, cognitive therapy, offers a systematic means to identify those triggers that are believed to be instrumental in causing suffering and then provides the means by which to reduce or change any unpleasant emotional response to one that is more measured, appropriate, and much less upsetting. There are different variations of the method developed as cognitive therapy (Aaron Beck),[13] rational-emotive therapy (Albert Ellis),[14] cognitive-behavior modification (Donald Meichenbaum),[15] and multimodal therapy (Arnold Lazarus),[16] as well as more recent developments such as acceptance and commitment therapy (Steven Hayes)[17] and mindfulness-based approaches (Jon Kabat-Zinn).[18]

Insight number two: Feelings do not arise out of thin air, nor are they caused by anything other than your own thoughts and interpretations. This is fabulous news, by the way! It means that any and every time you are upset about something, and you prefer not to feel that way, you can do something about it by the way you alter your perception of that event.

Let's say someone cuts you off on the freeway, a close call from which you barely survived. Once you recover you can feel your terror convert itself into rage, and you are about one second from exploding, chasing down the offender and giving him or her a piece of your mind. You are absolutely furious. And what had been a five-second scary episode could very well ruin the rest of your day—if you allow that to happen. You can tell yourself all kinds of things to keep the tension rising— "I can't believe that sonofabitch did that to me!" "Why does this sort of thing always happen to me?" "This just absolutely makes a crummy day even worse."

All of these internal thoughts are perfectly understandable even though they are both distorted and highly irrational. Why? Well, for one thing the person didn't actually do this to *you*; in fact, he didn't even see you; there was nothing personal involved, just an inadvertent mistake that almost hurt you. Frightening? Of course. But blaming the other person hardly changes what already happened and only makes it far worse. Second, this sort of thing doesn't *always* happen to you even though it may sometimes seem like it. Count the number of times someone almost hit you on the freeway, and I doubt it was even a handful during the year—and if it was more often, then it's time to look at your own driving practices. Third, this five-second experience doesn't ruin your whole day; it just throws a temporary glitch in things from which you can recover within minutes, if you so choose.

Insight number three: You have the power to almost instantly change how you are feeling about almost anything you ever experience, just by altering your interpretations of the event and substituting alternative thoughts. For example, if you tell yourself that the close call on the freeway was an unfortunate accident, one in which you can let go by calming yourself, slowing your speed, and being a little more defensive and vigilant on the road, you are likely not to feel nearly as upset about what happened.

There are so many things you can't control—the weather, the economy, world events, the stock market, fate, your genetics and physical limitations, what other people say or do—but one thing that is within your power is what you think inside your own head and how you respond to the things that happen to you.

Insight number four: Most people don't want what I'm selling. If I told you that I had the secret to never being upset about anything ever again, what would you give for this miracle? A year's salary? Your soul? Your first-born child? Your mobile device?

Alas, most people don't want to be responsible for their emotional lives. They think it's too much work, or it's just more satisfying to be able to blame others when things go wrong. What if every time you were miserable, disappointed, or upset about something, the first place you'd look is at yourself and what you are doing inside your own mind to create or exacerbate this situation?

That might sound pretty darn good, but it also means that there's nowhere else to look but at yourself when things aren't going the way you prefer. You are likely exaggerating things or making unrealistic demands of yourself or others. According to this perspective, almost all suffering is self-inflicted. People do or say annoying things. Fate laughs at our best-laid plans. Things don't go the way you expected or hoped. Disappointments, failures, and losses occur, all without your consent. Yet you have a choice about what you tell yourself about the incident.

For instance, compare these two very different series of internal responses to the same situations:

Event	Helpless perception	Empowered response
Trauma or disaster occurs without warning.	I'm a victim.	I'm a survivor.
Disappointment leads to unexpected setback.	This sort of thing always happens to me.	This is frustrating but I'm glad it happens so rarely.
Failure results after a concerted attempt.	I might as well give up because I'll never do it.	This is just another challenge for me to overcome.
Someone treats you poorly, without apparent reason.	This is so senseless and unfair.	There is a lesson to be learned from this.
In spite of best effort, things don't work out as preferred.	I have no options except to accept the situation.	There are some things I can control, and others I can't.

You can readily see that there would be very different emotional reactions to disappointments, failures, annoyances, and setbacks, depending on how they are interpreted and how you talk to yourself about it afterward. Even though you can't possibly control what other people say to you, or the seemingly inappropriate, insensitive, or careless things they do, you have virtually complete control on how you choose to react. Even though it may not feel that way, it is indeed a choice you can make.

DYSFUNCTIONAL BELIEFS

So far we have been examining internal reactions and self-talk as if they are situational. The goal, however, is to purge yourself of particular beliefs that consistently get in your way and program you for negative emotional responses. In one of the examples cited earlier, I mentioned the helpless response of telling yourself that things are not fair when they don't go your way. As long as you continue to subscribe to that belief, you are going to consistently be disappointed—because clearly the world is not fair and people don't get what they deserve.

Every time you demand that others live according to your preferred expectations or feel crushed when things don't go your way—even though you've done everything you can to make that happen—you are going to be pretty unhappy. I'm not saying that you should accept injustices, or avoid fighting for what's important to you, just that because there are many different perceptions of what is right and wrong, appropriate and out of bounds, it's inevitable that outcomes are not always going to work out the way you want. The world is sometimes an unfair, brutal environment. The natural world doesn't care in the least about anything that happens to you. There are people running around who have holes in their consciences, who are exploitive, manipulative, and deceptive. There are bullies, power-hungry tyrants, and evil individuals who live by different rules than the rest of us. Again, I'm not saying we shouldn't protect ourselves, but I am pointing out that demanding and expecting that the world treat you fairly, and then feeling shocked when you get a raw deal, only makes things more difficult for you to recover.

In addition to expecting that the world is fair and that you should be furious when things don't work out the way you want, there are several other dysfunctional beliefs that will result in unnecessary self-inflicted misery. These are essentially errors in logical reasoning, irrational beliefs, or in some cases, full-fledged delusions. The moments of clarity that can change your life occur when you catch yourself engaging in self-defeating thought patterns and alter them to include more reasonable and appropriate responses, given the circumstances.

Here are a few examples.

Overgeneralization. Based on a small sample of behavior, you make assumptions that apply to many other cases. This becomes a self-fulfilling prophecy that will end up confirming predictions: "Because this relationship ended, I'll never find anyone else to love me."

Discounting. If you selectively focus on negative aspects of a situation, you increase the likelihood that change will be avoided. Plus you have a good excuse for continued failure: "Sure, I got the report done on time, but I did a lousy job."

Mind reading. This involves making invalid assumptions about other people's behavior and motives, based on inaccurate data, poor observations, and fallacious reasoning: "He didn't call back because he probably never liked me in the first place."

Fortune telling. This is another variation of the theme that involves making pessimistic predictions with little evidence to support them: "There's no sense in even trying because I'll still get rejected anyway."

Disasterizing. Grossly exaggerating the magnitude of an annoyance or source of frustration way out of proportion to reality. This occurs when some minor disappointment or inconvenience occurs (rush hour traffic, delayed flight, cancelled appointment, rude comment), and your immediate internal response is something like: "This is the worst thing that could happen" or "This is absolutely awful" or "What a disaster this turned out to be."

If there is a theme that runs throughout all these examples of dysfunctional thinking, it is related to all the ways we tend to exaggerate things in our own minds ("This is horrible that it happened"), overpersonalizing things ("It's all my fault"), and holding on to unrealistic expectations for oneself or others ("Sure I got the job done on time but I never screw up like that"). The goal is no less than to change the ways we experience and make sense of our internal thoughts. The specific method employed, whether using a mindfulness-based approach to gently push disturbing ideas aside, or to more directly confront the upsetting cognitions, is probably less important than the very idea that you can exert more control over your inner world.

Self-efficacy and control can also be distorted and illusionary in that there are times when we overestimate what is within our power to change, and what time frames are realistic. Stress and discouragement increase with every failed attempt, accumulating hits to self-esteem and confidence. In the next chapter, we will look more carefully at the accumulative damage that occurs from repeated disappointments, but one final insight is the realization that there are limits to what you can reasonably do. Moments of clarity are required to honestly assess the attainability of goals and the capabilities that are within your grasp.

CONVERTING INSIGHTS INTO ACTION

It is one thing to experience a moment of clarity or transformative realization—and it is quite another to *do* something about it. Sometimes talking to yourself inside your head is not nearly enough when there has been a history of avoidance, denial, and fear. That's why people consult therapists, hire personal coaches, attend workshops, or read books like this. That's why people talk to friends and family, hoping that such disclosures will motivate them to work through their issues and follow through on their intentions.

Yet there has also been a distinguished tradition of using expressive writing to produce moments of insight and provide support for changes that have been launched and maintained. Journaling, for example, has been demonstrated to be an effective means by which to work through unresolved issues, reduce stress, and provide deeper levels of self-understanding that often lead to resolutions of stated problems.[19]

Scarlett had been bullied relentlessly in school. Every day she ran through a gauntlet of teasing, ridicule, and intimidation that ended up with her crying in the bathroom. She sat in the lunchroom eating by herself. She furtively walked the halls hoping never to draw attention to herself. Worst of all, she never understood what she had ever done to deserve this torture. And when she approached teachers and her counselor, they told her she was just being oversensitive.

Although Scarlett hoped that once she got into high school things would change, they actually became worse. She had nowhere to turn and felt that everything was hopeless. Then she discovered writing as an outlet for her pain and the means by which to make sense of her suffering, or at least come to terms with it: "I so badly wanted to talk to someone, a friend, a counselor, but all I had was my journal. All my thoughts, feelings, and opinions I could put down on paper. I could finally release everything that had been building up inside me. I was just so relieved that I didn't have to hold it all in anymore. I could say whatever I wanted without fear of judgment. It became part of my daily routine and it's what saved me."

Once she began college, Scarlett continued her daily writing, but no longer to recover from the trauma she'd been experiencing. Now it became a vehicle for her to make sense of her new world and come to terms with things from the past: "It was the one place where I could tune out everything else and just be with my own thoughts."

It is now many years later, and Scarlett still writes in her journal to prompt new ideas and insights, as well as to work through stress and confusion: "It's helped me become so much more comfortable with expressing myself and sorting out what I'm feeling."

It is precisely the clarity of insight that establishes—or rather, *re*establishes—some kind of control and pulls everything back together during a time of intense distress and disorientation.[20] As has been stated earlier, there may often be a gradual process of growth, learning, and skill acquisition, but at some point these changes must become assimilated into one's self-identity. Regardless of the particular means by which "conversation" takes place—with a friend or a therapist, during self-talk inside your head, or writing in a journal, it is the insights that are generated that help put things in perspective and provide some semblance of order in a world that so often feels chaotic and confusing.

CHAPTER 10
Reducing Stress and Facing Fears

The diver stood on a platform three stories high, his toes balanced over the edge of open space and the vertical drop below. Then he carefully, oh so slowly, adjusted his position so that he was actually doing a handstand with his feet pointed skyward. The crowd below collectively held their breath, watching, waiting to see what would happen next in the drama.

The answer: nothing. The man remained frozen in this awkward, precarious position for almost a minute. His arms started to quiver uncontrollably and he began to sway. His mother was in the crowd below and felt utterly helpless to do anything except watch in horror as her son began to lose complete control.

The man's name is Scott Donie. His "job" at the time was Olympic silver medalist in the high dive and one of the greatest, most exciting athletes of his generation. The scene just described occurred in the exact middle of his 10 scheduled dives in an Olympic qualifying event in 1993. Although he had stood on this same platform thousands of times during practices and performances—it was his second home—this particular moment Scott totally and literally froze.

He wouldn't have understood at the time that freezing during perceived moments of danger is among the most natural of instinctual responses, programmed in our evolutionary past to make us less visible to predators. Even children train themselves from the earliest age to play "frozen tag" as a kind of rehearsal for future scenarios they might face. But all Donie was aware of at that moment on the high dive was that he couldn't catch his breath and couldn't move.

It is a testament to the power of his resilience that eventually Scott Donie recovered from his panic attack and "reinvented" himself. Although he would not climb a 10-meter platform again, he devoted himself to excellence in the lower springboard event, placing fourth in the 1996 Olympics. Since that time he has become a coach for college athletes, having mentored over a dozen All-American champions.

What Donie experienced on the high dive most of us feel at some point in our lives when we are crippled by anxiety and frozen in fear. Our brains seem to shut down. All we hear in our heads is the panicked scream of our inner voice telling us that we are totally helpless and out of control. It is under such circumstances that we are most ripe for change, whether for better or worse. Stress and fears demand our attention like nothing else, requiring some adaptation in order to address the perceived threat.

EFFECTS OF STRESS

There is nothing more paralyzing than stress when it comes to making changes in your life. Although originally designed as an automatic defensive response to perceived danger, it is rare these days that we encounter predators that require us to do battle or run for our lives. Yet deep within our endocrine and nervous systems remains this "fight-or-flight response" that prepares us for emergency conditions. We may not run into warring tribes of enemies or saber-toothed tigers very often, but we still retain the capacity to respond as if we did when faced with challenges of the modern world.

If you were asked to give a speech in front of a large audience, confront a supervisor about some injustice, face off against a nemesis who is bullying you, or take any action that involves a *perceived* risk, your body reacts identically to a situation in which your life may be at stake. Signals are sent to activate all systems preparing for dire circumstances. Your heart rate increases to pump blood into your large muscles that will be needed to fight or run. Your breathing accelerates to bring more oxygen to your muscles. Your eyes dilate to better perceive danger. You start to sweat to cool off your body. You might feel tremors as a result of the cortisol, adrenaline, and other hormones flooding through your system. Your stomach feels tingly and your mouth becomes dry as your digestive system shuts down, saving energy for the upcoming emergency. You feel tension in your muscles as they prepare for instant reactions. But the problem is that you aren't *really* facing a life-and-death struggle but just a grossly exaggerated reaction to what you misinterpret as terrible danger.

Corresponding to these initial sensations triggered by the body's emergency responses to perceived danger is a long list of symptoms that can occur, most of them the result of prolonged exposure (see Table 10.1). It is, after all, when the switch is stuck in the "on" position that people become hypervigilant and see potential danger around every corner and that serious health problems can develop. Most of the symptoms are the logical consequences of chronic overload of physiological systems that were never designed for anything other than brief activation.

As you review the list of symptoms, you may notice that many of them are directly related to the fight-or-flight reflex. It would make sense, for instance, that if you have trouble turning off that response, you would continually feel your muscles tensing and fidgeting and your heart racing and experience feelings of unrelenting dread. It would also make sense that you'd have trouble sleeping and relaxing with excessive stress chemicals continuing to run through your body.

Table 10.1. MOST COMMON SYMPTOMS OF STRESS

Irritability	Anger
Fatigue	Inertia
Nervousness	Headache
Insomnia	Stomach ache
Loss of appetite	Overeating
Emotional volatility	Muscular tension or pain
Relationship conflicts	Dizziness
Reduced sex drive	Sexual dysfunctions
Teeth grinding	Depression or sadness
Disrupted menstrual cycle	Chest pain
Social withdrawal	Isolation
Alcohol or drug abuse	Pessimism/hopelessness
Inability to concentrate	Forgetfulness
Ruminations/obsessive thinking	Fidgeting/restlessness

This also helps explain why change is so difficult to sustain when there is a high level of negative emotional arousal that makes it difficult to remain in control.[1]

Causes of Stress

Stress often begins as a mere annoyance even though this isn't even recognized by most scholars as any different from frustration, mild anger, or aversion. Someone cuts in line in front of you. You are stuck in a traffic jam. A baby is crying, a dog is barking, or someone is talking loudly on the phone right next to you. A car alarm goes off. Your inbox is deluged by spam. Your flight is delayed. Any of them sound familiar?

Annoyances have three main characteristics.[2] First, they are unpredictable and, second, you don't know when they will end. Third, the experience is unpleasant in some way. If the irritation continues unabated, the intensity and duration building, eventually the relatively mild condition will blossom into full-fledged stress.

If you had to guess what the single greatest source of stress was in most people's lives you'd probably say that it has to do with either money or relationships. And you'd be right. There is a consistent pattern that every year roughly three quarters of the population mention their personal financial status or the economy as their greatest worry. This is followed by 60% of individuals describing their family responsibilities and relationships as being their biggest concern. Health and personal safety are mentioned by about half the population as a cause of their stress.[3]

Among those who are experiencing severe stress in their lives (which is the vast majority), three quarters of them say that their problems have little or no effect on their children and other family members. They believe they've mostly got things under control or at least are skilled at hiding their concerns. Well, talk about delusions: It turns out that 9 out of 10 children say they *do* know when their parents are really upset and worried because they observe their impatience, frustration, and complaints.[4] We are far more transparent in our misery that we'd like to believe.

There's Good Stress, Too

Stress not only inhibits behavior and reduces the likelihood that you can initiate constructive changes, but in more moderate doses it also actually *enhances* performance. Called "eustress," this is the condition when you feel a little bit anxious and jittery and find that this nervous energy helps you to focus better and even reach a higher level of optimal functioning. Your cognitive capacity is not impaired, nor are you so worked up that you can't maintain control. As long as the duration is short-term and there is balance between stimulation and recovery, the effects of the endocrine boost don't do any major damage. But once the stress switch is turned on and remains activated, the body systems begin to deteriorate to the point that you can develop all kinds of problems including ulcers, hypertension, chronic pain, colitis, stroke, and heart disease. It is as if acid is eating away at your arteries and neural pathways.

Stress responses in the body were designed originally to make it easier and more efficient for you to protect yourself in the same way that the immune system repels invaders. If you are participating in sports or a debate, presenting at a meeting, or just approaching an attractive stranger at a party, you will feel the familiar heart pounding in your chest and trickle of sweat down your back, telling you that your systems are activated to turbocharge your energy and give you fast access to resources you might need (glucose, oxygen, adrenaline, cortisol, nutrients, fast muscle twitch). The key, then, is to kick in just enough of a stress reaction to help you perform at peak levels, but not enough to override the off switch once the crisis or event is over.

Elizabeth, a lawyer who routinely works 80-hour weeks, would appear to meet every definition of a workaholic who labors under extraordinary stress. But there's a difference between the "classic workaholic" and the so-called "engaged workaholic" who loves what she's doing without regret.[5] "There's an excitement about what is around the corner," Elizabeth says. "I manage attorneys, the work product that goes out, my own caseload, business operations. I work with an iPad on, and a computer on, and I'm on the phone. It's kind of a fire that fuels itself."[6]

What is it that makes it possible for someone like Elizabeth to deal with the obvious stressors she must encounter on a daily basis? Well,

for one thing she's having fun! Engaged workaholics have certain characteristics that differentiate them those who fall victim to pressures on
the job: (1) they love their work; (2) they feel no resentment toward
the long hours they are putting in and devotion they are showing to
their work; it is their own choice and it feels that way; (3) they don't
experience much stress because they don't interpret the stimulation
that way; (4) they've developed effective ways to handle the stress they
do encounter; (5) they feel in control and know how to set limits; and
(6) they report (and it *is* a self-report) that they aren't compromising
other aspects of their lives they say are important to them.

In other words, some people have learned to interpret stress in ways
that they feel energized, stimulated, and challenged. This is especially
true with respect to individuals who feel a degree of control and power
over their lives, as well as the ability to influence others. In that sense,
people who are most successful tend to live longer than others.[7] In a
remarkable example of this, it has been observed that U.S. presidents
actually have a significantly longer lifespan than other citizens, even
with the extraordinary pressure they face on a daily basis and the stressful decisions they must make. The first eight presidents (Washington
through Van Buren) lived an average of 80 years, *double* the life span of
their contemporaries.[8] Just as surprising, CEOs of major corporations
also report significantly less stress than their subordinates.[9] It would
appear that crushing responsibility itself is not necessarily stressful but,
rather, the relative control you have to manage it. Of course, it also helps
to be in a privileged position so you have access to better diet, resources,
medical care, and environmental conditions.

MALADAPTIVE STRESS RESPONSES

We have seen how most often people don't exactly *choose* to change;
more often it is forced upon them by circumstances, whether that is
a crisis, developmental transition, health issue, relationship conflict,
or abject misery from a sense of helplessness. The first line of attack
is almost always the option that requires the least amount of effort
and expenditure of energy—ignoring the problem and hoping it goes
away. That rarely works and stress likely increases. After all, its essential

purpose is to get your attention in such a way that you can't ignore the message any longer and must do something to change things, whether you like it or not. Stress builds and builds until even sleep is no haven: "You do not rouse with the sunrise or the sound of your alarm clock. It's midnight, it's 2:02, it's 3:19, and you wake as though shot through a cannon, speeding through the air, arms flailing, stomach in knots. It is dark and it's quiet. And. You. Are. Flying."[10]

When turning a blind eye or deceiving yourself eventually wears thin, the next set of options often involves forms of self-soothing or self-medication. This can mean rather benign strategies, such as watching television, getting massages, masturbation, or escape reading, or it can involve far more potentially destructive habits that include alcohol or drug use, behavioral addictions, and acting out in hurtful ways.

In extreme cases, when stress continues to build and the messages are still ignored, a range of emotional responses can develop, most of them with very negative side effects. When false alarms continue to go off in response to any misinterpreted danger, internal systems wear down and eventually fall apart. Inaccurate threat assessments account for many irrational fears, while miscalculations lead us to ignore those problems that could really be dangerous. For instance, people commonly express fears of flying even though you are far more likely to be injured or killed on the drive to the airport. Similarly, the number of shark or bear attacks each year can be counted on one hand, yet people appear to remain oblivious to the very real dangers of obesity and heart disease.

Fears and Phobias

When changes are avoided, or experienced as too frightening, people lock themselves into rigid, familiar patterns to stabilize themselves. In their own way, the rituals become soothing and are often perceived as having magical properties to keep danger at bay (another form of self-deception).

Phobias represent extreme overreactions, developed during times of vulnerability (childhood, crisis, feeling threatened). Although common forms of this disorder involve the fear of heights (acrophobia), germs (mysophobia), or closed spaces (claustrophobia), there are also some rather unusual ones.[11] Queen Elizabeth I had an extreme fear of roses. Frederick the Great was terrified of water. Adolph Hitler was phobic about closed spaces, ironic considering he lived the last days of his life in a bunker. Edgar Allen Poe, master of terror, was claustrophobic. Napoleon, fearless warrior and conqueror of most of Europe, was frightened of cats.

Once locked into phobic patterns, change becomes extremely resistant. These have been learned, exaggerated responses that became self-reinforcing over time. For instance, it is perfectly reasonable to be cautious around heights, closed spaces, spiders, and snakes—even roses will prick you—but the fear becomes debilitating when it interferes with daily functioning.

Chronic Anxiety

If phobias and fears are situationally specific, anxiety also operates at a more global level. Approximately one quarter of Americans will suffer the symptoms at some time in their lives.[12] In our fast-paced, pressure-filled lives, it is almost inevitable that responsibilities will exceed time available. With mobile devices as constant companions, intrusions from texts, calls, messages, and e-mail are an ever-present connection to the world at large. There is no escape from the demands placed upon us—and eventually the body rebels.

In Chapter 8 we discussed the ways that travel can be transformative for people, under certain conditions. But recent polls show that 60% of people who return from a vacation are actually *more* stressed than before they left home because of accumulated work and responsibilities that built up while they were gone. In addition, almost half of the travelers check in with their offices every day, so they are hardly leaving stress behind while they're gone.[13]

Existential angst is another form of chronic anxiety that is even more universal and pervasive since it is the logical result of considering life's most thorny questions: What will happen after I die? What is my purpose in this life? It is virtually impossible to think about your mortality, your finite existence, your heart beating in your chest, just a muscle that is wearing out as we speak, without feeling a certain anxiety.

When anxiety or any of these other conditions take over your life, it is far more difficult to concentrate on growth; after all, it feels like you are drowning. On the other hand, suffering in any form can act as a strong incentive to change something about your life to make the pain go away. Without these symptoms you might likely accept a level of mediocrity in your life that limits potential to do far greater things. In that sense, anxiety, depression, and other symptoms of emotional disorders are "gifts" to get your attention until such time that you do something constructive to remediate whatever is wrong.

It's easy enough to recall a time when you felt extremely overstressed and highly anxious, especially if the condition persisted over time. Now consider the changes you had to make (or still need to make) in order to release the pressure: This is your body's way of telling you it will not cease the stranglehold until such time that you do some things differently.

Reasonable Responses to Crisis

From this very brief review of maladaptive stress responses, it is apparent that these are quite natural responses to crises or events that have spun out of control. It makes perfect sense that someone would become a basket case, or experience troubling emotional problems, after some major disappointment or tragedy. There is a healing process that begins but sometimes loses its original intent and focus. There are also new opportunities to turn trauma into growth.

When Samantha was notified that both her parents had killed themselves in a collective act of despair and hopelessness, she was understandably devastated. Who could imagine handling such news with anything less than overwhelming misery? Samantha was despondent, depressed, immobilized, anxious, and guilt ridden. How could she not have seen this coming? How could her parents abandon her life this, leave her to pick up the pieces of their fractured family?

Samantha remembered that her mother had sent her a letter explaining why she had been fired from her job: "She had been caught stealing drugs from the pharmacy in her hospital. This was the second time, and she felt terrible shame and guilt because she couldn't stop using drugs. My father was also unemployed, and they had a massive amount of debt. They felt that killing themselves was their only option."

Samantha just shakes her head in bewilderment. Even two years after her parents' death, she is still reeling from the loss. There were so many aspects of this event that affected her life on a massive scale. Of course, she lost both her parents: that's certainly enough to send anyone into a tailspin. But she was also left with the mystery of her parents' secret lives. She wondered how she could have missed all the signs of their trouble. She worried about how this would affect her young son, and her own future: "Maybe you can understand that at first I dealt with all the stress and anger and depression by isolating myself. I tried to bury my pain in food, and I gained 30 pounds in the first three months after they died."

Samantha binged on comfort foods in chain restaurants, eating junk, fried, synthetic substances that barely resembled anything remotely nutritious. She ate not only when she was hungry, but also when she was depressed and anxious. She even lost the ability to differentiate hunger from sadness and loneliness: "I just felt awful. I felt like a zombie. I couldn't breathe and could barely function or even play with my son who so needed me. I had become obese and hardly recognized myself under all the fat."

Friends told Samantha that she had to start moving again, getting some exercise, but she just had no energy. It was difficult enough just to crawl out of bed. And she was certain she'd die of a heart attack if she strained herself in any way. "One evening I was looking through some of my parents' scrapbooks, and I came across awards and ribbons they had both won for running in marathons and other races," she recalled. "They had both been excellent athletes, and exercise had always been important to them, at least until they came under the influence of the drugs."

It was while staring at the last memories of her parents, with tears running down her face, that Samantha asked herself what her parents would say to her in that moment. What would they want for her? If they were watching her right now, what would they tell her to do? The fantasy became so strong and vivid in her mind that it was as if they were both in the room talking to her. "I know they would have wanted me to be healthy," she admitted to herself. "They would see how I was suffering, as was my little boy. They would say he deserved to be happy and have a mother who is happy. It occurred to me in that moment that if I didn't take control of my life and change things around, I'd end up just like my parents. And that terrified me!"

This was one of those magic moments of clarity discussed in the previous chapter when change is possible on a scale and magnitude that is almost unimaginable. When stress and suffering take such a hold over a life that continued existence is intolerable, *that* is when things become interesting. It is a choice point when some people become so despondent that they give up, as Samantha's parents did, or...it presents an opportunity to refashion one's life and write a completely new script.

For Samantha, this was a turning point, sitting on the couch staring at the scrapbook with the last remnants of her parents' lives. Certainly other factors and influences played a role, leading up to this critical incident, but this was the moment that changed everything for her. She had tried therapy with modest results. She had rallied for her son and that helped. She felt support from friends and coworkers and that helped to stabilize her. But everything seemed to come together with the scrapbook on her lap, or at least what resembled a lap when her stomach pressed over it: "From that evening forward, I began to educate myself about healthy eating. I decided to make that a major priority, not only for myself but for my own family, which is now all that I had left. I lost 100 pounds, and I did it the old-fashioned way through exercise and careful, healthy eating. That also helped me to make a connection between mental and physical health. My depression and anxiety finally lifted."

The connection that Samantha noticed was that the same discipline that she had exhibited to work out six days a week and become a vegan was also operating in the ways she challenged her emotional suffering. She decided to forgive herself for not "saving" her parents. She let go of her guilt. She exorcised her shame by telling her story to others (including here) and honoring her parents' memory: "There were many times when I wanted to just give up, and that's when I would talk to my parents in my head and ask them what they wanted me to do. I found such strength in these moments because I could feel them cheering me on from the grave."

Samantha says this with such pride. She is amazed by what she has managed to do, how she has not only survived but flourished in the past year. She has never felt better about herself: "I chose to draw strength from my personal tragedy rather than crumbling under the weight of it."

CULTURAL CONSTRAINTS ON FREEDOM TO CHANGE

In Samantha's case, or any other that we've covered, the choices and responses selected are not only made based on individual preferences and circumstances but also limited and enhanced by contextual factors in the culture, environment, and personality structure.

Thus far I have been describing change processes as if they are just a matter of free will: If you want something, just go after it. We have already reviewed some of the biological constraints that limit options for people, based on their abilities, genetics, and life experiences, but this also holds true for relatively stable personality characteristics. Whether the result of Nature or nurture, people exhibit widely different responses to crises and challenges, as well as immunities to stress and inclinations to face fears. There are certain personality types that have been described as "codependent" or "helpless" and others that exhibit high levels of "hardiness" and "resilience." Let's set aside what actually causes such entrenched patterns and simply acknowledge that it's harder for some people to change than others.

Even the so-called "fight-or-flight response," which is supposed to be evolutionarily predetermined and universal, is actually more descriptive of characteristically male behavior. More recent evidence points to quite a different natural response to stress among women called "tend and befriend."[14] There are different hormonal responses operating for women under stress, releasing high levels of oxytocin, which drive affiliation and collaboration within social structures. The initial urge to flee or fight is thus augmented by another strong desire to seek social support. This is but another reason why women and men may respond so uniquely to situations and also initiate changes through different pathways.

Culture also exerts tremendous influences in the ways that people visualize changes that are possible. Those who live in "progress-resistant cultures" hold fatalistic beliefs that things are the way they are and it is best to accept one's station and situation in life. In contrast, those who reside in a "progress-prone" culture (like many in the West) view destiny as something that can be changed and altered depending on your creativity and drive.[15]

We live in one of the few places and times in history when people actually choose their mates and professions. Love marriages are relatively recent inventions, only a few hundred years old, and still the minority in the world in which arranged marriages are more the norm. Likewise, it has only been in the last century or two that we have the option of not following in our parents' footsteps with respect to a career choice. If you are a girl, you were married off to an appropriate suitor chosen by your family; if you were a boy, you did what your father and grandfather did before you as a blacksmith, farmer, soldier, or priest.

There are still many constraints placed on us by our culture, gender, socioeconomic class, geographic region, physical features, religion, race, and sexual orientation. The culture of poverty presents a whole different set of stressors that are quite different from those who are privileged, including increased risk of violence, crime, overcrowding, chaos, and feelings of oppression and lack of choices.

In so many ways, the change options available to us are programmed by the earliest training we received at home, school, and through media in our culture. To a great extent, what we tell ourselves is possible depends on what we've been told. These cultural injunctions can be overcome, of course, but in order to do so you must first become aware of the ways you are limited by them.

MANAGING STRESS THAT PREVENTS CHANGE

Stress has become such a universal problem that there exists a whole, billion-dollar industry designed to assist people. Antianxiety medications are the most commonly prescribed drugs in the world. Open almost anyone's medicine cabinet, and you will likely find prescriptions for Valium, Xanex, or sleeping pills. Alcohol consumption and abuse are so problematic because they've become such accessible coping strategies for dealing with stress. Marijuana has become an accessible and readily available means to take the edge off any discomfort or annoyance. Yoga classes, meditation centers, exercise regimens, fitness centers, retreat facilities, stress clinics, self-help books, and support groups are cropping up with unprecedented acceleration. The market is boundless for alleged new treatments or strategies for reducing stress or managing other negative feelings.

There is perfect legitimacy to the belief that stress is the main culprit that prevents constructive changes from taking place. When you are distracted and beaten down, you hardly have any extra energy to pursue lofty goals. The good news is that there are plenty of proven strategies for managing and preventing incapacitating stress. But the bad news is that none of them work for very long because very few people stick with them over time.

In the previous chapter, we already tackled one of the most effective ways for counteracting stress, or any other negative emotion, through self-talk or cognitive restructuring. This also happens to be one of the options that can most easily and permanently be incorporated into daily functioning. Somebody or something is giving you a hard time. You catch yourself thinking self-sabotaging thoughts ("This is awful, the worst thing that ever happened. I'll never be able to handle this.") and then challenge their veracity by substituting more rational and reasonable responses ("This is only difficult and only annoying.").

How do people most often deal with their increasing stress, which compromises changes they'd like to make? In descending order of frequency, music is most often mentioned as the favored antidote, followed by exercise, spending time with family, reading, watching television, praying, playing video games, taking a nap, enjoying a hobby, eating, attending religious services, drinking alcohol, shopping, smoking, getting a massage, playing sports, and meditating. Interestingly, consulting with a therapist or taking medications was, barely, if ever, mentioned in the surveys (less than 4%).[16]

Managing Time

It's really quite interesting how some people claim they never seem to have the time to do the things they say are most important. I think they are being honest when they say it *feels* that way, but I don't for a minute believe that's the way it has to be. Of course, we get stuck (or feel stuck) with obligations and responsibilities that are (or feel) thrust upon us, leaving precious little time to engage in the activities we enjoy the most. And it's also the case that some people really don't have a choice in the matter because of economic or family realities. But most of the time we really do make our own choices, even while we complain about them.

"You think I wouldn't *love* to quit this pitiful excuse for a job and, for that matter, get out of this crazy living situation?" one woman said angrily, when I point this out to her.

Although I was thinking to myself at the time that if she really didn't like being a martyr she really could do some things differently, I wisely kept my mouth shut. Some people don't want to hear that they have more control than they think they do. Even when there are some things you can't do much about you, still have choices about how, when, and where to do them, and on what terms. Nowhere is this more evident than in how you spend time.

Even for those who feel like they have few discretionary options, there are still ways that priorities can be changed. Simon feels "dead" inside, like an automaton who just goes through the motions of his life, which is so overprogrammed that he has to plan specific times to call his parents or he'd likely forget. When I asked him what he might do to alter this pattern, he looked at me like I was crazy. Then he looked at his watch, as if to tell me that I'd better hurry up and say what I want because he's got more important things to do. He was making me nervous just sitting in the same room with him.

Simon's homework (and he was very good at writing down instructions and following through) was to come back the following week with an exhaustive list of things he might do to reduce stress and free up more discretionary time. I told him that he had to come up with at least a dozen options and encouraged him to be as creative as possible and think outside the box. Most brainstorming exercises work best when participants are given permission to be as wild and crazy as possible since they've already exhausted the more obvious solutions.

Simon returned the following week with the paper, which initially he told me felt like just one more obligation that he couldn't wait to get done before moving on to the next thing on his list. But then a funny thing happened (or at least it was funny to him): clutching the paper in his hand, he mentioned he hadn't realized that actually there were a number of things he *could* do to free up more time, even if they didn't seem realistic, at least at first. He started rattling off his list—he could quit his job, ask for a demotion, sell all his belongings and travel around the world, open a pawn shop, lower his expenses, join the circus, live in a homeless shelter, get a loan and go back to school—the list went far beyond the mandatory dozen items. It seems he got a little carried away with the assignment, dizzy with the freedom of all the possibilities that really were available to him even if most of them weren't very realistic.

The point of the exercise was just to demonstrate that he wasn't trapped after all. He did have some choices he could make regarding his time, and how he managed it, *if* he were willing to live with the consequences, trading higher income and power for freedom.

Procrastination or postponing needed changes isn't necessarily the result of laziness or some personality flaw but represents a logical response with clear messages. The key to changing this pattern is directly related to decoding the meaning of the avoidance. This is often the case because of distractions that get in the way, ambivalence you feel about the consequences of changing (more work and effort required), and especially self-deceptive beliefs about what you say is most important. In each of these instances, avoidant behavior actually makes perfect sense. You will put off those activities or tasks about which you can't identify a clear and compelling reason to finish. That isn't the only reason, of course, since there are also times when procrastination really does indicate a form of self-defeating behavior that is punitive.

Psychological and Spiritual Rejuvenation

Sometimes the changes that need to be made involve not so much external changes as internal ones that keep you grounded, centered, and focused. It is easy to get distracted and diverted by daily pressures that make it difficult to remain appreciative of present moments. We get stuck in the past, reliving old memories that haunt us. We launch ourselves into the future with grandiose plans and fantasies of what might come true. But ultimately, all we ever have are the present moments, the now that is *right there*, or *was* there just a moment ago. Now it's gone.

Prayer is not only communion with a Higher Power, nor is it just ritual repetitions, but rather, it is an effective way to maintain calmness and focus in the face of challenges and adversity, providing significant relief from stress and even trauma.[17] Regardless of the religious tradition, the power of prayer is used for a variety of purposes—to ask for favors or express desires, to offer gratitude for gifts, to request support or wisdom during times of crisis, to engage in forgiveness, or to hope for some greater good. Even if the intention is to focus on a particular outcome (serenity, job promotion, healing, gratitude), the *process* of prayer resembles any other form of meditation.

Altered states of consciousness can be induced through a variety of portals including self-hypnosis, visual imagery, drugs, music, dance, and other mindfulness-based activities. The word "flow" was coined to describe the state of effortless concentration in which you are so totally immersed in the moment that you lose all conception of time and place. You are so completely involved in whatever you are doing that you lose your sense of self.[18]

All of us could do with a lot more flow in our lives in which we remain appreciative of the most ordinary daily tasks—just feeling heightened awareness of whatever is going on in the moment. It is during flow, or some other altered states, that all critical judgment is suspended, focus is dialed in, and performance is enhanced. You not only perform at a higher level but also enjoy the experience more because you are so fully engaged in the activity.

Meditation and related mindfulness-based practices are perhaps the most systematic way that people seek a state of inner stillness, if not enlightenment. There are moving meditations, as well as sitting forms. Yoga, tai chi, and other forms of exercise can also become ways to calm the mind and tune the body. Such activities are associated with all kinds of health benefits, including reduced stress, decreased metabolic rate and blood pressure, improved sleep, reduced chronic pain, improved concentration, and increased feelings of self-control.[19]

It's more than a little ironic that meditation-type practices are even associated with improved multitasking on the computer and Internet.[20] It supposedly allows people to notice all the distractions they encounter without letting it bother them. But even if that's really not the case (and it *does* seem counterintuitive) and it really doesn't improve efficiency, people who meditate seem to enjoy their multiple tasks more.

Whereas it does make sense that practicing meditation or mindfulness-based strategies would, indeed, help anyone to find greater satisfaction in any and every activity—including multitasking—hopefully the real lesson to be learned is the intrinsic pleasure of doing just one thing at a time. If there is one single change that most people would be well advised to make in their lives, almost without exception, it would be to demonstrate sufficient self-discipline, and respect for others, to turn off their mobile devices or leave them at home when they are already fully engaged with others. How often do you see a family or group of friends sharing a meal together, and each one of them is texting or calling *someone else*? How often have you been having an intense conversation with someone, just in the middle of saying something important, when the other person interrupts to answer a text or call? How often have you sat in a movie theater and see people texting or e-mailing while they are watching the film, projecting distracting light throughout the room? Some people even check their mobile devices while having sex or in the shower! There is absolutely no down time, no opportunities to focus on just doing one single thing with full commitment, passion, and attention. That is one of the benefits of mindful meditation or prayer: the object is to lose yourself in the special moment of communion with the divine, loved ones, or with yourself.

I realize, of course, that it feels good to remain connected to friends and family at all times with mobile devices, but not when it interferes with what you are doing with someone else at the moment. I was recently waiting at an intersection at a pedestrian crosswalk, and I couldn't help but overhear the conversation of the couple standing in front of me, two college students who were talking about something highly emotional. I leaned closer to them (okay, I'm nosy and always doing research), and I could hear the young woman telling the guy that her mother was dying of cancer. The young man was nodding his head as she continued to talk about her feelings, on the verge of tears. I was actually quite moved myself by the disclosure and envied their intimacy. Then the light changed, and as we started to walk across the street I noticed that all the while the woman was confiding her pain, the guy was texting on his phone to someone else! He was continuing to nod his head, indicating that he was mostly listening to her, although only looking at the screen on his phone. And here's the remarkable thing about that interaction: *It didn't seem to matter to the woman!* It's as if she was so used to having people's divided attention, even during moments of emotional significance, that she didn't seem the least annoyed by her friend's split attention.

There is probably no more significant and meaningful change that most anyone could make in their lives to enhance relationships, reduce stress, and enrich daily life than to focus on just one task, one conversation, one activity at a time and give it your full and complete attention. That would mean, of course, making conscious decisions to turn off your mobile devices, or even leaving them behind, which means sacrificing access to the constant flood of intrusive communications.

LIFESTYLE CHANGES

There are changes you make to fix something in your life that feels broken, and then there are things you do to enhance the quality of your life with respect to intimacy, productivity, health, and well-being. There doesn't have to be something wrong or dysfunctional in order to take certain steps to make things better.

Lifestyle refers to the attitudes, habits, priorities, values, practices, and behavior that encompass your life. They not only include things like your career, financial status, health, housing arrangements, leisure activities, and social connections, but also the choices you make on a regular basis. Health professionals consistently underestimate, or even ignore completely, the significance of lifestyle factors when assessing problems. This is all the more puzzling considering that just a few of them have a huge impact on life expectancy and health functioning—physical exercise, diet, alcohol use, and smoking.[21]

Physical Exercise

Obesity is among the most serious health issues in the Western world, foremost among Americans with over one third of the population significantly overweight (and literally growing). Even more alarming, and increasing rapidly, is that one in five children is considered obese.[22] Besides the health risks they might experience, children who are significantly overweight are more likely to have problems sleeping and report higher than normal headaches, stomach aches, anger, bed wetting, and social and academic difficulties. They worry a lot and also say they are concerned about their parents, who seem stressed all the time.[23]

You have been more than inundated with research findings about the benefits of exercise, not only to control weight for a variety of other effects—reducing stress; improving sleep; stabilizing moods; improving cardiovascular functioning; preventing diseases like diabetes, Alzheimer's, Parkinson's, and prostate cancer; improving endurance; increasing life expectancy; and improving sex, self-confidence, body image, pain tolerance, and mental focus. Most impressive is the way that regular exercise reduces depression and stress, as well as improves sleep, because of the endorphin release (runner's high) and increase in serotonin.[24] Studies completed with young people and the elderly, with rats and monkeys, repeatedly confirm that exercising even a few minutes each day improves memory, cognitive functioning, concentration, problem solving, and task performance.[25]

Everybody already knows that becoming more physically active is good for you even though more than half the population never gets any regular exercise whatsoever. Even with more and more evidence demonstrating how exercise prolongs life and improves life satisfaction, the number of people taking this seriously is not changing and, if anything, is becoming worse.[26]

Presenting information like this doesn't seem to have much impact on those of you reading this who still lead a sedentary lifestyle. Scolding doesn't work. Doctors' prescriptions have little effect. Even joining a gym or fitness club seems futile when four out of five members don't show up again after the first few visits, but they keep paying their dues anyway to appease their guilt.[27]

So, then, what works?

Good question. In one sense, nothing works very well, for very long. Just review the number of times people join a fitness center, attend exercise classes, begin a routine of walking or running, and then end up abandoning the effort through complacency or other commitments.

The situation is compounded by all the confusing advice you get.[28] You thought stretching before working out was important and later discover that it mostly leads to injuries and doesn't actually improve performance. Those expensive cardio machines with heart rate monitors? Their gauges tend to overestimate your pulse, and the machines provide less resistance than just playing or walking outside. The weight machines that resemble medieval torture instruments? They're outstanding physical therapy for injuries because they isolate individual muscles, but they're not nearly as good as free weights that exercise more natural body movements. And then there is all that advice you read in magazines, newspapers, and books like this telling you the secrets to perfect abs or sculpted delts. Good luck with that, too. What's a person to do?

For one thing, you have to want this really, really badly—so much that you are willing to make it as much a habit as brushing your teeth every day. No missed promises. No negotiation. No excuses. You just "do it" as the Nike slogan says, without a single reason to avoid it. No matter what.

Sure, it helps to have some external structures in place—companions to join you, a class to attend with a regular schedule, a pattern that you follow without exception. But deep down inside you have to believe that this is so important to your health, welfare, and peace of mind, that you couldn't possibly consider any other option except following through.

Eating Healthfully

Although the purpose of food is nutrition, the practice of eating has evolved to literally feed cravings from other sources, notably stress, depression, loneliness, boredom, and guilt. People eat for all kinds of reasons that have nothing to do with physical hunger, and the choices that are made regarding what we put into our bodies is nothing short of ridiculous. If you are not faint of heart, just take the time read the actual ingredients served by fast-food outlets such as dimethylpolysiloxane (silicone used as an antifoaming ingredient in chicken nuggets—and breast implants), ammonium sulfate (fertilizer ingredient in Subway's bread), or all the mystery ingredients like cellulose gum, disodium phosphate, and sorbitan monostearate contained in a 650-calorie medium-sized Frosty at Wendy's.

If we're here to talk about lifestyle changes that contribute to better health, greater longevity, and self-care, then it isn't so much where we choose to harvest or gather our food as it is the choices we make about what, when, and how much to eat. There is a recognizable stress-eating cycle that begins with a spike in perceived danger or challenge. This sets in motion that fight-or-flight emergency response surge of hormones that need additional stores of fuel. That's why you feel a craving for sugar and processed foods, which produce elevated insulin levels. Then you crash: sugar levels drop. Adrenaline and cortisol are still working their way through the system, leaving you feeling fatigued and worn down. You crave sugar and junk food again (plus caffeine) for a quick infusion of energy, and the cycle continues.

Drugs and Alcohol

Some form of institutionalized drug use has been around as long as humans figured out how to grow and distill plants. Eskimos are about the only culture on Earth that didn't have any regular use of intoxicants to regulate and enhance their moods, and that's only because they couldn't grow anything above the Arctic Circle. Once they were introduced to alcohol in the last century, they made up for lost time with one of the highest incidences of alcoholism. Apparently their bodies have no immunities.

Since some form of drug use has been around most of human history, it obviously serves important functions as social lubricants, communal rituals, and mood regulators. Every culture has some unique preferences and prohibitions about which drugs they consider acceptable: In our case it seems to be tobacco, caffeinated beverages, alcohol, and other drugs designated by those who have been deputized to dispense them (called doctors).

It's interesting to think about how certain drugs actually impact the whole creative and productive advancements of a culture. One intriguing theory posits that humans essentially emerged from the Dark Ages into the Renaissance largely as a result of a switch from beer to coffee as the social beverage of choice.[29] Since water was never very safe to consume, with all kinds of wicked germs and plague floating about, people used to drink mead (beer, ale, wine, or fermented cider) all day long, half-drunk while trying to get some work done. But once people started frequenting coffee establishments and made the switch from a depressant to a stimulant, wow, the paintings, sculptures, and scientific breakthroughs started to fly!

Drugs and alcohol are not intrinsically bad for you, any more than food is detrimental to your health. It's all about when, how, where, and why you consume them. Drinking a glass of wine per day is even associated with better health and longevity than abstaining altogether. But it's moderation that seems to be the key in most of the aspects of one's lifestyle that are worth review and adjustment.

Money, Sex, and Children

When couples arrive for counseling, there is an assumption that their problems will relate to one of three areas that involve their finances, sex life, or issues related to their children. Although there are certainly other problems that might crop up (health, addictions, depression), these are the most common. The first two problems would certainly apply to almost anyone else, and other family members (in-laws, siblings, parents) can easily be substituted for children.

Satisfying relationships with family and friends have been linked to all kinds of health benefits and stress reduction. There is research demonstrating that people who feel support from loved ones have reduced risk of strokes, depression, and even the common cold. They experience a "social cure" for other maladies and report higher quality of life and greater wisdom.[30] Given these benefits, it might not be surprising that one reason that stress is increasing is because people are actually spending much less time with their families than in the past, have fewer friends, and are less involved in civic and social activities.[31] When people are together, it is for shorter periods of time and with many other things on their minds that increase the likelihood of conflicts and fractured intimacy. As mentioned earlier, so much of the direct, face-to-face intimate contact that used to be more common has been replaced by brief texts, e-mail, tweets, and social media.

Monica and Sam both have busy lives managing their respective jobs, taking care of their two children, and trying to keep their heads above water with a number of financial pressures. They are "underwater" on their mortgage and can't get out of the obligation without destroying their credit. They are barely making ends meet as it is, but things are about to get much worse when their eldest child attends university the following year.

As is so often the case, Monica and Sam have been so consumed with making ends meet, keeping up with their work schedules, and transporting their children to various activities, that they have little time and energy left over for themselves. They can't remember the last time they had sex because they are so tired when they finish all their chores and get the kids settled down. All they want to do is get some sleep, which would be lovely, indeed, except they are both so pumped up they joke that they only need a single bed because one or the other of them is up restlessly watching television.

Monica and Sam have managed to attain the "trifecta," all three of the major problems that couples present. They worry constantly about money. Their sex life is nonexistent, and when they do manage to schedule time together, it feels more like another chore to get out of the way. Neither of them says they have the chance to get regular exercise, or even plan quality time together as a family. Their two children, who are rather high strung in the first place, are having numerous problems of their own as a direct result of the tension at home. Lately, more than ever, they have become obstinate and defiant, exacerbating the stress for all of them. At this point it's difficult to decode causes and effects since there is a circular dynamic operating in which each member of the family is both a source of difficulty for the others, as well as a recipient of others' negative effects.

In altering the stressful pattern evident in this family, it's clear that any changes that occur will have to take place within the larger context of their interpersonal dynamics since each person's stress is exacerbated by what's going on with the others. Monica decides she'd like to spend a romantic evening with Sam, but their plans are sidetracked when their daughter is grounded for getting in trouble at school. She, in turn, sets her brother into a rage because she's feeling so miserable about her situation. Sam comes home from work, looking forward to a relaxing evening with Monica, and then discovers a civil war in progress. He freaks out and yells at the children, setting off additional fireworks.

Since perhaps one in a hundred families would seek professional help for these problems, they are left to figure out things on their own. And it's not pretty. What eventually helped them to turn the corner and bring them together was still another stressor that would have affected all of them: Sam's job was changed, reducing his income and further limiting any possibility for further advancement. This meant they'd have to abandon their home, perhaps even move to another area and school district. Yet this crisis led all of them to realize that, ultimately, if they didn't pull together as a team they would all suffer the consequences. Both children decided (on their own, without parental pressure!) to get part-time jobs to help out. It wasn't their added income that made the difference, as much as their choice to take on adult responsibilities. Likewise, the fear that Monica and Sam felt motivated them to take better care of themselves and their relationship. They could afford to lose their home, and the material trappings of a comfortable life, but they now felt clear about what was most important. Both of them vowed— and actually followed through on their commitment—to spend more quality time with each other.

Here is where the story should end, just like in the movies,…and they lived happily ever after. But, alas, that wasn't to be—at least in the short run.

Sam and Monica eventually separated, realizing that it was mostly the children that were holding them together and that wasn't nearly enough. Even though they chose to make changes to go their separate ways, it gave each of them the opportunity to do things differently. Their two kids were initially pretty upset about the breakup of their parents' marriage, but the adversity that they had faced the preceding year helped them to become far more resourceful, independent, and responsible in the future.

ANTIDOTE TO STRESS AND PANACEA TO CURE MOST ILLS

Stress is unavoidable, just as it is impossible to hide from all fears. Among all the things we've reviewed that contribute to reducing stress most effectively, not to mention increasing resilience and promoting constructive changes, there is one that stands out above the rest.

Before you reach for a pad and paper to write this down, or a marker to underline these definitive words of wisdom, let me assure you that you will remember this. In fact, you already know this even if it may not be as much a priority as it could be.

I'm referring to a cure for stress, or almost anything else that bothers you, one that has conclusive and overwhelming empirical support. It has been found to significantly increase your life span and reduce the likelihood of dying from diseases by a factor of four. It not only improves your health but is also the single factor that most contributes to your sense of well-being and life satisfaction.[32]

Are you ready?

Da dum!

It's called "social capital" and refers to the sum total of your close connections to family, friends, and community. It is directly related to your attainment of so-called happiness (covered in Chapter 11) and also a significant part of the meaning you create for your life when those social interactions are involved in helping others in some way (see Chapter 12). What this means is that no matter what else is going on in your life, how many challenges you face, how many difficulties you encounter in work, love, or leisure, it is your relationships that sustain you.

CHAPTER 11
Creating Meaning and Happiness

Regardless of their life circumstances, most people harbor the belief that if only they could make a few adjustments in their lives—earn more money, find true love, switch jobs, improve their health or body image, reclaim their youth—they would achieve that illusive state of happiness. Ironically, it is precisely the belief that such changes produce ultimate happiness that ends up sabotaging efforts to keep momentum going. Happiness is just an illusive construct that is mostly built on myths, misconceptions, and exaggerations about our own abilities to completely transform ourselves and live blissfully ever after.[1]

You don't *find* happiness, but rather, you *create* it at little at a time. This is an active process of invention as much as discovery, one in which you shape the meaning of your own experiences in such a way that they inspire you to continue along the transformative path. These interpretations can soothe the most hollow spirit and hopeless despair.

Even those who suffer from extreme physical agony or disabilities, as well as those who manifest symptoms of emotional disorders, can choose their own path to happiness and create their own meaning from the challenges they face. As we've seen, life satisfaction and well-being are not determined by the circumstances in which we find ourselves but, rather, by the choices we make in how we decide to live with them. It turns out that your level of life satisfaction is determined, in part, by your genetic inheritance, which includes your general disposition, unique cognitive and emotional style, health markers, and other biological factors. It is estimated that about 50% of reported happiness is the result of genetics and another 10% is influenced by particular situations and contexts.² The good news is that this means that as much as 40% can be shaped, influenced, and controlled by strategic intentional actions.³ In other words, whereas there are, indeed, some things you can't control such as certain physical attributes, genetic inheritances, family background, past experiences, and unforeseen events, meaningful and significant changes can, indeed, take place largely as a result of your chosen attitudes, beliefs, and perspective.

SECRECY, SHAME, AND SELF-ACCEPTANCE

Vera's life has felt very much like she's been lost at sea in a storm. There have been a few placid periods when things appear calm, but that's but an illusion as she bobs gently in the eye of a hurricane. Most of the time, she is rudderless, exhilarated, and terrified as she rides the crest of gigantic waves that toss her around with indifference. She has no control whatsoever regarding the direction her life drifts, feeling completely helpless.

During the preceding seven years, Vera has been the victim of extreme mood swings. There are times she feels like superwoman with boundless energy, but those episodes don't seem to last nearly as long as the deep depressions that leave her wrecked and despondent, even suicidal. It is during that despair and hopelessness that she cuts herself, leaving ragged scars along the insides of her arms and thighs.

For many years Vera didn't know her "spells" had an official name or diagnostic label; she was just uncontrollably moody, sending her into surges of unbridled energy when she didn't seem to need rest. She'd sleep maybe a few hours each night for a week or longer, talking a mile a minute, rushing around doing one thing after another without pause. It looked exhausting and weird to her family and friends, but she found these periods to be quite fun and productive. "It was incredible all the things I could do when I was flying," she said. "I was taking five classes in school, working part-time, doing research on campus, volunteering with kids at an elementary school, running for office in a student organization. I had sticky notes everywhere with tasks for me to complete, to-do lists, and schedules. I was like superwoman!"

Then the crash would hit. Vera would run out of energy and sleep for days at a time, barely able to move. When she was at school or at her job, she'd fall asleep at her desk. One time she was out with friends at a restaurant and just passed out while sitting at the table.

Vera's boyfriend suddenly and unceremoniously ended their relationship, leaving her shocked and devastated. She'd been depressed before but nothing like the intensity of what she was feeling—or not feeling: "It was like I was dead inside. I was so empty, so sad, in such awful pain; all I could think of was that I wanted it to stop. With silent tears streaming down my face, not wanting to wake anyone up, I quietly made my way in the darkness to the kitchen and headed for the knife drawer. I remember purposely picking the biggest knife, and sharpening the blade just to be sure it would do the job I had in mind."

Looking back, Vera says it was as if she were totally disconnected from her body, as if someone or something else were in charge. She just remembers wanting the pain to end, wanting to be saved. But there was no hope for that, so she locked herself in the bathroom, gripping the butcher knife: "I began slicing my left arm starting from my elbow down towards my wrist. Then my right arm. Each cut was deep and about two inches long, and I could see all the blood and pieces of skin stuck to the knife. I was staring at all the damage when I heard the voice of my best friend on the other side of the door. She had known that something was wrong and showed up just in time to save my life."

Vera survived the suicide attempt, but she remembered how the physical pain of cutting herself had distracted her from her emotional misery. That was something she'd remember and repeat for many years to come. Vera was forced to go to therapy, which she enjoyed, but there were many things that she kept hidden, including her secret solution to dull the psychic pain by cutting herself: "Whenever I felt sad, or angry, or rejected, or out of control, I'd take a razor blade or sometimes a safety pin and start cutting parts of my body where I could hide the incisions—on my thighs or hips. I knew what I was doing was crazy but I was helpless to stop."

Things continued in a downward spiral for Vera until one night she was taking a shower in preparation for an upcoming religious festival, La Virgin de Guadalupe. She still felt terrible guilt over her suicide attempt, which was against her Catholic beliefs, so she tried hard to renew her devotion. She recalls: "While I was in the shower, distracted and relaxed, my thoughts started roaming from one thing to another when suddenly these unexpected and abrupt flashbacks started coming back to me, one after another, as I froze in place with the water running down my face. All at once I remembered that I had been molested by a boy when I was a child and started to sob and break down. I was so upset that I jumped out of the shower with shampoo still in my hair and soap on my body."

The first thing Vera thought to do was call her boyfriend and tell him what had happened to her. But instead of responding with compassion and sympathy, he became angry with her for hiding this from him. She tried to explain that it was just that moment that the traumatic memory became clear to her, but he questioned how she could forget such a thing: "His rejection and lack of understanding only deepened my feelings of despair. I also started to think that if my brain had buried that memory from so long ago, what else was hiding there? I felt like I couldn't any longer trust myself or anything that I thought was true. I cut myself to hide from that agony."

With little improvement in therapy, Vera was eventually referred for psychiatric care and finally diagnosed with bipolar disorder and stabilized on medication. Although those interventions certainly would have helped, Vera credits her recovery and subsequent growth with a single day in her life in which she attended a lecture by a guy who had survived jumping off the Golden Gate Bridge: "His story was so powerful and inspiring that I couldn't stop crying. I just had to talk to him and tell him how I admired his courage to tell his story. I told him a little about my situation and he told me he was honored that I trusted him. Just as his story had helped me, maybe my story would inspire others."

The incredible thing about Vera's story (which is bringing tears to my own eyes as I write this) is that her breakthrough and quantum growth are taking place this very second as you read these words. It is/was the act of sharing her pain and recovery with others, finding meaning in her suffering, that has helped to heal her. She has since appeared on panels and given talks about recovery from emotional disorders and posttraumatic growth after trauma.

Vera hopes that telling her story may help others who have lost hope or surrendered to their suffering. It was keeping her secrets that was eating her alive as much as the initial traumas and mood disorder. She found meaning and strength by talking about her problems rather than by privately torturing herself with knives and razor blades.

It has now been four years since her last depressive episode and three years since she last cut herself. She decided to stop taking her medication to see if she could handle her mood swings on her own. So far, so good, but she is cautiously and carefully monitoring herself, prepared to seek medical and psychological help if it is needed for support. She is also well aware that 95% of people with her condition will experience another episode within five years. Far more than that, Vera became so interested in the research related to bipolar disorder and early trauma that she made a decision to devote a part of her life to helping others.

If you're still wondering how Vera manages to control her continued impulses to hurt herself to cover up painful feelings, she has been remarkably creative: "I still struggle with thoughts about cutting, and I don't think they will be going away for a while. But now I have the willpower to look past those urges. When the impulse is really strong, instead of cutting myself I will often take a knife and stab other objects such as pillows or plastic bottles, which I realize can be viewed as weird behavior but it works for me. When the urges are less intense, I take a red sharpie and write in my notebook, 'I want to cut myself,' over and over and the feelings go away. This might also sound strange to you, but I also use a red sharpie when writing this because part of the satisfaction that comes from cutting is seeing the blood that trickles out from my cuts and so the color red reminds me of blood, which calms me down."

Vera accepts that she has a bipolar disorder, with all the highs and lows that come with it. She is realistic about what she can and can't do on her own, and when and how she will need to ask for help if things escalate beyond what she can handle. In some ways she feels proud to be a member of an exclusive club of manic-depressives that included Abraham Lincoln, Winston Churchill, and Ted Turner. But regardless, she is done with secrecy and shame.

WHAT IS HAPPINESS, ANYWAY?

Vera's goal was never to attain happiness, that elusive, ethereal construct that is supposed to be our inalienable right, guaranteed by the Constitution. But alas, happiness is almost unattainable because of its association with constant cheerfulness, complete satisfaction, and exclusivity. There's only so much you can actually control given that supposedly half of your potential to achieve happiness is genetic, and another chunk controlled by your circumstances. As mentioned, that still leaves about 40%, which isn't anything to sneeze at, but there are limits to what can be done when you're so inundated by advice, indoctrination, and advertising, about what supposedly leads to the good life—a three bedroom home, a BMW in the garage, 2.3 children, and the most coveted new technological gadget.

Surprisingly, what people want for the "good life" hasn't changed in thousands of years, whether we are talking about ancient Mesopotamia, Rome, or Greece, or contemporary New York, Belfast, Kathmandu, Cairo, or Havana. Most people, wherever they live, are reasonably content if they enjoy good health, have a few friends whom they can trust, a supportive family, adequate space and shelter, a voice in government, and opportunities to pursue aesthetic interests and meaningful work.[4] Most people in Western countries have greater wealth, larger homes, and far more luxuries than their parents but are also markedly less happy.[5] We are among the most miserable population in the Western world, not even in the top 10 industrialized nations in terms of expressed life satisfaction.[6] All the Scandinavian countries, plus Canada, make us pale in comparison, mostly because of their better health care systems, social policies, and closer social networks. Just as important, because Americans have higher expectations for themselves and their perceived opportunities for advancement, they tend to be more disappointed—and unhappy—when things don't turn out as expected.[7] In addition, happiness is a somewhat fickle and transient description of felt experience, one that is dependent on context and situations. Just because you feel lonely or upset about something doesn't mean you aren't happy. To make matters still more challenging, some people are flat out destined to be unhappy compared with others as a function of personality traits described as neuroticism, which means a tendency to worry a lot and overreact to minor annoyances.[8] Although this is a core vulnerability in these individuals, it can be managed by learning skills to counteract the negative thinking such as those described throughout the book.

It's also more than a little ironic, if not downright paradoxical, that the passionate pursuit of happiness pretty much ensures you'll never find it. If, after all, you have to ask yourself if you're happy, you've probably got your answer: you're not. Studies support this contention in that the more people value happiness as a life goal, the less likely they are to obtain it.[9] The whole "happiness system" evolved, and continues to operate, as a means for us to continuously improve ourselves. We are continuously scanning "the horizon on the lookout for a better environment, a better social network, a better mode of behavior."[10] We will eternally search for something better than what we already have, and find ourselves always just short of perfection.[11] This has been described as a "hedonistic treadmill" because no matter what we attain in terms of wealth, status, achievement, possessions, and friendships, it is just not quite enough.[12]

It is for this reason that researchers now prefer to use the terms "well-being" or "flourishing," which are much easier to define and measure. "I actually detest the word *happiness*," states Martin Seligman, one founder of the positive psychology movement and originally responsible for some of the most well-designed studies on the subject.[13] He has since retracted this term, preferring alternatives that are more practical and realistic, and that emphasize increased positive emotions, engagement, accomplishments, intimate relationships, and life meaning—all things that represent a *process* of ongoing development.

This change in focus fits better with Vera's account of her own development and growth, seeking meaning in her life, and discovering ways that she can increase her sense of well-being, even while struggling with lifelong mood swings and self-destructive urges.

With that said, I don't have the same problems as Seligman with "happiness" as an idea, used interchangeably with well-being, life satisfaction, flourishing, contentment, or whatever else you want to call it. We are all pursuing essentially the same life goals. We want to remain secure and safe from harm. We want sufficient resources to live comfortably. We want a certain degree of status and respect from others. We want loving relationships with those we trust. We want an active sex life. We want to be healthy and feel good on a daily basis. We want to be productive and do something meaningful with our lives. We want to learn new things and be stimulated by new experiences. And when things don't go our way, which is sometimes the case, we want the resources and ability to do something about that so we are back on track. I think all of these things are reasonably attainable for most of us, much of the time. And I think the hope in reading books like this is to help us get closer to the wisdom and life satisfaction that we seek.

WHAT MAKES PEOPLE HAPPY—AND WHAT DOESN'T

If someone asks you if you're happy, usually you don't consider the question in terms of whether you feel joy at that moment, but rather, you take inventory of your relative pleasures versus pain. On this global balance sheet, you add up all the things for which you feel grateful and appreciative, then deduct those items that are annoying, frustrating, disappointing, or otherwise unsatisfying. Happiness thus has different levels of meaning, as a momentary feeling of exhilaration, a comparison between the current state of affairs versus hopes and expectations, or as a general assessment of life quality in terms of fulfilling your potential or flourishing in the way you are capable of being.[14]

It's not all that easy to assess this third level of happiness that encompasses so many aspects of experience and judgment. You can be in the midst of tremendous stress, struggles, and burdens, even subjected to difficult challenges, and yet still feel like that the accompanying growth, achievement, and meaning is definitely worth the effort and makes you insanely happy.[15] People have different standards of contentment and expectations for what they want and deserve. Some just want to avoid pain and suffering as much as possible and consider that the single best measure of well-being. As long as you are out of trouble, in reasonably good health, and avoiding conflict, life is good. Many of the philosophers of the past century (Nietzsche, Sartre, Schopenhauer, Wittgenstein, Freud) shared this pessimistic view that you are born in pain, alone, and pretty much on your own, and that's the way you die. Everything else in between is just getting through the days without too much anguish.

Others have a much higher standard that goes far beyond mere avoidance of pain or even the active pursuit of pleasure. They don't much mind a little suffering along the way if it leads to higher achievements of enlightenment, wisdom, growth, productivity, or service. Abraham Maslow and the subsequent positive psychologists and humanistic philosophers have set a much higher standard that goes far beyond meeting basic needs and instead seeking a sense of belongingness and self-actu-alization. There is a price paid for this ambitious goal in that it is often accompanied with a certain amount of rejection, failure, and setbacks (Figure 11.1).

Happiness is thus as much a state of mind as it is life circumstances. It is all about cognitive style and optimism, a favorable outlook toward life events, situations, circumstances, and challenges. Perhaps more than any other ingredient, having a positive, optimistic attitude predisposes you to a range of benefits, many of them associated with happiness. These include better cardiovascular fitness, protection against colds and the flu, lower risk of death, healthier lifestyle habits, and a more robust immune system.[16] There are good reasons for this, even though it may strike you, at first, as rather mysterious. If you look at the world through rose-colored glasses, try to see the best in things, and maintain a positive outlook toward the future, you are likely to take better care of

Figure 11.1: The wealthy are admired and envied for the accumulation of material possessions, yet they are no more happy and satisfied with their lives than almost anyone else in the middle class who is living reasonably comfortably. Howard Hughes (pictured above) had everything that anyone could possibly want yet struggled throughout his life to find some semblance of peace. There is a set point (roughly $50,000 to $100,000 dollars per year, depending on the region and cost of living) after which additional income produces no significant increase in life satisfaction or well-being. We may have been told this many times. We may even believe it. But it doesn't seem to change people's behavior when they continue to pursue greater wealth, sacrificing their health and families along the way. (Photo courtesy of Associated Press.)

yourself in all sorts of ways. You would see a clear connection between your behavior and favorable outcomes, leading you to listen to medical advice, watch your diet, exercise regularly, and avoid smoking. You would have more friends and social support because optimists are more attractive and fun to hang around. Your body would be more finely tuned because you would have developed ways to minimize stress. And generally you feel empowered to change things you don't like because you optimistically view that is possible.[17]

Do What You Love—A Lot

This assumes you really do know what you love, which might be more of a stretch than you think. There are some advantages to being flexible with respect to your personal goals and especially the way that you measure success in achieving them. Those who are most happy, or at least satisfied with their lives, are those who are willing to alter their objectives when faced with immovable obstacles. Or in the words of Crosby, Stills, and Nash, if you can't be with the one you love, then love the one you're with. If you generalize that to almost all other aspects of life, then there is a body of research to support the notion that the happiest people are those who are most willing to adjust their visions and change their objectives in light of experience and feedback regarding what is working and what is not.[18]

Social scientists and philosophers have been obsessed with exploring the roots of happiness for millennia. And the results are pretty clear as far as what most contributes to it:[19]

1. Focus on positive feelings and try to make the best of those that are unpleasant.
2. Hold onto an optimistic perspective, looking at the best in people and things whenever possible.
3. Live in the present and honor those moments when you can.
4. Do good work for which you feel proud.
5. Spend quality time with those you love the most.
6. Forgive those who have hurt you and let those resentments go.
7. After you figure out what you love, make a habit of doing those things as often as possible.

It all sounds so simple. Just let yourself admit what truly makes you most happy (but not necessarily in terms of immediate pleasure and satisfaction). If you don't know the answer to that, then back up one step and figure out what that might be. And if you can't do that either, then you've got a *lot* of work to do.

It might be surprising to learn that many people don't really know what's good for them. They make awful choices about relationships, job decisions, or lifestyle. They are so influenced by others' opinions and clever marketing strategies that they can't sort out what is dear to their own hearts.

"What do you love doing the most?" is an interesting question to consider. I asked myself that question as I was writing these words and felt self-satisfied, and a bit smug, when my immediate answer was, "I love to write." Well, that's good because it's what I'm doing right now. But then I dug deeper and made a list that included such items as being with friends, getting together as a family, being creative, and skiing. It was this last item that got my attention because I say that I love skiing and it makes me happy, but I had to admit that it had been three years since I've been out on the slopes! That either makes me a liar in that it really isn't much of a priority after all, or else I've been ignoring some of those things in my life that most contribute to my well-being. Before I even wrote this next sentence, I checked online and arranged to make three different ski trips during the upcoming season. Now, *that* is when insight leads to action.

It's All About Relationships

Being content with your life, or far more than that, feeling really, really good about the way things are going, is probably more complicated than just figuring out what you like and doing it more often. Although that helps, there are so many other nuances that contribute to the belief that you are living the good life.

Based on evidence compiled by 100 researchers who investigate what leads to happiness, there are several factors that are most important, some of which are surprising (see Table 11.1).[20] For instance, we spend so much time and effort in our lives focused, if not obsessed, with achievement in our work and the accumulation of wealth, yet beyond

Table 11.1. WHAT LEADS TO HAPPINESS AND UNHAPPINESS?

Happiness	Unhappiness
Achievements and productivity	Envy and comparison with others
Comfortable level of income	Unmet basic needs
Friendships (4–12 relationships)	Isolation
Perception of choices	Too many choices or lack of control
Flexible goals	Rigid goals
Forgiveness	Rumination over past
Optimism	Pessimism
Recognition of fluctuations	Unrealistic expectations
Altruism and generosity	Mistrust/suspicion of others
Creative expression	Boredom of routines
Enjoying possessions	Accrued debt from possessions
Romantic relationship	Living alone
Permission to be unhappy, sad, or disappointed	Obsession with happiness and need satisfaction

a certain point that meets basic needs, there is no appreciable difference between those who live reasonably comfortably and others who are considered rich.

But, then, you *know* these things. That's the thing about advice like this: it doesn't usually have much impact.[21] You can know things, really *know* them, and still not follow what is so self-evident. Everyone knows that smoking, excessive drinking, carrying extra weight, and lack of exercise are very bad for you, but this awareness doesn't alter behavior. Likewise, most people realize that money doesn't buy happiness. Yet on some level many people feel powerless to stop pursuing the things that won't make much difference. If you already have accumulated enough wealth to live comfortably, what difference would a little (or even a lot) more make?

The satisfaction derived from what you already have is directly related to the comparisons you make with others around you. If you have a million dollars sitting in the bank and live in a mini-mansion, but your friends or neighbors have ten million dollars and own more expensive possessions, then you might very well feel just as much discontent as the homeless person who admires a "neighbor" who lives in a more sturdy refrigerator box.

So, material possessions are not the answer to life satisfaction or well-being, at least up to a certain point. If making money and moving up the ladder don't fundamentally change things, then it is a reasonable question to ask just what does make a difference? What if you could ask people on the very last legs of their life journey, those who are about to face death, what *they* wish they could have changed or done differently? Faced with their imminent mortality, with just a few weeks or days left to live, what would they say they regret the most?

Based on a report by those involved in palliative care who help people to die with dignity and greater clarity, the two most common regrets are precisely those things we take most seriously—pleasing others and working hard.[22] Most dying patients face the reality that they have lived their lives trying to meet others' expectations rather than their own. Along the way, they neglected their own dreams to serve those of others. Many of their life goals will remain unfulfilled.

Second on the list of regrets is that they spent too much time working and convincing themselves that this was more important than spending time with loved ones. Almost nobody on his or her deathbed looks back on his or her life and says, "Gee, I wish I had worked harder and put in more hours." On the contrary, they wish they had spent more time with their partners and lament that they missed so much of their children growing up. Hardly anyone ever confesses, "If only I had earned more money and bought a bigger house or a nicer car, then I could look back and feel like my life was a success."

During the past half-century, the standard of living in the United States has consistently risen. People now live in bigger homes, have more discretionary income, and enjoy greater comforts and luxuries, and yet this has made no appreciable difference in their level of happiness. Whatever fantasy you have about winning the lottery, or hitting the jackpot, or inheriting a fortune, I have some revealing news: There's just as much chance that this sudden influx of wealth will only make you more miserable.[23] Your trust in others will be compromised. You will find that the cash doesn't make you genuine friends, nor does it buy you the things you thought would make such a difference. You will be a constant target of fraud and manipulation. And all you'll think about is how you can hold on to what you've got—and perhaps for good reason because there's a high probability you'd blow it all anyway.

Meaningful Work Matters, Too

The operative word in this heading is "meaningful." Work isn't necessarily what you do to earn a living, if it doesn't feel meaningful or productive to you; it is just something you do to survive. But enjoying what you do, whether making widgets on an assembly line, creating or selling ideas, or painting houses, cars, or canvases, is far more important that what you do.

"This might sound a little peculiar to you," Iris explained. "But I really like what I do."

"You mean chopping vegetables?"

"Exactly." She shrugged.

Iris felt a little apologetic because although she had a Ph.D. she was working in a kitchen as a sous chef. Most of her time was spent with an eight-inch chef's knife in her hand: "I like the fact that at the end of a shift I produced a heaping mound of onions. I can see the progress. I can measure it. Chopping puts me in this whole other universe where nothing else exists but the blur of the blade, the fragrant smells of the food, and the tapping sounds of the knife on the board. I go home at night tired from being on my feet but also really satisfied."

Prior to her kitchen job, Iris worked as a therapist, and although she found the work meaningful, she couldn't really tell if and when she helped people. She hated sitting in a chair all day. She hated just listening to people. She wanted to do something with her hands, something where she could turn her ever-whispering brain off completely and just concentrate on doing one thing really well. Iris is looking forward to graduating into sauces next, but she's in no hurry and describes herself as perfectly happy with her present situation.

In the context of well-being and happiness, work involves some consistent activity that provides satisfaction and a sense of accomplishment. Whereas that often does take place during paid employment, it can involve many other options. In that sense, work could be defined as something you *have* to do and play what you *choose* to do. Again, attitude is almost everything since there are many people who don't even think about what they do as a form of forced labor but rather as a forum for them to express their creative spirit and accomplish goals that are important to them.

"I was an energy lawyer for several years," Jay explained. "I worked with huge multinational corporations on their new acquisitions, mostly minimizing their risk and handling the closings. I didn't hate my job by any means, but neither did it seem all that interesting after a while. I could have stayed around and made partner, made a zillion dollars, and been reasonably content. But I wanted something more."

Jay would not have described himself as unhappy as much as restless and unfulfilled. He wanted to do something more with his life, leave something behind that was meaningful. It wasn't that he felt unproductive at the law firm; on the contrary, he was doing important things that advanced corporate growth. But he felt like he could easily have been replaced by hundreds of others. So Jay quit his job: "Friends thought I was crazy to give up so much security and future wealth, but I just wasn't happy there. It scared me to think that I would be doing basically the same things for the rest of my life. I felt like I needed a challenge. And I didn't want to minimize risk for others—I wanted to be a risk taker."

Jay joined an alternative energy start-up company that had an audacious plan to build infrastructure to support solar and wind farms. It was high risk but provided endless opportunities for him to broaden his skills beyond the practice of law to include learning about project management, federal regulations, engineering, and natural sources of energy.

Jay has many reasons to describe himself as happy and satisfied besides anything to do with work. He adores his wife and new baby. He has a vast network of friends. He diversifies his life to include lots of different leisure and athletic activities. "I think what I enjoy most," he said at the end, "besides that I'm learning so much, is that I feel like I have some control over what I do and how I do it. Sure, I answer to a few others and have to be accountable for my time, but it feels like it is mostly on my own terms." What Jay didn't say explicitly is that he also finds tremendous satisfaction in feeling like the projects he is working on will make the world a better place—and that's important to him.

Not everyone has the flexibility, opportunities, or the courage, to quit their jobs and find something else more meaningful and socially useful. But then again, meaningful work doesn't have to take place during a day job. Most of the world must remain content with finding employment that pays the bills and takes care of financial needs but doesn't necessarily fill that need for ultimate productivity and satisfaction that is associated with happiness. Some people volunteer their time to work on service projects (see Chapter 12). Some see their meaningful work as related to supporting their families or raising their children. Some take great satisfaction doing whatever job is assigned to them with the best of their abilities. Some treat their leisure activities as their identified "job" whether that is gardening, carpentry, photography, or writing poetry.

HAPPINESS IS OVERRATED

We have reviewed already several reasons why happiness is often an unattainable goal. Our genetic inheritance, personality characteristics, and environmental and contextual factors all program us in certain ways and limit us in others. Happiness, as a construct, is an ideal that can't be reached in ultimate form. However good you feel, however content you are, however satisfied you are with the way things are going, you can't help but look around you and wonder how things could be even better if only...

"If only" is the kicker. Once you start thinking about what could be, once you start comparing what you have or what you've accomplished, to what others have done, it's hard to feel completely satisfied. This is what encourages many people to strive for a better life, if not for themselves, then for their loved ones.

Then there is the other side of this debate from the media and experts in which we aren't ever supposed to be unhappy, even for a little while. There are designer drugs to make you feel better—Lexapro, Prozac, Zoloft, Xanax, Valium, plus alcohol, caffeine, marijuana, nicotine, Ecstasy, uppers, downers, and in-betweeners. "How ya' doin'?" you are regularly asked throughout the day, expected to answer with the standard response, "Just fine. How 'bout yourself?"

We've lost our right to be melancholic or sad, as if it is no longer allowed except in the lyrics of country western songs. People have to apologize for not being at the top of their game or joyous every moment of the day. "What's wrong?" you would immediately be asked if you don't sport a beaming smile. Yet suffering also holds an honorable place in human experience, one that is hopefully short lived but also useful at times to promote growth, creativity, and needed change. To the Buddhist, life *is* suffering. It is one of the Noble Truths that teaches us tolerance, self-discipline, and acceptance of all things in life, the painful with the pleasurable. It is ironic that by reducing desire and craving for something more, something else, we free ourselves from suffering.[24]

Here's the good news: ultimate happiness isn't that important to enjoy life and make the most of the experience. That's why researchers have most recently abandoned the term altogether. And that's why philosopher John Stuart Mill observed that people are only happy "who have their minds fixed on some object other than their own happiness. Aiming thus at something else, they find happiness along the way."[25] So we return to the hedonic paradox in that the more deliberately you pursue happiness, the less likely you will ever attain it.

Practically speaking, that means going after other things that give life greater meaning and looking elsewhere for sources of well-being. Although that can occur through work, many people also turn to their faith and spiritual beliefs, to their leisure interests, or to serving others in need. Just as companies diversify in order to protect themselves against uncontrollable market swings, so too should we all create/discover/manufacture other sources of pleasure and satisfaction that may, ultimately, lead to an approximation of so-called happiness. I mention an "approximation" because, once again, the whole idea of happiness may not even be valid. Because it is so integrally linked to cheerfulness and joy, both fleeting states, it isn't even necessarily a desirable goal.[26] For instance, building a circus may produce more exuberant joy than a library, but that doesn't mean we should be dismantling libraries and schools in favor of theme parks.

The great majority of people do report that they are more happy than unhappy, although very few describe themselves as completely happy. And this is true in most countries around the world, irrespective of their gross national product or economic development. We can't really help ourselves for wanting more than whatever we have. We are programmed that way from our culture, our peers, and also our biology. Our neurological systems reward us with sensations of pleasure when we do things that provide surges of temporary happiness, whether stimulated by sex, drugs, music, or food. We experience similar spikes of pleasure when we manage to increase our status or position in relation to others. And all of this is highly adaptive: "The idea of happiness has done its job if it has kept us trying," writes one scholar who is summarizing conclusions from the research. "In other words, evolution hasn't set us up for the attainment of happiness, merely its pursuit."[27] Happiness is just a fantasy, a construct, a goal that we might think about yet never reach. And that's just fine as long as you realize that what you've already got is more than enough to sustain you.

"Are you happy?" is the wrong question to ask, any more than it is meaningful to ask, "Are you fulfilled?" The obvious answer is, "Up to a point." We are all happy, fulfilled, satisfied, and content some of the time, maybe even most of the time. Ambition and dreams can very well lead you to want more, and that desire can also be constructive if it leads you to savor additional achievements. But such unfulfilled desire can also be the main source of unhappiness when (not if) you usually fall short.

Remember that although each of us is limited by genetic determinants and circumstances, you still have it within your power to control much of what happens to you and how you choose to deal with it![28] This is this capacity that allows you to alter most aspects of your life that could be upgraded. You are far more likely to be successful in any change effort when you forget altogether about some rigid definition of success or happiness and instead concentrate on doing the best you can to get closer approximation to where you'd like to be.

CHAPTER 12

Changing People's Lives While Transforming Your Own

In the previous chapter, we explored the paradoxical nature of happiness. It is counterintuitive that we are likely to experience joy and fulfillment not by trying endlessly to satisfy our own interests but, rather, by serving others in greatest need. It is also the case that one of the pathways to change in our own lives occurs through the actions we take on behalf of others. It isn't that happier people are significantly more generous than others, but that generous people tend to be happier. Even when we make personal sacrifices that are not in our own best interests—giving away time, money, and resources to those who are less fortunate—this investment pays off big time in terms of increased well-being and personal satisfaction.[1]

In the search for happiness and greater meaning in life, the first place we usually begin is through *self*-reflection, *self*-understanding, and *self*-discovery. We enter therapy, attend seminars, read *self*-help books, and do all kinds of other *self*-initiated growth activities to produce desired changes. "I feel like I've spent my whole life searching for answers," one woman summed up her quest. "I've traveled the world looking for some semblance of truth and meaning in my life and to figure out who I am. I've spent endless hours in therapy, attended universities, sought spiritual enlightenment, traveled the world, trying to find my way. It's as if I climbed a mountain, retreated to an island, or read a book, I'd know who that person really is inside my body."

Even with all her devotion and commitment to further growth, this woman felt unfulfilled. Her journey became a compulsion to find the next, best thing—the hottest self-help rage, the most challenging yoga postures, the latest best-selling book, the most remote destination. "I will tell you that I've yet to find the profound insights that I'd been looking for," she confessed, "at least as long as I focused on myself. But this year I had a breakthrough. I was traveling with a group to work on a service project in South Asia. I was sharing tea with two young girls. They didn't speak English and I didn't speak their language. But I felt this connection between us that was incredible! I realized, in that moment, that this experience wasn't about me at all but rather about giving to others. In that instant, sitting with the girls in their tiny hut, I realized more about myself while serving others than anything I've ever done to serve myself."

WHY DOES ANYONE HELP OTHERS AT GREAT PERSONAL COST?

It is an intriguing question, indeed, as to why some people would give away their hard-earned money or risk their life to save a perfect stranger. I'm not talking about "reciprocal altruism" in which, as a result of generosity, you expect something in return—status, indebtedness, or future benefit. I don't just mean philanthropists who donate a portion of their fortunes, or soldiers who fight for their friends, but rather those extraordinary cases when individuals literally sacrifice themselves to save someone they don't even know. It doesn't seem to make any sense.

On a freezing winter night in 1982, an Air Florida plane took off from Washington, D.C., and immediately crashed into a bridge and then the Potomac River, killing almost everyone on board. There were only six passengers who managed to survive, among them Arland Williams, a bank examiner who had a terrifying fear of the water.

Spectators and news crews watched helplessly as the plane began to slowly sink in the icy water. Just when all hope was lost, a rescue helicopter arrived on the scene, dropping a rope to haul up the few survivors. Williams, who had been hanging perilously onto the tail section of the plane, freezing to death, received the lifeline to attach and haul himself to safety but instead passed it on to other passengers. Five of the survivors were eventually rescued while Williams perished, voluntarily giving up his life to save others. Dubbed "The Man in the Water" (Figure 12.1), Williams' heroism inspired a song, as well as several tributes to his selfless acts: "The man in the water pitted himself against an implacable, impersonal enemy; he fought it with charity; and he held it to a standoff. He was the best we can do."[2]

We are left to wonder why anyone would do such a "crazy" thing, to give up his life for people who are not his relatives, or even his friends. There's the old formula first proposed by the geneticist J. B. S. Haldane that he'd risk his life for two siblings or eight cousins, meaning that from the perspective of maximizing the survival of our gene pool, it only makes sense to put your life at risk if enough of your genetic material will continue through direct kin.[3] From the point of view of evolutionary theory, it doesn't seem to make any sense to die without any biological reward.

But how do we explain such altruistic behavior that ultimately results in one's own demise? Although this question has driven evolutionary

Figure 12.1: When Air Florida flight 90 crashed into the Potomac River in 1982, all but six passengers were killed instantly. Five of those remaining in the freezing water were rescued through the heroic actions of a few courageous individuals who risked their own lives to save strangers. This dramatic altruistic behavior is not only the result of a biological imperative to serve the greater good of the community, but produces a number of benefits (if one survives). (Photo courtesy of Associated Press.)

biologists to distraction for many years, trying to account for voluntary self-destruction with no apparent *personal* benefit, it turns out that Nature isn't as concerned with any individual surviving as much as what might be for the greater good of the community or species. In one spectacular example that has been described as deserving an epic poem, the lowly brainworm (*Dicrocoelium dendriticum*), a parasite that lives inside a cow's intestines, is eventually excreted in feces, after which it is devoured by ants that apparently have rather undiscriminating palettes.[4] Once inside the ants, most of the brainworm is converted into cysts that eat through the ant's stomach and live happily ever after in their freedom. But one of these creatures volunteers (or is selected) to head up to the ant's brain, where it does enough damage that it forces or guides the ant to hang helplessly at the tip of a blade of grass. Guess what happens next? You got it: The grass gets eaten by a cow, after which the cycle begins anew. And this is the typical way that biologists view altruism, that one individual sacrifices itself so that others may thrive.

There are all kinds of other examples from the animal kingdom in which individual members will deliberately sacrifice themselves so that others in their communities (not necessarily relatives) will survive. Among wolves and other pack animals, a perfectly healthy, virile male will elect not to mate so that the alpha male's genes will have priority to produce the most fit offspring. When chimpanzees discover new sources of food, they will alert the rest of their troop rather than keep the prize to themselves. In other instances, a member will deliberately attract the attention of a predator so that others can escape. Squirrels and birds will do the same thing to sound an alarm, drawing certain attention from a hawk or eagle, but ultimately accepting death as the reward.

It has long been assumed that when chimpanzees engage in "prosocial behavior" it was for some instrumental purpose in the future. They will share food sources, work together for communal responsibilities, and engage in grooming tasks with peers, but all for some reciprocal favor in the future. Yet in studies that examined the motives of altruistic acts, it was discovered that in spite of their selfish and competitive nature, they would willingly offer assistance to others without any tangible reward.[5]

Among insects, sacrificial acts are even more the norm. Bees launch kamikaze missions to prevent threats to their hive or protect their queen. Termites volunteer for suicide missions to block tunnels when under attack by rivals. Why should it be so different that human animals would engage in selfless acts of kindness, generosity, or sacrifice, for some greater good? Armed services personnel risk their lives to protect their nations (but mostly squad mates). People donate their kidneys and other precious organs to help those in need. And with increasing interest, more and more people are volunteering their time to help others.

WHY PEOPLE HELP

In addition to being programmed by evolution to serve our communities, or species, there must be other benefits and rewards that accrue to those who willingly help others. There are, of course, obvious self-serving motives. One way to attain status and respect in the community is by developing a reputation as being generous. It's good for business and inflates your image. As mentioned, there is often an implicit "deal" made that if I help you now, you owe me in the future. It can be seen as a ticket to heaven in that God will open the pearly gates more readily because of this act of generosity.

On the other hand, selflessly assisting others is the most natural of human instincts. It can represent a sense of justice or fairness, which actually arises at the earliest age. Even as early as one year old, infants will offer help like retrieving objects, offering hugs of comfort, or opening cabinets without any notion that this will pay off for them in the future. They do this spontaneously as soon as they recognize they are in a position to be helpful. A number of such studies highlight the ways that altruism appears to be both naturally inborn and intrinsically rewarding.[6] People thus can experience personal satisfaction, leading to significant life changes as a result of their work serving others.

Ebenezer Scrooge Effect

There's plenty of evidence to indicate that people who are generous with their time and resources are much more likely to enjoy better health and greater happiness. They have lower blood pressure, less likelihood of depression and chronic pain, and feel greater congruence and satisfaction in their lives acting on their moral convictions. As you well know, there is a whole lot of preaching and posturing out in the world about our responsibility to help those who are less fortunate but precious little sustained action. People will make donations for the tax deductions or service awards they receive. They will begin some compassionate gesture but lose interest after a while, moving on to the next thing. They have hidden agendas to pad resumes for future jobs or seek public office.

Feelings of compassion and empathy are, themselves, intrinsically rewarding. It just feels good to know you made a difference in someone's life and this contributes to your own self-worth. It is like the "Ebenezer Scrooge effect" in that the character from Dickens' *A Christmas Carol* transforms himself from a mean, ornery, self-centered miser into a heroic, much happier person.

Helper's High

Most intriguing of all is the concept of a "helper's high."[7] This is thought to be similar to a "runner's high" in which the limbic system sends out "feel good" chemical transmitters like oxytocin and vasopressin as a reward for doing something helpful for others. This makes such gestures habit forming over time.[8] There are also associated lowered amounts of stress hormones like cortisol and epinephrine after engaging in altruistic behavior.[9] Roughly two thirds of people who engage regularly in helping activities report a number of physical sensations in their bodies, including feeling "high," increased energy and well-being, reduced discomfort, and a sense of calmness.[10]

"I feel like I'm operating in another dimension altogether," one person admits after regularly volunteering in developing countries. "I just lose myself completely. I see these kids, and my heart just goes out to them. They are so brave and they never complain. And I have so much back home, and yet I'm always thinking about what I want next. But when I'm there with them, I'm transported to a place where I have no needs except to give more of myself. I feel the chills right now just talking about it. I remember so vividly the buzz I get. Even when I'm in this pretty hairy situation and I'm just overwhelmed with what's going on around me, I have this huge grin on my face. I've never felt more alive. It's like I'm reborn every time I do this."

In a review of scientific studies that investigated altruism and benevolence, it was concluded that doing good has even greater health benefits than regular exercise in terms of reducing stress, prolonging life, improving immunity to diseases. Studies have demonstrated that when elderly people volunteered to help others as few as five hours a week, it increased their life span by 44%.[11] A similar study looking at coping strategies of those patients with chronic pain found that when they assisted others with a similar condition they experienced less pain themselves, and felt less disabled and depressed.[12] Even watching films of others doing good deeds provides a spike in antibody levels.[13]

For the Greater Good

Most communal species, humans among them, function as part of a tribe or herd. Individual needs and interests are important only because they don't compromise what is good for the majority. If our laws, moral codes, and cultural norms weren't designed to encourage fairness and justice, the organization that holds us together would fall apart. Evolution has similarly prepared us to make personal sacrifices if they result in significant benefits for the community.

It's interesting to consider the ways that bees, ants, and other insects don't really function as separate individuals but rather as part of a single organism that operates for the benefit of the unit. They "become a single animal," observed biologist Lewis Thomas, "as if they share a single thought and universal goal."[14]

There are wide variations in the extent to which cultures place an emphasis on individual versus collective needs. Western nations, for example, are well known for their tolerance of individual pursuits of freedom and prosperity. But even the United States, perhaps the most individualistic culture of all, contains within it prominent individuals such as Bill and Melinda Gates, Warren Buffett, George Soros, and many others who have achieved extraordinary wealth and chosen to redistribute it through their charitable work. They seem to do this, not because it furthers their corporate interests but, rather, because they feel a moral imperative to use what they've attained for the benefit of the larger community (Figure 12.2).

Figure 12.2: It appears to be part of human nature to feel empathy and caring for others who are suffering. This empathic arousal creates a degree of vicarious discomfort that can be reduced by either closing your eyes to the pain or else reaching out to offer help. You can't look at an image like this without feeling a strong urge to do something constructive to make a difference. (Photo courtesy of Associated Press.)

THE BENEFITS OF HELPING

Whether motivation stems from concern for the greater good, or as a result of empathic arousal, altruistic acts that are intended to help others have a number of reciprocal benefits for those who extend themselves.[15] As we've seen, helping others has been associated with many benefits, including the reduction of self-centeredness, greed, envy, and jealousy. The role of service has been universally promoted, not just to change the world, but because it does so much good for the individuals involved. It is conceived not so much as making sacrifices as actually promoting self-interest.[16] This is especially true when people are motivated by a sense of personal responsibility, moral duty, and internal choice, rather than social pressure from others.[17]

Being Part of Something Bigger Than Yourself

One thing that leads to unhappiness is the obsession with your own needs and interests. Regardless of your own personal demons and struggles, we have seen how well-being and life satisfaction are more readily achieved when we get outside ourselves and stop focusing on our problems. There are some things that you truly cannot change and other things that, at least for now, that you can't do much about. Self-pity and complaints won't change that.

Once you involve yourself actively in a greater cause, it makes your own problems pale in comparison. When you see people who can't even enjoy the most basic needs, it sure makes your own shortcomings less significant. When you see people who don't even have a pair of shoes, or who can't figure out where they're going to get their next meal, you can't help but feel grateful for what you do have rather than obsess about what is out of reach.

When you touch others with love and caring and compassion, when you get outside yourself, that is when you can sometimes reach a state of spiritual transcendence. It is as if you exist to serve others rather than only yourself. You feel a connection to the world at large, and a greater commitment to make a difference with whomever you can.

Experiencing a Parallel Process

There's much to be learned observing others struggle with issues that resonate with our own. This is the essence of vicarious learning that occurs with regularity in group therapy and other settings. It is also one of the incredible gifts that accrue to those who help others for a living. When Jon Carlson and I interviewed many of the world's greatest living theorists and practitioners, we asked them to talk about the clients who changed them the most, either personally or professionally. There were several prominent themes reflecting a parallel process of simultaneous growth.[18]

First and foremost, the therapists mentioned an empathic bond that developed between them and their most impactful clients. The felt a transcendent connection that was both special and unprecedented. They felt extraordinarily moved by the encounter in such a way that they would never forget it. In some cases, the relationship became so close at times that it was difficult to separate their own issues that were triggered from those of their clients. This was both disturbing and exhilarating, which is one reason why the experience was so memorable.

Besides the intimacy that was shared, there was also a high level of emotional arousal that was felt. This could have been a positive experience, when the therapist was moved to tears of joy or pride, or extremely negative when fear or anger were elicited. Regardless of the particular kind of emotion, if its magnitude was high, it was often unforgettable.

Therapists tend to remember those helping encounters that were out of the ordinary in some way, and that makes sense if we remember the power of any novel experience to promote change. There were times when the usual boundaries were collapsed, leading to a different kind of therapeutic relationship that might have been more informal, relaxed, and nontraditional. These eminent clinicians shared examples of taking a client to a bar to learn how to meet women, or running a marathon with a client, or disclosing more of their own lives to make the sessions more personal.

Therapists were most often changed themselves when they were witnesses to profound transformations in their clients. There was something quite extraordinary about being present when someone is undergoing a major life-altering shift. It is even more powerful when you realize that you played a significant or supporting role in these dramatic changes. It beats anything you could ever see on television or the movies because of the immediacy of the moment when you hold your breath in wonderment. It is magical, indeed, to see such changes in action and virtually impossible not to be affected in a profound way.

Not surprisingly, the final theme that emerged from our interviews is related to helpers being challenged in new ways. Just as in travel experiences, or other examples we have covered throughout the book, when you encounter something you've never seen before and are required to invent something altogether brand new in order to deal with it, you are more likely to remember that experience and learn from it.

In any effort to help others, whether as a therapist, coach, parent, teacher, friend, nurse, or volunteer, there is often a reciprocal process of influence taking place. Whereas the stated purpose of helping is to put aside our own needs in service to others, there are so many opportunities to learn and grow as a result of our participation in this fertile process that seeks to examine behavior critically and devise more effective ways to function. As long as you are paying attention, it is almost impossible to help others without also helping yourself along the way.

Gaining New Perspectives

There are a number of studies that demonstrate the power of volunteering and service to change the lives of those who work on others' behalf.[19] Those who participate in ongoing projects report that they feel a greater sense of purpose to their lives. As a result of their work in environments, and with people, they ordinarily would never encounter, they have much wider interests and expanded worldviews. They describe themselves as far more flexible than they ever thought was possible.

"Look, when you see how other people live and see what they have to do just to survive, it sure makes you think about all the crap that we whine about." This person just returned from a service trip in which he confronted all kinds of things he'd never even imagined before—that eight people in a family would live in a single room, that some people eat basically the same thing for every meal, that people can't find work no matter how hard they try, and most importantly, no matter what their deprivations they can still maintain a positive, loving, optimistic outlook and feel grateful for the few things they do have.

Twenty years of research indicates fairly clearly that when people are experiencing positive emotions, such as those that usually accompany helping activities, they are more prone to expanding their thinking in a variety of ways. This includes not only the potential for greater innovation, flexibility, and creative breakthroughs, but also the opportunity to see the "bigger picture" of their lives.[20]

Being Part of a Caring Community

Most successful service projects represent collaborations among people rather than solo efforts. There's a good reason for this because the work is so challenging and the size of the problems so huge that it literally takes a community to effect significant change. Although there are all kinds of interpersonal conflicts, political squabbles, and complex systemic dynamics that occur in any group, especially one doing such stressful work, there is also tremendous comfort and support within a caring group of people who are working together (Figure 12.3).

Figure 12.3: It's both surprising and intriguing the ways that getting outside yourself to help others actually improves your own well-being, not to mention increases life expectancy, prevents diseases, and improves general health. (Photo courtesy of istockphoto © MShep2)

"My favorite part of what we do," one person mentioned who travels to far-flung places to volunteer in schools, "are the friends I've made along the way. There was this one school in India where the teachers didn't bother to show up the days we were visiting. I guess they figured since we were there they could take a holiday or something. So we show up, and there are all these classrooms, each one filled with at least 50 kids, and they're going crazy. If you think kids back home love a substitute teacher as permission to play a bunch of games, what do you think happens when you get these subs showing up from another country who have no clue what's going on?

"Our group got together in a huddle, made a plan, and then split up to tackle each of the classrooms. I got to tell you it was hilarious. Things were so out of control in my class, all we figured out to do was play pin-the-tail-on-the-elephant. I don't know how I got through the day, or the next one, or the one after that, but the really fun part was getting together at night to share our experiences and commiserate about the situation that was so over our heads. Somehow we got through the situation and probably even did some good, but, you know, some of those people with us became my lifelong friends. It was just amazing to all be thrown in there together. I could never have done it alone."

Leaving a Legacy

It might seem peculiar to imagine that people engage in acts of service to deal with their own fears of death. Our purpose here on earth is to create someone, or something, that we leave behind, a legacy in the form of offspring, creative products, or advancement of knowledge. You hear athletes, artists, writers, or politicians speak frequently about their legacies. It's important for them to be remembered for something unique or meaningful. In one sense, we live forever as long as someone remembers us. Our spirit continues to flourish long after our physical body has left this world.

Some people find redemption through their advocacy and services. Much of the discussion thus far has been about changes experienced by an individual, yet groups are sometimes transformed in mass even if they have individualized coping responses. Such social movements have resulted in constructive attempts to turn tragedies into some benefit for the common good. These have taken the form of organizations to promote social responsibility (Physicians for Social Responsibility), restorative justice (Nuremberg Trials, Truth and Reconciliation Commission of South Africa), collaborative self-help groups (12-step programs), prevention of tragedies (Mothers Against Drunk Driving), or political action. Many of these movements began as a result of someone who felt helpless and grief stricken after a loss and decided to do something constructive to honor the loved one's memory.

Paying Something Back

Service to others doesn't always have to be the result of some moral imperative; guilt is a legitimate motive as well. Those of us who consider ourselves fortunate or privileged in some way enjoy our life situations partly as a result of effort, but also of luck that we happened to be born where we were and have access to resources that are unimaginable to others. One way to appease our consciences is by giving something back. That's why some people donate to charities or volunteer for a civic organization, but it is also why people take action on a much larger scale.

From an opposite point of view, it may very well be the suffering rather than the privileges that people experienced which leads to altruism. It is actually a myth that negative early experiences necessarily lead survivors to antisocial behavior or helpless conditions. We've seen in Chapter 6 about the opportunities presented by posttraumatic growth, and that applies equally to those who feel increased commitment and motivation to help others who are disadvantaged, suffering, or oppressed. Labeled as "altruism born of suffering," this phenomenon describes people who have been abused, neglected, tortured, imprisoned, or persecuted, and find themselves even more strongly motivated to help others as a result of their trauma.[21] They were helped to recover from their difficulties and feel sufficient gratitude that they want to pass along what they learned. It also gives their lives greater meaning to feel that what they went through was somehow worth it if they can make a positive contribution.

Taking a Stand for Social Justice and Advocacy

There are all kinds of injustices and inequities in the world. Some people are victims of oppression or genocide. Thousands of children are starving to death every day. Thousands more are forced into sex trafficking or other forms of slavery. Many communities around the world don't have safe water to drink. Violence and wars are a continual threat to safety. There are many places where there is no access to medical care whatsoever, and others where diseases are out of control.

It doesn't matter what the cause or injustice, whether the result of poverty, racism, sexism, prejudice, or oppression of minority groups, but each of us has some important issue that matters to us, some problem that we would like to help eradicate, even if just a modest effort. Many people find that advocating on behalf of a neglected or disadvantaged group helps redeem their own lives.

"I do this not just for the children I teach," remarked one woman who volunteers to work in schools in Haiti a few times each year, "but for myself." It is one of the highlights of her already full life, but she feels that her commitment to work in areas of poverty and neglect are important to show her own children what a life of service really means. Already, as a family, they take their "vacations" building houses in Central America or teaching in Haiti.

People get involved in social justice in different ways. They might seek to challenge systemic inequities within their organizations or communities, trying to change the status quo. They try to transform social institutions (schools, agencies, government institutions) that are neglectful or inefficient. They work on behalf of marginalized groups to give them a voice. They bring attention to issues that they consider important, especially those that limit access to resources for anyone who might require help. They speak out on behalf of those who have been denied rights. And their deeds follow their words: they volunteer their time and energy to make a difference where they can.

SERVICE IN ACTION

Imagine, if you will, that you are in a remote village somewhere in the world. You learn that young girls are "disappearing" and so question the school principal about what is going on. He shrugs and tells you that some families are so poor that they have no choice but to keep their girls at home where the lucky ones are forced into early marriage by age 12—and those not so "fortunate" end up sold, kidnapped, or tricked into sex slavery, smuggled across the border into India where they will end up raped 15–20 times per day and eventually die of HIV within a few years. This may be one of the most horrific tales you've ever heard, but so far it is just a story among all the tragic, inhumane injustices around the world. But, what if this principal standing next to you points to a young girl talking to her friends and tells you that she will be "disappeared" next? What would you do then?

What if you asked the principal what it would take to keep this little girl in school and away from harm, and he told you that it would cost $50? What if you reached into your pocket impulsively and gave the principal the money to save this girl's life and then learned that unless you were prepared to revisit this village and check on this girl, she and the money would likely disappear? *Then* what would you do?

It wasn't courage or nobility or altruism that led me on this path. Since I don't subscribe to luck or fate, I believe that my present course is the logical consequence of a life spent taking risks, acting impulsively, and trying to do the most good that I can in the limited time I am allotted. And that is why, so many years later, I now find myself somewhere in the Himalayan foothills, three planes, a bus ride, and long walk, mostly uphill, to this ridge where I'm walking with a group of volunteers and the dozens of the scholarship children we support.

In this moment I'm just resting on a rock, trying to catch my breath in the thin, cold air. For the past half hour we have been snaking our way up a narrow trail leading to a *stupa*, a Buddhist shrine, perched high over a Himalayan village. I turn and look downward, noticing with relief that I'm not the only one who stopped to rest: there are 55 girls strung out behind and ahead of me, the youngest 10 years old and the eldest in her late teens. They have all been transported here from their villages across Nepal, each of them supported by a scholarship to keep them in school.

I wonder what I'm really doing here? My first thought is that I'm hiding from my responsibilities back home, or maybe hiding from myself. But no, that's not it. I've been ready for a change in my professional life for some time. Throughout my career I've periodically felt stale doing therapy, tired of hearing my same old anecdotes and stories, but I've managed to revitalize myself by reinventing how I work every few years. I've felt trapped by my routines, stuck in the template that has become my life. And lately I've felt more and more like a hypocrite as I urge my clients and students (and readers) to take new risks to nourish and stimulate their lives. It's getting harder to live with myself when I realize that whatever time I have left is passing me by at a pace that is more than a little disturbing.

There's one other thought that bothers me as I sit idly on this rock catching my breath—as important as my work is back home seeing clients, teaching therapists, writing about change—more and more it feels like I'm replaceable, that there are so many others who could—and can—do what I do. But I look at these children surrounding me on this mountain, all waiting for direction about where we are going next, and I wonder where they would be without our support?

As I've done every year during the past 15 years, I've brought a team of volunteers with me to rescue and support girls who would otherwise have no chance at survival (Figure 12.4). We have spent the prior week conducting home visits, consulting with parents and teachers,

Figure 12.4: Neglected girls in Nepal who are receiving scholarships, mentoring, and support from generous volunteers at www.empowernepaligirls.org. (Photo courtesy of author.)

awarding new scholarships, providing supplies and resources for the children. We have been mentoring and helping them to support one another given the challenges they face from poverty, catastrophic illness in their families, and often a parent who abandoned them. For many of the girls, this is the first time they've ever left their villages; some traveled for three days to arrive at our location, huffing and puffing as we climb the steep incline.

As I try to breathe deeply and gather my energy for the climb to the summit, I think about the morning's activities. We had arranged the girls in small groups, each from a different village. They had been asked to share something in their lives about which they felt pride, as well as some difficult struggle they were facing. Since most of the girls are from the "untouchable" caste, it was not surprising that many shared economic hardships. Most of them lived in small huts in which their families slept together on the floor. I also knew well about the challenges they faced as girls in a country in which women have few opportunities for advancement, especially living in such remote areas. But I was surprised by how many of the girls had lost parents, some from disease, many from abandonment, and one father was eaten by a tiger! Others had parents who were alcoholics or incapacitated. As they were telling their stories, the girls were trying to hold back tears. Me, too. I was just so amazed by their courage and resilience.

We are here supposedly to help these children, but they have done so much for me. Many of them, and their families, are so poor they don't even have shoes. They have nothing, and expect nothing, yet appear to accept their fate with cheerfulness and joy; maybe the next life will be better. As for me? I come to Nepal each year not only to help these children, but also to help myself. It is when I'm here that I feel most alive. And at least for the few months after I return, I feel clear about what is most important to me, none of which includes ambition and materialism. Ah, if only the effects would last!

I am at a crossroads, quite literally, as the trail we are following splits in two directions, but also in my life. I wonder whether it is truly within my power to refashion my life in the ways I preach to others? With the perception of limited time that comes with aging, I'm asking myself more and more often what I want to do with the opportunities I have left. More often than not, the answer I hear in my heart is that my life is most redeemed when I extend myself to others.

I walk behind the girls in front of me, creating some distance and privacy because I feel myself losing control: I start to sob in a hoarse voice I barely recognize as my own. I am scaring myself with the raw power of the emotions I am feeling. I've done a lot of good things in my life. I've helped a lot of people as a therapist or teacher or supervisor. I look for opportunities every chance I get to help little old ladies cross the street, lost tourists to find their destinations, or anyone else I meet to find what they're looking for. But of everything I've ever done, nothing seems to come close to what I can do to help a young girl to survive by providing such minimal financial and emotional support.

After an experience like this, how do I ever go back to my life back home and expect to be the same? I've spent half of the last year traveling around the world working on service projects. I've told myself I could never afford to do something like this. I remember when I was a much younger man I met a woman who told me she was taking a year off to travel around the world. When I remarked how lucky she was to do that she became furious. "Are you freaking kidding me?" she screamed. "Do you know what I used to do for a living? I was a secretary barely making minimum wage. But I quit my job, sold all my stuff, and invested all my savings in this adventure. *Anyone* can do this if they are willing to pay the price."

That scolding has always haunted me. Whereas I have never had much interest in traveling around the world for its own sake, I've always fantasized what it would be like to buy out some of my time so I could work in regions of the world where they need help the most. What stops me from doing that except my own imposed limits?

It's been just a few months since I returned from Nepal. I lost so much weight that none of my clothes fit and I walk around in a daze. I am haunted by what I've witnessed and sometimes begin crying uncontrollably for reasons I don't understand. I think constantly about the hundreds of girls we support, wondering how they're doing throughout the year until I visit again. I feel so helpless and frustrated that we can't help more of them. But there is nothing I've ever done that feels more satisfying—and more challenging. And here's the most important part for me: I know I'm making a difference! Each year I see these girls grow into poised young women who have dreams and opportunities for education and professional careers. They want to be teachers and doctors and engineers, the first girls in their village to ever receive higher education. They are learning things they never knew were possible—and so am I!

I thrive on new stimulation and challenges, all the while I complain about how difficult and annoying they are. I feel better about myself when I encounter people who have so much less—and I'm talking about children in the Himalayas who don't even have shoes! When I return from the field, I feel this ecstatic transformation, which, unfortunately, only lasts a few months before I feel my familiar materialistic, ambitious stirrings once again. I like that when I'm working in such difficult, challenging, overwhelming situations I can forget about myself and my own troubles.

When I own my personal motives for doing this sort of work I could go on and on about feeling smug and superior, feeling like a martyr, escaping from the mundane aspects of my life, hiding from issues I'd rather avoid, having an excuse to travel, and having access to the forbidden or exotic that few outsiders have ever witnessed.

But most of all, I so hunger for the intimacy and caring I experience with my team members, the parenting role I enjoy with the hundreds of children, and the close relationships that develop over time. It is so much fun to commiserate with our team members about the difficulties we faced, bitch and moan about the annoyances we encounter (squat toilets, limited food choices, armed Maoist rebels, traffic jams, fuel and electricity shortages, garbage strikes, incomprehensible cultural rituals). I love what I learn about the world—and what I learn about myself.

So I keep trying to reinvent myself—not so much to improve my effectiveness as to entertain myself. I just so crave creative expression and opportunities to do things differently than I've ever encountered before. I see my clients and students making exciting changes in their lives and I want some of that, too!

Throughout all the investigations and writing I've done throughout my career, I've been wrestling with the ultimate question that is the focus of this book: What *really* makes a difference in the lives of those who require help? There are all kinds of answers to this question, depending on your orientation, professional context, and personal style. But ultimately there is this amazing collaboration that takes place with those we help, whoever they might be. They become our teachers—not just about improving the effectiveness of our interventions but also about those things that matter most in our own lives. I love the fact that I've chosen a profession that allows me to learn so much—requires me to grow so much—every day. And yet as great as those benefits are, I find them magnified ten-fold when working in the field. I even like the idea that I'm *not* being paid for my efforts, that it is truly an act of love.

"MY LIFE IS MY MESSAGE"

There is a story told of Mahatma Gandhi, who was hurrying to catch a train when he was approached by someone who begged for a spiritual message that he could spread to his friends and relatives back in his village. Although distracted and rushed, Gandhi took the time to write down a brief message on a piece of paper, folded it, and handed it to the man as he boarded the train. Watching the train depart the station, the villager opened the paper to read, "My life is my message."[22]

Indeed.

In what has been described as "ordinary grace," there are several common elements that characterize those who give of themselves without concern for personal benefit and thereby enjoy greater meaning and satisfaction in their lives.[23] There is no predictable demographic that describes those who are most likely to be altruistic and devote themselves to service as a life priority. They are both rich and poor, privileged and disadvantaged. Some have suffered terribly and want to help those who share this plight; others have been sheltered from most of life's discomforts but still feel a responsibility, if not an obligation, to make a difference.

First, those whose lives are their messages feel a deep connection to the human race. They don't see themselves exclusively as a member of their own family, religion, ethnic group, or "tribe" but, rather, feel a strong identification with others from around the world. They have unwavering faith in the goodness of people, even with anomalies that show up with manifestations of evil. They don't view that helping people, or extending themselves, is much of a sacrifice—even with the very real challenges, difficulties, and discomforts that are part of service. Instead, they view helping others as a privilege that offers its own gifts. Their actions are often not planned or premeditated but arise in the moment when a need is recognized and they are in a position to do something useful. And has already made clear, those who practice compassion, caring, and ordinary grace as a way of being enjoy a life with greater meaning, joy, and satisfaction. They not only live longer, in better health, but feel a greater sense of appreciation and awe for everything around them.

CHAPTER 13

Soliciting Support and Resolving Conflicts in Relationships

I saved the most difficult subject for the end. If, as we've seen, that relationships are the foundation for recovering from trauma, preventing stress, and increasing well-being and happiness, as well as initiating and maintaining changes, then their rupture is among the most serious of obstacles. We spend a significant part of our waking lives worrying about family, ruminating over perceived slights by friends, recovering from abuse or hurt that occurred in the past, navigating complex interpersonal issues with coworkers, avoiding awkward situations with strangers, and always looking for greater intimacy without the corresponding anguish that is common during squabbles, disagreements, and misunderstandings. If relational connections are the sustenance of life, then they are also the scourges that can make us utterly miserable.

Any changes that are initiated and actually maintained over time require some kind of ongoing assistance from family, friends, and coworkers. Without such support it is almost impossible to keep momentum and morale at high levels. In those cases in which there is active conflict or disengagement with loved ones, the prognosis for success is pretty dismal unless steps are taken to resolve the issues or at least take constructive action to minimize the collateral damage.

MOST CHANGES TAKE PLACE IN
A RELATIONAL CONTEXT

Bibi and Poldi had been married for more years than they could remember. They'd been through hard times when just getting through the days was difficult, and they'd enjoyed plenty of good times by each other's sides. But lately things had gone from bad to worse. The couple would barely speak to one another, and when they did decide to acknowledge one another they could be heard arguing constantly. The last straw occurred when their verbal skirmishes turned into physical abuse. Bibi, who was somewhat larger than her husband, viciously attacked him, causing serious injury.

Finally, they were mandated to attend counseling, and a professional attempted to help them sort out their disagreements. After 36 years together, it seemed a shame that their current conflicts would end their marriage. The counselor tried bonding and communication exercises, arranged for them to enjoy romantic meals together, and urged them to change their patterns of interaction, all without success.

After almost four decades together, Bibi and Poldi, two giant tortoises who were both 115 years old and living in an Austrian zoo, called it quits. They just couldn't stand living together any longer and had to be separated in different cages. Now I'm not saying that the interpersonal conflicts between two reptiles necessarily has all that much to do with intractable human squabbles, but it does illustrate the ways in which some disagreements escalate to the point that it seems impossible to alter the patterns, even with professional help. In fact, there's nothing that dooms a relationship more definitively than high-intensity, chronic conflicts that manifest hostility and overt contempt.[1]

If you think about the changes you'd like to make in your own relationship landscape, they would likely take place in several different contexts:

1. Changing the patterns of those that are frustrating, unsatisfying, or unfulfilling
2. Setting boundaries for relationships that aren't meeting your needs or are taking a bite out of your soul

3. Reducing the level and intensity of conflicts with others, especially those locked into repetitive patterns
4. Ending relationships that don't seem amenable to necessary changes
5. Enhancing intimacy with friends and loved ones
6. Feeling and expressing more love and caring in current relationships
7. Initiating and broadening new relationships that meet interests and needs that are currently unsatisfied
8. Experiencing more authentic, caring, honest, respectful, and fun exchanges with people on a daily basis
9. Processing and recovering from perceived slights and relational difficulties in the past
10. Practicing forgiveness to let some things go and move forward without lingering resentment
11. Learning from past mistakes, misjudgments, and relationship breaches in order to enhance future connections

That's quite a basketful of work, given that almost every week, if not on a daily basis, you encounter some sort of relationship problem that plagues you. Your boss rudely tells you to do something without the slightest concern for your overloaded schedule. A family member ignites a familiar argument that you've already lived through a hundred times. A supposed friend is talking behind your back. Another always talks and never listens. You get a text from someone who strikes you as catty or insensitive. You send a message and the person doesn't bother to respond at all, leaving you wondering what the heck is going on. A person bumps you on the street and then gives you a dirty look as if it's all *your* fault. A driver runs a stop sign, almost hitting you, and then gives you the finger. Then of a far more serious nature, there is ongoing tension and an uneasy truce with your spouse or partner. You are fighting a lot with a child or parent, without any sign that things are going to get better soon. You feel frustrated because of the superficiality of so many of your relationships or else feel just plain lonely because there are so few meaningful connections in your life.

From this brief listing of only a few possibilities, it's fairly clear that when you are experiencing relationship conflicts in your life it's difficult to feel good about most anything else. Making changes in those patterns is especially difficult because a lot of the issues aren't completely within your control.

REVISITING THE PAST

Although it is frequently said that if you can't remember the past, you are doomed to repeat it, the opposite is also true: if you can't let go of the past, you will keep reliving it. The problem with conflicts is that they are often not related to what appears to be happening in the present—the argument about which movie to see, the feud over whose turn it is to wash the dishes, the disagreement about who really said what and who started the damn fight in the first place. Often such conflicts are reenactments of unresolved struggles, some of which are not only continuations of what happened months or years previously but also sometimes generations in the making. Think Cain and Abel, Mary Queen of Scots and Elizabeth I, or the Hatfields and the McCoys.

It's especially challenging to resolve issues that are so integrally linked to the past. Memories become distorted. Resentments build over time. Little slights get blown way out of proportion. Scorecards keep track of who did what and whose fault it was. Heated conversations sound ridiculous to observers who can't make sense of why people are fighting over such seemingly inconsequential matters like who was the last person to take out the trash, or who is most responsible for dinner being late or an assignment not fully completed. As such, in order to work through interpersonal difficulties it's often important to revisit the past.[2]

An interesting question to consider is what the *real* issues are at the core of a fight or ongoing conflict. As mentioned, it's often not about the issue at hand but connected more deeply to something that occurred previously, either with this same antagonist, or further in the past in another situation that triggers a negative memory. In that respect there are several common themes that may be related.[3]

Historical Legacy

Each of us inherits a history that is part of our culture and family of origin. It isn't all that surprising to find that the same interpersonal struggles that confronted grandparents and parents are passed on to their own children and reenacted in similar ways. This is a pattern that has been observed in a lot of family dynamics and is a routine part of the assessment that takes place during therapy when the question is posed: "How does this strike you as familiar in terms of what you witnessed growing up?"

Unresolved Issues With Authority Figures

Sometime in our lives, each of us was subjected to perceived abuse or oppression at the hands of others who wielded power unjustly. We carry within us the resentments and anger from these experiences, and sometimes those feelings seep out at unexpected moments. We sometimes react to people not as they are in the moment but, rather, as we distort them and turn them into antagonists from the past.

Hunger for Freedom

Nobody wants their freedom of choices limited or their options blocked as a result of some rule or tradition that was established some time in the past without our consent or agreement. This is especially the case when the particular limitation is not one that we subscribe to or even makes sense to us. After all, there are still laws and moral imperatives on the books that were devised eons ago when the world was a very different place. It makes sense there would be times when you would feel a strong urge to be able to act outside the rigidly drawn lines of what is considered appropriate.

Fears of Intimacy

Most anyone who has ever felt devastated by betrayal, or who is still licking wounds from a relationship that ended poorly, or who has been neglected or abused, is going to have some justifiable hesitation about trusting others. Conflict is sometimes "used" in such circumstances as a way to maintain distance and safety. If you examine the peculiar times and situations when people fight, when it doesn't seem to make any sense, it is often because one or both parties are unknowingly protecting him or herself.

Pattern of Enmeshment

Codependency in a relationship creates all kinds of interesting problems that have been programmed in the past. One person feels a strong need to be protected while the other takes on the role of protector. Other family or systems dynamics develop in the past in which it's difficult to sort out where one person begins or the other ends. While all the parties may claim that everything is just peachy the way it is, there are occasionally expressions of independence or self-assertion that will trigger all kinds of protective responses to keep the pattern intact.

HOW CONFLICTS ARE HELPFUL

Before you can hope to change the nature of conflicts, or prevent them from occurring in the future, you first have to understand what useful purposes they may be serving you. We talked about this idea previously in the context of secondary gains that "reward" people for remaining the same. Sometimes these patterns that are most resistant to change are precisely those that are functional to you in some way even if that seems peculiar. After all, who enjoys fighting with people?

You'd be surprised.

Preparing Readiness

Every time Cal and Marti are just on the verge of settling their disputes and finally picking a date for their wedding, one or the other of them (they actually seem to take turns!) fabricates some rigid position from which they won't budge. First it was agreeing on a wedding date, then a drag-out fight about whether the ceremony should take place in a church or park, followed by a prolonged battle about the invitation list. One would justifiably wonder whether they should remain together in the first place, given their passionate arguments over everything related to their wedding. The funny thing is that they never had these kinds of conflicts until they become engaged.

Funny, indeed. So the question to ask is: what are these fights doing for them that is useful? What if both of them were extremely apprehensive about the commitment involved in their marriage? What if they felt pushed by family members to proceed with the nuptials before they felt ready? What if Cal had long-standing concerns about whether he was even fit for marriage considering problems he had maintaining long-term relationships in the past? What if Marti had once been betrayed by a previous partner and feared it might happen again? Under such circumstances, it would seem that the ongoing conflicts between them were actually quite useful in stalling and slowing down their plans until such time that they could (hopefully) become more comfortable with them.

Attracting Attention to Issues That Have Been Ignored

As can be seen in the case of Cal and Marti, conflicts sometimes emerge as a way to bring your attention to issues that you have long been ignoring. As is often the case with annoying symptoms, they are designed to let you know that things aren't working properly. They can sometimes be "gifts" of a sort in that they keep the pressure on until such time that you make needed changes.

If conflicts persist over time, or even become worse, it is because you've been ignoring things that must be addressed. If you are absolutely miserable at work because your boss is unreasonable, if not abusive, and you continue to subject yourself to this stressful situation, increased conflicts will turn up the heat sufficiently that you have to do something differently. That could involve changing the way you deal with your boss, or the way you process the experiences internally, or it could mean something more radical such as a direct confrontation, initiating a rebellion, consulting with advocates, or even quitting and starting over. But regardless, the conflicts may escalate until such time that you do something constructive to alleviate the underlying problem.

Releasing Tension

You have to admit that conflicts make life exciting, perhaps not in a way that you'd prefer, but nevertheless they do create a certain amount of drama. They also let off steam, like a pressure valve, even if the negative repercussions linger for some time.

Temper tantrums, screaming matches, and emotional explosions are satisfying for some people, especially those who have the remarkable ability to recover immediately afterward with no apparent signs of distress. Sometimes they enjoy the ways they can intimidate others, but for some people they just feel a sense of release after a "good" argument, which presumably means one that ends well.

The stress from conflicts can be extremely toxic as we've already covered extensively in Chapter 10. Yet there's some evidence that the worst possible outcomes for those involved in quarrels are when they can't seem to let them go and they lose sleep over them, producing all kinds of health-related problems as well as affecting mood and functioning for days afterward.[4]

Promoting Reflection and Growth

Just as it is true for most any situation in life that is challenging, conflicts often provoke significant learning and growth. After all, you can't help but reflect on what's going on, what your own role in the trouble has been, and what you might do differently. It is just as interesting to think about how this particular incident is similar to others during previous times and contexts and how this might relate to other patterns.

Conflict, by definition, means that what you normally do to resolve interpersonal issues is not working. This requires you to stretch yourself in new ways, to rethink the ways you respond to people and situations, and hopefully, to devise ways to broaden your behavioral options. Once you can work through a conflict successfully, you are better equipped to deal with similar encounters in the future.

"I let myself by terrorized by a department head for years," reveals Mika, a petite woman in her thirties. "The guy just scared the crap out of me. He was a bully, and a mean one at that. I tried over and over to just ignore the jerk's actions as much as I could. I would keep my head down and try to ignore him as much as possible. I'd stand by and watch on the sidelines when he was so cruel and vindictive toward others. When he'd attack me, I'd just swallow my pride and take it…until I couldn't any longer. Not one more friggin' minute!"

Mika takes a deep breath to compose herself. Even after all these years, she can feel the tears coming when she thinks about how long she suffered. It was some small consolation that there were so many others in a similar predicament: "First, I went to the head of the whole unit and told him what was going on. I had detailed notes with lots of supporting evidence, so there's no way he could ignore me. I'd also lined up others who agreed with that I was saying. It was like I was starting a revolution."

Mika laughs at this, but with a nervous tinge. It's obvious that although she's proud she took action, it was not something that she did willingly until she felt like there was no other choice: "The next time that guy [her boss] got in my face, I just let him have it right back. It's like all those years of frustration and anger were bottled up inside me and they just all exploded at once. I could see how shocked others were—and you better believe they could hear me bellowing right back at the a-hole. And here's the funny thing: he just sat there and took it with his mouth clamped shut. I'm guessing that the head guy had already talked to him and let him know he was being watched."

What Mika learned from this experience, asserting herself and standing up to abuse and injustice, had far greater implications than merely protecting herself at work. You wouldn't be surprised to learn that she was somewhat submissive and complacent in almost all her relationships, allowing others to take advantage of her and push her around. But a line had been crossed when she stood up for herself (and others) in the office. She felt proud of what she had done and received a lot of support and respect from her coworkers. After this first glimpse of her power, she was able to take what she learned and apply it other areas of her life.

FIXING CONFLICTS—OR LEARNING TO LIVE WITH THEM

There are all kinds of simplistic advice offered in popular magazines, most of it logical and sound but little of it actually helpful. Change yourself since you can't change anyone else. Don't let people push your buttons. Look at the best parts of the relationship instead of focusing on the annoying parts. Don't blow things out of proportion and keep them in perspective. Don't keep doing the same things that aren't working over and over. Disengage from conflict when you feel yourself becoming upset. Avoid power struggles. Choose your battles carefully. Stay true to yourself. Give people a chance, but not more than three strikes before you walk away.

It all makes perfect sense, right? If only it were that easy.

The main problem isn't only related to the conflicts you face but, rather, their repetitious nature without resolution, accompanied by ongoing perseveration. Whether you can actually ever resolve an ongoing struggle or not, recovery from the chronic tension is critical. The extent to which people can "cool down" after a disagreement is one of the best predictors of a stable and satisfying relationship.[5] Likewise, the inability to disengage from uncomfortable interactions also spells serious trouble in the future, especially when things escalate at inappropriate times and places such as public settings, when others are present, or when participants are fatigued or preoccupied.[6]

A process of self-regulation is required that allows people to let go of what is bothersome, at least until the timing and context is more conducive to civil and respectful negotiations. This involves setting and enforcing boundaries and utilizing self-talk strategies to decompress and calm down.[7] It also means resisting the urge to start up the unsatisfying interaction once again when the repeated outcome is virtually certain.

After all, it is curious that one of the most difficult things for people to do is to *stop* doing what they are already doing that clearly hasn't been working. Until ineffective behaviors are blocked, it isn't possible to experiment with other options that will likely be far more useful and constructive. Earlier in the book, I presented a case of a belligerent adolescent who challenged her parent, and the conflict became intractable because of their stubborn pattern that kept repeating itself. This sort of thing happens frequently whenever you try to make a point or present an argument, encounter resistance, and yet persist in pressing onward rather than changing tack in a different direction.

Whereas you don't know what *might* work to get through to this person, you have pretty compelling evidence that what you are already doing will *never* work, even though you persist in the face of clear data. That is one factor that contributes to chronic conflicts: we keep relying on the same strategies that are proven worthless. Until such time that you can step back and stop doing what is not working (after three or four tries), it's time to try something else, *anything* other than what you are already doing. This could mean changing your position or agreeing with the other person to see what would happen. It could involve changing your tone or voice, your style or manner. It could mean bringing in humor or a distraction. It could involve changing direction and appealing to reason instead of emotion, or doing just the opposite. It could also mean just giving up and realizing that you aren't going to get what you want, so it's time to move on. Probably most useful of all would mean getting outside of yourself long enough to imagine what the other person is feeling and thinking, and why things have gotten so out of control.

Surrendering Blame

It sure feels good to find fault with someone else when things aren't going well. Absolved from responsibility for your misery, at least you can take comfort in the belief that you are a victim of someone else's awful behavior. This was exactly what April was thinking after her boyfriend ended their relationship in order to "find himself." It was particularly devastating for her because this was her first long-term relationship. She felt abandoned, betrayed, grief stricken, and angry, more so after she discovered he'd been seeing someone else: "I couldn't figure out how someone I loved and trusted so much could break my heart and cause me so much pain. I was so confused because I still loved him all the while I hated him. I blamed him for everything. He was the one who ruined everything. He was the perpetrator, which in turn, made me the victim. And I didn't like that one bit."

April and her boyfriend had engaged in an ongoing conflict for months prior to their final breakup. Things became progressively more tense and awkward, and April felt more and more depressed, until she decided to stop being a victim: "I realized that I needed to think about what I do have in my life, instead of what I don't have, like the boyfriend I once loved. It wasn't doing me much good to blame him for everything that happened; even if it was mostly his fault, that wasn't helping me much. I've learned to appreciate the love I have in my other relationships with friends and family."

April was able to change the nature of the conflict from "us" or "him" to herself: "I realize now that this was more about me and my feelings. The only way I could let go and move on was to practice forgiveness instead of blame. I understand that people make mistakes and do bad things, but I still have to free myself from bitterness and negativity that is eating me alive."

April acknowledges she's still got a lot of work yet to do, but she feels so much better when she's able to let go of her resentments and anger. Sure, it feels good to think that she had done nothing wrong, but that doesn't help much when she considers some day being in another relationship. Her sense of control and peace comes from being able to accept the situation, even if she didn't much like it, and try to do some things differently in the future.

There are also dangers, of course, in unilateral forgiveness in that you can become a doormat for others to take advantage of you and then expect absolution—so they can do it again.[8] When a valuable relationship is recovered as a result of forgiveness, then it is clearly worth the effort. In addition, there's considerable evidence that forgiving a transgressor or antagonist is a significant part of reducing depression, stress, and helplessness.[9] It helps significantly to let go of resentments that are eating you up inside.

It Really *Is* About You

So often the ways we describe conflicts are in terms of what other people are doing that we find so abhorrent or difficult. It's the idea that if only *they* would stop doing things that are hurtful or annoying to us then everything would be fine. If only they would be more like us.

Stop nodding your head in agreement because it's not going to happen.

The first line of attack in any conflict situation is usually to try to change other people. This ordinarily doesn't work out very well because they are perfectly happy the way they are: Their problem is *you*.

The only real power we have to at least try to change others' behavior is related to our own children when they are young—and even that doesn't always work out the way we'd prefer. Otherwise, any continued focus on trying to get others to act differently, just because you don't like it, is often futile. That doesn't mean that you shouldn't try, but you'd better have some other options available when that doesn't work very well. And the next place to begin is with yourself. The good news is that you really do have tremendous power to change many aspects of yourself, including the ways you frame the conflict in the first place.

For as long as she can remember, Kristi has been stressed out by her mother. Her parents divorced when she was an infant, and with her father gone, Kristi eventually grew into the role of her mother's caretaker. Her mother became severely depressed after the divorce and relied on alcohol as her main coping strategy. Kristi then took on the job of being her mother's caretaker, believing that without such dedicated help there's no way her mother could possibly survive: "That was my job until I turned 18. I've spent more than half my life in therapy trying to come to terms with this crazy, codependent relationship. I've been trying to give up responsibility for her welfare, but how do you do that when you've been recruited, trained, and programmed your whole life? How do you let go when you are used to hosting your own birthday party since you are five because your mother is passed out in the bedroom?"

Recently, things between Kristi and her mother have become much worse. Her mother is showing early signs of dementia and other health problems from the chronic drinking. Her memory is shot, and she keeps falling and injuring herself. It has fallen on Kristi to take care of her and try to keep her safe even if these actions are never appreciated and are rarely successful: "My mother has rarely followed any of my suggestions or done anything I tell her to do. She completely ignores me. So many times I tried to get her to stop drinking and always failed. She was drunk and out of control at my wedding, and I felt like an eight-year-old carrying her to bed and tucking her in."

Many family members have told Kristi that she is not her mother's parent, nor is she responsible for her. And even if she were in charge, she's been singularly ineffective considering that all her complaining, cajoling, and arguing have had no appreciable effect. She'd been told over and over again, as well as observed herself, that her helpful efforts only seem to make things worse. Her mother doesn't want her help, nor does she ever respond graciously to it. You'd think Kristi would have realized this after so many years, but they've been locked into this struggle for decades. And that's what makes it so easy for Kristi to blame her mother for all these problems. It occurred to her to wonder why, if her mother really didn't want her advice or help, she was so focused on giving it? "That's when I realized that all this time I had been doing it for *me*," she explained. "When I was a child, it was all about self-preservation. I had to keep her sober and alive to keep me safe and alive. Over time this became my identity and reason for being. All those years in therapy, all the tears and struggle, prepared me for the moment when I truly listened and heard my mother absolving me of the responsibility. Really, I was absolving myself, but the point is that I was able to step back and make a change because I truly listened to what she was trying to communicate to me (and probably had been for a long time). I didn't want to have this codependent relationship, so I stopped engaging in it. I let it go. I gave myself permission to let it go because I realized that my behavior wasn't serving her and it certainly wasn't serving me."

This is another example of the kind of insight or moment of clarity discussed in Chapter 9 that can change *everything*.

When You Have to Protect Yourself

Conflicts basically involve two types, those composed of combatants who are of roughly equal status and power, and more commonly, those in which there is a distinct inequity. It is in this latter case that rights are most often ignored or abused and people are exploited, especially when they don't feel safe standing up for themselves because of a fear of consequences. Whether you like it or not, there are people in the world who live by very different rules, either from a sense of entitlement or psychopathy. They just don't flat out care what you or anyone else thinks, as long as they get what they want. They have no sense of conscience when it comes to exploiting or manipulating others since they believe they are special and much better than you.

In school these individuals were bullies who enjoyed provoking and controlling others they perceived as weaker and less worthy. As they grew into adults, their methods of dominating others became more sophisticated and complex. They aspire to positions of power. They gravitate toward politics or other opportunities that feed their narcissism and self-centeredness. And, alas, they actually enjoy being in conflict with others since they seem to have developed an immunity to wounds (remember, they don't care what others think) and like the feelings of power that comes with knowing they've gotten under others' skin.

If you have the misfortune to be stuck with individuals like this in your world, you don't have the option of just making the best of the situation because they will interpret that as weakness to be exploited further. And when I'm speaking of "they," I am drastically overgeneralizing since difficult people come in so many different forms, not all of them universally distressing. Nevertheless, there are some common configurations. There is the person who challenges your sense of competence, undermining and criticizing you at every possible opportunity. There's the aggressive or hostile bully that I profiled earlier. The whiner or complainer is not satisfied no matter what you do and how you try to provide accommodations. There's the person who is passive aggressive, smiling and friendly to your face but doing whatever possible to hurt you behind your back.

Patricia has been struggling with her father most of her life. She describes him as "a man who has been blessed with everything and appreciates nothing. He is an arrogant man who views himself as wise. He is both racist and religiously biased. He treats everyone as though they are beneath him. In brief, he is a representation of everything that I despise."

It was especially difficult for Patricia watching the way her father treated her mother and siblings while they were growing up: "My father's yelling and belittling his wife and children in public has always been the norm and brings him a sick sense of pleasure. He has refused to financially support his children because he said he never wanted us in the first place. We were an embarrassment to him and the objects of his criticism and constant ridicule. He would constantly mock me and call me names. It was unbearable."

Perhaps not surprisingly, Patricia has had difficulty in her relationships with other men throughout her life as a direct result of the conflicts with her father. She has come to resent her own culture because of the macho crap that her father constantly unloaded on all of them, using his background as an excuse to be so cruel. But here's the thing: 15 years have now passed since she moved out of the house, and things now feel very different to her: "Of course, my father is still the same man. Nothing has changed. If anything, he's worse than ever. He hasn't worked in a long time and he's become increasingly bitter. He has more time to hate and criticize everyone."

What's different, however, is that Patricia has changed a lot to protect herself and come to terms with this man who has been such an ongoing source of conflict in her life: "I just don't expect anything from him. No matter how much I cry and beg, he'll never be any different. I realize how insecure and troubled he is. That doesn't mean I allow him to treat me poorly anymore, but it helps me to understand and forgive him for being the way he is. I feel so much more control and strength knowing that he can't hurt me anymore."

And Sometimes You Have to Fight Back

Another variation of this theme related to difficult people who aren't "trainable" is described by another woman who has continuous trouble with her mother-in-law, who neither respects her, nor treats her with a modicum of kindness. "Even when I first started dating my husband, she would ignore me," Melissa remembered. "Right in front of me, she'd start talking about my husband's old girlfriends and how great they were. She'd make fun of my son and compare him to other boys his age. I really had reservations even going through the wedding because this lady was such a witch."

The mother-in-law turned up late for the wedding and wouldn't even pretend to be civil, her disapproval on display for anyone to notice. Melissa just shakes her head in astonishment: "I just loathe being around my husband's mother, even for a few minutes. I've tried so often to extend invitations to her, but she does nothing but try to embarrass me in front of my family and friends. There are times when I've had to ask my husband to keep a muzzle on her, not that she would ever listen. I tell you, the woman is downright evil."

Finally, Melissa decided that enough was enough: "I was tired of living in terror of this woman and allowing her to ruin my life. I never did anything to her, so there's no reason for her to be so rude all the time. One day I decided I'd had enough and I just exploded. I told her that she needed to cut all this shit out and be nice to me because I'll be the one taking care of her in her old age. I said I'd throw her in a nursing home and leave her in diapers. As soon as I blurted out all of that, I felt terrible but, you now what? That changed everything! She started to be careful around me after that."

There are, indeed, times when it's necessary to stand up for yourself, even if you are generally conflict avoidant. Many people just hope that if they hold their breath, and wait long enough, the problem will resolve itself; it almost never does.

Time Flies When You Loathe Someone

Theresa has been in active conflict with someone for over 25 years. "Time flies when you loathe someone," she says, but you can tell it's not funny at all. This was someone who used to be her best friend, who introduced Theresa to her husband, and now happens to be her sister-in-law: "We used to spend so much time together. Next thing I know, she and her husband buy a house near us. She started planning the timing of her firstborn to be in sync with me, so our kids could grow up together to be best friends. Sounds good, huh?"

Not so good. Theresa felt smothered, and it was impossible to get away from her friend/sister-in-law: "I sat down and talked to her about it one night. I told her we needed our own space and that I was not sure what was going to happen in the future so I needed her to back off. That was a huge mistake because it really hurt her feelings. She couldn't understand where I was coming from, so I got angry and just did my own thing from then on."

It's been many years since that conversation, and now they barely speak to one another. It's awkward for everyone in the family, especially during those times when they are all forced to be together: "We both put on our fake smiles and pretend that nothing is amiss. But you cut the tension with a knife. At least our kids our friendly even if they're not the best friend cousins that she had planned."

Like Patricia in the previous section on protecting oneself, Theresa had been effective in setting boundaries, but at a price that she didn't like. She now realizes that the dispute between them was as much her fault as her sister-in-law's. She feels so sad about that now and yet also helpless and confused about how to turn things around. As she says these words, she makes a commitment to herself, and out loud, that it is time to end this feud that is creating so much unhappiness for everyone. She vows to sit down soon and sort this out, apologize if necessary, but somehow, some way, negotiate a truce.

I heard variations of this story again and again from people who were still licking their wounds after an important friendship ended badly and still haunts them with unresolved issues and regrets. Unlike Theresa, who wants someday to reconcile with her sister-in-law, another person has come to terms with the breach by accepting that things are for the best: "I believe that everything happens for a reason even though my friend and I were once so close. The thing is that people change, so it's natural that sometimes we'd grow apart or lose interest in the same things. In our case, we just grew into completely different people. I know that sounds sad, but I think it's for the best that we went our separate ways."

Reconciling Divergent Paths

The phenomenon of people in close relationships who are changing, but in different directions, is not only common but inevitable in some ways. It makes perfect sense that two friends, or two partners or spouses, would find that over time that they are growing in different (but parallel) directions. As long as there is open dialogue about the changes, negotiation and compromise along the way, such divergent interests can often enhance relationships and make things far more interesting. But other times, splits between friends or couples can be traced to their deviating paths, especially when there wasn't much conversation about the process and what it might mean.

Keira describes her husband as rather controlling. This was particularly a problem in their relationship when he was the primary breadwinner and thus used money as leverage to exert his influence. She was so appalled by this situation that she vowed she'd never be dependent on him or anyone else. The dynamic of their relationship that evolved is that he tries to bribe her with things in order to win back what he sees as a loss of control. As a result she feels grateful for their nice home and all the financial benefits they enjoy together. The problem is that he still expects payback in the form of her complete devotion and availability.

Keira is extraordinarily busy in her life. She is a full-time graduate student. She studies classical guitar and Celtic music, earning money as a professional musician. She is busy with the children they share, from their marriage as well as a previous one. And yet with everything she already has on her plate, Keira's husband expects her to be more willing to do the things that he enjoys most. "We're at a critical point in our relationship," Keira realized, "where something has to give one way or the other. My music and studies are important to me but he [her husband] doesn't always respect that. I don't need his permission to do these things, but he can make things pretty miserable for me if I don't agree with his preferences. I know this might sound selfish, since he still earns most of the money in our family and supports us, but aren't my interests important, too?"

Keira is resolved that there are some things about which she just won't compromise, even if it means that her marriage must end: "I just don't know how this is going to end, but I know for sure that although he wants me to help him with his business, that's just not my path. I wish he'd understand that I have my own vision of what I want to do with my life and it's just not the same as his."

Keira realizes that the conflict they are having is not really about their different interests and priorities but, rather, how they negotiate them. Their lives could be enriched by what each of them brings to the table (literally). Different agendas, interests, and goals can be useful, diversifying their lives and making things more stimulating. But they can also pull people apart. Nevertheless, Keira remains optimistic: "If we can work this out, I think it could be good for our relationship. I'd be bringing in more money, which would take some pressure off my husband. I know for sure I would feel better and probably even be more willing to compromise on other things. I'm so grateful for everything he's done for us, and I need to tell him that more often. But I can't repay his generosity by giving away a part of myself that is also important."

As yet, there is no resolution to Keira's ongoing conflict with her husband. And this is such a common pattern that most couples struggle with in some form or another. It just isn't reasonable to expect that two people in a friendship, partnership, or marriage are going to remain in lockstep over time without taking divergent paths at times. The resolution of such disagreements takes place at a level at which the participants feel like they are heard and understood. This is the essence of successful mediation when outcomes are not determined by each person necessarily getting what they want as much as by the parties understanding far better what the other is experiencing and what it means to them.[10]

Sometimes Conflicts Can't Be Resolved

It's often a good idea to avoid using the word "problem" a lot of the time since it implies there's a solution, even a single best answer to whatever is bothering you. We were raised on multiple-choice tests in which we were presented with questions that were accompanied by only four possible answers, and one of them was supposedly the "correct" one. We've often taken that experience to heart, believing that when we are faced with conflict situations that they can be successfully negotiated if only we can figure out the single right answer among the few choices available. But, alas, the number of options is almost infinite, and most of the time it's not even possible to figure out if the one you selected was preferable over all the others. Sometimes there isn't *any* satisfactory solution to the problems that confront us.

Larissa grew up in a strict Southern Baptist home. As she grew older, she became less devout and started to question her faith, or at least her belief in traditional religious observance. Understandably, this created some problems in the family, especially with her brother, who was incensed that she had "turned away from God."

Larissa tried to explain to him that this was not at all the case, that she was just exploring her own spiritual path, but her brother found this extremely upsetting, if not threatening. The wedge between them continued to grow over the years to the point where they could barely have a civil conversation: "I think the conflict between us is really about frustration. He loves me so much that he can't stand the thought of me going to Hell, which is what he believes will happen to me unless I convert back to his way of thinking. He has tried multiple times to convince me without success. He is stubborn, just like me, and is frustrated that I will not believe the same way he does. I, too, am frustrated that he cannot accept me as I am. I want a closer relationship with him, but he believes this is impossible given our different religious views. Both of us would like things to be different and feel powerless to change the other."

Larissa feels like she is the cause of the conflict because if only she changed her views—or *said* she had—things would resume the way they had been. But this was also a matter of principle to her. During moments of clarity, she would agree that it was just as much her brother's rigidity and judgmental nature that was the source of their conflict. "I made things so much worse by letting things get so far out of hand and not attending to the issues earlier," she explains. "As such, the distance between us has grown wider. Recently, he reached out to me. He had heard a sermon about forgiveness, being Christlike, and not closing doors on nonbelievers. After that, we have been e-mailing each other regularly with genuine questions and information about our lives. It has definitely helped mend the distance although we are by no means close. I also sent his daughter a card and some stickers (she is two) out of the blue. It meant a lot to him because he thought that my moving away from him was a sign that I had no interest in building a relationship with his daughter."

Larissa is trying. She's doing her best to patch things up. But she recognizes that, given their differences, there isn't a way to truly ever be close again. The nature of her brother's beliefs is that they don't seem to permit him (or that's his excuse) to accept his sister where she is. Although Larissa isn't all that crazy about her brother's lifestyle, she accepts that it works for him. She just doesn't see any way that they can ever truly bridge their gap and work things out. So her growth edge has been to accept what she can't do much about and concentrate instead on what is within her power to change. Her brother may not take forgiveness to heart, since it seems to be conditional on her taking on board a different religious stance, but she has found it useful to do her best to just accept that this is the best they can do.

SOMETIMES IT REALLY DOES TAKE A VILLAGE

There is a tribe in the northern part of Uganda, the Karimojong, by name, that have particularly vicious, violent, and bloody conflicts. The people fight over honor, over territory, over mates, and over imagined slights, and these do not just involve verbal combat. Yet among this pre-literate people they have devised a method of conflict resolution that follows one of their proverbs: "You can't kill a louse with one finger." Actually it takes at least two fingers to pinch the sucker and squeeze it to death. In the case of extreme conflicts, it takes a whole community to intervene, and the results are often nothing short of miraculous. In a study of almost three dozen such serious conflicts among the Karimojong, every single one of them was resolved in such a way that justice, peace, and forgiveness prevailed.[11]

There are some situations that you just can't tackle on your own. As we've seen, those most directly involved in conflict often feel powerless and stuck, locked into patterns that only aggravate the situation and further increase the intensity and vehemence of the struggle. That's why people seek the services of a therapist or mediator to help them work things out. But among most indigenous people around the world, conflict becomes a concern for the whole community because it is potentially destabilizing and has collateral effects on many others.

In the final chapter that follows, we will once again take up the discussion of how to make changes last. One of the most universally effective strategies is one in which support is mobilized from trusted others, not to take sides in the struggle (which would make things worse) but, rather, to provide an environment that is more conducive to resolution. When the "village" (social group, work unit, neighborhood, home, etc.) will no longer tolerate the continued conflicts, that is when the participants are required, if not demanded, to put the troubles behind them and move forward—if not for themselves, then for the sake of the community.

CHAPTER 14

Why Changes Don't Often Last

It is both realistic and inevitable to assume that most changes will not persist, for all kinds of good reasons. Perhaps the results did not produce the desired outcome that had been anticipated since oftentimes losing weight, relocating, going back to school, or changing jobs doesn't produce the miracle that was anticipated. In addition, it's just too much work to continue the sustained effort, or it's easy to "forget" what once seemed so important. In any case, lapses, mistakes, and slips are not only commonplace but also necessary: they provide valuable feedback about what is working best and what adjustments need to be made to prevent backsliding in the future. It doesn't count as an "official" relapse until such time that you surrender completely and admit your feelings of powerlessness. In the meantime, as long as setbacks are treated simply as useful intelligence that can be used to improve performance in the future, they are no more disappointing or discouraging than any other input that helps you improve what you do.

WHY LASTING CHANGE HAS BEEN IGNORED

Before we discuss why it's so difficult to maintain the changes that you make, it's interesting to speculate about why this important issue has been so often ignored. Most books about change and growth almost never have a section on the subject. Therapists and teachers talk a lot about how to get people to alter their behavior but rarely expand the conversation to include what happens afterward. I actually have no idea what impact this book had on you, the reader, since direct feedback is rare except by reviewers who may have their own agendas. So it is the same with the practice of teaching in that we are required to do thorough assessments of what students liked and didn't like about their learning experiences, but we are rarely asked to track them down years later to find out what stuck with them over time. It is the same with therapy in that we are encouraged, if not mandated, to do follow-up evaluations but that doesn't happen very often. We're just too busy dealing with what's in front of us rather than what passed through the rearview mirror a long time ago. Besides, it might be better, after all, to just hold our illusions that things turned out happily ever after.

To add to the problem, and as stated in the very first chapter, we don't really understand change because of its complexity. When stunning transformations do occur, we don't completely understand what happened and why. It's not like a pathologist can do an autopsy to figure out what killed the patient, or a car mechanic can complete a computer diagnostic on the vehicle, identify the faulty part, and then replace it. There are all kinds of other factors that are involved in people's lives, making it difficult to sort out what caused what. People also attribute all kinds of reasons and sources for why they have managed to maintain their progress in the face of obstacles and distractions—God, fate, vitamins, friends, coincidence, drugs, or just luck. Most of the time they just shrug and chalk it up to the unknown.

A second reason why professionals and researchers have so often neglected to study why and how changes last is because the news is often so discouraging. The relapse rate for depression is nearly 75%; for some addictions it can be as high as 90%; and for people who quit smoking, over 60% will give up within the first week and as many as 95% within a year, often requiring five or six attempts before finally becoming successful.[1] No wonder there's reluctance to measure effects of recovery when the long-term prognosis is often discouraging.

Third, it's really quite difficult to even define what constitutes a "relapse." If you regress back to old patterns or "forget" to stick with a program, does that necessarily mean that it was a failure or simply a temporary setback and opportunity for further growth? There are natural fluctuations in behavior, especially anything to do with human moods, emotions, and attitudes, that make it challenging to pin down stable conditions.

Professionals and researchers employ many different measures of what constitutes a successful change effort, sometimes arbitrarily picking a time limit for changes considered to be stabilized (one month, one year). Similarly, what qualifies as a successful or failing treatment can also be somewhat peculiar. "I work on a psych unit," a nurse explained as a preamble to her amazing story. "And we admitted this lady who said she had over a 100 poisonous snakes crawling around inside her belly. We are under such pressure to discharge patients as fast as we can that the medical team decided she had been 'cured' because we had reduced the number of poisonous snakes in her stomach to less than a handful."

There are times when people make a conscious decision to temporarily postpone a change effort because of the current stress levels in their lives and then resume the effort at some later time in the future when they feel better equipped to sustain the momentum. With such difficulties assessing what it means for change to be "permanent," it is often far easier to just stick with initial measures of progress.

Measurement of change is also complicated by the unreliability of the instruments employed and their limited scope for examining specific variables that may, ultimately, not be that significant in the grand scheme of things. People lie—a lot—during interviews and on questionnaires, often shading nuances of their experiences, presenting themselves in the best (or worst) possible light, and seeking to earn researchers' approval. In addition, participants often disappear, making it difficult to follow up during long-term studies. There also isn't much of an incentive for scholars to conduct longitudinal research because of their need to earn promotion and tenure within a finite number of years.

Finally, it's very difficult to assess a moving target. It is the nature of the world that everything is in a constant state of flux and evolution, even though the changes may be beyond our awareness. The universe is always expanding. Geological time is measured in eons rather than years. Every single second our bodies and minds are continuing to grow, as well as deteriorate. There are often delayed effects in which particular incidents, experiences, programs, and treatments may initially have seemed to be inconsequential, and then months or years later their impact is felt with surprising power and influence. There are books you've read, films you've seen, conversations you've had, or experiences you lived that haunt you years later, invading your dreams, surprising you with their lingering influences.

WHY CHANGES DON'T OFTEN LAST

Changes you make aren't maintained for a lot of very good reasons, not all of them necessarily undesirable. Often things last as long they're useful, after which they disappear. You tend to forget things that you don't use on a regular basis, practice very often, or are no longer meaningful to you.

Limits of Will

Intention is never enough. There are limits to willpower and the *desire* to do something that you say is important. There are so many things that happen between the time you commit to an action and actually follow through on it. It isn't that you changed your mind as much as other diversions and distractions interrupted the focus.

To add to the difficulties, we don't have nearly as much control over our lives as we'd like to believe.[2] Our behavior is regulated by all kinds of influences, many beyond our awareness. Close to half of all the actions that people engage in during a typical day aren't guided by any conscious decisions but, rather, represent habitual responses.[3] We unconsciously employ "mental butlers" that create grooved, neurological pathways to make our lives easier through habitual patterns.[4] Evolutionarily speaking, this provides distinct advantages because it allows the complicated human brain to function at a significantly smaller size than would otherwise be possible (consider the challenges of childbirth if the head were any larger). It allows us to respond instantly to certain situations or dangers without the needlessly time-consuming delay of making conscious decisions. This makes it so much easier for us to drive home taking familiar routes or mindlessly completing morning grooming tasks, but it also makes it much more challenging to alter these ingrained habits. One reason for this is that it turns out that old habits are never ever completely wiped out but remain permanently etched in the basal ganglia region of the brain. The best we can do is attempt to override and reroute the neural pathways so that new habits replace the old ones (Figure 14.1).[5]

Advertising and marketing strategies influence our tastes and preferences in surprising and unimaginable ways, deviously planning strategies to build habitual responses in our behavior. Consumer products are even designed in such a way as to provide cues that signal automatic responses. For instance, there is no other reason to include foaming ingredients in shampoo or toothpaste other than to provide a signal that the product is supposedly working its magic.[6] Companies deliberately design their products with particular scents, appearances, chemical actions, and properties to optimize immediate "rewards" in the brain so that habits will be formed.

In addition to marketing campaigns that plant cues for habit formation, social media and popular culture also shape our beliefs. Peer pressure and environmental constraints affect behavior. Sanctioned

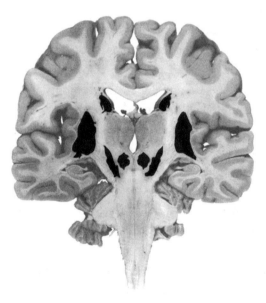

Figure 14.1: Left to its own device, the human brain would habituate as many behaviors as possible to save energy and speed up automatic responses. Such habits are housed in the basal ganglia. If this region is destroyed or injured in some way, the person becomes functionally paralyzed and overwhelmed, unable to make any decision or initiate any action.
Source: Graybiel (2010).

religious, community, and political figures also try their best to control our actions, leaving us with the illusion that we actually have free will.

Unrealistic Expectations (or Lousy Goals)

Change is sometimes doomed from the beginning when expectations aren't realistic and the objectives are not realistically attainable. It's easy to become discouraged when initial efforts aren't successful and then continued progress is abandoned.

Tabitha had never felt more stoked to lose weight. She had a breakthrough in her resolve when diagnosed with type 2 diabetes, although she'd been experiencing a number of obesity-related health problems for years, including sleep apnea and stomach problems. Now, finally, she was ready to transcend all the faddish diets and simplistic weight control cures and begin eating sensibly, incorporating new eating habits into her lifestyle.

She had been attending a weight loss support group in which participants were expected to make public commitments and declare their goals for the following week. Caught up in her enthusiasm and excitement, Tabitha vowed she would lose five pounds. For some reason nobody thought to challenge her rather ambitious goal, especially considering that she hadn't been able to lose any significant weight in over a year. Instead, everyone applauded, rewarding her for reaching way beyond what might be realistic for her.

In all fairness, Tabitha practically starved herself during the week, picturing how it would feel when she returned to the group and weighed in in front of everyone, basking in their approval. She would pacify her hunger pains with fantasies about how her extraordinary self-discipline might inspire others to follow her lead.

Tabitha resisted the urge to check her weight until the morning she was going to return to the group. She wanted the final outcome to be a surprise and even entertained the idea that she would have far exceeded her five-pound goal given how dedicated she'd been to her diet and healthful eating throughout the week. When she looked down at the scale she was devastated because she "only" lost four pounds. Immediately, she concluded (I'm not saying this was rational) that she'd failed in her effort because she didn't reach her stated goal. She felt totally embarrassed to return to the group and face their scrutiny, imagining that they, too, would see her as a failure (which couldn't have been further from the truth).

Needless to say, Tabitha's momentum was stopped abruptly. She never returned to the group and quickly regained the four pounds she'd lost.

Dysfunctional Beliefs

The only thing more obstructive and counterproductive than setting goals that can't be reached involves harboring pessimistic internal thoughts such as those covered in Chapter 9. If you are telling yourself that you probably won't be successful or that, ultimately, your fate is out of your hands, then there will often be a self-fulfilling prophecy. Defeatist attitudes will reduce the likelihood that the changes will last (see Table 14.1).

One especially virulent example of this is the belief that if you make one mistake, or slip up, it will inevitably lead to a relapse. Lapses are inevitable, predictable, and virtually impossible to prevent completely, but the problem is when you tell yourself, "What the hell! I might as well give up now that I've *completely* blown it." The operative word here, "completely," implies that all the effort has been for naught and there's no use trying anymore; it's hopeless. That's a very different internal response than telling yourself something quite different such as the following: "Gee, this is disappointing. I wonder what happened and what

---

Table 14.1. COMPARISON BETWEEN DEFEATIST AND EMPOWERED BELIEFS

"This is crazy and senseless."	"It would be interesting to figure out what this means."
"I'm a victim, and there's nothing I can do about it."	"I'm a survivor and can make the best of the situation."
"I just don't have any other options."	"I can't think of many alternatives right now, but I need to explore some other possibilities and get some help."
"This is God's will and I must accept it."	"God is giving me a message that I must be strong and resilient."
"There's no hope in even trying since I already know what's going to happen."	"This is an interesting challenge that I must somehow overcome."

I need to change in order to make sure this doesn't happen again, at least in this context? Just because I slipped this one time doesn't necessarily mean anything other than I'm human and sometimes make mistakes. Time to move forward and learn from this."

Responsibility and Blame

Assigning blame for problems does have its pleasures and satisfactions, but also considerable side effects. Blaming others when things go wrong might absolve you of responsibility but also potential control to resolve the situation and get back on track. Blaming yourself when things go awry is laudable in some situations in that it does lead to acceptance of responsibility, but can also produce feelings of discouragement. While it is important to figure out what went wrong, and what led to the problems, it is also critical to forgive the transgressions, learn from the setback, and move forward (Figure 14.2).

Figure 14.2: Emily Seebohm was the overwhelming favorite to win a gold medal at the London Olympics in the 100 meter backstroke, and Australia's best hope for a sure thing. After coming in second she was still tearful days later, searching for a reason to explain her sub-par performance. She blamed it on being distracted by social media, saying that she couldn't concentrate and "can't get into my own mind." When people offer excuses for disappointing behavior, blaming external factors, it initially lets them off the hook but at the price of feeling out of control. (Photo courtesy of Associated Press.)

The Benefits of Remaining Stuck

Sometimes changes don't continue because of the realization that it just doesn't seem like a worthwhile use of time and effort. Sure, you could make more money, but only if you are willing to trade discretionary time and make other sacrifices. Yes, you could have the body of a world-class athlete but only if you are willing to spend five hours each day working out and conform to the diet of a monk. Certainly you could have more friends and intimacy in your life, but that would involve taking some major risks. And it would absolutely be possible for you earn promotions and move up the ladder at work—*if* you are willing to meet all the demands that are required. Sometimes you make a choice (conscious or otherwise) that you don't really want it after all. Other times you are so ambivalent about what's involved that you just end up surrendering through complacency.

We covered in Chapter 2 the benefits of remaining stuck and avoiding change. Just as a review, here is a list of some very good reasons to relapse:

1. You get to feel sorry for yourself and feel like a victim.
2. You can blame others or factors outside of your control.
3. You have a ready excuse for avoiding the hard work involved; after all, you can't help it.
4. You can continue to enjoy the sympathy from others.
5. You don't have to risk abandoning what's familiar for the unknown, which could be worse, or at least more uncomfortable initially.
6. You have a good reason for not being more productive or completing tasks that are annoying—you can't help it since you're stuck.
7. You can control others through passivity, withdrawal, and helplessness.
8. You can distract yourself from other issues and problems that are even more disturbing.
9. You can be rude, insensitive, noncompliant, and uncooperative and blame it on your chronic condition.
10. You can remain miserable on your own terms.

Once you are aware of the underlying reasons for self-sabotage, it's much harder to get away with them. As we've covered earlier, that's one of the "gifts" of insight, at least the kind that really sinks into your core: such self-knowledge prevents you from engaging in behavior that is now completely within your awareness.

Lack of Support

One of the main purposes of therapy is to provide support during periods of transition and transformation. Yet one reason why the effects from treatment don't last as long as they could, and why relapses occur, is that the one hour of conversation per week represents less than one percent of your waking time. You'll be alive something like 700,000 hours, so how can you expect that a few hours spent reading a book, attending a lecture, or being in therapy are going to have much lasting impact? Of course, such influence happens all the time, but the instances when the effects continue are most associated with ongoing reinforcement of those changes.

The only thing worse than not having enough support or "social capital" to reinforce changes is having people in your world who work to actively sabotage the effort. Some people are threatened when someone initiates action since it means that they, too, would no longer have an excuse. A common example is when one person in a group gives up alcohol or drugs and tries to remain clean and sober; others may feel uncomfortable by the recovery. Given a choice between changing themselves or persuading their friend to give up the effort, the latter is far easier. That's why you will notice supposedly well-meaning friends tempt and tantalize one among them who they know is working hard to make changes: "Come on, one drink won't hurt you!"

The roles that religion and spirituality play in people's lives are often as much about social support as they are about sacred rituals. "Throughout time," observed physician Mehmet Oz, "religion has been about not just worship but also life lessons, self-improvement, and redemption, with earthly accountability to the community and congregation to help keep us in line."[7] Indeed, it is the congregational support and accountability to others that maintains changes and moral behavior in the face of earthly temptations. In spite of some of the oppressive and negative effects of religious and spiritual traditions, researchers have discovered a number of mental and physical health benefits including reduced stress, depression, and drug abuse; lower rates of cancer, heart disease, and stroke; and increased marital satisfaction, number of friendships, social support, and even lifespan.[8]

Traits and Moods

We have also covered in earlier chapters how chronic depression, stress, or anxiety, not to mention other serious emotional problems, make it far more difficult to stay on stable footing because of volatile mood swings. Two of the most accomplished feminist writers of the past century, novelist Virginia Woolf and poet Sylvia Plath, both desperately wanted to change the self-destructive nature of their lives. Both had recurrent episodes of debilitating depression, followed by repeated suicide attempts (which eventually succeeded). Both of them had some support in their lives from therapists, medical professionals, and their families. Both found their creative output actually fueled by their misery and so found reasons to create meaning from their suffering. And yet each of them could never find and maintain stable emotional footing because of biologically based mood disorders that utterly controlled their lives.[9]

In spite of one's best intentions and desires, sometimes results are compromised, or at least made far more difficult, by inborn personality traits (or disorders), underlying physiological conditions, and emotional disorders that produce additional unstable and unpredictable obstacles.

Poor Skills or Preparation

If you've been waiting for the good news, here it is: with adequate training anyone can better prepare themselves for the inevitable setbacks and relapses that are certain to occur. Change almost never occurs in a predictable, incremental, and progressive trajectory. There are a few steps of progress forward, and then a slip or slide backward. There are moments of extraordinary pride of accomplishment, followed by disappointment that the results have not been repeated.

It's interesting that the best antidote for ultimate failure is to deliberately prompt a setback so as to practice recovery skills. After rehearsing such strategies ahead of time, therapists often prescribe small relapses as homework assignments just to demonstrate that it is quite feasible to put it behind you and move onward. This is most dramatically illustrated by encouraging people on strict diets to deliberately eat a forbidden food, just to show that they can do so without losing all control. The cure for most any fear is to confront it in small doses until such time that an immunity is developed.

MAKING CHANGES LAST

The prognosis for maintaining changes can sometimes be pretty dismal for some conditions including addictions, weight loss, smoking, criminal or antisocial behavior, and other habitual patterns. Even for relatively common complaints related to emotional problems, whereas the initial success is pretty impressive, the long-term prognosis is rather guarded. For instance, there are dozens of successful treatments for depression that produce positive outcomes, including many different drugs, therapies, and lifestyle changes, but without the most optimistic prospects that the progress will become stabilized. When researchers do follow-up studies, the usual accepted intervals are three and six months after treatment ended, but rarely five or ten years later. In one representative study of depressed adolescents who were treated with antidepressant medications and therapy, the results were absolutely spectacular in that a whopping 96% responded favorably to the program with an absence of symptoms. Yet when they were checked five years later, half of them had relapsed.[10]

Based on what we've covered in this book, not to mention your own numerous, frustrating experiences, you can appreciate the daunting challenges involved in preventing regression and relapses after hard-earned gains. People have been stabilized for years, even decades, and then apparently, out of nowhere, they appear to fall off a cliff and end up worse than they've ever been. But here's what you've been waiting for: there are some relatively effective means by which you can increase the likelihood that any changes you've made will continue to grow. Many of these strategies have been empirically validated and tested for decades, ever since the first systematic studies of relapse prevention therapy, which was designed from the outset to address concerns about maintaining changes.[11]

Check Commitment and Motivation

Often it is the case when changes don't stick that there was some ambivalence about the eventual outcome that may not have been as satisfying as anticipated or perhaps had some undesirable side effects. When Darcy and Dan declared that they wanted to spend more quality time together, they were utterly sincere about their intention. Yet once they began setting aside more time than usual for their planned activities, they both noticed (but didn't mention) that they felt greater stress and found themselves in conflict more often. It's no wonder that one of them, then the other, found reasons to postpone their plans, soon returning to their previous pattern.

The strength and resolution of a commitment to maintain changes is directly related to several factors,[12] the first of which is that it was your own decision to take action in the first place. Obviously people are far more motivated to complete and continue tasks if they believe that it is their own choice rather than the result of pressure or coercion by others. Related to that, it is also critical that there are clear, articulated reasons and consequences for initiating the change, as well as definite incentives and rewards for continuing them. In the case of Darcy and Dan, rather than feeling rewarded for the changes they had initiated, they only felt more harassed. They could have structured things much differently in such a way that it felt like a gift rather than an obligation to spend extra time together.

It also helps to make a public commitment of intentions, making it far more difficult to go back on promises. One of the powerful components of support and therapy groups is that members often declare specific goals they wish to reach and then are held accountable for their actions. You may hesitate or find excuses to avoid working out, completing a task, or continuing to follow through on something you said was important, but once you realize that you have to face your peers who will ask you what happened, there is an extra incentive to do what you say you will.

Study the Patterns and Change Losses Into Gains

The first and perhaps most important step is to increase awareness of what you do, when you do it, and what triggers the behavior. Hundreds of obese individuals who had tried everything to lose weight and keep the pounds off were asked to do one simple thing—spend one day recording everything they ate. That's it! Nothing more. What happened was truly remarkable in that, without specific prompting, many of them began studying the patterns of their eating behavior, identifying particular cues that triggered cravings even though they weren't hungry. They noticed the times they ate when they were bored, or unhappy, or just triggered by images, smells, or others' behavior. That was enough for many of them to alter their patterns and eliminate the inappropriate cues.[13]

Increasing awareness of when, how, and why you engage in certain behaviors, and what triggers them, is crucial to understanding your usual routines. This is particularly important when you find yourself in the throes of chaos and disorientation that accompany sudden losses, whether a job, valued possession, emotional stability, or loved one. These are times when people are most vulnerable for self-medication and self-defeating behaviors.

It is often the exception rather than the rule that life changes are planned and chosen; sometimes fate steps in, or more often, other people in your life who set in motion circumstances that are beyond your control. Tiffany was a senior in high school when her father announced he was leaving and that a divorce was inevitable. To say that she was surprised and devastated would be an understatement: "My childhood had been easy, happy, fun, and carefree overall. Not perfect, but what you envision childhood should be. And then just like that, it was gone."

Tiffany points to that single day in her life when her childhood ended: "Life changed instantly. I literally grew up over night. Roles changed. I become a parent figure to my parents. I become totally independent and yet their caregiver. My vision of love and marriage was shattered. My parents were no longer my perfect mom and dad, but normal parents with problems, issues, failures, mistakes, and weaknesses. I had to learn how to set boundaries. I became much more blunt, outspoken, and vocal. I started to take charge of my life more and do things for me."

None of this occurred by Tiffany's choice, nor did she feel the slightest gratitude for this newfound responsibility; it all felt like a burden, and she resented the hell out of it at the time. Yet eventually, years later, she realized that she felt empowered as a result of the circumstances she found herself in. She learned to reach out to others—teammates on her basketball team, friends, and the support of a therapist. All of this began with the awareness of her previous dependent life patterns. In some ways she felt herself set free after the loss of illusions about her supposedly perfect family.

Identify and Carefully Document the Triggers

Based on studying unique patterns, one thing that will jump out is that there are certain cues that consistently provoke automatic responses. Once these are thoroughly investigated, it becomes possible to alter them, or at least reduce their power to control you. It's also helpful to learn to avoid them if that's possible.

One of the reasons that diets don't often work is because they don't include *permanent* solutions that are incorporated into daily life forever after. Sure, eating grapefruits, acai berries, cabbage soup, apple cider vinegar, leeks, celery, chocolate, baby food, miracle juice, low carbs, low protein, a tapeworm (yes, these are all actual published diets!) will probably all result in weight loss, but unless you are prepared to stick with this limited regimen for the rest of your life, the progress will be temporary, and within weeks you will likely return to your original baseline (or worse).

On the other hand, you can pretty much lose weight eating anything and everything you want as long as you do so in minimal or moderate amounts, eat only when you're hungry, and make lifestyle changes to prevent binges. This is possible only if you're completely aware of the vulnerable times and triggers for impulsivity. For instance, if you decide ahead of time exactly what you will eat on any given day (including any foods that appeal to you), with no departures from the plan without exception, write it out, and stick to it, then a pattern has been set that can be maintained throughout a lifetime.

Practice Lapses Before They Become Relapses

When Alan Marlatt, a pioneer researcher in relapse prevention, first began studying ways to solidify progress with addicts, one key aspect of his program was to help people to identify high-risk situations that they feared (like barreling down a mountain on two wheels), train them in the skills they need to deal with the adversity and temptations, and practice recovery from lapses before they became full-fledged relapses.[14] It is not much of a problem to take a step or two backward as long as it doesn't lead to permanent regression.

There's much to be learned from so-called failures.[15] When you succeed in something, you often tend to forget about it and move forward, but failures get your attention, forcing you to reflect on what happened and why. They encourage a degree of reflection, a time-out to consider where things went awry and what can be done to prevent such difficulties in the future. In that sense, they are valuable feedback about your behavior, providing key information that helps you make needed adjustments. Let's say, for instance, that you want to become more proactive, inviting new people in your life. You approach several individuals who seem interesting and attractive to you, but it's fairly obvious that they aren't reciprocating. It would be natural that you might then feel rejected, and perhaps even discouraged, but if you reflect on what happened, critically analyze the interactions, you'd likely gain valuable information that may help you to adjust your approach with the next people you encounter. Perhaps you were too aggressive and threatening? Maybe you came across as too needy? Next time you decide you'll hang back a little and try an approach that is more restrained.

Failure is an excellent teacher in that it helps you to become more flexible and adaptable. It teaches you humility and improves your tolerance for frustration. And most critically, after you recover and lick your wounds, you are even better prepared for handling new challenges in the future.

Find Different Social Support

This is the basis of 12-step programs and one reason why they often work. Apart from any other facet of Alcoholics Anonymous and related programs, such as taking a fearless inventory, or turning yourself over to a Higher Power, it is the social support provided that seems to make all the difference.[16] No matter what changes you attempt in your life, if you are surrounded by people who don't support what you've done, it is virtually impossible to maintain the progress. As mentioned previously, family or friends may actually attempt to undermine or sabotage you if they feel threatened by the changes. This is exactly what happens with many clients who attend therapy, without the consent or active support of their families. It is all very well to talk to a professional about all the things you'd like to change, but if you return to living situation, peer group, or environment that is less than amenable to what you plan, there is definitely an uphill battle with lots of unnecessary obstacles.

It is a common experience that when people go back to school they often encounter radical changes in their relationships with family members, coworkers, and friends. In this enriched learning environment, they are learning so many new things about themselves, about others, and about the way things work in the world. They develop greater intellectual curiosity and new standards for intimacy as a function of their enhanced interpersonal skills. They may feel less patient with superficial conversations. They develop greater insight and awareness of relationship dynamics. And every day they come to school there is a risk that they are leaving loved ones behind—unless they bring them along for the ride by talking about all that they are learning. Even with this warning, many students discover (happily it turns out most of the time) that many of their old relationships will end as new ones begin. They are no longer satisfied being part of social groups that hold values they have outgrown or no longer find as meaningful in their lives.

"I had this group from way back in high school that I've always been close to," one student remarked. "We used to hang out together all the time, text and talk every day. But they started to make fun of what I was doing, which I just accepted because we always tease one another. But then I noticed that a few friends would try to persuade me to skip classes or not do a paper and instead go out and play with them. I finally realized that I just didn't have much in common with them anymore. I didn't care much about the things they were into, and they certainly weren't interested in what I was doing. Every time I'd get excited about something I was learning and tell them about it, they'd abruptly change the subject and kind of make fun of me. Who needs friends like that?"

Although she sounds matter of fact about dumping her peer group, she is actually quite sad about what happened. In retrospect, she accepts that this is inevitable, that when you completely change the direction of your life, of course it means that all relationships will change as well.

Substitute a Better or Different Habit

One of the realities of change efforts is that there are sometimes collateral effects or substitution of new symptoms for previously maladaptive behavior.[17] This was originally observed by Sigmund Freud during the early years developing psychoanalysis, although it has not been consistently verified empirically.[18] Thus, people who stop smoking may gain weight with new oral fixations to feed their anxiety or manage stress. It is not unusual that people who end destructive romantic relationships end up in another one that follows a similar pattern. Those who give up particular detrimental habits may take up different ones that present their own negative side effects.

Addictions and habits can be destructive, as well as highly adaptive and healthy. There are so-called "positive addictions" that can be used to replace those that produce undesirable outcomes.[19] Exercise is an excellent example of this in that almost everyone begins such a regimen at some time during the year, whether involving walking, running, aerobic classes, yoga, or joining a fitness center.

Exercise is considered a "keystone" habit, one with far-reaching consequences that changes so many other aspects of a person's behavior, including diet, smoking, work productivity, stress levels, and lifestyle.[20] As such, once the regimen begins, it can become highly rewarding at a neurochemical level, producing the so-called "runner's high" or endorphin rush that is associated with regular exercise. More than two thirds of people who work out regularly say they do so because they feel a sense of personal accomplishment, and over 90% do so because they say it makes them feel good.[21]

If it seems too daunting to attempt a major shift in your routines, whether altering eating patterns, beginning an exercise program, or making a lifestyle adjustment, there's some evidence that initiating little changes can eventually lead to much bigger ones. I've mentioned that those who exercise regularly experience other healthy changes in their lives related to diet and other self-disciplined routines. Likewise, making simple and small changes to your life such as eating together as a family, turning off your mobile device when with loved ones, and altering the time in which you usually do something, can have far-reaching consequences. So if a bad habit is too difficult to stop altogether, an alternative is to just reconfigure a tiny aspect of the way you engage in it, at least demonstrating some small degree of control.

If you are frustrated and disappointed because you've been unable to completely stop an undesirable behavior, begin with a small adjustment in terms of when, where, with whom, or how you engage in it. It's also important to rehearse new behaviors over and over again until they are second nature and so much a part of you that you don't have to even think about them any longer. In his book on habit formation, Charles Duhigg[22] mentions the training program at Starbucks as one example in which new employees are drilled over and over again to practice responding to the two most frequent challenges—when a customer becomes irate and abusive, and when staff become flustered when there are long lines of people waiting less than patiently for their caffeine fixes. They drill new workers over and over to practice responding to these critical incidents, thinking of their aprons as shields to avoid taking any problems personally. This is precisely the intent of role-playing strategies that are used in therapy when people are encouraged to practice responding to anticipated difficulties.

One of the things that distinguish world-class athletes from those who never reach such acclaim isn't just what they are able to do with their bodies, but also their minds. Visualization and mental rehearsal are as much a part of their training regimens as physical conditioning. Negative thinking is counteracted through the development of mental skills that helps performers to control their emotional arousal, utilize constructive and soothing self-talk, and slip into comforting and familiar routines.[23]

Build in Consistent Rewards

We do the things that we do, even the unhealthy habits, because they provide some level of reinforcement. That's one reason why it is so difficult to change those habits and addictions that provide immediate physiological responses (pleasure, stimulation, arousal) such as coffee, tobacco, drugs, alcohol, and junk food. The goal, then, is to find other ways to reward yourself for unsatisfied needs, especially those that are healthier and contribute to greater well-being. In the same sense that it isn't *that* much of a sacrifice for dieters to substitute low-fat for whole milk in their coffee or cereal, adjustments can be made to include rewards that do their intended job but without the collateral damage.

Whereas attractive incentives are important to maintain continued vigilance and commitment, there are times when the urge to regress, or engage in self-defeating behaviors, is so strong that you can barely concentrate on anything else. That's one reason that mindfulness or distraction techniques have become such an integral part of relapse prevention programs.[24] This means equipping yourself with internally based methods for regaining control, possibly through breathing or meditative-type exercises or reassuring self-talk. Once such techniques are fully embedded into your way of being, they become automatic responses during times of stress or discouragement (Figure 14.3).

ILLUSIONS OF KNOWING AND UNDERSTANDING

Throughout our time together, we have been exploring extensively what often leads to relatively permanent changes in people's lives. We've learned that such shifts can occur with striking suddenness, forever transforming people's worlds, or they can evolve so slowly that there is barely any awareness of what's happening at the time.

If you've learned anything from our investigation, it is that it takes a combination of factors, on different levels and dimensions of experience, to produce quantum changes that endure. There is often a catalyst or two—a critical incident, trauma, conflict, impactful story, adventure, or insight—that gets things going. If the change is to grow and dig in roots for many seasons, then it is internalized and personalized in such a way that meaning is created. Then, there must be some kind of ongoing support to reinforce the changes and help them to spread to other areas.

It all begins with the belief, if not the certainty, that change is not only possible but also necessary. If you hold doubts, if you second-guess

Figure 14.3: One useful strategy favored by athletes and performers is to build invariant rituals into their behavior that help ground them, clear their minds, and keep them conforming to precise routines. Their high levels of excellence are the result, in part, of consistency in their behavior, setting themselves up to do the same things the same exact way. You do the same thing in some aspects of your life, which is why you don't "forget" to brush your teeth in the morning or take a pill in the evening.

Olympic swimmer Michael Phelps (above) swings his arms back and forth three times before he steps up on the block. These all become self-rewarding habits because of their soothing, consistent, familiar effects. They help lock in and cue optimal patterns that have already been practiced and ingrained. (Photo courtesy of Associated Press.)

yourself, you make it that much harder to persevere in the face of so many obstacles. Then again, change is not often a choice you make but, rather, the consequences of events that felt out of your control. Sometimes all you can do is go along for the ride, making the best of the situation.

So, what *really* makes a difference in recovery, growth, or producing lasting change? Is it even possible to compose a definitive answer, especially one that truly captures the essence, much less the nuances, of human experience?

Moments of inspiration that produce changes are often portrayed as an epiphany that forever changes everything—or at least that's how people often describe their transformations. As I've said, such reports are often unreliable. People don't really remember what exactly happened. Or, they don't know. They simplify and abbreviate the process. Sometimes they even make things up—and then they believe what they say.

We present these illusions, perhaps deceptions, that true understanding is both possible and desirable. It is, indeed, perfectly reasonable that we can accept the limits of what we understand about our own transformations and ourselves. Even within such parameters, we can become far better students of our own internal processes, especially those that are related to changes that we initiate.

We began this journey together by acknowledging that change is, indeed, a mystery in many ways. But that doesn't mean that we can't better understand and harness those forces that are most influential in assisting us during times of need. If it's important to you, really, really important, that you hold onto something in this dialogue between us, that you remember it, apply it, use it in constructive ways, then it is within your power to do so. *That is what really makes a difference.*

NOTES

PREFACE

1. Bergsma, A. (2008). Do self-help books help? *Journal of Happiness Studies, 9,* 341–360.
2. Beutler, L. E., Forrester, B., Gallager-Thompson, D., Thompson, L, & Tomlins, J. B. (2012). Common, specific, and treatment fit variables in psychotherapy outcome. *Journal of Psychotherapy Integration, 22*(3), 255–281. Castonguay, L. G., & Hill, C. E. (Eds.). (2012). *Transformation in psychotherapy: Corrective experiences across cognitive, behavioral, humanistic, and psychodynamic approaches.* Washington, DC: American Psychological Association. Kazdin, A. E. (2009). Understanding how and why psychotherapy leads to change. *Psychotherapy Research, 19*(4–5), 418–428. Norcross, J. C. (Ed.). (2011). *Psychotherapy relationships that work* (2nd ed.). New York: Oxford University Press.
3. Evans, I. (2013). *How and why people change: Foundations of psychological therapy.* New York: Oxford University Press. Kottler, J. A. (2001). *Making changes last.* New York: Routledge. Miller, W. R., & Rollnick, S. (2012). *Motivational interviewing: Preparing people for change* (3rd ed.). New York: Guilford. Ogden, J., & Hills, L. (2008). Understanding sustained behavior change: The role of life crises and the process of reinvention. *Health, 12*(4), 419–437. Polivy, J., & Herman, C. P. (2002). If at first you don't succeed: False hopes of self-change. *American Psychologist, 57*(9), 677–689.

CHAPTER 1

1. A number of sources summarize some of the unexplained mysteries of evolutionary theory: Dawkins, R. (2006). *The selfish gene: 30th anniversary edition.* Upper Saddle River, NJ: Prentice-Hall. Wright, D. (1994). *The moral animal: Why we are the way we are.* New York: Random House. Barash, D. P. (2012). *Homo mysterious: Evolutionary puzzles of human nature.* New York: Oxford University Press. Miller, A. S., & Kanazawa, S. (2007). *Why beautiful people have more daughters.* New York: Perigee.
2. Kottler, J. A. (1996). *The language of tears.* San Francisco: Jossey-Bass. Lutz, T. (2001). *A natural and cultural history of crying.* New York: W.W. Norton.

3. Carey, T. A., Carey, M., Mullan, R. J., Murray, L. K., & Spratt, M. B. (2006). Psychological change: What changes and how does it occur? A critical review. *Counselling Psychology Review, 21*(4), 28–38.
4. Evans, I. (2013). *How and why people change: Foundations of psychological therapy.* New York: Oxford University Press.
5. Duhigg, C. (2012). *The power of habit.* New York: Random House.
6. Gianakis, M., & Carey, T. A. (2008). A review of the experience and explanation of psychological change. *Counselling Psychology Review, 23*(3), 27–38.
7. Knight, T. A., Richert, A. J., & Brownfield, C. R. (2012). Conceiving change: Lay accounts of the human change process. *Journal of Psychotherapy Integration, 22*(3), 229–254.
8. Van Hoose, W., & Kottler, J. (1977). *Ethical and legal issues in counseling and psychotherapy.* San Francisco: Jossey-Bass. Kottler, J., & Brown, R. (1985). *Introduction to therapeutic counseling.* Belmont, CA: Brooks/Cole. Kottler, J. (1987). *On being a therapist.* San Francisco: Jossey-Bass. Kottler, J., & Blau, D. (1989). *The imperfect therapist: Learning from failure in therapeutic practice.* San Francisco: Jossey-Bass. Kottler, J. (1991). *The compleat therapist.* San Francisco: Jossey-Bass. Kottler, J. (1992). *Compassionate therapy: Working with difficult clients.* San Francisco: Jossey-Bass. Kottler, J., Sexton, T., & Whiston, S. (1994). *Heart of healing: Relationships in therapy.* San Francisco: Jossey-Bass. Kottler, J. A. (2000). *Doing good: Passion and commitment for helping others.* New York: Routledge. Kottler, J. A. (2001). *Making changes last.* New York: Routledge. Kottler, J. A., & Carlson, J. (2003). *The mummy at the dining room table: Eminent therapists reveal their most unusual cases and what they teach us about human behavior.* San Francisco: Jossey-Bass. Kottler, J. A., & Carlson, J. (2006). *The client who changed me: Stories of therapist personal transformation.* New York: Routledge. Kottler, J. A., & Carlson, J. (2009). *Creative breakthroughs in therapy: Tales of transformation and astonishment.* New York: Wiley. Kottler, J. A., & Montgomery, M. (2011). *Theories in counseling and psychotherapy.* Thousand Oaks, CA: Sage.
9. One of the most influential movements in the field of psychotherapy is examining common factors that operate in all approaches. See: Bohart, A., & Tallman, K. (1999). *How clients make therapy work: The process of active self-healing.* Washington, DC: American Psychological Association. Castonguay, L. G., & Beutler, L. E. (Eds.). (2006). *Principles of therapeutic change at work.* New York: Oxford University Press. Wampold, B. (2001). *The great psychotherapy debate.* Mahwah, NJ: Lawrence Erlbaum. Higginson, S., & Mansell, W. (2008). What is the mechanism of psychological change? *Psychology and psychotherapy: Theory, research, and practice, 81,* 309–328. Hubble, M. A., Duncan, B. L., & Miller, S. D. (2009). *Heart and soul of change* (2nd ed.). Washington, DC: American Psychological Association. Kazdin, A. E. (2009). Understanding how and why psychotherapy leads to change. *Psychotherapy Research, 19*(4–5), 418–428. Kottler, J. (1991). *The compleat therapist.* San Francisco: Jossey-Bass. Kottler, J. A., & Carlson, J. (2008). *Their finest hour: Master therapists share their greatest success stories* (2nd ed.). Bethel, CT: Crown Publishing. Kottler, J. A. (2010). *On being a therapist*

(4th ed.). San Francisco: Jossey-Bass. Norcross, J. C. (2011). *Psychotherapy relationships that work*. New York: Oxford University Press.

10. Greenberg, L. S. (1991). Research on the process of change. *Psychotherapy Research, 1,* 3–16. Duncan, B., & Miller, S. (2000). The client's theory of change: Consulting the client in the integrative process. *Journal of Psychotherapy Integration, 10,* 169–187. Carey, T. A., Carey, M., Mullan, R. J., Murray, L. K., & Spratt, M. B. (2006). Psychological change: What changes and how does it occur? A critical review. *Counselling Psychology Review, 21*(4), 28–38. Carey, T. A., Carey, M., Stalker, K., Mullan, R. J., Murray, L. K., & Spratt, M. B. (2007). Psychological change from the inside looking out: A qualitative investigation. *Counselling and Psychotherapy, 7*(3), 178–187.

11. Solomon, R. C. (2002). Back to basics: On the very idea of "basic emotions." *Journal for the Theory of Social Behavior, 32,* 115–144. Burum, B. A., & Goldfried, M. R. (2007). The centrality of emotion to psychological change. *Clinical Psychology: Science and Practice, 14*(4), 407–413.

12. Insel, T. R. (2012). Next-generation treatments for mental disorders. *Science Translational Medicine, 4,* 19–155.

13. Quoidbach, J., Gilbert, D. T., & Wilson, T. D. (2013). The end of history illusion. *Science, 339*(6115), 96–98.

14. Haidt, J. (2006). *The happiness hypothesis: Finding modern truth in ancient wisdom.* New York: Basic Books.

15. Heath, C., & Heath, D. (2010). *Switch: How to change when change is hard.* New York: Broadway.

16. Gould, R. A., & Clum, G. A. (1993). A meta-analysis of self-help treatment approaches. *Psychology Review, 13,* 169–186. Bohart, A., & Tallman, K. (1999). *How clients make therapy work: The process of active self-healing.* Washington, DC: American Psychological Association. Carey, T. A., Carey, M., Stalker, K., Mullan, R. J., Murray, L. K., & Spratt, M. B. (2007). Psychological change from the inside looking out: A qualitative investigation. *Counselling and Psychotherapy, 7*(3), 178–187.

17. Ptacin, M. (2012). Running. In L. Smith (Ed.), *The moment: Wild, poignant, life-changing stories* (pp. 129–131). New York: HarperCollins.

18. Each of these models is described in: Gianakis, M., & Carey, T. A. (2011). An interview study investigating experiences of psychological change without psychotherapy. *Psychology and Psychotherapy: Theory, Research, and Practice, 84,* 442–457.

19. See: Norcross, J. C., Krebs, P. M., & Prochaska, J. O. (2011). Stages of change. *Journal of Clinical Psychology, 67*(2), 1–12.

20. Carey, T. A., Carey, M., Stalker, K., Mullan, R. J., Murray, L. K., & Spratt, M. B. (2007). Psychological change from the inside looking out: A qualitative investigation. *Counselling and Psychotherapy, 7*(3), 178–187.

21. Examples of the search for common factors include: Cameron, M., & Keenan, E. K. (2012). *Direct practice using the common factors model: Conditions, processes, and strategies for facilitating change.* Upper Saddle River, NJ: Prentice-Hall. Lambert, M. (2004). *Handbook of psychotherapy and behavior change* (5th

ed.). New York: Wiley. Kazdin, A. E. (2005). Treatment outcomes, common factors, and continued neglect of mechanisms of change. *Clinical Psychology, 12*(2), 184–188. Duncan, B. L., Miller, S. D., Wampold, B. E., & Hubble, M. A. (2010). *The heart and soul of change* (2nd ed.). Washington, DC: American Psychological Association. Evans, I. (2013). *How and why people change: Foundations of psychological therapy.* New York: Oxford University Press.

22. Appelbaum, S. A. (1976). The dangerous edge of insight. *Psychotherapy: Theory, Research, and Practice, 13*(3), 202–206. Haley, J. (1993). *Uncommon therapy.* New York: W. W. Norton.

23. Evans, I. (2013). *How and why people change: Foundations of psychological therapy.* New York: Oxford University Press.

CHAPTER 2

1. Dostoyevsky, F. (1866/1993). *Crime and punishment.* New York: Vintage.
2. Kottler, J. A. (2001). *Making changes last.* New York: Routledge.
3. Csikszentmihalyi, M. (2000). *Beyond boredom and anxiety.* San Francisco: Jossey-Bass.
4. Joseph, S. (2011). *What doesn't kill us: The new psychology of posttraumatic growth.* New York: Basic Books.
5. Lyubomirsky, S. (2013). *The myths of happiness.* New York: Penguin.
6. Higginson, S., & Mansell, W. (2008). What is the mechanism of psychological change? *Psychology and Psychotherapy: Theory, Research, and Practice, 81,* 318.
7. Burns, D. (2013, January/February). Living with the devil we know: We may be anxious but not anxious to change. *Psychotherapy Networker,* 28–29.
8. Norcross, J. C., Krebs, P. M., & Prochaska, J. O. (2011). Stages of change. *Journal of Clinical Psychology, 67*(2), 1–12. Prochaska, J., & DiClemente, C. (1986). Toward a comprehensive model of change. In W. Miller & N. Heather (Eds.), *Treating addictive behavior.* New York: Plenum. Prochaska, J. O., Norcross, J. C., & DiClemente, C. C. (1994). *Changing for good.* New York: Morrow. Selig, M. (2010). *Changepower.* New York: Routledge.
9. Duhigg, C. (2012). *The power of habit.* New York: Random House.
10. Carey, T. A., Carey, M., Stalker, K., Mullan, R. J., Murray, L. K., & Spratt, M. B. (2007). Psychological change from the inside looking out: A qualitative investigation. *Counselling and Psychotherapy, 7*(3), 178–187.
11. Freud, S. (1913). On beginning the treatment. *The standard edition of the complete psychological works of Sigmund Freud.* London: Hogarth.
12. Glasser, W. (1999). *Choice theory: A new psychology of personal freedom.* New York: Harper Perennial. Miller, W. R., & Rollnick, S. (2012). *Motivational interviewing: Preparing people for change* (3rd ed.). New York: Guilford.
13. Diamond, J. (2011). *Collapse: How societies choose to fail or succeed* (Rev. ed.). New York: Penguin.
14. Duncan, B., & Miller, S. (2000). *The heroic client.* San Francisco: Jossey-Bass. Castonguay, L. G., & Beutler, L. E. (Eds.). (2006). *Principles of therapeutic change at work.* New York: Oxford University Press. Norcross, J. C. (Ed.).

(2011). *Psychotherapy relationships that work* (2nd ed.). New York: Oxford University Press.

15. Heath, C., & Heath, D. (2010). *Switch: How to change when change is hard.* New York: Broadway.

16. Bergman, P. (2009, March 11). The easiest way to change people's behavior. *Harvard Business Review.* Retrieved from http://blogs.hbr.org/bregman/2009/03/the-easiest-way-to.html

17. Maddi, S. R. (2002). The story of hardiness: Twenty years of theorizing, research, and Practice. *Consulting Psychology Journal, 54,* 173–185. Seligman, M. E. P. (2011). *Flourish.* New York: Free Press.

18. Fernandez-Alvarez, H., Clarkin, J. F., Salgueiro, M., & Crutchfield, K. (2006). Participant factors in treating personality disorders. In L. G. Castonguay & L. E. Beutler (Eds.), *Principles of therapeutic change at work* (pp. 203–218). New York: Oxford University Press.

19. Duhigg, C. (2012). *The power of habit.* New York: Random House.

20. Dixon, M., & Habib, R. (2010). Neurobehavioral evidence for the near-miss effect in pathological gamblers. *Journal of Experimental Analysis of Behavior, 93*(3), 313–328. Chase, H., & Clark, L. (2010). Gambling severity predicts midbrain response to near-miss outcomes. *Journal of Neuroscience, 30*(18), 6180–6187.

21. Kottler, J. A. (2006). *Divine madness: Ten stories of creative struggle.* San Francisco: Jossey-Bass.

22. Evans, I. (2013). *How and why people change: Foundations of psychological therapy.* New York: Oxford University Press.

23. Kottler, J. A., & Chen, D. (2011). *Stress management and prevention: Applications to daily life* (2nd ed.). New York: Routledge.

24. Ballou, M., & Brown, L. S. (2002) *Rethinking mental health and disorder: Feminist perspectives.* New York: Guilford.

25. Tough, P. (2012). *How children succeed.* New York: Houghton Mifflin.

26. Bargh, J. A., & Chartrand, T. L. (1999). The unbearable automaticity of being. *American Psychologist, 54,* 462–479. Park, D. C. (1999). Acts of will? *American Psychologist, 54,* 461.

27. University of Scranton. (2012). New Year's resolution statistics. http://www.statisticbrain.com/new-years-resolution-statistics. Accessed January 15, 2013.

28. Norcross, J. C., Ratzin, A. C., & Payne, D. (1989). Ringing in the new year: The change processes and reported outcomes of resolutions. *Addictive Behaviors, 14,* 205–212.

29. Polivy, J., & Herman, C. P. (2002). If at first you don't succeed: False hopes of self-change. *American Psychologist, 57*(9), 677–689.

30. Burkeman, O. (2012, December 24). The New Year's resolutions that won't fail you. *Newsweek,* 46–49.

31. Amabile, T., & Kramer, S. (2011). *The progress principle: Small wins to ignite joy, engagement, and creativity at work.* Boston: Harvard Business School Press.

32. There have been a number of previous studies of changes made outside of therapy, including: Kottler, J. A. (1997). *Travel that can change your life.*

San Francisco: Jossey-Bass. Miller, W. R., & Rollnick, S. (2002). *Motivational interviewing: Preparing people for change* (2nd ed.). New York: Guilford. C'de Baca, J., & White, W. L. (2004). Transformational change: A historical review. *Journal of Clinical Psychology, 60*(5), 461–470. Mahoney, A., & Pargament, K. I. (2004). Sacred changes: Spiritual conversion and transformation. *Journal of Clinical Psychology, 60,* 481–492. Wilbourne, P. (2004). Quantum change: Ten years later. *Journal of Clinical Psychology, 60*(5), 531–541. Lampropoulos, G. K., & Spengler, P. M. (2005). Helping and change without traditional therapy: Commonalities and opportunities. *Counselling Psychology Quarterly, 18*(1), 47–59. Higginson, S., & Mansell, W. (2008). What is the mechanism of psychological change? *Psychology and Psychotherapy: Theory, Research, and Practice, 81,* 309–328. Gianakis, M., & Carey, T. A. (2008). A review of the experience and explanation of psychological change. *Counselling Psychology Review, 23*(3), 27–38. Carey, T. A., Carey, M., Mullan, R. J., Murray, L. K., & Spratt, M. B. (2006). Psychological change: What changes and how does it occur? A critical review. *Counselling Psychology Review, 21*(4), 28–38. Bohart, A., & Tallman, K. (1999). *How clients make therapy work: The process of active self-healing.* Washington, DC: American Psychological Association.

33. See: Seligman, M. (2002). *Authentic happiness.* New York: Free Press. McMahon, D. M. (2006). *Happiness: A history.* New York: Atlantic Monthly Press. Haybron, D. M. (2008). *The pursuit of unhappiness: The elusive psychology of well-being.* New York: Oxford University Press. Seligman, M. (2011). *Flourish: A visionary new understanding of happiness and well-being.* New York: Free Press.

CHAPTER 3

1. Friedlander, M. L., Lee, H. H., & Bernardi, S. (2012, May). Corrective experiences in everyday life: A qualitative investigation of transformative change. *The Counseling Psychologist,* 1–27.

2. White, W. L. (2004). Transformational change: A historical review. *Journal of Clinical Psychology, 60*(5), 461–470.

3. Maslow, A. (1968). Toward a psychology of being. New York: Wiley.

4. Webber, R. (2010, September). Big moments. *Psychology Today.*

5. Miller, W. R., & Rollnick, S. (2002). *Motivational interviewing: Preparing people for change* (2nd ed.). New York: Guilford.

6. White, W. L. (2004). Transformational change: A historical review. *Journal of Clinical Psychology, 60*(5), 461–470.

7. Illest, B. (2009, February 28). June 12, 1970: Dock Ellis took a bunch of LSD and pitched a no-hitter [Video file]. Retrieved from http://www.youtube.com/watch?v=PgOqHLeKGH0

8. WFMU Blog. (2009, September 13). *Just what the doctor ordered* [Web log post]. Retrieved from http://blog.wfmu.org/freeform/2009/09/just-what-the-doc-ordered-lsd-and-the-strangest-moment-in-major-league-history.html

9. A short film by James Blagden, "Dock Ellis & the LSD No-No" can be found at: http://www.dockshort.com/dockshort/. Comedian Robin Williams did a comedy routine based on the incident: http://www.youtube.com/

watch?v=oO281JqXQdc. Todd Snider wrote and performed a song: http://www.youtube.com/watch?v=KG2SPjcKM4M

10. Much of the background about his life comes from several sources including: Hall, D. (1989). *Dock Ellis in the country of baseball*. New York: Fireside. Elliot, H. (2008, May 13). Ellis is trying to strike back at a tough foe. *Los Angeles Times*. Goldstein, R. (2008, December 21). Dock Ellis, All-Star pitcher who overcame longtime addictions, dies at 63. *New York Times*, p. 43. Silver, M. (2007). Dock Ellis. *Sports Illustrated, 107*(1), 126. Torre, P. S. (2010). A light in the darkness. *Sports Illustrated, 112*(26), 72–79. Witz, B. (2010, September 4). For Ellis, a long, strange trip to a no-hitter. *New York Times. Jet Magazine.* (1984, April 30). Former star Dock Ellis says fear of success drove him to use drugs, *66*(8). Madden, B. (2008, December 22). From no-hitter on LSD to hair curlers to feuds, Dock Ellis was free spirit. *New York Daily News*. Retrieved from http://articles.nydailynews.com/2008-12-20/sports/17912792_1_dock-ellis-no-hitter-yankees

11. Norcross, J. C., Krebs, P. M., & Prochaska, J. O. (2011). Stages of change. *Journal of Clinical Psychology, 67*(2), 1–12.

12. C'de Baca, J., & Wilbourne, P. (2004). Quantum change: Ten years later. *Journal of Clinical Psychology, 60*(5), 531–541.

13. Allsop, S., & Saunders, B. (1989). Relapse and alcohol problems. In M. Gossop (Ed.), *Relapse and addictive behavior*. New York: Routledge. Annis, H. K. (1986). A relapse prevention model for treatment of alcoholics. In D. Curson, H. Rankin, & E. Shepherd (Eds.), *Relapse in alcoholism*. Northhampton, UK: Alcohol Counseling and Information Service. Brownell, K. D., Marlatt, G. A., Lichenstein, E., & Wilson, G. T. (1986). Understanding and preventing relapse. *American Psychologist, 4*, 765–782. Hendershot, C. S., Witkiewitz, K., George, W. H., & Marlatt, G. A. (2011). Relapse prevention for addictive behaviors. *Substance Abuse, Treatment, Prevention, and Policy, 6*, 1–17. Marlatt, G. A., & Gordon, J. R. (1985). *Relapse prevention: Maintenance strategies in the treatment of addictive behaviors*. New York: Guilford.

14. Ogden, J., & Hills, L. (2008). Understanding sustained behavior change: The role of life crises and the process of reinvention. *Health, 12*(4), 419–437.

15. Gianakis, M., & Carey, T. A. (2011). An interview study investigating experiences of psychological change without psychotherapy. *Psychology and Psychotherapy: Theory, Research, and Practice, 84*, 442–457.

16. Heatherton, T. F., & Nichols, P. A. (1994). Personal accounts of successful versus failed attempts at life change. *Personality and Social Psychology Bulletin, 20*, 664–675. Miller, W. R. (2004). The phenomenon of quantum change. *Journal of Clinical Psychology, 60*, 453–460. Prochaska, J. O., Norcross, J. C., & DiClemente, C. C. (1994). *Changing for good*. New York: Morrow.

17. Hartmann, M., Gerhardt, W., & Eich, W. (2012). Pain perception in athletes compared to normally active controls: A systematic review with meta-analysis. *Pain, 153*(6).

18. Gifford, B. (2012, July). The transcendent pain. *Bicycling*, 84–85.

19. Ibid, p. 448.

20. Keroac, J. (1957). *On the road*. New York: Viking Press, p. 16

21. Boxer, S. (2002, November 18). Woody, do you feel like talking about it? *The Age.* Retrieved July 1, 2012, from http://www.theage.com.au/articles/2002/11/17/1037490050537.html

22. Watzlawick, P., Weakland, J., & Fisch, R. (1974). *Change: Principles of problem formation and problem resolution.* New York: W. W. Norton. Fraser, J. S., & Solovey, A. (2007). *Second-order change in psychotherapy: The golden thread that unifies effective treatments.* Washington, DC: American Psychological Association.

23. Ogden, J., & Hills, L. (2008). Understanding sustained behavior change: The role of life crises and the process of reinvention. *Health, 12*(4), 419–437.

CHAPTER 4

1. Speer, N., Reynolds, J., Swallow, K., & Zacks, J. (2009). Reading stories activates neural representations of visual and motor experiences. *Psychological Science, 20,* 989–999.

2. Gottschall, J. (2012). *The storytelling animal: How stories make us human.* New York: Houghton Mifflin.

3. MacAdams, D. P. (1993). *The stories we live: Personal myths and the making of the self.* New York: Guilford.

4. Woods, S. (2012, July). The last word: Michael Caine. *Men's Journal,* 138.

5. Vali, K., & Revonsuo, A. (2009). The threat simulation theory in light of recent empirical evidence: A review. *American Journal of Psychology, 122,* 17–38.

6. Nigam, S. K. (2012). The storytelling brain. *Science and Engineering Ethics, 18,* 567–571. Gottschall, J., & Wilson, D. S. (Eds.). (2005). *The literary animal: Evolution and the nature of narrative.* Chicago: Northwestern University Press. Hsu, J. (2008). The secrets of storytelling: Our love for telling tales reveals the workings of the mind. *Scientific American Mind, 19*(4), 46–51.

7. Leitch, W. (2012). Introduction. In L. Wilson (Ed.), *A Friday night lights companion* (p. 2). Dallas, TX: Benbella Books.

8. Campbell, J. (1968). *The hero with a thousand faces* (2nd ed.). Princeton, NJ: Princeton University Press.

9. Lazar, A., Karlan, D., & Salter, J. (2006). *The 101 most influential people who never lived.* New York: Harper.

10. Arana, M. (2008). Five life stories that changed my life. *Washington Post.* Retrieved from http://voices.washingtonpost.com/shortstack/2008/03/five_life_stories_that_changed.html

11. Kreider, T. (2008, September 24). When books could change your life. *City Paper.* Retrieved from http://www2.citypaper.com/news/story.asp?id=16743

12. Lazar, A., Karlan, D., & Salter, J. (2006). *The 101 most influential people who never lived.* New York: Harper.

13. Boyd, B. (2009). *On the origin of stories: Evolution, cognition, fiction.* Cambridge, MA: Harvard University Press.

14. Gottschall, J. (2012). *The storytelling animal: How stories make us human.* New York: Houghton Mifflin.

15. Green, M., & Donahue, J. (2009). Simulated worlds: Transportation into narratives. In K. Markman, W. Klein, & J. Suhr (Eds.), *Handbook of imagination and mental stimulation* (pp. 241–254). New York: Psychology Press.
16. Lazar, A., Karlan, D., & Salter, J. (2006). *101 most influential people who never lived.* New York: Harper.
17. Poniewozik, J. (2012, July 16). The greatest American antihero. *Time,* 60–61.
18. Kottler, J. A. (2011). *Lust for blood: Why we are fascinated by death, horror, and violence.* Amherst, NY: Prometheus Press.
19. Burns, G. W. (Ed.). (2007). *Healing with stories.* New York: Wiley.
20. Lankton, C., & Lankton, S. (1989). *Tales of enchantment: Goal-oriented metaphors for adults and children in therapy.* New York: Brunner/Mazel.
21. The story is described in: Kottler, J., & Carlson, J. (2009). *Creative breakthroughs in therapy: Tales of transformation and astonishment.* New York: Wiley.
22. Haley, J. (1973). *Uncommon therapy: The psychiatric techniques of Milton H. Erickson, M.D.* New York: W.W. Norton.
23. Kottler, J. A., Carlson, J., & Keeney, B. (2004). *An American shaman: An odyssey of ancient healing traditions.* New York: Routledge.
24. Kottler & Carlson (2009), p. 27.
25. Levitin, D. J. (2008). *The world in six songs: How the musical brain created human nature.* New York: Plume.
26. DeWall, C. N., Pond, R. S., Campbell, W. K., & Twenge, J. M. (2011). Turning in to psychological change: Linguistic markers of psychological traits and emotions over time in popular U.S. song lyrics. *Psychology of Aesthetics, Creativity, and the Arts, 5*(3), 200–207.
27. Kottler, J. A. (2014). *Stories we've heard, stories we've told: Life-changing narratives in therapy and everyday life.* New York: Oxford University Press.
28. Levitt, H. M., Rattanasampan, W., Chaidaroon, S. S., Stanley, C., & Robinson, T. (2009). The process of personal change through reading fictional narratives: Implications for psychotherapy practice and theory. *The Humanistic Psychologist, 37,* 326–352.
29. Solomon, G. (2001). *Reel therapy: How movies inspire you to overcome life's problems.* New York: Lebhar-Friedman Books.

CHAPTER 5

1. White, W. L., & Miller, W. R. (2007). The use of confrontation in addiction treatment: History, science, and time for a change. *The Counselor, 8*(4), 12–30.
2. Miller, W. R., & Rollnick, S. (2012). *Motivational interviewing: Preparing people for change* (3rd ed.). New York: Guilford.
3. Weisel, F. (2011). *Teller.* Indianapolis, IN: Dog Ear.
4. Forcehimes, A. A. (2004). De profundis: Spiritual transformations in Alcoholics Anonymous. *Journal of Clinical Psychology, 60*(5), 503–517.
5. Castonguay, L. G., & Beutler, L. E. (Eds.) (2006). *Principles of therapeutic change at work.* New York: Oxford University Press.

6. Miller & Rollnick (2012).
7. Kurtz, E. (1979). *Not-God: A history of Alcoholics Anonymous.* New York: Hazelden, p. 61.
8. Shoemaker, S. (1936). *National awakening.* New York: Harper & Row.
9. Griffith, K. D. (2007). The impact of rock-bottom experiences on the alcohol recovery process. *Dissertation Abstracts International, 67*(9-B), p. 5402.
10. Young, L. B. (2011). Help seeking among Alcoholics Anonymous members. *Journal of Social Work Practice in the Addictions, 11*(4), 321–335.
11. This story was coauthored with Sarah Childers, whose honesty, courage, and resourcefulness demonstrate the incredible power to change, especially with help from family and friends.
12. Luborsky, L., Barber, J. P., & Diguer, L. (1992). The meaning of narratives told during psychotherapy: The fruits of a new observational unit. *Psychotherapy Research, 2,* 277–290.

CHAPTER 6

1. This story is based on interviews and collaboration with Rodney Anderson, a basketball player for California State University, Fullerton, who was gunned down in a case of mistaken identity.
2. An excellent review of the research can be found in: Joseph, S. (2011). *What doesn't kill us: The new psychology of posttraumatic growth.* New York: Basic Books.
3. Dalgleish, T., Joseph, S., & Yule, W. (2000). The Herald of Free Enterprise disaster: Lessons from the first six years. *Behavior Modification, 24,* 673–699.
4. Rollins, J. (2012, February). The transformative power of trauma. *Counseling Today,* 40–43.
5. Heatherton, T. F., & Nichols, P. A. (1994). Personal accounts of successful versus failed attempts at life change. *Personality and Social Psychology Bulletin, 20,* 664–675.
6. Lyubomirsky, S. (2013). *The myths of happiness.* New York: Penguin. Seery, M. D., Holman, E. A., & Silver, R. C. (2010). Whatever does not kill us: Cumulative lifetime adversity, vulnerability, and resilience. *Journal of Personality and Social Psychology, 99,* 1025–1041.
7. Tedeschi, R. G., Park, C. L., & Calhoun, L. G. (Eds.) (1998). *Posttraumatic growth: Positive changes in the aftermath of crisis.* Mahwah, NJ: Lawrence Erlbaum.
8. Frankl, V. (1975). *Man's search for meaning.* New York: Pocket Books.
9. Hilbert Caesar was interviewed in: Ruane, M. E. (2005, November 26). From wounds, inner strength. *The Washington Post.*
10. Dekel, S., Mandl, C., & Solmon, Z. (2011). Shared and unique predictors of post-traumatic growth and distress. *Journal of Clinical Psychology, 67*(3), 241–252.
11. Tedeschi, R. G., & McNally, R. J. (2011). Can we facilitate posttraumatic growth in combat veterans? *American Psychologist, 66*(1), 19–24.
12. Hefferon, K., Grealy, M., & Mutrie, N. (2009). Post-traumatic growth and life threatening physical illness: A systematic review of the qualitative literature.

British Journal of Health Psychology, 14, 343–378. Park, C. L., & Calhoun, L. G. (Eds.). (1998). *Posttraumatic growth: Positive changes in the aftermath of crisis.* Mahwah, NJ: Lawrence Erlbaum. Tedeschi, R. G., & McNally, R. J. (2011). Can we facilitate posttraumatic growth in combat veterans? *American Psychologist, 66*(1), 19–24. Joseph, S., Linley, P. A., & Harris, G. J. (2005). Understanding positive change following trauma and adversity: Structural clarification. *Journal of Loss and Trauma, 10,* 83–96.

13. Frazier, P., Tennen, H., Gavian, M., Park, C., Tomich, P., & Tashiro, T. (2009). Does self-reported posttraumatic growth reflect genuine positive change? *Psychological Science, 20*(7), 912–919.

14. Huppert, F., & So, T. (2009). *What percentage of people in Europe are flourishing and what characterizes them?* The Well-Being Institute. http://www.isqols2009.istitutodeglinnocenti.it/Content_en/Huppert.pdf. Accessed August 4, 2012.

15. Levine, S. Z., Laufer, A., Stein, F., Hamama-Raz, Y., & Solomon, Z., (2009). Examining the relationship between resilience and posttraumatic growth. *Journal of Traumatic Stress, 22,* 282–286.

16. Seligman, M. (2002). *Authentic happiness.* New York: Free Press. Seligman, M. (2011). *Flourish: A visionary new understanding of happiness and well-being.* New York: Free Press.

17. Kottler, J. (1994). *Beyond blame: A new way of resolving conflict in relationships.* San Francisco: Jossey-Bass.

18. Mitchell, J. T., & Everly, G. S. (1993). *Critical incident stress debriefing: An operations manual for the prevention of traumatic stress among emergency services and disaster workers.* Ellicott City, MD: Chevron Publishing. Sakran, J. V., Kaafarani, H., Houawad, N. J., & Santry, H. P. (2011). When things go wrong. *Bulletin of the American College of Surgeons, 96*(8), 13–16.

19. Kagee, A. (2002). Concerns about the effectiveness of critical incident stress debriefing in ameliorating stress reactions. *Critical Care, 6*(1), 88. Greenberg, N. (2001). A critical review of psychological debriefing: The management of psychological health after traumatic experiences. *Journal of Royal Naval Medical Services, 87*(3), 158–161. Groopman, J. (2004, January 26). The grief industry: How much does crisis counseling help or hurt? *The New Yorker.* Lebow, J. (2002, November/December). From research to practice: Outing the unproven. *Psychotherapy Networker.*

20. Shalev, A. Y., Ankri, Y., Israeli-Shalev, Y., Peleg, T., Adessky, R., & Freedman, S. (2012). Prevention of posttraumatic stress disorder by early treatment. *Archives of General Psychiatry, 69*(12), 166–176.

21. American Psychological Association. (2012). *The road to resilience.* http://www.apa.org/helpcenter/road-resilience.aspx/. Accessed August 18, 2012.

22. Hefferon, K., Grealy, M., & Mutrie, N. (2009). Post-traumatic growth and life threatening physical illness: A systematic review of the qualitative literature. *British Journal of Health Psychology, 14,* 343–378.

23. Joseph, S. (2011). *What doesn't kill us: The new psychology of posttraumatic growth.* New York: Basic Books. Seligman, M. (2011). *Flourish: A visionary new understanding of happiness and well-being.* New York: Free Press.

Tedeschi, R. G., & McNally, R. J. (2011). Can we facilitate posttraumatic growth in combat veterans? *American Psychologist, 66*(1), 19–24. Meichenbaum, D. (2006). Resilience and posttraumatic growth: A constructivist narrative perspective. In L. G. Calhoun & R. G. Tedeschi (Eds.), *Handbook of posttraumatic growth: Research and practice* (pp. 355–367). Mahwah, NJ: Erlbaum. Schiraldi, G. (2009). *Post-traumatic stress sourcebook: A guide to healing, recovery, and growth* (2nd ed.). New York: McGraw-Hill. Werdel, M. B., & Wicks, R. J. (2012). *Primer on posttraumatic growth: An introduction and guide.* New York: Wiley.

24. Kottler, J. A., & Chen, D. (2012). *Stress management and prevention: Applications to daily life* (2nd ed.). New York: Routledge. Stahl, B., & Goldstein, E. (2010). *A mindfulness based stress reduction workbook.* Oakland, CA: New Harbinger. Davis, M., Eshelman, E. R., & McKay, M. (2008) *The relaxation and stress reduction workbook* (6th ed.). Oakland, CA: New Harbinger.

25. Lang, M. (1995, September/October). Shadow of evil. *Family Therapy Networker.*

CHAPTER 7

1. Smith, M., Glass, G., & Miller, T. (1980). *The benefit of psychotherapy.* Baltimore: Johns Hopkins University Press. Howard, K., Orlinsky, D., & Lueger, R. (1994). Clinically relevant outcome research in individual psychotherapy. *British Journal of Psychiatry, 165,* 4–8. Consumer Reports. (1995, November). Mental health: Does therapy help? *Consumer Reports,* 734–739. Seligman, M. E. P. (1995). The effectiveness of psychotherapy: The *Consumer Reports* study. *American Psychologist, 50,* 965–974. Norcross, J. C. (Ed.). (2011). *Psychotherapy relationships that work* (2nd ed.). New York: Oxford University Press. Castonguay, L. G., & Beutler, L. E. (Eds.). (2006). *Principles of therapeutic change at work.* New York: Oxford University Press.

2. Lambert, M. J., & Shimokawa, K. (2011). *Collecting client feedback. Psychotherapy, 48*(1), 72–79. Hatfield, D., McCullough, L., Plucinski, A., & Krieger, K. (2010). Do we know when our clients get worse? An investigation of therapists' ability to detect negative client change. *Clinical Psychology and Psychotherapy, 17,* 25–32.

3. Howard, K. I., Kopte, S. M., Krause, M. S., & Orlinsky, D. E. (1986). The dose-effect relationship in psychotherapy. *American Psychologist, 41,* 159–164. Talmon, M. (1990). *Single-session therapy.* San Francisco: Jossey-Bass. Hoyt, M. F. (1994). Single session solutions. In M. Hoyt (Ed.), *Constructive therapies* (pp. 140–159). New York: Guilford. Bloom, B. L. (2001). Focused single-session psychotherapy: A review of the clinical and research literature. *Brief Treatment and Crisis Intervention 1*(1), 75–86. Biancoviso, A. N., Fuertes, J. N., & Bishop-Towle, W. (2001). Planned group counseling: A single-session intervention for reluctant, chemically dependent individuals. *Journal for Specialists in Group Work, 26*(4), 319–338. Young, J., Weir, S., & Rycroft, P. (2012). Implementing single session therapy. *Australian and New Zealand Journal of Family Therapy, 33*(1), 84–97. Stalker, C. A., Horton, S., & Cait, C.

A. (2012). Single-session therapy in a walk-in counseling center. *Journal of Systemic Therapies, 31*(1), 38–52.

4. Examples include: French, T. M. (1933). Interrelations between psychoanalysis and the experimental work of Pavlov. *American Journal of Psychiatry, 89,* 1165–1203. Kubie, L. S. (1934). Relation of the conditioned reflex to psychoanalytic technique. *Archives of Neurology and Psychiatry, 32,* 1137–1142. Rosenzweig, S. (1936). Some implicit common factors in diverse methods in psychotherapy. *American Journal of Orthopsychiatry, 6,* 412–415. Thorne, F. C. (1950). *The principles of personal counseling.* Brandon, VT: Clinical Psychology Publishing. Strupp, H. (1973). On the basic ingredients of psychotherapy. *Journal of Consulting and Clinical Psychology, 41*(1), 1–8. Frank, J. (1961). *Persuasion and healing.* Baltimore: Johns Hopkins Press. Hobbs, N. (1962). Sources of gain in psychotherapy. *American Psychologist, 17,* 740–747. Truax, C. B., & Carkhuff, R. R. (1967). *Toward effective counseling and psychotherapy.* Chicago: Aldine. Watzlawick, P., Weakland, J. H., & Fisch, R. (1974). Change: Principles of problem formation and problem resolution. New York: W. W. Norton. Wachtel, P. (1977). *Psychoanalysis and behavior therapy: Toward an integration.* New York: Basic Books. Goldfried, M. (1980). Toward the delineation of therapeutic change principles. *American Psychologist, 35,* 991–999. Driscoll, R. H. (1984). Pragmatic psychotherapy. New York: Van Nostrand Reinhold. Kottler, J. (1991). *The compleat therapist.* San Francisco: Jossey-Bass. Prochaska, J. O., Norcross, J. C., & DiClemente, C. C. (1994). *Changing for good.* New York: Morrow. Wampold, B. E. (2001). *The great psychotherapy debate: Models, methods, and findings.* Hillsdale, NJ: Erlbaum. Castonguay, L. G., & Beutler, L. E. (Eds.). (2006). *Principles of therapeutic change at work.* New York: Oxford University Press. Gianakis, M., & Carey, T. A. (2008). A review of the experience and explanation of psychological change. *Counselling Psychology Review, 23*(3), 27–38. Kazdin, A. E. (2009). Understanding how and why psychotherapy leads to change. *Psychotherapy Research, 19*(4–5), 418–428. Evans, I. (2013). *How and why people change: Foundations of psychological therapy.* New York: Oxford University Press.

5. Van Hoose, W., & Kottler, J. (1977). *Ethical and legal issues in counseling and psychotherapy.* San Francisco: Jossey-Bass. Kottler, J., & Brown, R. (1985). *Introduction to therapeutic counseling.* Pacific Grove, CA: Brooks/Cole. Kottler, J. (1987). *On being a therapist.* San Francisco: Jossey-Bass. Kottler, J., & Blau, D. (1989). *The imperfect therapist: Learning from failure in therapeutic practice.* San Francisco, Jossey-Bass. Kottler, J. (1991). *The compleat therapist.* San Francisco: Jossey-Bass. Kottler, J. (1992). *Compassionate therapy: Working with difficult clients.* San Francisco: Jossey-Bass. Kottler, J. (1993). *Advanced group leadership.* Pacific Grove, CA: Brooks/Cole. Kottler, J., Sexton, T., & Whiston, S. (1994). *Heart of healing: Relationships in therapy.* San Francisco: Jossey-Bass. Kottler, J. A. (Ed.). (1996). *Finding your way as a counselor.* Alexandria, VA: American Counseling Association. Kottler, J. A. (1999). *The therapist's workbook: Self-assessment, self-care, and self-improvement exercises for mental health professionals.* San Francisco: Jossey-Bass. Kottler,

J. A. (1999). *Exploring and treating acquisitive desire: Living in the material world*. Thousand Oaks, CA: Sage. Kottler, J. A. (2001). *Learning group leadership: An experiential approach*. Boston: Allyn and Bacon. Kottler, J. A. (2002). *Theories in counseling and therapy: An experiential approach*. Boston: Allyn and Bacon. Kottler, J. A., & Carlson, J. (2002). *Bad therapy: Master therapists share their worst failures*. New York: Brunner/Routledge. Kottler, J. A., & Carlson, J. (2003). *The mummy at the dining room table: Eminent therapists reveal their most unusual cases and what they teach us about human behavior*. San Francisco: Jossey-Bass. Kottler, J. A., & Jones, W. P. (Eds.). (2003). *Doing better: Improving clinical skills and professional competence*. Philadelphia: Brunner/Routledge. Kottler, J. A., & Carlson, J. (2005). *Their finest hour: Master therapists share their greatest success stories*. Boston: Allyn and Bacon. Kottler, J. A., Carlson, J., & Keeney, B. (2004). *An American shaman: An odyssey of ancient healing traditions*. New York: Brunner/Routledge. Kottler, J. A., & Carlson, J. (2006). *The client who changed me: Stories of therapist personal transformation*. New York: Brunner/Routledge. Kottler, J. A., & Carlson, J. (2009). *Creative breakthroughs in therapy. Tales of transformation and astonishment*. New York: Wiley. Kottler, J. A. (2010). *The assassin and the therapist: An exploration of truth in psychotherapy and in life*. New York: Routledge. Kottler, J. A., & Carlson, J. (2011). *Duped: Lies and deception in psychotherapy*. New York: Routledge. Kottler, J. A., Carlson, J., & Englar-Carlson, M. (Eds.). (2013). *Helping beyond the 50 minute hour: Therapists involved in REAL social action*. New York: Routledge. Kottler, J. A., & Shepard, D. (2013). *On becoming a master therapist: Practicing what we preach*. New York: Wiley.

6. Kottler, J. A., & Carlson, J. (2002). *Bad therapy: Master therapists share their worst failures*. New York: Routledge.

7. Norcross, J. C., & Lambert, M. J. (2012). Evidence-based therapy relationships. In J. C. Norcross (Ed.), *Psychotherapy relationships that work* (2nd ed., pp. 3–21). New York: Oxford University Press. Wampold, B. E. (2001). *The great psychotherapy debate: Models, methods, and findings*. Mahwah, NJ: Lawrence Erlbaum. Roth, A., & Fonagy, P. (2004). *What works for whom? A critical review of psychotherapy research*. New York: Guilford. Duncan, B. L., Miller, S. D., Wampold, B. E., & Huggle, M. A. (2010). *The heart and soul of change* (2nd ed.). Washington, DC: American Psychological Association.

8. Knight, T. A., Richert, A. J., & Brownfield, C. R. (2012). Conceiving change: Lay accounts of the human change process. *Journal of Psychotherapy Integration, 22*(3), 229–254.

9. American Psychological Association Task Force on Evidence-Based Practice. (2006). Evidence-based practice in psychology. *American Psychologist, 61,* 271–285.

10. Kottler, J. (2010). *The assassin and the therapist: An exploration of truth in psychotherapy and in life*. New York: Routledge. Kottler, J., & Carlson, J. (2011). *Duped: Lies and deception in psychotherapy*. New York: Routledge.

11. Ariely, D. (2012). *The (honest) truth about dishonesty*. New York: HarperCollins. Trivers, R. (2011). *The folly of fools: The logic of deceit and self-deception in human life*. New York: Basic Books. Smith, D. S. (2004). *Why we lie: The*

evolutionary roots of deception and the unconscious mind. New York: St. Martin's Press.

12. Lebow, J., Kelly, J., Knoblock-Fedders, L. M., & Moos, R. (2011). Relationship factors in treating substance use disorders. In L. G. Castonguay & L. E. Beutler (Eds.), *Principles of therapeutic change at work* (pp. 293–317). New York: Oxford University Press.

13. Alarcon, R. D., & Frank, J. B. (2012). *The psychotherapy of hope.* Baltimore: Johns Hopkins University. Fish, J. (1973). *Placebo therapy.* San Francisco: Jossey-Bass. Larsen, D. J. & Stege, R. (2010). Hope-focused practices during early psychotherapy sessions. *Journal of Psychotherapy Integration, 20*(3), 271–292. Bjornsson, A. S. (2011). Beyond the psychological placebo: Specifying the nonspecific in psychotherapy. *Clinical Psychology: Science and Practice, 18*(2), 113–118.

14. Kottler, J. A., & Carlson, J. (2014). *Master therapists: Practicing what you preach.* New York: Wiley. Miller, S., & Hubble, M. (2011, March/April). The road to mastery. *Psychotherapy Networker,* 22–31.

15. DeFife, J. A., Hilsenroth, M. J., & Gold, J. R. (2008). Patient ratings of psychodynamic psychotherapy session activities and their relation to outcome. *Journal of Nervous and Mental Disease, 196*(7), 538–546. Reese, R. J., Toland, M. D., and Slone, N. C. (2010). Effect of client feedback on couple psychotherapy outcomes. *Psychotherapy: Theory, Research, Practice, and Training, 47*(4), 616–630. Frankel, Z., & Levitt, H. M. (2009). Clients' experiences of disengaged moments in psychotherapy: A grounded theory analysis. *Journal of Contemporary Psychotherapy, 39,* 171–186. Paulson, B. L., Turscott, D., & Stuart, J. (1999). Clients' perceptions of helpful experiences in counseling. *Journal of Counseling Psychology, 46*(3), 317–324. Manthei, R. J. (2005). What can clients tell us about seeking counselling and their experience of it? *International Journal for the Advancement of Counselling, 4,* 541–555. Manthei, R. J. (2007). Clients talk about their experience of the process of counselling. *Counselling Psychology Quarterly, 20*(1), 1–26. Hodgetts, A., & Wright, J. (2007). Researching clients' experiences: A review of Qualitative Studies. *Clinical Psychology and Psychotherapy, 14,* 157–163. Jinks, G. H. (1999). Intentionality and awareness: A qualitative study of clients' perceptions of change during longer term counselling. *Counselling Psychology Quarterly, 12*(1), 57–71. Carey, T. A., Carey, M., Stalker, K., Mullan, R. J., Murray, L. K., & Spratt, M. B. (2007). Psychological change from the inside looking out: A qualitative investigation. *Counselling and Psychotherapy, 7*(3), 178–187. Clarke, H., Rees, A., & Hardy, G. E. (2004). The big idea: Clients' perspectives of change processes in cognitive therapy. *Psychology and Psychotherapy: Theory, Research, and Practice, 77,* 67–89. Lambert, M. J., & Shimokawa, K. (2011). Collecting client feedback. *Psychotherapy, 48*(1), 72–79. Binder, P., Holgersen, H., & Nielsen, G. H. (2009). Why did I change when I went to therapy? A qualitative analysis of former patients' conceptions of successful psychotherapy, *Counselling and Psychotherapy, 9*(4), 250–256.

16. Cheavens, J. S., Michael, S. T., & Snyder, C. R. (2005). The correlates of hope: Psychological and physiological benefits. In J. Eliott (Ed.),

Interdisciplinary perspectives on hope (pp. 119–132). Hauppauge, NY: Nova Science. Larsen, D. J., & Stege, R. (2012). Client accounts of hope in early counseling sessions: A qualitative study. *Journal of Counseling and Development, 90*, 45–54.

17. Cheavons, J. S., & Gum, A. M. (2010). From here to where you want to be. In G. W. Burns (Ed.), *Happiness, healing, enhancement* (pp. 51–87). New York: Wiley.
18. Clarke, H., Rees, A., & Hardy, G. E. (2004). The big idea: Clients' perspectives of change processes in cognitive therapy. *Psychology and Psychotherapy: Theory, Research, and Practice, 77*, p. 75.
19. Clarke et al. (2004), p. 78.
20. Binder, P., Holgersen, H., & Nielsen, G. H. (2009). Why did I change when I went to therapy? A qualitative analysis of former patients' conceptions of successful psychotherapy. *Counselling and Psychotherapy, 9*(4), 250–256. Hodgetts, A., & Wright, J. (2007). Researching clients' experiences: A review of Qualitative Studies. *Clinical Psychology and Psychotherapy, 14*, 157–163.
21. Manthei, R. J. (2005). What can clients tell us about seeking counselling and their experience of it? *International Journal for the Advancement of Counselling, 4*, 541–555. Manthei, R. J. (2007). Clients talk about their experience of the process of counselling. *Counselling Psychology Quarterly, 20*(1), 1–26.
22. Manthei (2007). Farber, B. A. (2003). Patient self-disclosure: A review of research. *Journal of Clinical Psychology, 59*, 589–600. Rennie, D. L. (2004). Anglo-North American qualitative counselling and psychotherapy research. *Psychotherapy Research, 14*, 37–55.
23. Jinks, G. H. (1999). Intentionality and awareness: A qualitative study of clients' perceptions of change during longer term counselling. *Counselling Psychology Quarterly, 12*(1), 57–71.
24. Carey et al. (2007).
25. Paulson, B. L., Turscott, D., Stuart, J. (1999). Clients' perceptions of helpful experiences in counseling. *Journal of Counseling Psychology, 46*(3), 317–324. Jinks, G. H. (1999). Intentionality and awareness: A qualitative study of clients' perceptions of change during longer term counselling. *Counselling Psychology Quarterly, 12*(1), 57–71.
26. Kottler, J. A. (1991). *The compleat therapist.* San Francisco: Jossey-Bass.
27. Reese, R. J., Toland, M. D., and Slone, N. C. (2010). Effect of client feedback on couple psychotherapy outcomes. *Psychotherapy: Theory, Research, Practice, and Training, 47*(4), 616–630. Frankel, Z., & Levitt, H. M. (2009). Clients' experiences of disengaged moments in psychotherapy: A grounded theory analysis. *Journal of Contemporary Psychotherapy, 39*, 171–186. Lambert, M. J., & Shimokawa, K. (2011). *Collecting client feedback. Psychotherapy, 48*(1), 72–79. Miller, S., & Hubble, M. (2011, March/April). The road to mastery. *Psychotherapy Networker*, 22–31.
28. Treadway, D. C. (2004). *Intimacy, change, and other therapeutic mysteries.* New York: Guilford, p. ix.

29. Interviewed in: Gibney, P. (2012). Reimagining psychotherapy: An interview with Hillary and Bradford Keeney. *Psychotherapy in Australia, 18*(3), p. 67.
30. Gibney (2012), p. 67.
31. Kottler, J. A., Carlson, J., & Keeney, B. (2004). *An American shaman: An odyssey of ancient healing traditions.* New York: Brunner/Routledge.
32. Keeney, H., & Keeney, B. (2012). *Circular therapeutics: Giving therapy a healing heart.* Phoenix, AZ: Zeig, Tucker.

CHAPTER 8

1. Kottler, J. A. (1997). *Travel that can change your life: How to create a transformative experience.* San Francisco: Jossey-Bass. Kottler, J. A. (2002). Wisdom along the way: Frying onions. In J. Canfield, M. Hansen, & S. Zikman (Eds.), *Chicken soup for the traveler's soul: Stories of inspiration and insight to celebrate the spirit of travel.* Deerfield Beach, FL: Health Communications. Kottler, J. A. (2001). The therapeutic benefits of structured travel experiences. *Journal of Clinical Activities, Assignments, and Handouts in Psychotherapy Practice, 1*(1), 29–36.
2. Stone, G. W. (2012). Famous great travelers. *National Geographic.* Retrieved from http://travel.nationalgeographic.com/travel/famous-travelers/
3. Grogan, E. S., & Sharp, A. H. (1902). *From the Cape to Cairo: The first traverse of Africa from South to North.* London: Hurst and Blackett, p. 326.
4. Maddux, W. W., & Galinsky, A. D. (2009). Cultural borders and mental barriers: The relationship between living abroad and creativity. *Journal of Personality and Social Psychology, 96*(5), 1047–1061.
5. Stark, F. (1946). *Baghdad sketches.* UK: John Murray.
6. Salak, K. (2004). *Cruelest journey: Six hundred miles to Timbuktu.* Margate, FL: National Geographic.
7. Hiss, T. (2012). *In motion: The experience of travel.* Chicago: Planners Press.
8. Iyer, P. (2001). Why we travel. In P. Thoroux (Ed.), *The best American travel writing* (p. 146). Boston: Houghton Mifflin.
9. Ross, S. L. (2010). Transformative travel: An enjoyable way to foster radical change. *ReVision, 32*(1), 54–61.
10. Maslow, A. (1968). *Toward a psychology of being* (2nd ed.). New York: Van Nostrand Reinhold. McDonald, M. G., Wearing, S., & Ponting, J. (2009). The nature of peak experience in wilderness. *The Humanistic Psychologist, 37,* 370–385.
11. Knight, T. A., Richert, A. J., & Brownfield, C. R. (2012). Conceiving change: Lay accounts of the human change process. *Journal of Psychotherapy Integration, 22*(3), 229–254.
12. Kottler, J. A., & Marriner, M. (2009). *Changing people's lives while transforming your own: Paths to social justice and global human rights.* New York: Wiley. Brown, S., & Lehto, X. (2005). Traveling with a purpose: Understanding motives and benefits of volunteer vacationers. *Current Issues in Tourism, 8*(6), 479–496.
13. Rapoport, R., & Castanera, M. (Eds.). (1994). *I should have stayed home: The worst trips of great writers.* Berkley, CA: Book Passage Press.

14. Morris, M. (1994). Introduction. In R. Rapoport, & M. Castanera, M. (Eds.) (1994), *I should have stayed home: The worst trips of great writers* (p. 1). Berkley, CA: Book Passage Press.
15. Robertson, D. N., Jr. (2002). Modern day explorers: The way to a wider world. *World Leisure, 3,* 35–42.
16. Carson, R. (1965). *The sense of wonder.* New York: Harper and Row.
17. Hiss, T. (2010). *In motion: The experience of travel.* Chicago: Planners Press, p. 54.
18. For more information see: www.EmpowerNepaliGirls.org. Kottler, J. A. (2012, May). What *really* makes a difference? *Psychotherapy Networker.* Kottler, J. (2008, September/October). Transforming lives. *Psychotherapy Networker,* 42–47.
19. Olsen, D. H., & Timothy, D. J. (2006). Tourism, religion, and spiritual journeys. New York: Routledge. Ross, S. L. (2010). Transformative travel: An enjoyable way to foster radical change. *ReVision, 32*(1), 54–61.
20. Stone, G. W. (2012). Famous great travelers. *National Geographic.* Retrieved from http.//travel.nationalgeographic.com/travel/famous travelers/
21. Kottler, J. A., & Carlson, J. (2007). *Moved by the spirit: Discovery and transformation in the lives of leaders.* Atascadero, CA: Impact.
22. Pargament, K. I. (1997). *The psychology of religious coping.* New York: Guilford. Miller, W. R., & C'deBaca, J. (2001). *Quantum change.* New York: Guilford.
23. White, W. L. (2004). Transformational change: A historical review. *Journal of Clinical Psychology, 60*(5), 461–470.
24. Kurtz, E. (1979). *Not-God: A history of alcoholics anonymous.* New York: Hazelden.
25. Newberg, A., & Waldman, M. R. (2006). *Why we believe what we believe: Uncovering our biological need for meaning, spirituality, and truth.* New York: Free Press.
26. Hall, S. (2007, May 6). The older-and-wiser hypothesis. *New York Times.*
27. Walsh R. (2011). Lifestyle and mental health. *American Psychologist, 66*(7), 579–592.
28. James, W. (1902/1958). *Varieties of religious experience.* New York: Modern Library.
29. Sandage, S. J., Jankowski, P. J., & Link, D. C. (2010). Quest and spiritual development moderated by spiritual transformation. *Journal of Psychology and Theology, 38*(1), 15–31.
30. Berman, M. G., Jonides, J., & Kaplan, S. (2008). The cognitive benefits of interacting with nature. *Psychological Science, 19,* 1207–1212.
31. McDonald, M. G., Wearing, S., & Ponting, J. (2009). The nature of peak experience in wilderness. *The Humanistic Psychologist, 37,* 370–385.
32. Kaplan, R., & Kaplan, S. (1989). *The experience of nature: A psychological perspective.* New York: Cambridge University Press.
33. Benson, J. (1996). *Transformative getaways for spiritual growth, self-discovery, and holistic healing.* New York: Henry Holt. Kaye, R. (2006). Soul of the wilderness, the spiritual dimension of wilderness. *International Journal of*

Wilderness, 12(3), 4–7. Rountree, K. (2002). Goddess pilgrims as tourists: Inscribing the body through sacred travel. *Sociology of Religion, 63*(4), 475–497.

34. Forcehimes, A. A. (2004). De profundis: Spiritual transformations in Alcoholics Anonymous. *Journal of Clinical Psychology, 60*(5), 503–517.

35. Ross (2010). Kottler, J. A., & Montgomery, M. (2000). Prescriptive travel and adventure-based activities as adjuncts to Counseling. *Guidance and Counselling, 15*(2), 8–11. Benson, J. (1996). *Transformative getaways for spiritual growth, self discovery, and holistic healing*. New York: Henry Holt. Mitchell, R. G. (1983). *Mountain experience: The psychology and sociology of adventure*. Chicago: University of Chicago Press. Schoel, J., Prouty, D., & Radcliffe, P. (1988). *Islands of healing: A guide to adventure-based counseling*. Hamilton, MA: Project Adventure. Walsh, V., & Colins, C. (1976). *The exploration of the outward bound process*. Denver: Colorado Outward Bound Publications. Zikman, S. (1999). *The power of travel: A passport to adventure, discovery, and growth*. New York: Tarcher. Zurick, D. (1995) *Errant journeys: Adventure travel in a modern age*. Austin: University of Texas Press. Leed, E. J. (1991). *The mind of the traveler*. New York: Basic Books. Olsen, D. H., & Timothy, T. J. (2006). *Tourism, religion, and spiritual journeys*. New York: Routledge. Norris, J. (2011). Crossing the threshold mindfully: Exploring rites of passage models in adventure therapy. *Journal of Adventure Education and Outdoor Learning, 11*, 109–126.

CHAPTER 9

1. Sternberg, R. J., & Davidson, J. E. (Eds.). (1995). *The nature of insight*. Cambridge, MA: MIT Press. Bowden, E. M., Jung-Beeman, M., Fleck, J., Kounios, J. (2005). New approaches to demystifying insight. *Trends in Cognitive Science, 9*, 323–328.

2. Carey, T. A., Carey, M., Mullan, R. J., Murray, L. K., & Spratt, M. B. (2006). Psychological change: What changes and how does it occur? A critical review. *Counselling Psychology Review, 21*(4), 28–38.

3. Bidney, M. (2004). Epiphany in autobiography: The quantum changes of Dostoyevsky and Tolstoy. *Journal of Clinical Psychology, 60*(5), 471–480.

4. Dostoyevsky, F. (1985). *The diary of a writer*. Salt Lake City, UT: Peregrine Smith, p. 210.

5. Kottler, J. A. (2006). *Divine madness: Ten stories of creative struggle*. San Francisco: Jossey-Bass.

6. Tolstoy, L. (1940). *A confession, the gospel in brief, and what I believe*. London: Oxford University Press, p. 65.

7. Bidney (2004), p. 479.

8. Burum, B. A., & Goldfried, M. R. (2007). The centrality of emotion to psychological change. *Clinical Psychology: Science and Practice, 14*(4), 407–413.

9. Greenberg, L. S., & Safran, J. D. (1987). *Emotion in psychotherapy: Affect, cognition, and the process of change*. New York: Guilford.

10. Carey, Carey, Stalker, Mullan, Murray, & Spratt (2007), p. 186.

11. Haley, J. (1985). *Ordeal therapy: Unusual ways to change therapy.* San Francisco: Jossey-Bass.
12. Evans, I. (2013). *How and why people change: Foundations of psychological therapy.* New York: Oxford University Press.
13. Beck, A. T. (1976). *Cognitive therapy and emotional disorders.* New York: International University Press.
14. Ellis, A. (1962). *Reason and emotion in psychotherapy.* New York: Lyle Stuart.
15. Meichenbaum, D. (1979). *Cognitive-behavior modification: An integrative approach.* New York: Plenum.
16. Lazarus, A. A. (1976). *Multi-modal behavior therapy.* New York: Springer.
17. Hayes, S., Strosahl, K. D., & Wilson, K. G. (2003). *Acceptance and commitment therapy: An experiential approach to behavior change.* New York: Guilford.
18. Kabat-Zinn, J. (2005). *Coming to our senses: Healing ourselves and the world through mindfulness.* New York: Hyperion.
19. Pennebaker, J. W., & Seagal, J. (1999). Forming a story: The health benefits of narrative. *Journal of Clinical Psychology, 55,* 1243–1254. Pennebaker, J. W., & Chung, C. K. (2007). Expressive writing, emotional upheavals, and health. In H. Friedman & R. Silver (Eds.), *Handbook of health psychology* (pp. 263– 284). New York: Oxford University Press. Hoyt, T., & Yeater, E. A. (2011). The effects of negative emotion and expressive writing on post-traumatic stress symptoms. *Journal of Social and Clinical Psychology, 30*(6), 549–569.
20. Carey, T. A. (2006). *The method of levels: How to do psychotherapy without getting in the way.* Hayward, CA: Living Control Systems.

CHAPTER 10

1. Burum, B. A., & Goldfried, M. R. (2007). The centrality of emotion to psychological change. *Clinical Psychology: Science and Practice, 14*(4), 407–413.
2. Palca, J., & Lichtman, F. (2011, May 29). What's bugging you? *Los Angeles Times.*
3. American Psychological Association. (2012). *Stress in America: Our health at risk.* Washington, DC: APA. http://www.apa.org/news/press/releases/stress/2011/final-2011.pdf. Accessed May 10, 2013.
4. APA. (2012).
5. Hakanen, J. J., & Schaufeli, W. B. (2012). Do burnout and work engagement predict depressive symptoms and life satisfaction? A three-wave seven-year prospective study. *Journal of Affective Disorders,* March. http://dx.doi.org/10.1016/j.jad.2012.02.043
6. Doheny, K. (2012, February 13). When it's all work. *Los Angeles Times,* E1–E5.
7. Friedman, A. S., & Martin, L. R. (2012). *The longevity project.* New York: Plume.
8. Goldbaum, G. (2012). Accelerated aging of U.S. presidents. *Journal of the American Medical Association, 307*(12), 1254.
9. Sherman, G. D., Lee, J. J., Cuddy, A. J., Renshon, J., Oveis, C., Gross, J. J. et al. (2012). Leadership is associated with lower levels of stress. *Proceedings of the National Academy of Sciences,* September.

10. Dorment, R. (2011, November). What moderate to severe anxiety feels like. *Esquire, 163.*

11. Resnick, J. (2011). Far-out philias and phobias. *Psychotherapy in Australia, 17*(4), 65–66.

12. National Institute of Mental Health. (n.d.). *Anxiety disorders.* http://www.nimh.nih.gov/health/publications/anxiety-disorders/complete-index.shtml. Accessed August 8, 2012.

13. Clark, J. (2012, July 24). Why we no longer feel rested after a vacation. *USA Today.*

14. Taylor, S. E., Klein, L. C., Lewis, B. P, Gruenewald, T. L, Gurung, R. A. R., & Updegraff, J. A. (2000). Biobehavioral responses to stress in females: Tend-and-befriend, not fight-or-flight. *Psychological Review, 107,* 441–429. Taylor, S. (2006). Tend and befriend: Biobehavioral bases of affiliation under stress. *Current Directions in Psychological Science, 15*(6), 273–277.

15. Harrison, L. E. (2006). *The central liberal truth: How politics can change a culture and save it from itself.* New York: Oxford University Press.

16. American Psychological Association. (2012).

17. Harris, J. I., Erbes, C. R., Engdahl, B. E., Tedeschi, R. G., Olson, R. H., Winskowski, A. M., et al. (2010). Coping functions of prayer and posttraumatic growth. *International Journal for the Psychology of Religion, 20,* 26–28.

18. Csikszentmihalyi, M. (1977). *Beyond boredom and anxiety.* San Francisco: Jossey-Bass. Csikszentmihalyi, M. (2008). *Flow: The psychology of optimal experience.* New York: Harper.

19. Kabat-Zinn, J. (2005). *Coming to our senses: Healing ourselves and the world through mindfulness.* New York: Hyperion. Chu, L. C. (2010). The benefits of meditation vis-à-vis emotional intelligence, perceived stress, and negative mental health. *Stress and Health, 26*(2), 169–180.

20. Meyer, R. (2012, July 24). Studies trickle in on how mindfulness meditation actually improves multitasking. *The Atlantic.* Retrieved from http://www.theatlantic.com/technology/archive/2012/07/studies-trickle-in-on-how-mindfulness-meditation-actually-improves-multitasking/260263/

21. Walsh, R. (2011). Lifestyle and mental health. *American Psychologist, 66*(7), 579–592.

22. Center for Disease Control. (2012). *Prevalence of obesity in the United States.* http://www.theatlantic.com/technology/archive/2012/07/studies-trickle-in-on-how-mindfulness-meditation-actually-improves-multitasking/260263/. Accessed July 27, 2012.

23. American Psychological Association. (2012).

24. Deslandes, A., Moraes, H., Ferreira, C., Veiga, H., Silveria, H., Mouta, R., & Laks, J. (2009). Exercise and mental health: Many reasons to move. *Neuropsychobiology, 59,* 191–198.

25. Parker-Pope, T. (2011, November 30). How exercise benefits the brain. *New York Times.* Griffin, E. W., Mullally, S., Foley, C., Warmington, S. A., O'Mara, S. M., & Kelly, A. M. (2011). Aerobic exercise improves hippocampal function and increases BDNF in the serum of young males. *Physiological Behavior, 104*(5), 934–941.

26. Gallup-Healthways. (2012). *Well-being index.* http://www.well-beingindex.com/. Accessed July 28, 2012.

27. Green, A. (2012, January 2). 4 out of 5 gym memberships go unused—Except the first days of the new year. *The Oregonian.* Retrieved from http://www.oregonlive.com/health/index.ssf/2012/01/four_out_of_five_gym_membership.html

28. Duane, D. (2010, November). Everything you know about fitness is a lie. *Men's Journal.* Retrieved from http://www.mensjournal.com/magazine/everything-you-know-about-fitness-is-a-lie-20120504

29. Johnson, S. (2010). Where good ideas come from. *Ted.* http://www.ted.com/talks/steven_johnson_where_good_ideas_come_from.html. Accessed August 1, 2012.

30. Jetten, J., Haslam, C., Haslam, S. A., & Branscombe, N. R. (2009). The social cure. *Scientific American Mind, 20,* 26–33.

31. Putnam, R. D. (2000). *Bowling alone: The collapse and revival of American community.* New York: Simon & Schuster. McPherson, M., Smith-Lovin, L., & Brashears, M. E. (2006). Social isolation in America: Changes in core discussion networks over two decades. *American Sociological Review, 71,* 353–375.

32. Post, S. G. (2011). *The hidden gifts of helping: How the power of giving, compassion, and hope can get us through hard times.* San Francisco: Jossey-Bass.

CHAPTER 11

1. Lyubomirsky, S. (2013). *The myths of happiness.* New York: Penguin.

2. Lyubomirsky, S. (2008). *The how of happiness: A new approach to getting the life you want.* London: Penguin.

3. Bergsma, A. (2010). The state of the art in happiness advice; Can we escape the dodo-verdict? *Journal of Happiness Studies, 11,* 649–654.

4. Land, K. C., Michalos, A. C., & Sirgy, M. J. (Eds.). (2008). *Handbook of social indicators and quality of life research.* New York: Springer.

5. Sandler, L. (2011, March/April). The American nightmare. *Psychology Today,* 70–78. Post, S. G. (2005). Altruism, happiness, and health: It's good to be good. *International Journal of Behavioral Medicine, 12*(2), 66–77.

6. Earth Institute. (2012). *First world happiness report launched at the United Nations.* New York: Columbia University. http://www.earth.columbia.edu/articles/view/2960

7. Graham, C. (2009). *Happiness around the world: The paradox of happy peasants and miserable millionaires.* New York: Oxford University Press.

8. Hayes, N., & Joseph, S. (2003). Big five correlates of three measures of subjective well-being. *Personality and Individual Differences, 34,* 723–727.

9. Mauss, I. B., Tamir, M., Anderson, C. L., & Savino, N. S. (2011). Can seeking happiness make people unhappy? Paradoxical effects of valuing happiness. *Emotion, 11*(4), 807–815.

10. Nettle, D. (2005). *Happiness: The science behind your smile.* New York: Oxford University Press, p. 62.

11. *National Child Development Study.* http://www.esds.ac.uk/longitudinal/access/ncds/l33004.asp. Retrieved May 10, 2013.

12. Brickman, P., & Campbell, D. T. (1971). Hedonistic relativism and planning the good society. In M. H. Appley (Ed.), *Adaptation level theory* (pp. 287–305). New York: Academic Press.
13. Seligman, M. (2011). *Flourish: A visionary new understanding of happiness and well-being.* New York: Free Press, p. 9.
14. Nettle (2005).
15. Ryff, C. D., & Keyes, C. L. (1995). The structure of psychological well-being revisited. *Journal of Personality and Social Psychology, 69,* 719–727.
16. Rasmussen, H., Scheier, M., & Greenhouse, J. (2009). Optimism and physical health: A meta-analytic review. *Annals of Behavioral Medicine, 37,* 239–256.
17. Seligman (2011).
18. Diener, E., & Biswas-Diener, R. (2008). *Happiness: Unlocking the mysteries of psychological wealth.* Malden, MA: Blackwell.
19. Bergsma, A. (2010). The state of the art in happiness advice; Can we escape the dodo-verdict? *Journal of Happiness Studies, 11,* 649–654.
20. Bormans, L. (Ed.). (2010). *The world book of happiness.* Singapore: Page One.
21. Bergsma, A. (2008). Do self-help books help? *Journal of Happiness Studies, 9,* 341–360.
22. Ware, B. (2012, January 21). Top 5 regrets of the dying. *Huffington Post.* Retrieved from http://www.huffingtonpost.com/bronnie-ware/top-5-regrets-of-the-dyin_b_1220965.html
23. Adams, S. (2012, November 28). Why winning Powerball won't make you happy. Forbes, November 28. Retrieved from http://www.forbes.com/sites/susanadams/2012/11/28/why-winning-powerball-wont-make-you-happy/
24. Dalai Lama, & Cutler, H. C. (2009). *The art of happiness: A handbook for living.* New York: Riverhead.
25. Mill, J. S. (1909/2006). Autobiography. In *Collected works of John Stuart Mill* (Vol. 1). Liberty Fund.
26. Seligman (2011).
27. Nettle (2005), p. 168.
28. Lyubomirsky, S. (2013). *The myths of happiness: What should make you happy doesn't, what shouldn't make you happy, but does.* New York: Penguin.

CHAPTER 12

1. Graham, C., & Lora, E. (2009). *Paradox and perception.* Washington, DC: Brookings Institution.
2. Rosenblatt, R. (1982, January 25). The man in the water. *Time.*
3. Haldane, J. B. S. (1955). Population genetics. *New Biology, 18,* 34–51.
4. Sigmund, K., & Hauert, C. (2002). Altruism. *Current Biology, 12*(8), R270–R272.
5. Warneken, F., & Tomasello, M. (2006). Altruistic helping in human infants and young chimpanzees. *Science, 311,* 1301–1303.
6. Warneken, F., & Tomasello, M. (2009). The roots of human altruism. *British Journal of Psychology, 100,* 455–471.

7. Luks, A. (1988). Helper's high: Volunteering makes people feel good, physical and emotionally. *Psychology Today, 22*(10), 34–42.

8. Post, S., & Neimark, J. (2007). *Why good things happen to good people.* New York: Doubleday. Van der Linden, S. (2011, December 23). The helper's high. *Ode Wire.* Retrieved from http://odewire.com/176916/the-helper's-high.html

9. Field, M. F., Hernandez-Reif, M., Quintino, O, Schanberg, S., & Kuhn, C. (1998). Elder retired volunteers benefit from giving massage therapy to infants. *Journal of Applied Gerontology, 17,* 229–239.

10. Post, S. G. (2005). Altruism, happiness, and health: It's good to be good. *International Journal of Behavioral Medicine, 12*(2), 66–77.

11. Oman, D., Thoresen, C. E., & McMahon, K. (1999). Volunteerism and mortality among community-dwelling elderly. *Journal of Health Psychology, 4*(3), 301–316.

12. Arnstein, P., Vidal, M., Wells-Federman, C., Morgan, B., & Caudill, M. (2002). From chronic pain patient to peer: Benefits and risks of volunteering. *Pain Management Nursing, 3*(3), 94 103.

13. Post, S. G. (2011). *The hidden gifts of helping: How the power of giving, compassion, and hope can get us through hard times.* San Francisco: Jossey-Bass.

14. Thomas, L. (1979). *The medusa and the snail.* New York: Viking, p. 10.

15. Kottler, J. A. (2000). *Doing good: Passion and commitment for helping others.* New York: Routledge.

16. Walsh R. (2011). Lifestyle and mental health. *American Psychologist, 66*(7), 579–592.

17. Gebauer, J., Riketta, M., Broemer, P., & Mai, G. (2008). Pleasure and pressure based prosocial motivation: Divergent relations to subjective well-being. *Journal of Research in Personality, 42,* 399–420.

18. Kottler, J. A., & Carlson, J. (2006). *The client who changed me: Stories of therapist personal transformation.* New York: Routledge.

19. Kottler, J. A., & Marriner, M. (2009). *Changing people's lives while transforming your own: Paths to social justice and global human rights.* New York: Wiley. Post, S. G. (Ed.). (2007). *Altruism and health: Perspectives from empirical research.* New York: Oxford University Press.

20. Fredrickson, B. L. (2003). The value of positive emotions: The emerging science of positive psychology is coming to understand why it's good to feel good. *American Scientist, 91,* 330–335.

21. Staub, E. (2003). *The psychology of good and evil: Why children, adults, and groups help and harm others.* Cambridge, UK: Cambridge University Press. Volhardt, J. R. (2009). Altruism born of suffering and prosocial behavior following adverse life events: A review and conceptualization. *Social Justice Research, 22,* 53–97.

22. Ram das and Bush, M. (1992). *Compassion in action.* New York: Bell Tower, p. 102.

23. Brehony, K. A. (1999). *Ordinary grace.* New York: Riverhead.

CHAPTER 13

1. Woodin, E. M. (2011). A two-dimensional approach to relationship conflict: Meta-analytic findings. *Journal of Family Psychology, 25*(3), 325–335. Gottman, J. (1994). *What predicts divorce? The relationship between marital processes and marital outcomes.* Hillsdale, NJ: Lawrence Erlbaum.
2. Tint, B. (2010). History, memory, and intractable conflict. *Conflict Resolution Quarterly, 27*(3), 239–256.
3. Kottler, J. A. (1994). *Beyond blame: A new way of resolving conflicts in relationships.* San Francisco: Jossey-Bass.
4. Hicks, A. M., & Diamond, L. M. (2011). Don't go to bed angry: Attachment, conflict, and affective and physiological reactivity. *Personal Relationships, 18,* 266–284.
5. Salvatore, J. E., Kuo, S. I., Steele, R. D., Simpson, J. A., & Collins, W. A. (2011). Recovering from conflict in romantic relationships: A developmental perspective. *Psychological Science, 22*(3), 376–383.
6. Gottman, J. M., & Levinson, R. W. (1999). Rebound from marital conflict and divorce prediction. *Family Process, 38,* 287–292.
7. Gross, J. J., & Thompson, R. A. (2007). Emotion regulation: Conceptual foundations. In J. J. Gross (Ed.), *Handbook of emotional regulation* (pp. 3–24). New York: Guilford.
8. Luchies, L. B., & Finkel, E. J. (2011). The doormat effect: On the dangers of resolving conflict via unilateral forgiveness. In J. P. Forgas, A. W. Kruglanski, W. Arie, & K. D. Williams (Eds.), *The psychology of social conflict and aggression* (pp. 217–230). New York: Psychology Press.
9. Ysseldyk, R., Matheson, K., & Anisman, H. (2009). Forgiveness and the appraisal-coping process in response to relationship conflicts: Implications for depressive symptoms. *Stress, 12*(2), 152–166.
10. Winslade, J., and Monk, G. (2000). *Narrative mediation: A new approach to conflict resolution.* San Francisco: Jossey-Bass. Winslade, J., & Monk, G. (2008). *Practicing narrative mediation: Loosening the grip of conflict.* San Francisco: Jossey-Bass.
11. Jabs, L. B. (2010). "You can't kill a louse with one finger:" A case study of interpersonal conflict in Karamoja, Uganda. *Peace and Change, 35*(3), 483–502.

CHAPTER 14

1. Polivy, J., & Herman, C. P. (2002). If at first you don't succeed: False hopes of self-change. *American Psychologist, 19,* 76–83. Brandon, T. H., Vidrine, J. L., & Litvin, E. B. (2007). Relapse and relapse prevention. *Annual Review of Clinical Psychology, 3,* 257–284. Christensen, A., Atkins, D. C., Baucom, B., & Yi, J. (2010). Marital status and satisfaction five years following a randomized clinical trial comparing traditional versus integrative behavioral couple therapy. *Journal of Consulting and Clinical Psychology, 78*(2), 225–235. U.S. Department of Health and Human Services. (2010). *Results from the national survey on drug use and health: Summary of national findings.*

http://www.samhsa.gov/data/NSDUH/2k10NSDUH/2k10Results.htm.
Burcusa, S. L., & Iacono, W. G. (2007). Risk for recurrence in depression. *Clinical Psychology Review, 27*(8), 959–985. Hajek, P., Stead, L. F., Jarvis, M., & Lancaster, T. (2009). Relapse prevention interventions for smoking cessation. *Cochrane Collaboration, 1*. Retrieved from http://www.thecochranelibrary.com.lib-proxy.fullerton.edu/SpringboardWebApp/userfiles/ccoch/file/World%20No%20Tobacco%20Day/CD00999.pdf

2. Park, D. C. (1999). Acts of will? *American Psychologist, 54,* 461.

3. Verplanken, B., & Wood, W. (2006). Interventions to break and create consumer habits. *Journal of Public Policy and Marketing 25*(1), 90–103.

4. Bargh, J. A., & Chartrand, T. L. (1999). The unbearable automaticity of being. *American Psychologist, 54,* 462–479.

5. Duhigg, C. (2012). *The power of habit.* New York: Random House.

6. Duhigg (2012).

7. Oz, M. (2012, September 17). Goal power. *Time,* pp. 47–49.

8. George, L. K., Ellison, C. G., & Larson, D. B. (2002). Explaining the relationship between religious involvement and health. *Psychological Inquiry, 13,* 190–200. McAdams, D. (2006). *The redemptive self: Stories Americans live by.* New York: Oxford University Press. Mochon, D., Norton, M. I., & Ariely, D. (2011). Who benefits from religion? *Social Indicators Research, 101*(1), 1–15. Spilka, B., & Ladd, K. L. (2013). *The psychology of prayer: A scientific approach.* New York: Guilford.

9. Kottler, J. A. (2006). *Divine madness: Ten stories of creative struggle.* San Francisco: Jossey-Bass.

10. Curry, J., Silva, S., Rohde, P, Ginsburg, G., Kratochvil, C., et al. (2005). Recovery and recurrence following treatment for adolescent major depression. *Archives of General Psychiatry, 68*(3), 263–270.

11. Marlatt, G. A. (1985). *Relapse prevention.* New York: Guilford. Marlatt, G. A., & Donovan, D. M. (Eds.). (2007). *Relapse prevention: Maintenance strategies in the treatment of addictive behaviors* (2nd ed.). New York: Guilford.

12. Kottler, J. A. (2001). *Making changes last.* New York: Routledge.

13. Hollis, J. F., Gullion, C. M., Stevens, V. J., Brantley, P. J., Appel, L. J., et al. (2008). Weight loss during the intensive intervention phase of the weight-loss maintenance trial. *American Journal of Preventive Medicine, 35,* 118–126.

14. Marlatt & Donovan (2007).

15. Kottler, J., & Blau, D. (1989). *The imperfect therapist: Learning from failure in therapeutic practice.* San Francisco, Jossey-Bass. Kottler, J. A., & Carlson, J. (2002). *Bad therapy: Master therapists share their worst failures.* New York: Routledge.

16. Groh, L. A., Jason, L. A., & Keys, C. B. (2008). Social network variables in Alcoholics Anonymous: A literature review. *Clinical Psychology Review, 28*(3), 430–450. Kelly, J. F., Magill, M., & Stout, R. L. (2009). How do people recover from alcohol dependence? A systematic review of the research on mechanisms of behavior change in Alcoholics Anonymous. *Addiction Research and Theory, 17*(3), 236–259.

17. Evans, I. (2013). *How and why people change: Foundations of psychological therapy.* New York: Oxford University Press.
18. Kazdin, A. E. (2000). Symptom substitution, generalization, and response covariation: Implications for psychotherapy outcome. *Psychological Bulletin, 91,* 349–365. Tryon, W. W. (2008). Whatever happened to symptom substitution? *Clinical Psychology Review, 28*(6), 963–968.
19. Glasser, W. (1976). *Positive addiction.* New York: Harper and Row.
20. Blair, S. N. (2009). Relationships between exercise or physical activity and other health behaviors. *Public Health Reports, 100,* 172–180.
21. Krystina, A., Finlay, D. T., & Villarreal, A. (2002). Predicting exercise and health behavioral intentions: Attitudes, subjective norms, and other behavioral determinants. *Journal of Applied Social Psychology, 32,* 342–356.
22. Duhigg (2012).
23. Mockenhaupt, B. (2013, January). Get your head in the game. *Outside,* 71–75.
24. Bowen, S., Chawla, N., & Marlatt, G. A. (2011). *Mindfulness-based relapse prevention for addictive behaviors: A clinician's guide.* New York: Guilford. Witkiewitz, K., Lustyk, M. K. B., & Bowen, S. (2012). Retraining the addicted brain: A review of hypothesized neurobiological mechanisms of mindfulness-based relapse prevention. *Psychology of Addictive Behaviors, July,* 1–15.

INDEX